Other books by Jack E. Fryar, Jr.

- The Coastal Chronicles Volume I (2002)
- A History Lover's GD to Wilmington & The Lower Cape Fear (2003)
- The Coastal Chronicles Volume II (2003)
- The Story of Brunswick Town & Fort Anderson, with Franda D. Predlow (2005)
- Charles Towne on the Cape Fear: The Rise and Fall of the First Barbadian Settlement in Carolina (2019)
- The Coastal Chronicles Vol. III (2022)
- When the British Came: Revolution in the Cape Fear, 1765-1782 (2024)

Books authored in "The Young Reader's Series of North Carolina History"

- Plantations: Living and Working on North Carolina's Great Estates (2022)
- 1898: The Violent Taking of a Southern City (2022)
- The Yellow Death: Wilmington & the Yellow Fever Epidemic of 1862 (2008)
- Under Three Flags: The Fort Johnston Story (2008)
- "King George and Broadswords!" The Battle at Widow Moores Creek (2007)
- Pirates of the North Carolina Coast (2007)
- The Battles for Fort Fisher (2006)

Books edited

- Lossing's Pictorial Field-Book of the Revolution in the Carolinas & GA (2005)
- Chronicles of the Cape Fear River: 1660-1916 (2005)
- Derelicts: An account of ships lost at sea in general commerce traffic and a brief history of blockade runners stranded along the North Carolina coast 1861-1865 (2006)
- Blue Tide Rising: A Memoir of the Union Army in North Carolina (2007)
- Buccaneers & Pirates of Our Coasts (2007)
- One Good Man: Rev. John Lamb Pritchard's life of faith, service & sacrifice (2007)
- Lossing's Pictorial Field-Book of the Revolution in Virginia & Maryland (2008)
- A Sketch of the Life of Brig. Gen. Francis Marion (2008)
- Big Book of the Cape Fear River (2009)
- A James Sprunt Reader (2009)
- Revolutionary Incidents: Sketches of Character, Chiefly in the Old North State, Vol. I (2010)
- Revolutionary Incidents: Sketches of Character, Chiefly in the Old North State, Vol. II (2010)

All books are available at your favorite local bookstore,
or at www.dramtreebooks.com

When the British Came

Revolution in the Cape Fear, 1765-1782

By Jack E. Fryar, Jr.

©2024 by Jack E. Fryar, Jr..

All rights reserved. No part of this book may be reproduced in any form or by any electronic or mechanical means, including information storage and retrieval systems, without written permission from the publisher, except by a reviewer who may quote brief passages in a review.

Published in the United States of America by Dram Tree Books

Publisher's Cataloging-in-Publication data

(CIP provided by DRT Press)

Names: Fryar, Jack E., author.
Title: When the British came : revolution in the Cape Fear, 1765-1787 / Jack E. Fryar, Jr.
Description: Includes bibliographical references and index. | Wilmington, NC: Dram Tree Books, 2024.
Identifiers: ISBN: 978-0-9814603-5-2 (hardcover) | 978-0-9814603-7-6 (paperback)
Subjects: LCSH Cape Fear River Valley (N.C.)--History, Military--18th century. | Wilmington (N.C.)--History--18th century. | North Carolina--History--Revolution, 1775-1783. | United States--History--Revolution, 1775-1783. | BISAC HISTORY / Military / United States | HISTORY / Revolutions, Uprisings & Rebellions | HISTORY / United States / Colonial Period (1600-1775) | HISTORY / United States / Revolutionary Period (1775-1800) | HISTORY / United States / State & Local / South (AL, AR, FL, GA, KY, LA, MS, NC, SC, TN, VA, WV)
Classification: LCC E230.5.N8 F79 2024 | DDC 975.6/2--dc23

10 9 8 7 6 5 4 3 2 1

Dram Tree Books
P.O. Box 7183
Wilmington, N.C. 28406
www.dramtreebooks.com
dramtreebooks@gmail.com

For the family and friends that shaped me:
Jack E. Fryar, Sr., Arlene C. Fryar, Charles and Carrie Bell Fryar, George and Alma Collins, Carol and Phil Hines, Ann and John Wingo, cousins Troy, Julia, Wes, Travis, and best friend Jon Dennison

For the teachers and historians who have made a difference:
Dr. Alan D. Watson, Dr. Chris E. Fonvielle, Jr., Jason Howell, Jim McKee, Shannon Walker, John Mosely, Jim Steele, Ray Flowers, Becky Rowles Sawyer, Beverly Tetterton, Hunter Ingram, Kim Sincox, Christine Jamet Lamberton, Dale Williamson, Jeanna Boyd, Judy Martinez, Steven Roberts, Russ Adams, Jennifer Robbins, Steve Wood, Hunter Moon, Meagan Thornton Surface, Dr. Larry Usilton, Dr. Paul Townend, Dr. Eva Mehl, Jason Collins, Mary Strickland, Dr. David LaVere, Bert Dunkerly, and too many others to mention

For the students who became friends:
Alejandra, Alexa, Alexis, Arabeny, Bart, Caroline, Dylan, Jon, Lilian, Kailee, Maddi, Victor, and Benji

But most of all, this book is dedicated to
Cherie
for literally everything

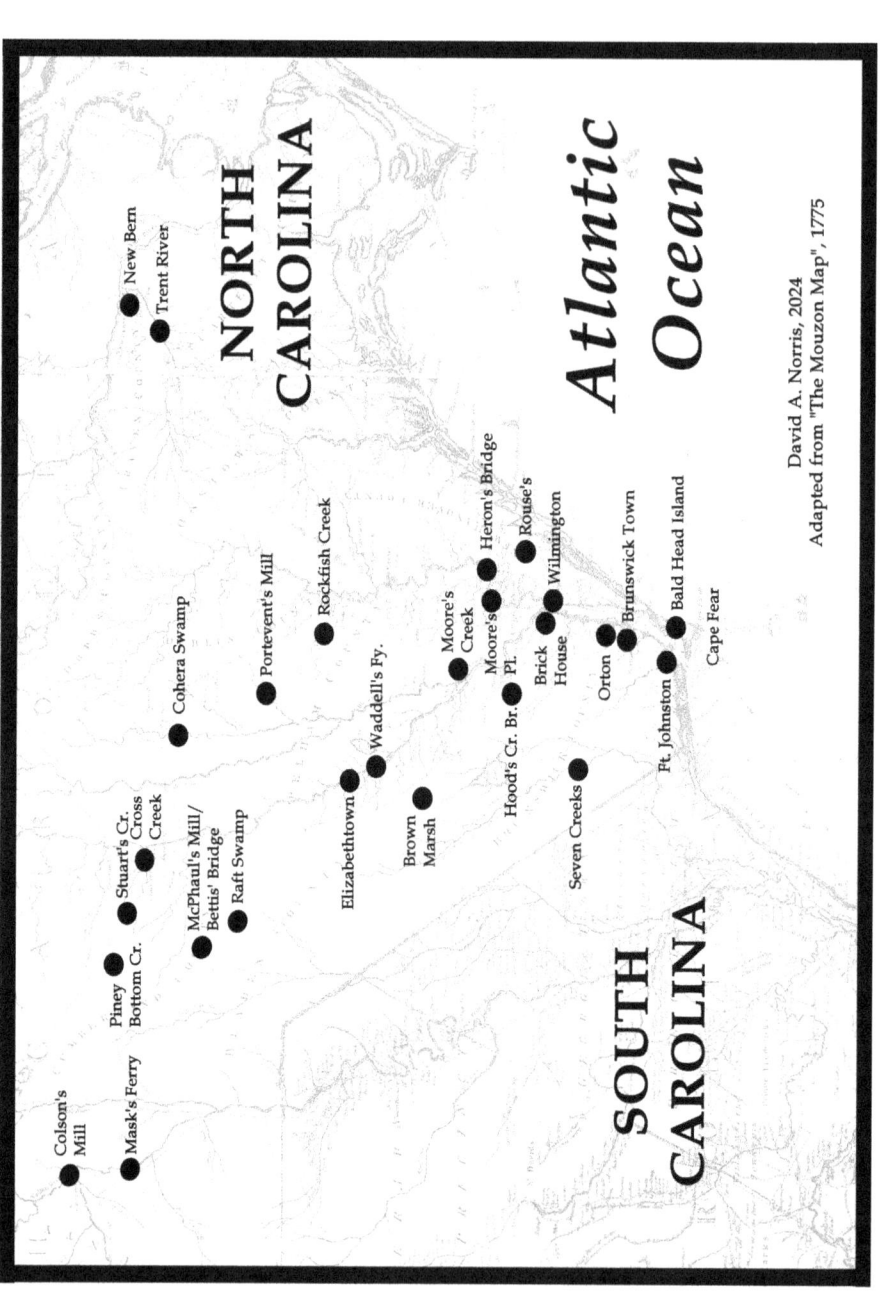

Sites of significant fighting in the Lower Cape Fear during the American Revolution. (Map by David A. Norris)

Contents

Origins
7

1765-1766
31

1767-1773
49

1774-1775
73

1776
111

1777-1780
169

1781
191

1782
323

Bibliography
333

Index
343

Revolutionary War Clashes in the Lower Cape Fear

Modern locator maps identifying where military clashes occured in southeastern North Carolina during the Revolutionary Era.

Maps by J.D. Lewis, from his website (www.carolana.com)

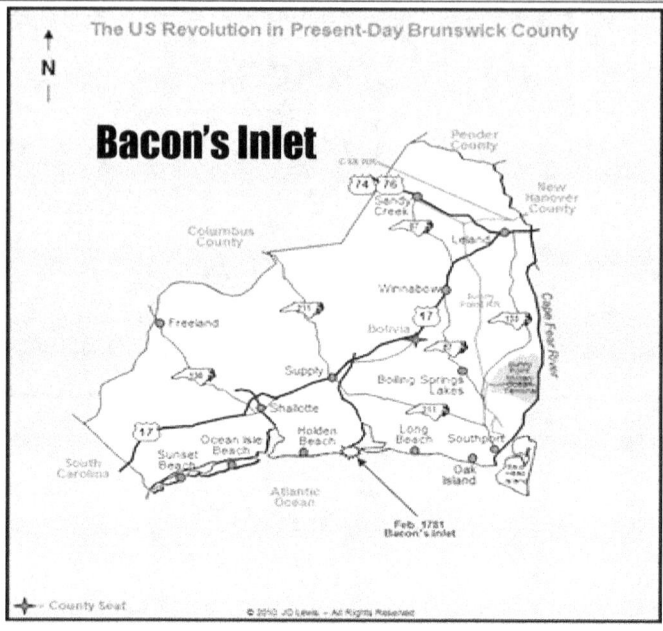

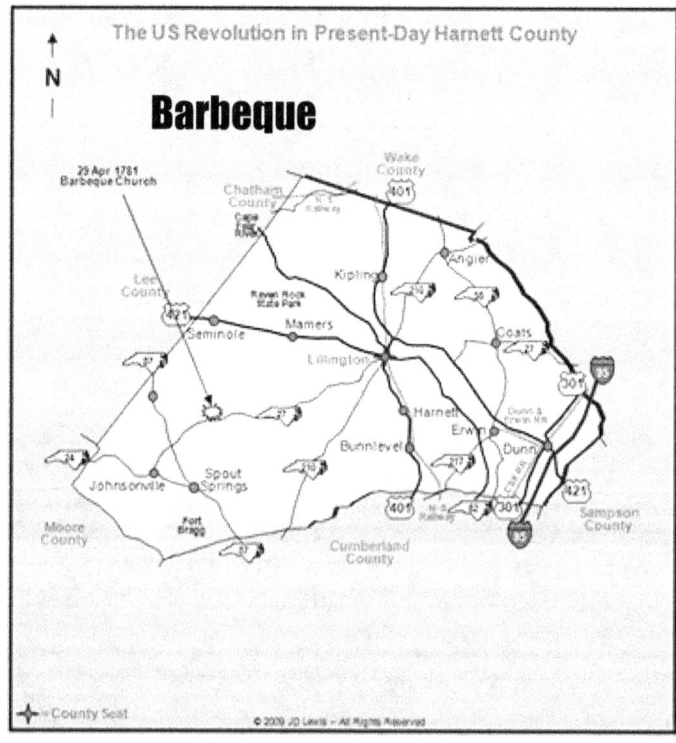

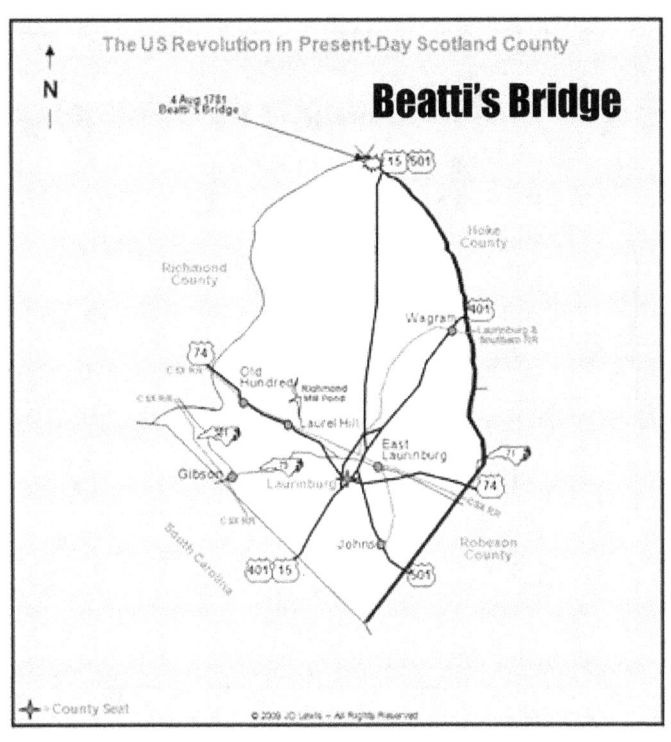

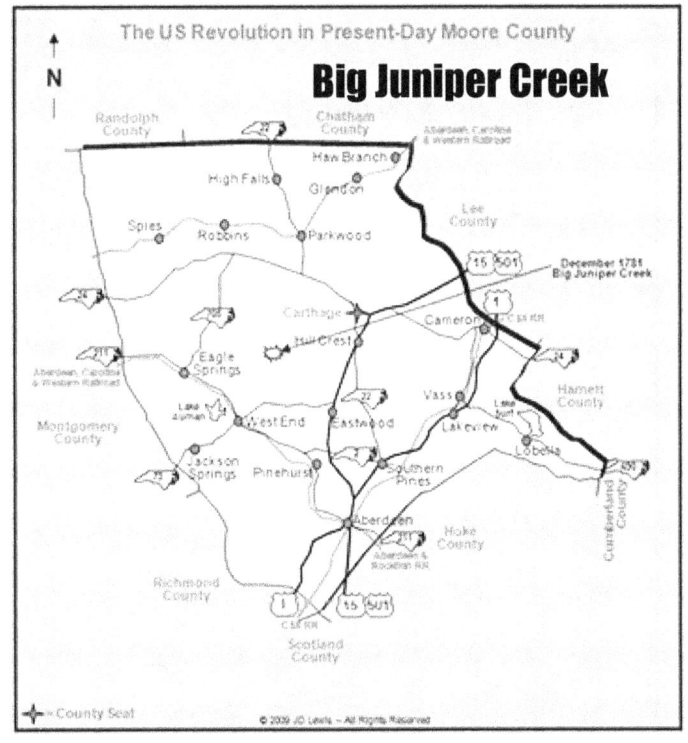

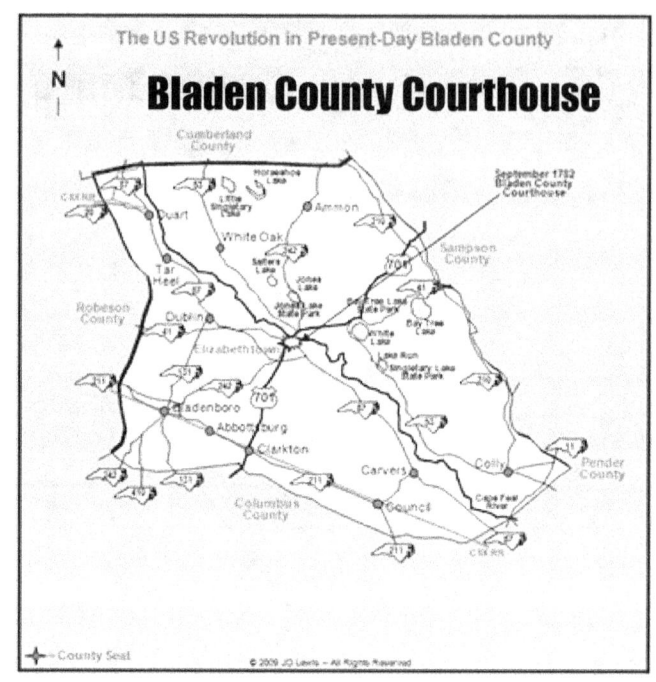

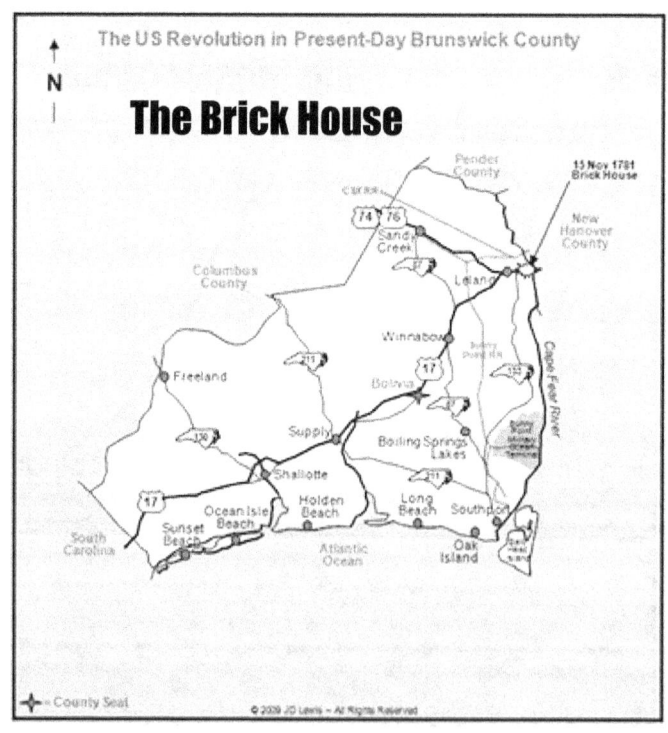

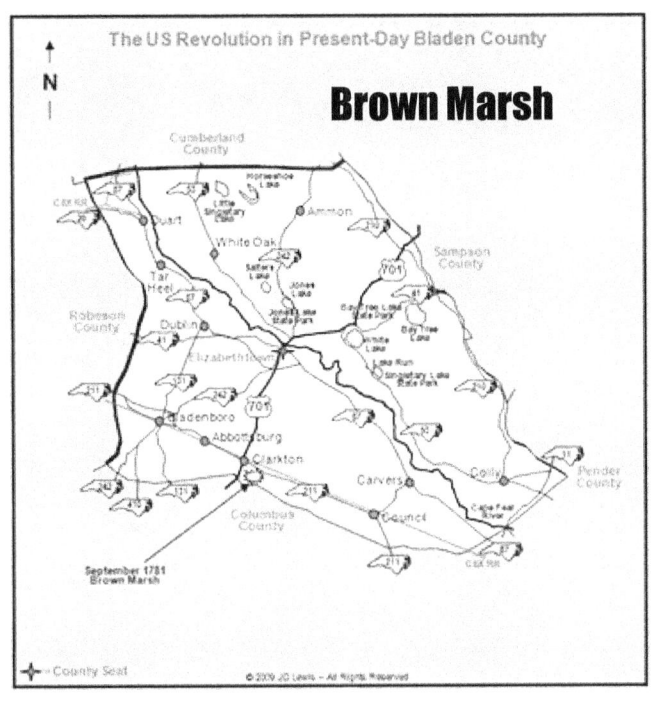
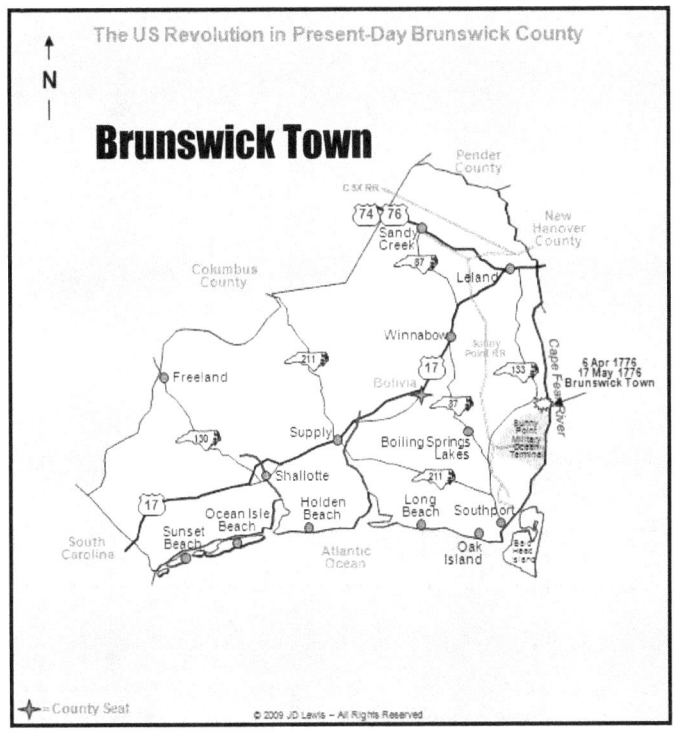

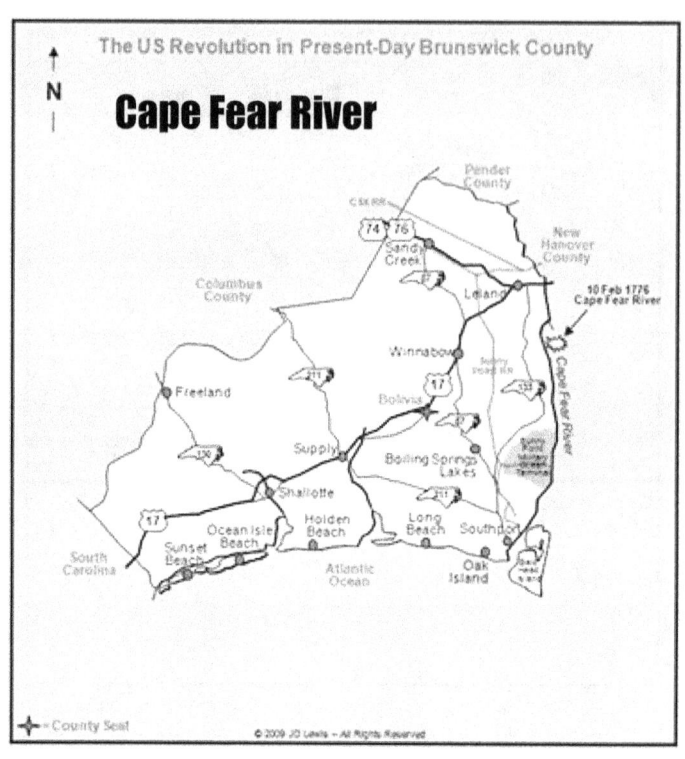

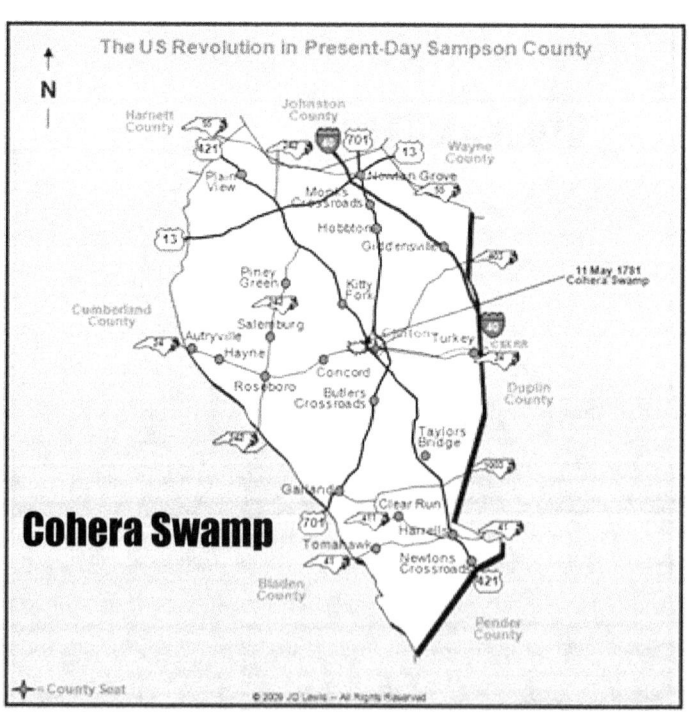

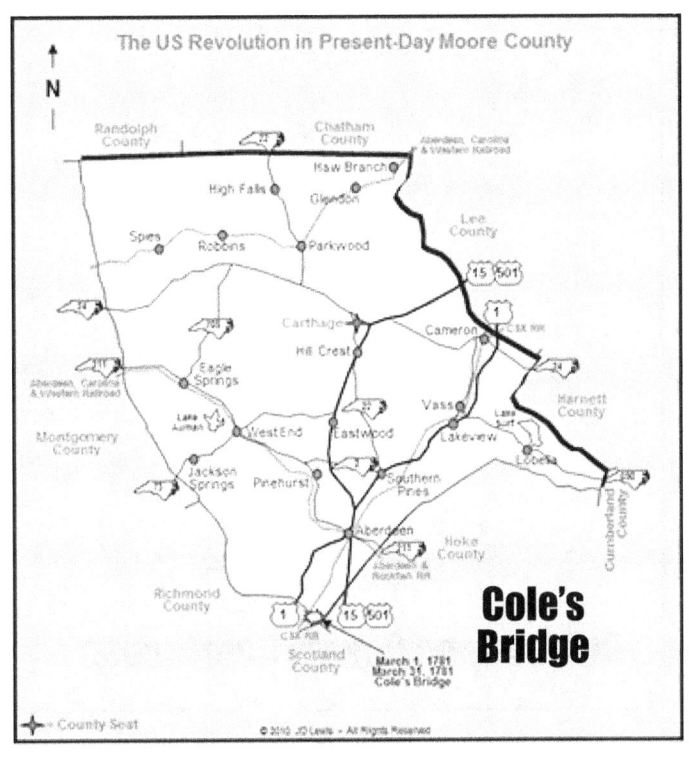

Cole's Bridge

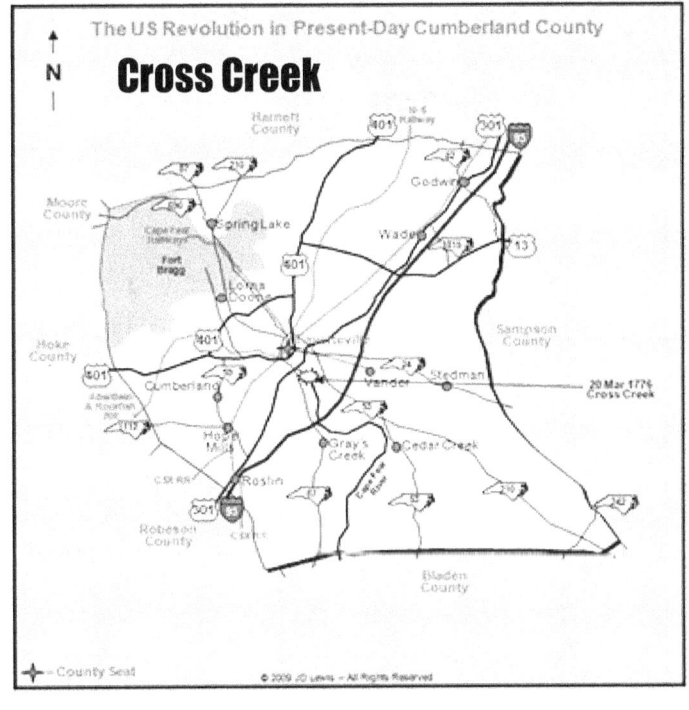

Cross Creek

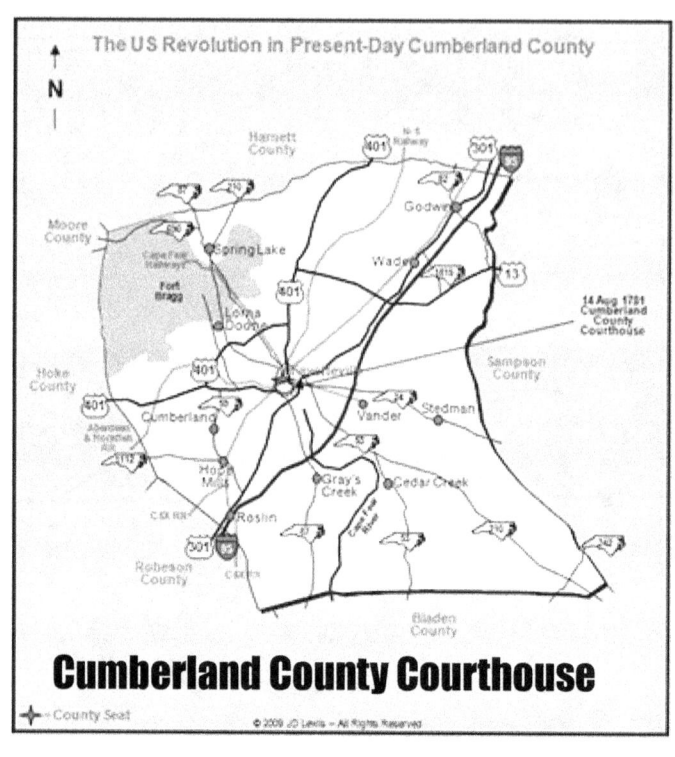

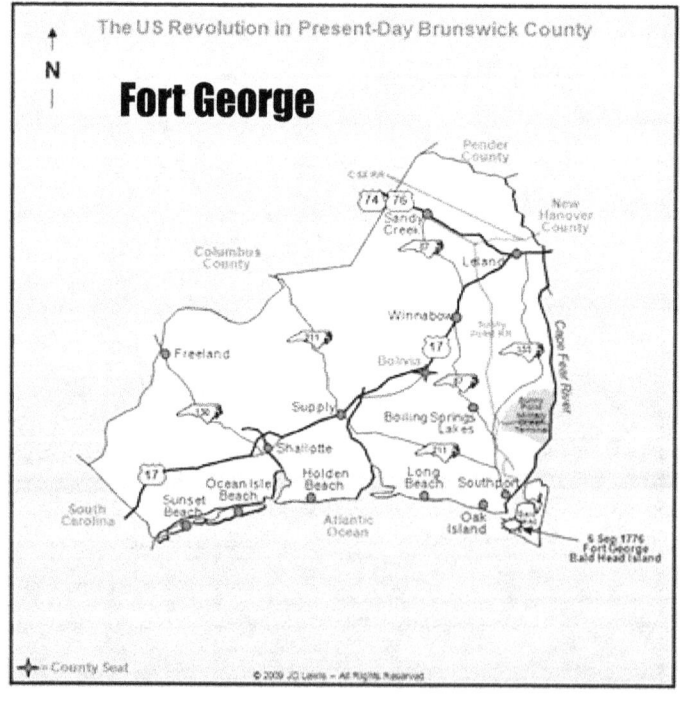

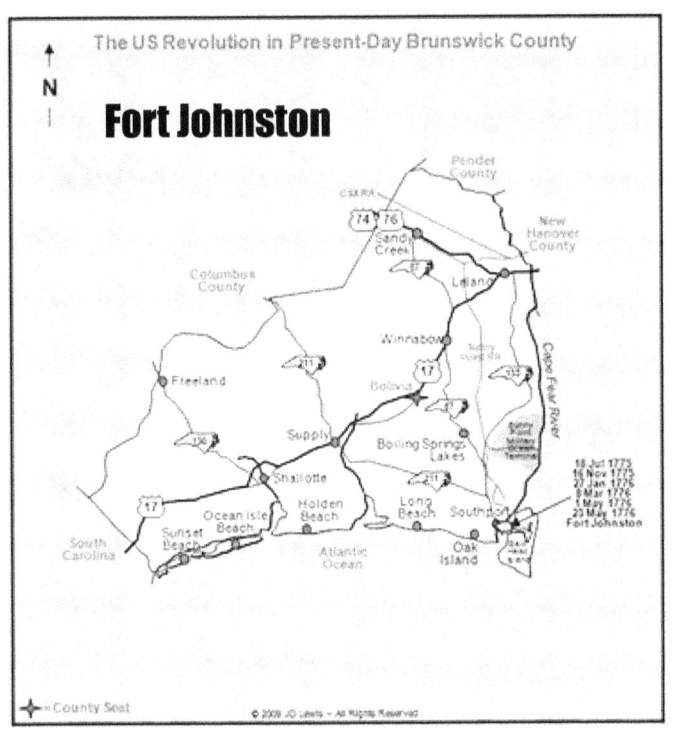

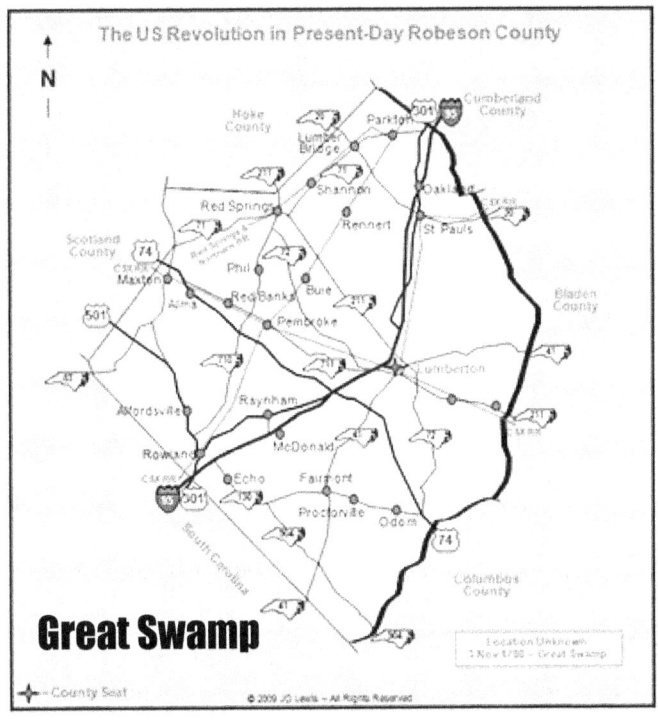

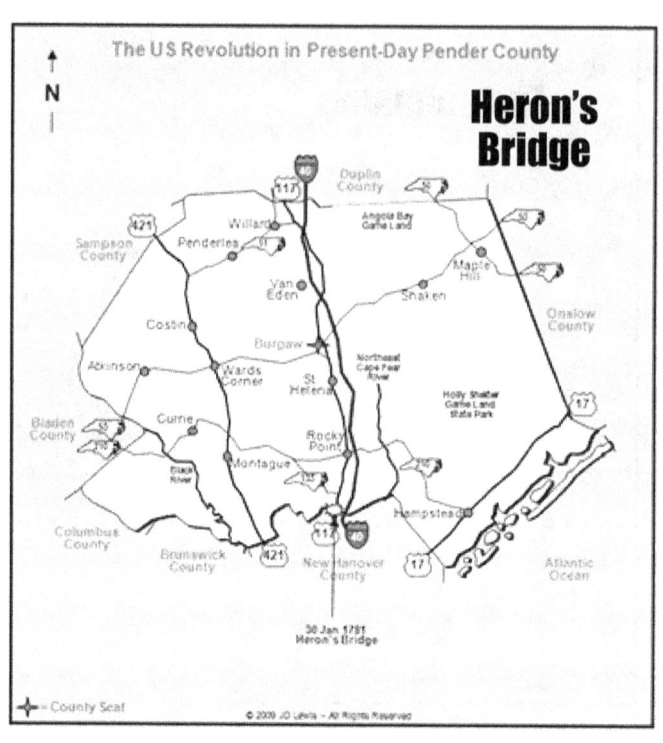

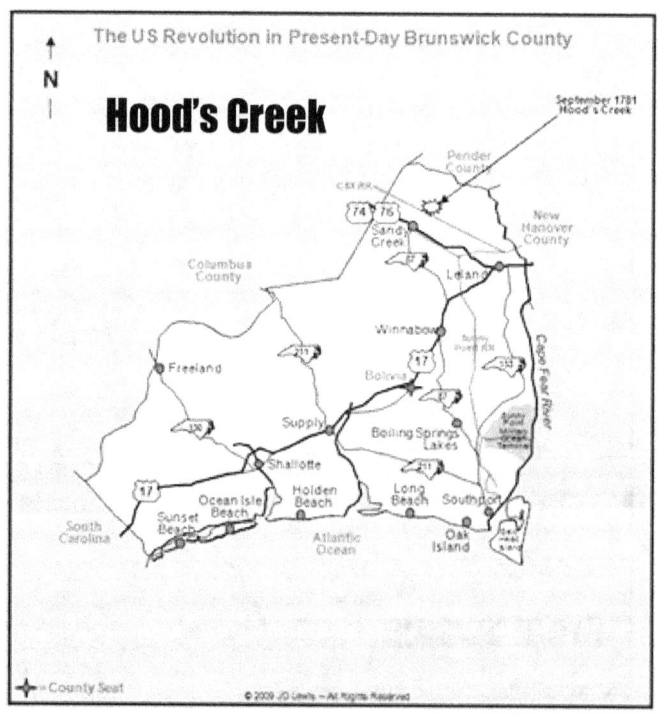

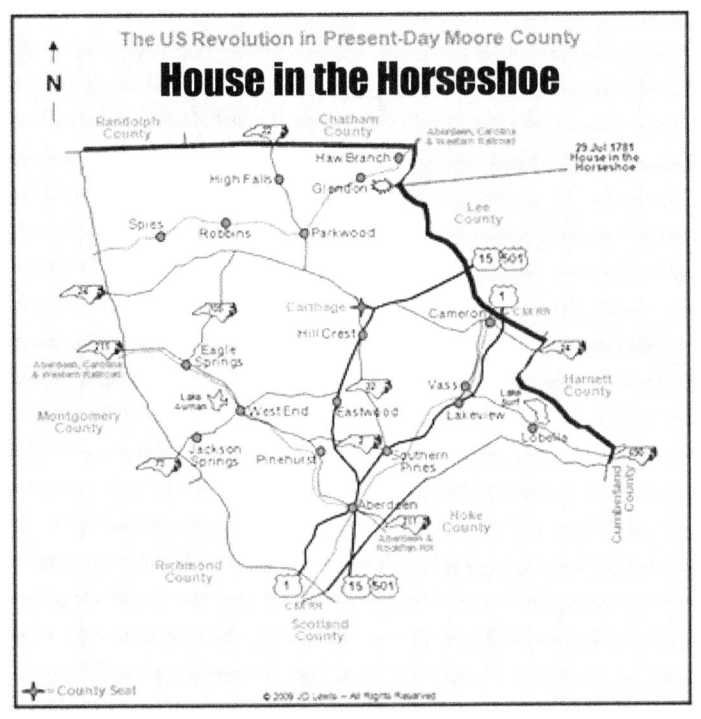

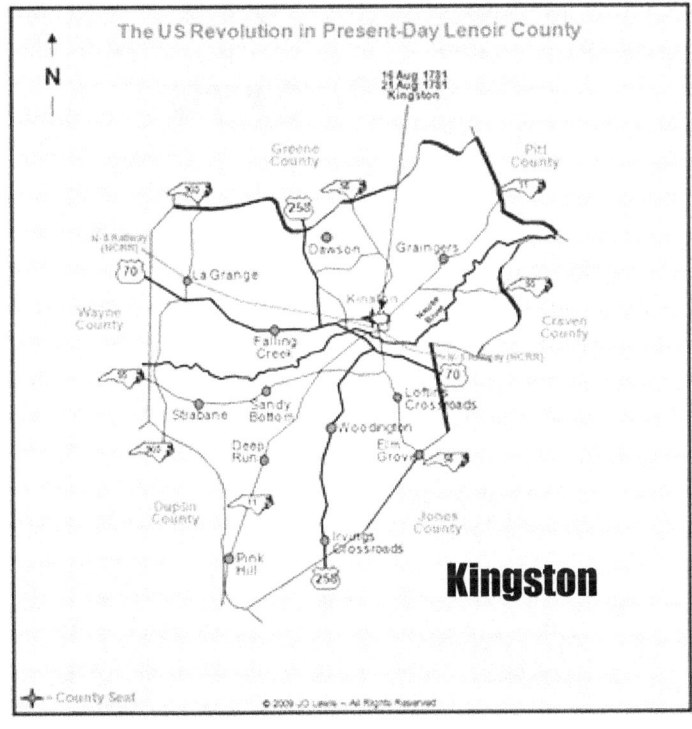

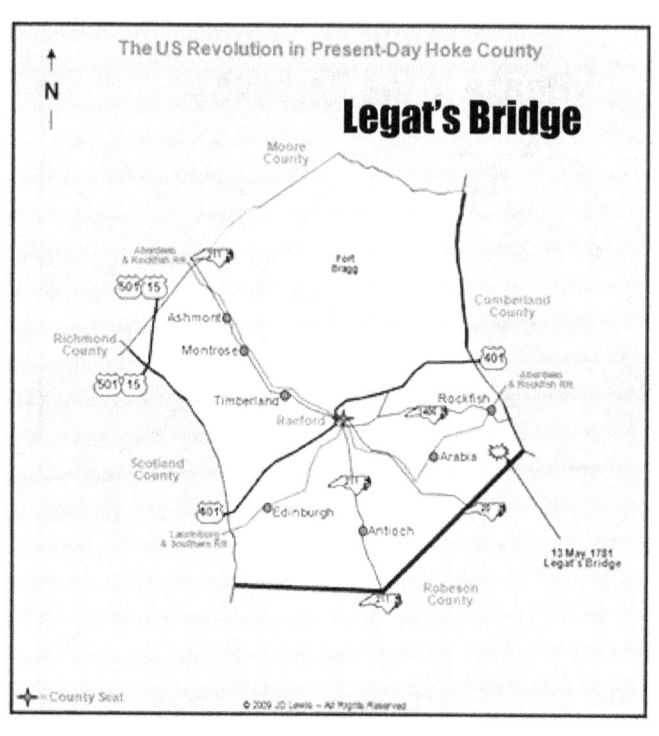

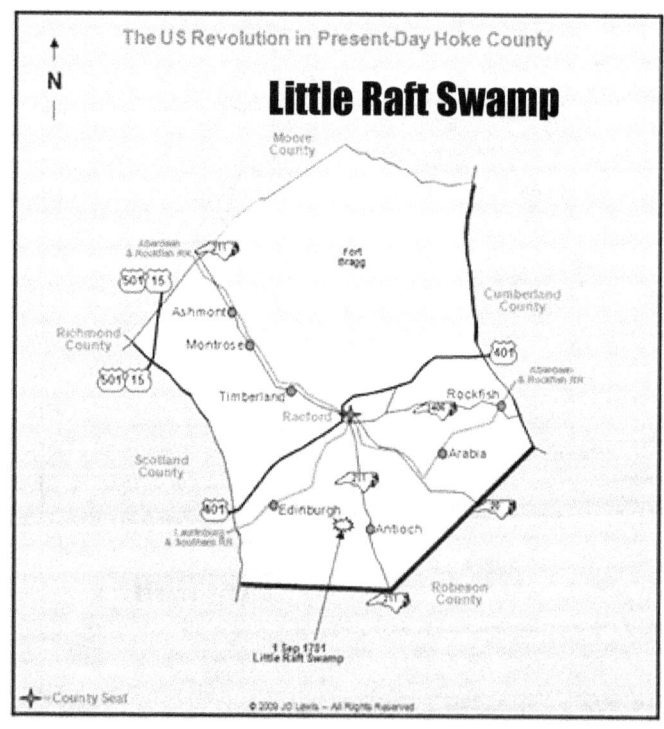

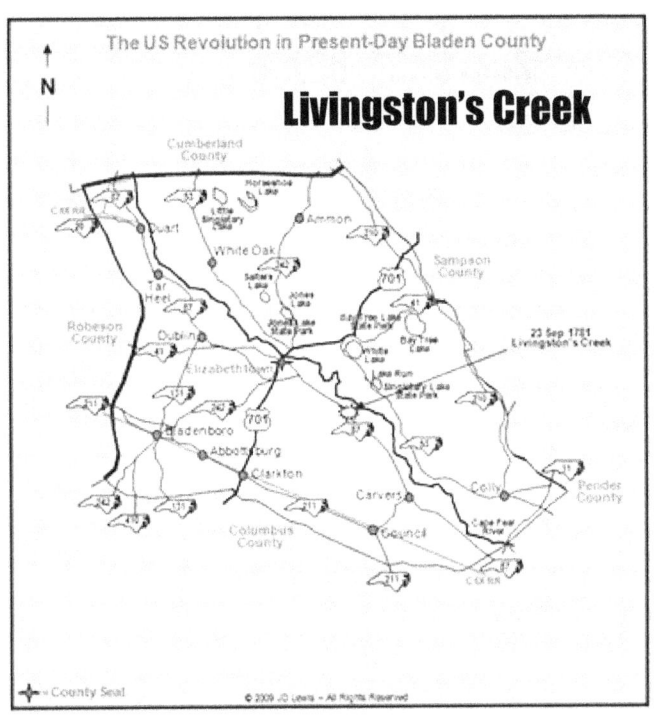

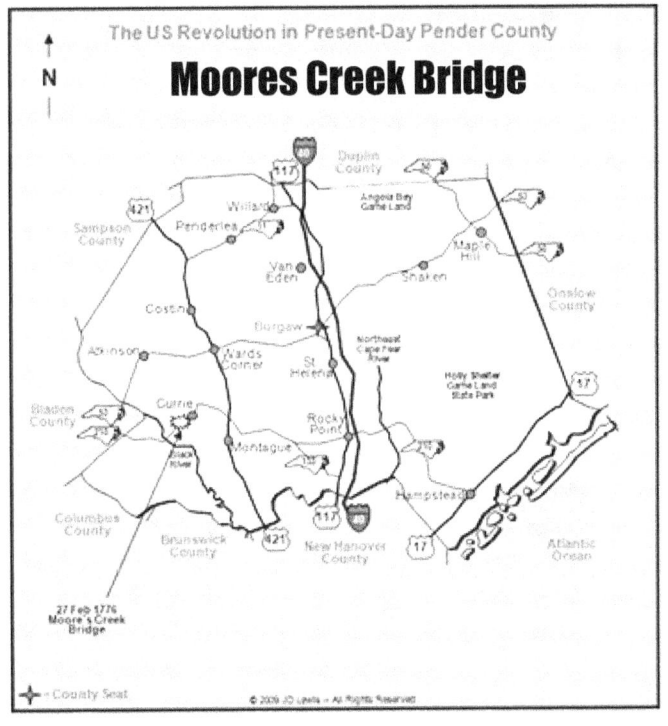

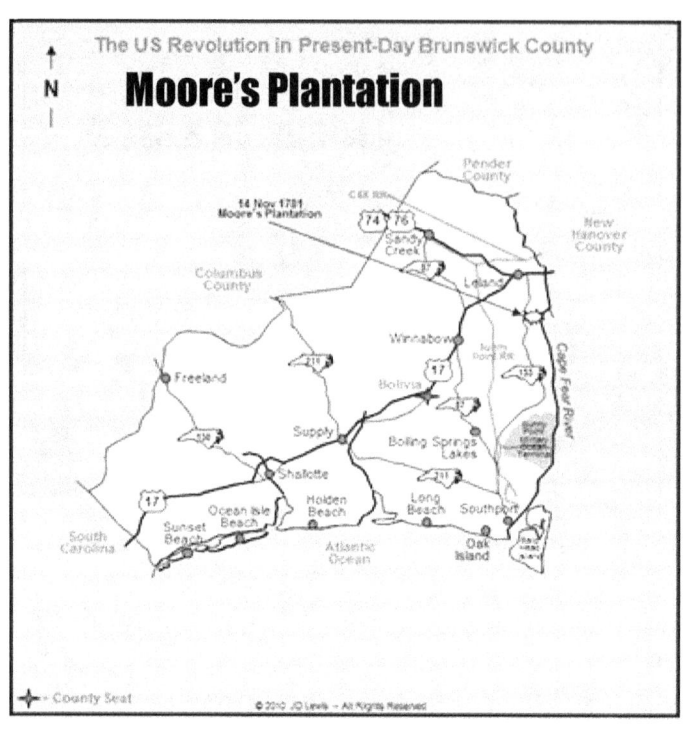

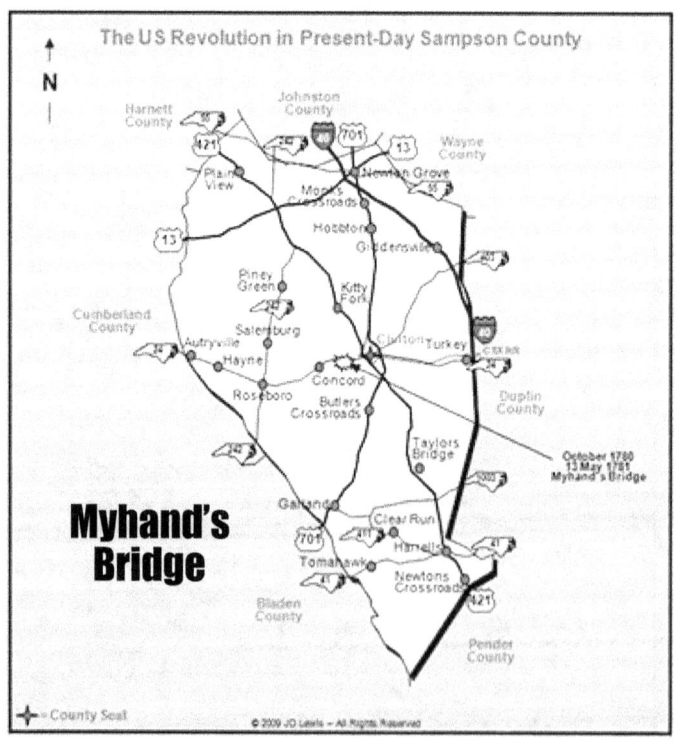

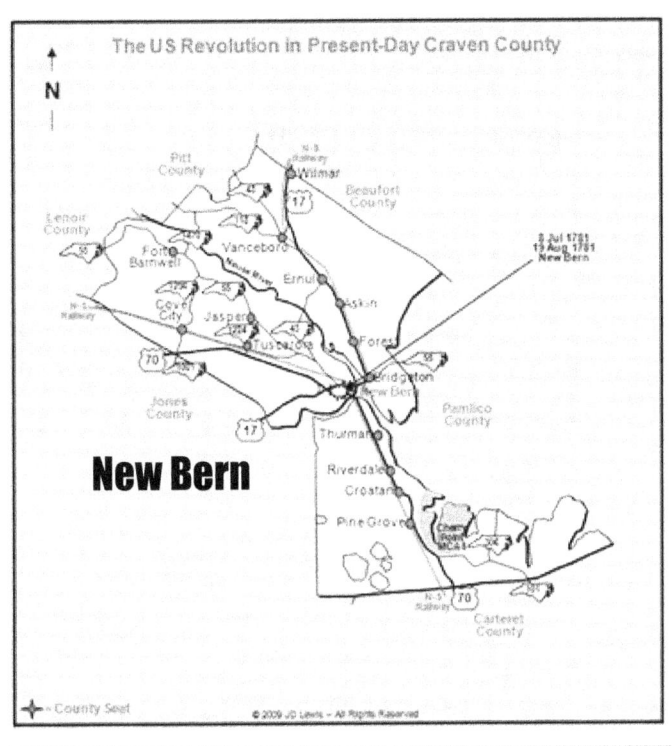

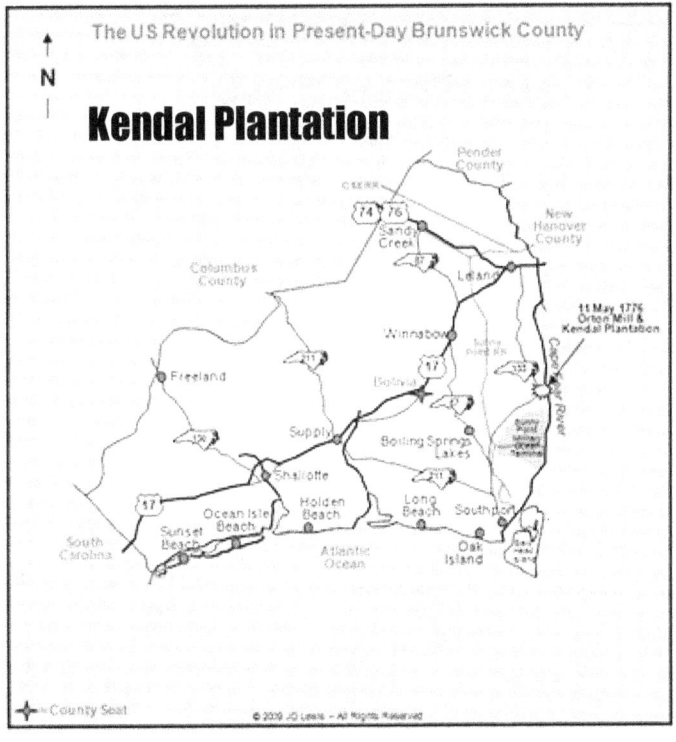

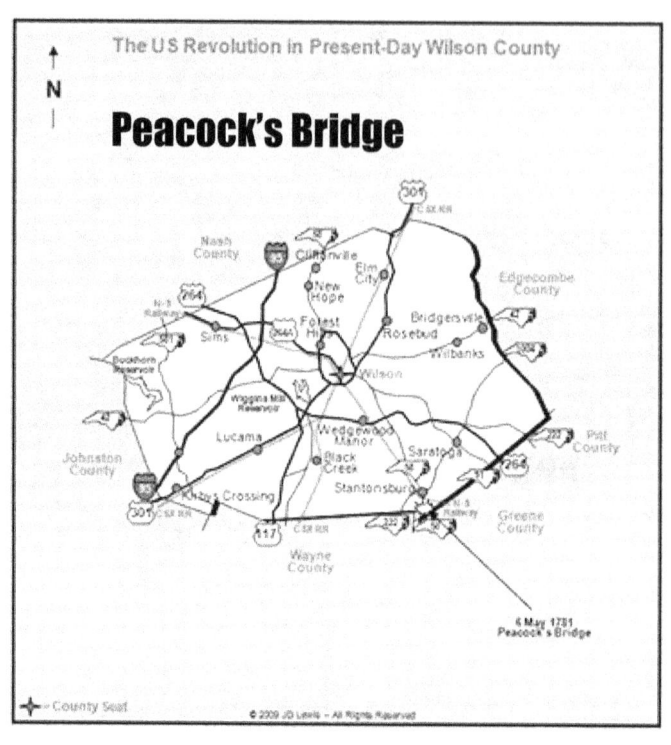

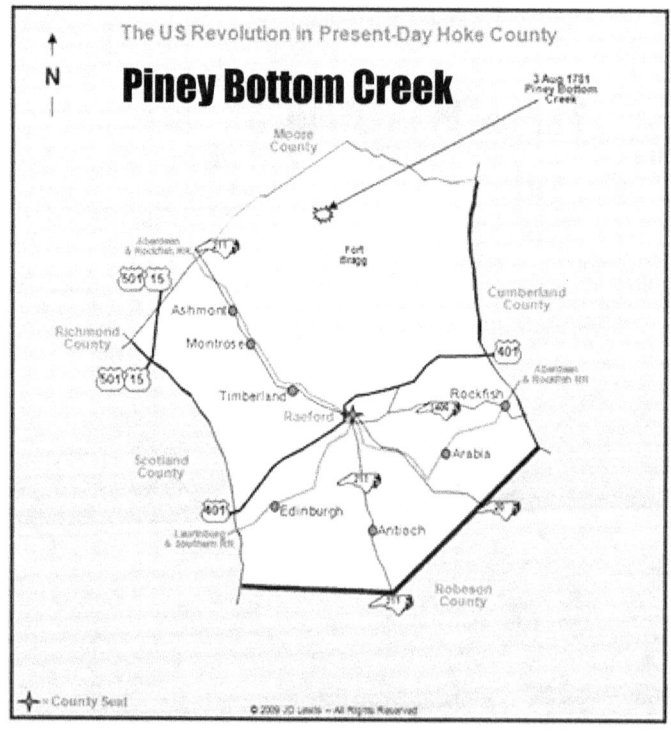

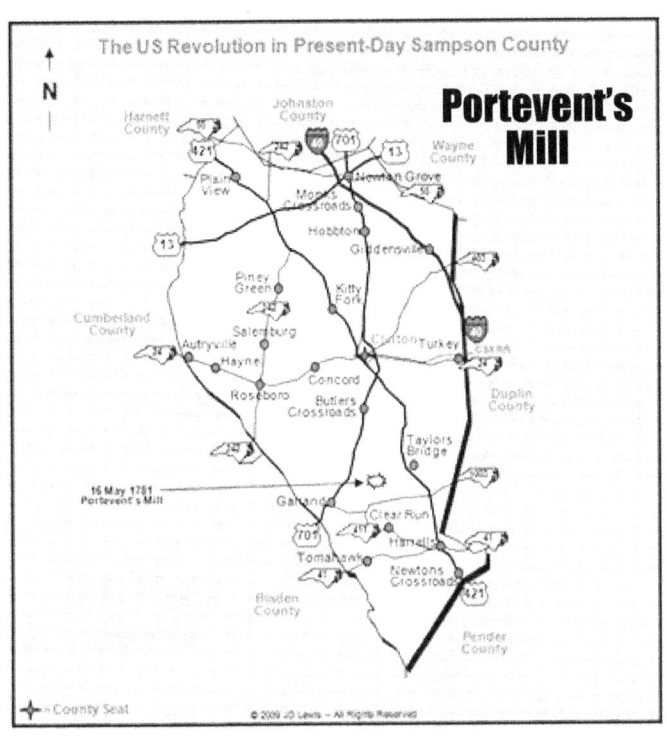

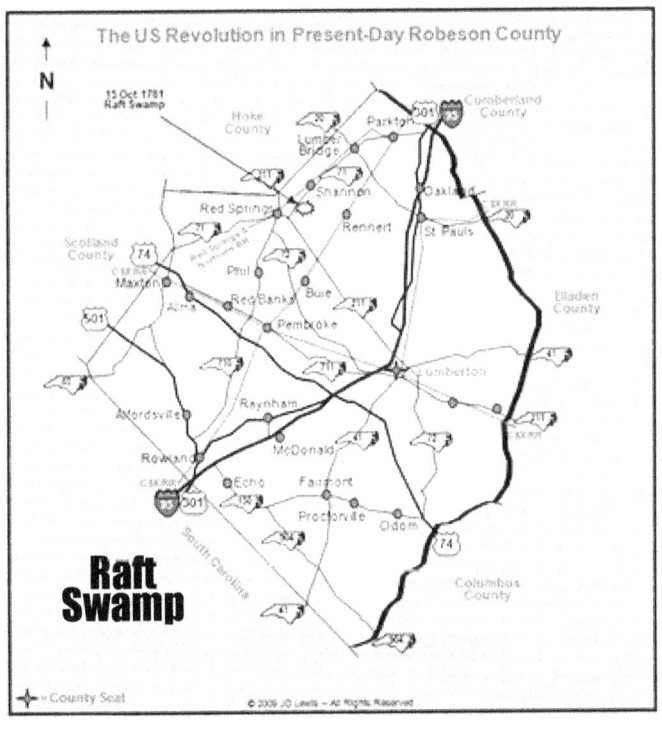

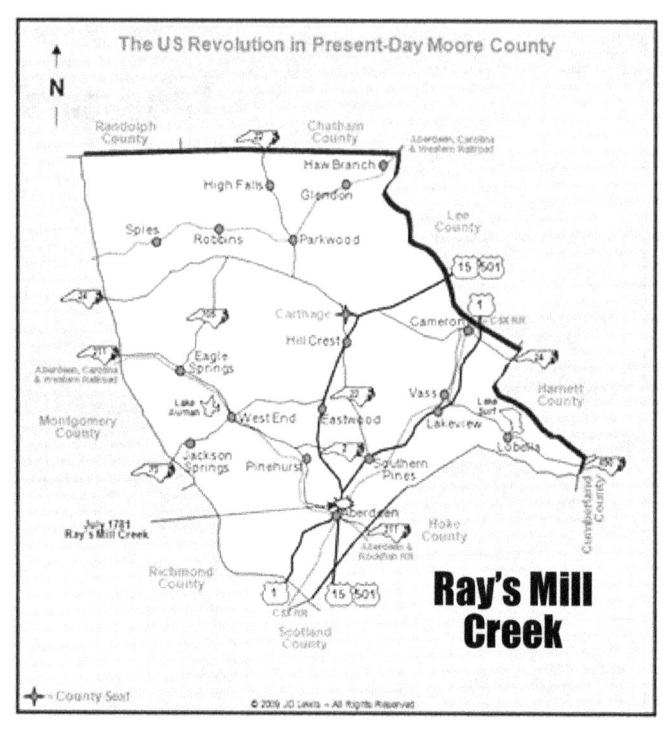

Ray's Mill Creek

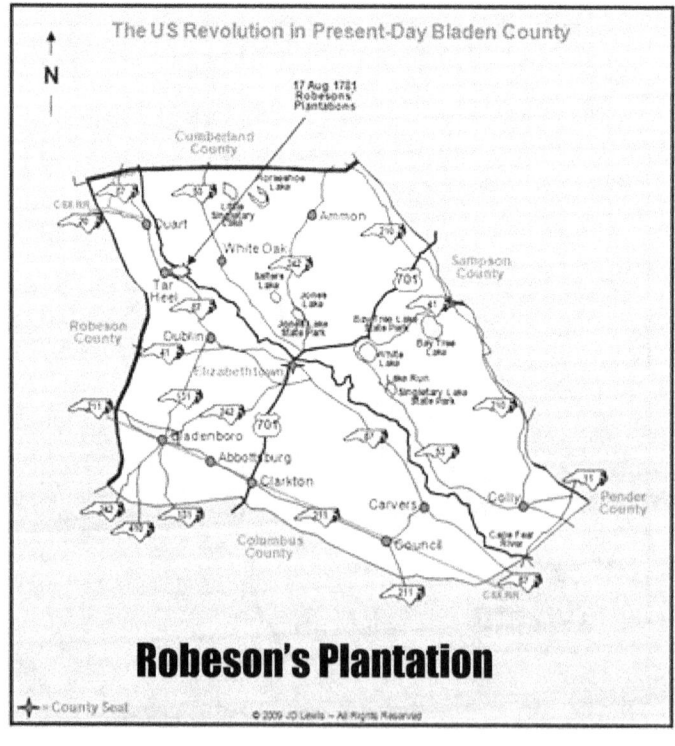

Robeson's Plantation

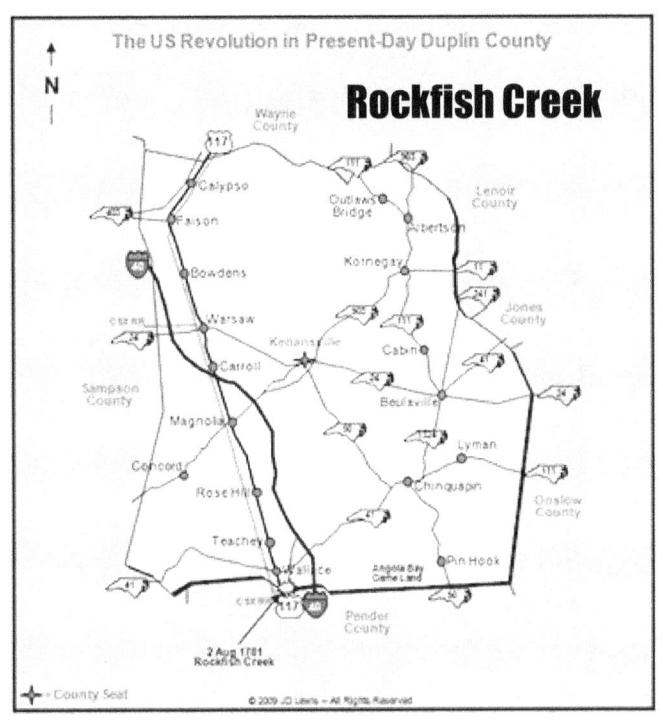

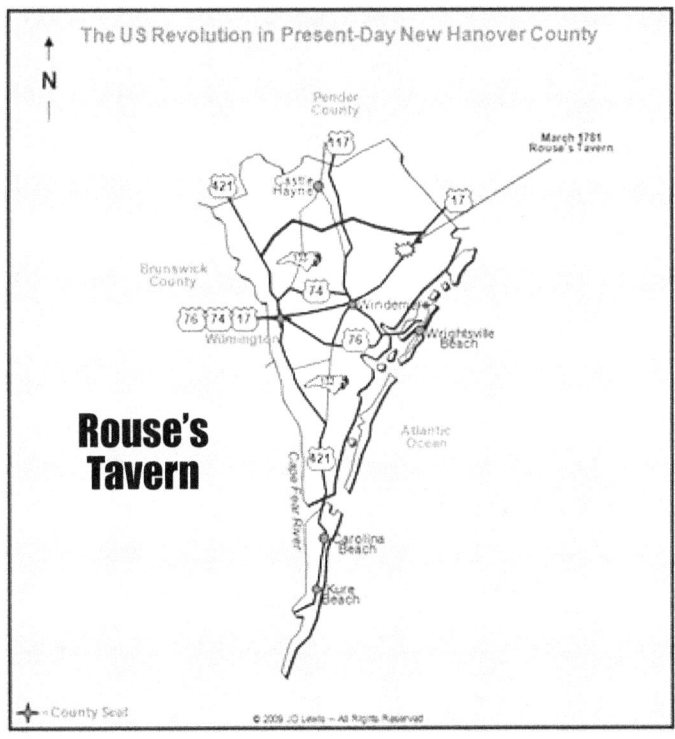

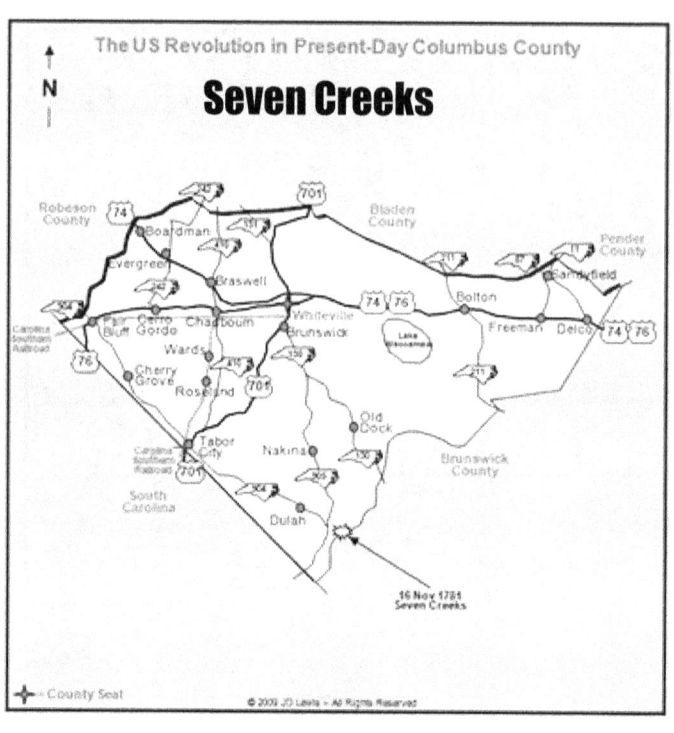
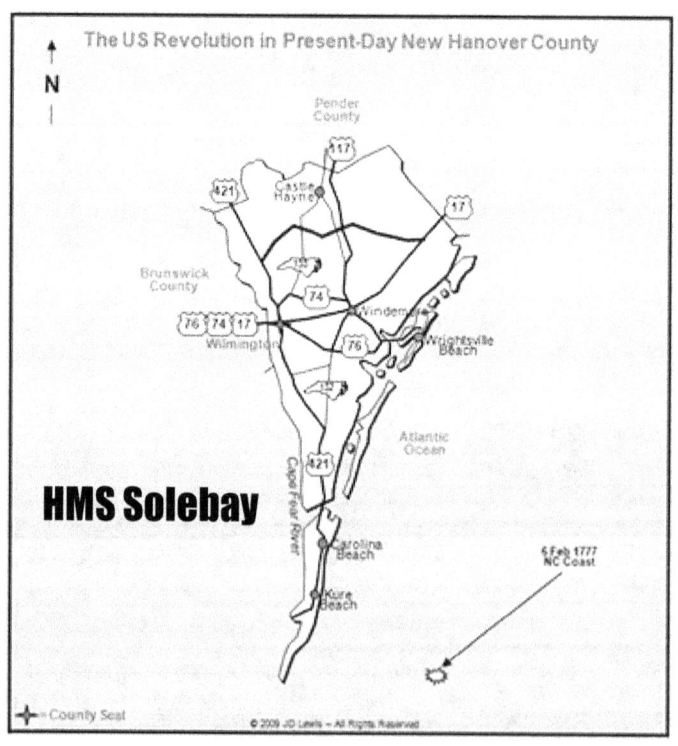

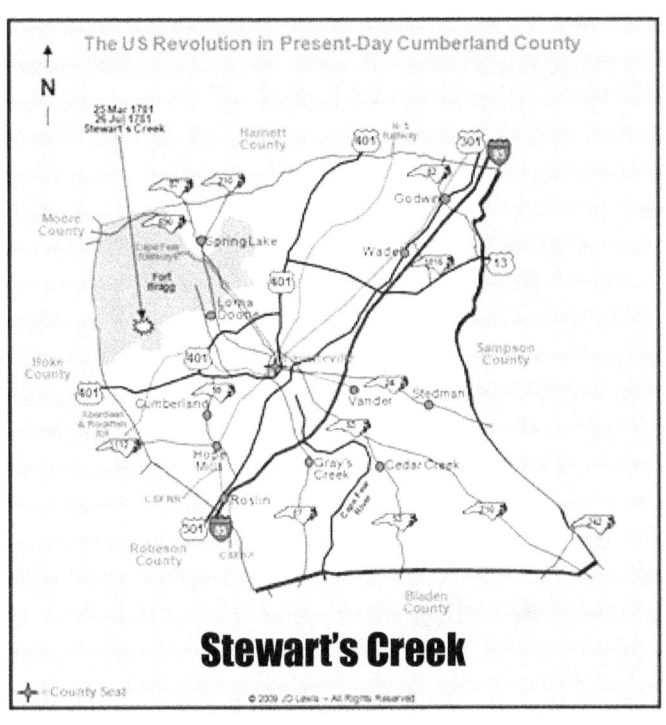

Stewart's Creek

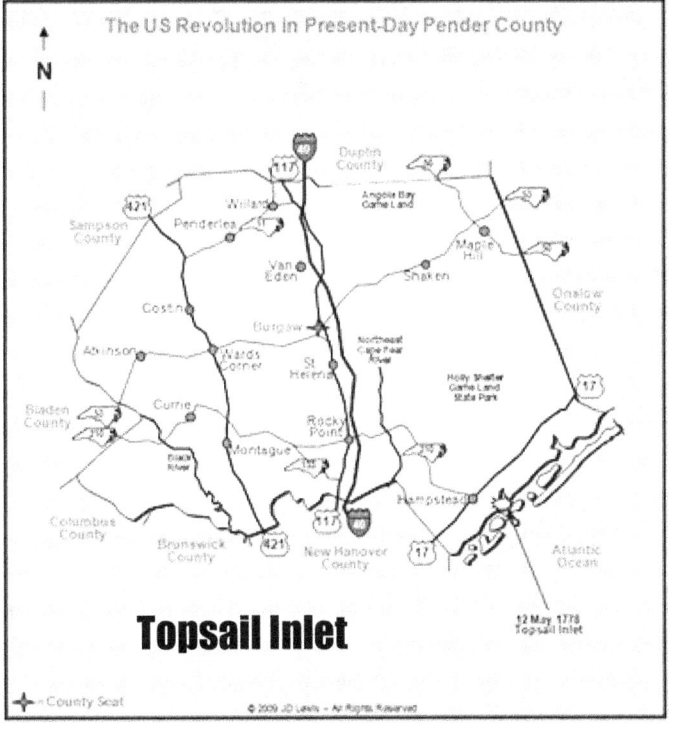

Topsail Inlet

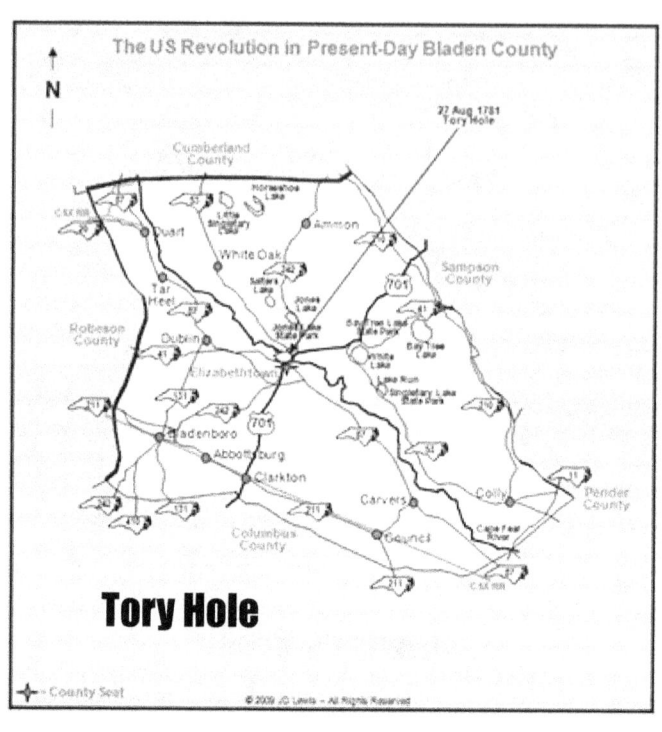

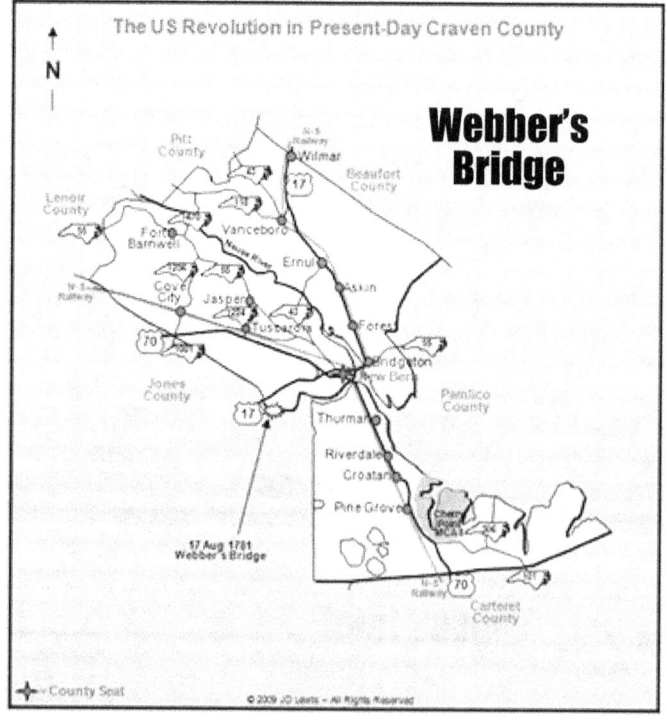

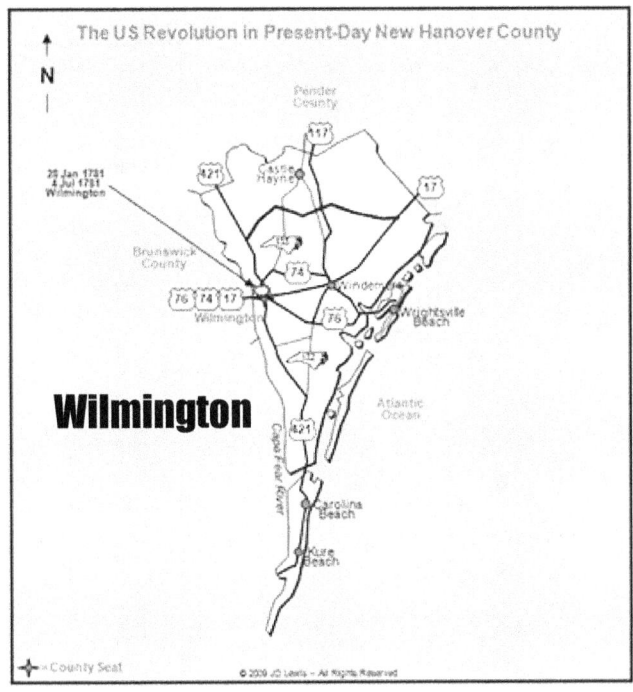

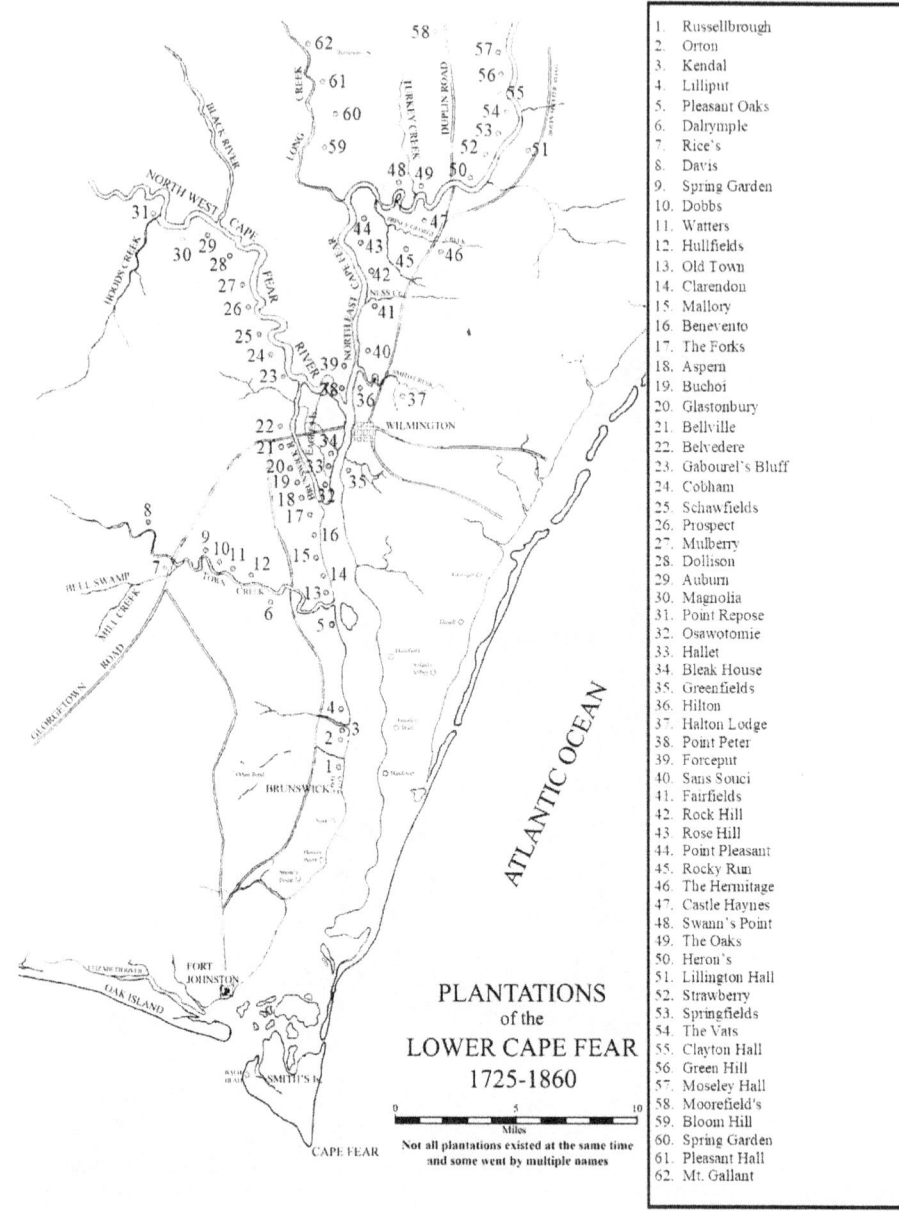

Timelines of Revolution in the Cape Fear, 1765-1782

Lower Cape Fear Revolutionary War Timeline

1765
3/18 - The Simpson-Whitehurst duel is fought at Brunswick Town by two British officers competing for the affections of the same local girl.
10/19 - 500 people meet in Wilmington to protest the Stamp Act.
10/31 - Wilmington stamp protestors hold a mock funeral for "Liberty."
11/1 - The Stamp Act goes into effect.
11/16 - Duplin County's Dr. William Houston - unknown to him - is made stamp master. Wilmington protestors confront him and force his resignation.
11/18 - Royal Gov. William Tryon invites 50 Cape Fear men to dinner to reason with them regarding the Stamp Act.
11/28 - The stamps arrive in the Cape Fear aboard *H.M.S. Diligence*.

1766
Mid-January - Merchant sloops *Dobbs*, *Patience*, and later the *Ruby*, arrive at Cape Fear River without the required stamps for their cargoes. The ships are seized by British officials.
2/18 - Cape Fear men pledge to stop enforcement of the Stamp Act.
2/19 - Roughly 1,000 men of New Hanover and Brunswick Counties march on Brunswick Town to prevent the landing of the stamps.

2/19 - Later, Gov. Tryon is confronted at his Bellefont home (Russelborough) by protestors.
2/20 - Protestors seize the impounded ships' papers from Port Collector William Dry.
2/20 - Comptroller of Customs Captain William Pennington seeks refuge from the protestors at Gov. Tryon's home.
2/21 - Col. James Moore and Cornelius Harnett lead a force of several hundred men to surround Bellefont and confront Pennington and the governor.
3/18 - The Stamp Act is repealed, but in its place the Declaratory Act goes into effect.
11/3 - Robert Howe assumes command of Fort Johnston at the mouth of the Cape Fear River after the death of John Dalrymple.

1767
11/4 - Howe's command at Fort Johnston is short-lived, as British Capt. John Abraham Collet arrives with a commission to assume command.
6/67-7/67 - The Townshend Acts passed and result in nonimportation agreements across the colonies, including in N.C. The acts are repealed in April 1770.

1768
The Regulator Rebellion begins.

1769
9/69 - Cape Fear Sons of Liberty enter into a nonimportation agreement to boycott British tea and goods.

1770
6/70 - Representatives from the lower Cape Fear meet in Wilmington to reaffirm their commitment to the nonimportation agreement.
12/14 - Josiah Martin appointed the new royal governor of N.C.
12/20 - Herman Husband is expelled from N.C. by the General Assembly for his role in the Regulator Rebellion.
12/31 - Gov. Tryon warns the Assembly that Regulators are assembling at Cross Creek (modern Fayetteville).

1771
3/1771 - Gov. Tryon and the Supreme Court bring charges against the Regulators under the Riot Act.

4/24 - Tryon and an army made up mostly of coastal planter elites depart New Bern to hunt down the Regulators.
5/16 - Tryon's army and the Regulators meet in the climactic Battle of Alamance.
7/11 - Royal Gov. Josiah Martin arrives in the Cape Fear.
8/1771 - New governor Josiah Martin issues a proclamation promising death to anyone who attacks Fort Johnston. Cornelius Harnett and the Wilmington Committee of Safety declare Martin an enemy of the people.

1772
Summer - Royal Gov. Josiah Martin and his family tour the N.C. back-country.

1773
1/30 - Adam Boyd starts publishing the *Cape Fear Mercury* newspaper, the lower Cape Fear's first.
3/30 - Josiah Quincy visits Cornelius Harnett at his Hilton Plantation (site of Wilmington's Sutton Water Treatment Plant).
12/1773 - N.C. General Assembly forms a Committee of Correspondence to maintain communications with the other twelve colonies.

1774
3/30 - Gov. Martin dissolves the General Assembly.
6/1 - Wilmington citizens send a ship with supplies to Boston in response to the Boston Port Bill.
7/21 - Wilmington citizens call for a Provincial Congress to select delegates to the first Continental Congress.
8/25 - The first Provincial Congress of N.C. meets in New Bern.
9/8 - William Hooper, Joseph Hewes, and Richard Caswell chosen to represent N.C. at the Continental Congress in Philadelphia.
11/23 - Wilmington forms a Committee of Safety (later to merge with the New Hanover Committee of Safety).
12/1 - Following a resolution of the Continental Congress, N.C. imposes an import ban on tea and slaves from Great Britain and the British East India Company.

1775
1/1 - New Hanover Committee of Safety formed (later to merge with the Wilmington Committee of Safety).
3/1 - A ban issued on the consumption of British tea.

4/7 - The Second Provincial Congress meets in New Bern. They approve N.C. joining the Continental Association, calling for a trade boycott of British merchants in the colonies.
4/8 - Royal Governor Josiah Martin dissolves the General Assembly as a result of its rebellious actions.
7/1775 - The Wilmington Committee of Safety decrees mandatory militia membership for all white males between 16-60 years of age.
7/18 - Robert Howe leads a Patriot force in burning Fort Johnston (modern Southport) to deny it to the British. The fort's cannons are spiked by the British and dumped onto the riverfront.
9/10 - A ban on exports to Great Britain and the West Indies goes into effect.

1776

Late 1775-Early 1776 - Royal Gov. Martin begins planning what would become the Moores Creek campaign.
1/1776 - Patriot militias begin to fortify Wilmington and seize Fort Johnston.
1/1 - Col. Robert Howe's First Regt. of the N.C. Continental Line arrives in Norfolk, VA in support of Patriot forces at the Battle of Great Bridge.
1/3 - Gov. Martin receives word that his plan to raise Loyalists in the N.C. interior and link them up with British regulars to put down the rebellion has been approved by Lord Dartmouth.
1/5 - The Wilmington Committee of Safety orders all Cape Fear River pilots into custody to prevent them being used by any potential British force.
1/10 - Royal Gov. Martin issues a proclamation denouncing the growing rebellion and raising the royal standard.
1/20 - British general Sir Henry Clinton sails from Boston with a flotilla to support Martin's plan.
1/27-1/28 - *H.M.S. Scorpion* fires 26 rounds at Fort Johnston. *H.M.S. Cruizer* attempts a raid on Wilmington, but is turned away by heavy musket fire coming from along the river banks.
2/1 - Gen. Donald MacDonald raises the king's standard at Cross Creek (modern Fayetteville).
2/5 - Col. James Moore of the Second Regt. of the N.C. Continental Line reports hostile actions by British warships in the Cape Fear River.
2/9 - Col. Moore learns Loyalists are gathering at Cross Creek.
2/10 - Militia colonels Alexander Lillington and Richard Caswell are ordered to mobilize their men, along with the militias of Dobbs, Johnston, Pitt, and Craven Counties.

2/10 - *H.M.S. Cruizer* captures the Patriot privateer *America* in the Cape Fear River.
2/12 - Gen. MacDonald arrives at Cross Creek to find no Regulators have assembled there yet.
2/13 - Admiral Sir Peter Parker's fleet departs Cork, Ireland carrying troops under Gen. Sir Charles Lord Cornwallis to support Martin's plan in N.C.
2/14 - Wilmington is in a frenzy on the rumor that *H.M.S. Cruizer* is coming upriver to support Loyalists.
2/14 - Duplin, Onslow, and Brunswick County militiamen arrive in Wilmington to bolster the town's defenses.
2/15 - Fifteen hundred Scots and Regulators gather at Cross Creek in response to Royal Gov. Martin's call to arms.
2/15 - Col. Moore and 650 men of the Second N.C. Continental Line march for Rockfish Creek outside Cross Creek to block any movement by MacDonald's Loyalist army.
2/18 - Scottish heroine Flora MacDonald waves at the largely Highlander Loyalist army as it departs Cross Creek for the coast. Her husband is an officer in the force.
2/23 - MacDonald learns Col. Richard Caswell's men are camped at Corbett's Ferry on the Black River. The Loyalists sneak past them by floating a sunken flat in the river and using it to cross over.
2/25 - The Loyalists camp at James Rogers' sawmill, six miles from Moores Creek Bridge.
2/25-2/26 - Militia under Col. Alexander Lillington and Col. Richard Caswell prepare their defenses on the east side of Moores Creek Bridge.
2/26 - Gen. MacDonald dispatches James Hepburn to deliver an ultimatum to Patriot forces at Moores Creek, and to collect intelligence on their dispositions.
2/27 - *H.M.S. Cruizer* anchors off Wilmington and demands supplies from the town, threatening bombardment if the town refuses.
2/27 - The Battle of Moores Creek occurs twenty-two miles northwest of Wilmington. It is a resounding victory for Patriot forces under Richard Caswell and Alexander Lillington.
3/1776 - Whig militias establish encampments along the Cape Fear River to oppose an expected British landing.
3/8-3/12 - *H.M.S. Cruizer* exchanges fire with Patriot defenders at Fort Johnston.
3/12 - Local slaves escape from area plantations to join Clinton's British forces. These escapees become the basis of the Black Pioneers (a.k.a. the

Ethiopian Regiment) that worked for British forces throughout the war.

3/12 - James Moore marches 120 men of the 2nd N.C. Continental Line to Brunswick Town to join militia already deployed there.

3/12 - Admiral Sir Henry Clinton's fleet arrives in the Cape Fear River. It is joined by additional ships and troops in May. The British begin conducting raids up and down the river.

3/20 - Loyalist forces under Capt. Thomas Reid capture a larger force of Patriot militia at Cochrane's Mill near Cross Creek.

4/6 - Royal Navy begins patrolling the Cape Fear River below Wilmington, foraging, looking for targets of opportunity, and recovering Loyalist survivors of Moores Creek.

4/12 - N.C. instructs its delegates to the Continental Congress to vote for independence from Great Britain.

5/76 - N.C. Assembly orders the imprisonment of all who took up arms against Patriot forces at Moores Creek.

5/3 - The entire British fleet (both Clinton's and Parker's flotillas) is finally together in the Cape Fear River off Fort Johnston. The forces numbers as many as 70 ships.

5/1-5/3 - Major General Clinton orders Fort Johnston destroyed.

5/2 - Clinton orders ten companies out to eliminate annoying Patriot snipers along the riverbanks.

5/7 - The British land two regiments (600 men) who are joined by escaped slave guides for a raid on Robert Howe's plantation.

5/7 - In Wilmington, three of William Hooper's slaves burn down his home (on modern 3rd Street) enroute to join the British. The slaves are captured and jailed.

5/11 - Troops under Gen. Cornwallis raid Howe's Kendal Plantation. From there they march to Orton Mill and burn it after a short clash with Moore's Continentals.

5/15 - The British deploy five regiments around Fort Johnston, and one more to Bald Head Island tasked with constructing an outpost there they name Fort George.

5/17 - Cornwallis leads a raid on Brunswick Town, but finds it deserted. They still sack the town and damage St. Philip's Anglican Church there.

5/20 - Patriot forces send a fire raft downriver in an attempt to sink the troop transport ship *Glasgow Packet*.

5/23 - During a bad storm, Patriots attack British troops in Fort Johnston after the redcoats reoccupy it.

5/31 - With the failure of Martin' plan after Moore Creek, Clinton decides to abandon the Cape Fear in favor of attacking Charleston, S.C. instead.

He leaves behind three warships and enough troops to garrison Fort George.

6/15 - The Loyalist DuBois family is exiled from Wilmington.

7/14 - N.C. Continentals at Wilmington mutiny. Militias are called out to restore order.

9/1776 - Robert Howe is promoted to Major General, and given command of the Southern Department. Howe would be the highest ranking Southern officer in George Washington's army.

9/6-9/7 - Col. Thomas Polk's Continentals conduct a raid by boat on Fort George. The raid is unsuccessful, but it could possibly be the first amphibious assault ever conducted by American forces.

10/8 - The last British warships depart the Cape Fear River.

11/76 - Loyalist property is declared subject to seizure. As well, all males ages sixteen and up are required to swear allegiance to the rebellion or leave N.C.

11/12 - The N.C. Declaration of Rights is adopted.

1777

2/6-2/8 - British warship *H.M.S. Solebay* patrols off Cape Fear, taking several merchantman prizes

4/15 - Brigadier General James Moore dies from "gout of the stomach," or perhaps malaria. His kinsman, Judge Maurice Moore, died in the same house on the same day.

5/1777 - British warships conduct a naval raid into the Cape Fear River to destroy several merchant ships anchored there.

6/11 - Most N.C. Continental regiments, under the command of BGen. Francis Nash, participate in the Battle of Bradywine.

1778

2/1778 - MGen. Robert Howe is sent to Georgia to aid in reorganizing their military forces, and to plan an expedition against Florida.

5/12 - Privateers burn a captured brig at Topsail Inlet, east of modern Hampstead.

12/29 - The British capture Savannah, defeating Robert Howe's much smaller force there.

1780

2/19 - BGen James Hogun's Continentals arrive in Wilmington enroute to reinforcing Charleston, S.C.

5/6 - LtCol. William Washington's cavalry retreat to Wilmington with seventy-five survivors of Banastre Tarleton's raid at Lenud's Ferry on the Santee River in S.C.

5/12 - The British capture Charlestown after BGen. Benjamin Lincoln surrenders Patriot forces there, including one third of the N.C. Continental Line.

5/24 - After the fall of Charlestown, S.C. governor John Rutledge warns N.C. governor Abner Nash that the British might target Wilmington next.

8/28 - Pursued by British forces, Francis Marion's partisans retreat to White Marsh (modern Whiteville) in N.C.

9/12 - Fifty-seven prisoners from the Maryland and Delaware Continental Line regiments freed by Francis "The Swamp Fox" Marion arrive in Wilmington.

9/24 - Francis Marion's guerilla force departs White Marsh and returns to S.C. after two weeks hiding from pursuing British dragoons.

10/1780 - Duplin militia skirmish with Loyalists at Myhand's Bridge in Duplin (modern Sampson) County, southwest of modern Clinton.

10/14 - Militia units from Bladen, Caswell, Guilford, Orange, and Rowan counties participate at the Battle of Shallow Ford on the Yadkin River near colonial Salem, N.C.

11/3 - A skirmish is fought between Loyalist and Patriot militias at Great Swamp in Bladen (modern Robeson) County.

1781

1/81 - MGen. Nathaniel Greene dispatches his chief engineer to Cross Creek to arrange for boats to be built for his army, possibly for use at Trading Ford.

1/1-1/7 - Col. James Kenan of the Duplin County militia defeats a Loyalist force in a skirmish at Drowning Creek (today the Lumber River).

1/7-1/8 - Cornwallis orders that Wilmington be taken to provide a logistics base for his Southern Campaign through the Carolinas.

1/11 - Alexander Lillington (of Moores Creek fame) awaits Col. James Kenan's troops at Cole's Mill.

1/21 - British forces under Maj. James Henry Craig depart Charlestown for Wilmington.

1/25 - Craig's 300 redcoats of the 82nd Regt. of Foot (a Highlander regiment) land at Ellis Plantation on the Cape Fear River, nine miles below Wilmington.

1/27 - A committee of Wilmington citizens meet with Maj. Craig to discuss terms of the town's surrender.

1/28-1/29 - Craig's forces occupy Wilmington under the protection of naval guns aboard three British galleys anchored in the river.

1/30 - The first skirmish at Heron's Bridge on the Northeast Cape Fear River occurs. Craig's redcoats clashed with militia from New Hanover County, Wilmington, Bladen County, Brunswick County, Duplin County, and Onslow County. The British succeed in scattering the Whig forces and burn part of the bridge.

1/31 - British forces under Craig seize or destroy several vessels on the Cape Fear River

2/1 - Two British galleys are turned back by heavy musket fire from militiamen at Bacon's Inlet (east of modern Holden's Beach).

2/2 - Patriot and Loyalist militia skirmish at Thomas Owen's Bladen County plantation.

2/7 - N.C. General Assembly issues a call to raise more militia to oppose Craig's redcoats at Wilmington.

2/18 - British naval units supporting Craig depart the Cape Fear River except for several galleys and gunboats.

2/21 - MGen. Richard Caswell orders the Kingston (modern Kinston) militia to the Wilmington area.

2/22 - A British burial party from *H.M.S. Delight* is fired on and driven off by militia on Eagles Island.

2/20 - Cornelius Harnett is captured at Col. John Spicer's Onslow County plantation and brought back to Wilmington bound and draped across a horse. He is jailed in the Bull Pen at 2nd and Market Streets.

2/28 - Harnett dies in captivity at Wilmington and is buried at St. James Episcopal Church.

Early March 1781 - British troops raid Rouse's Tavern (a.k.a. Eight Mile House, in modern Ogden) and kill Patriot troops there.

3/1 - Craig writes Cornwallis that he has been unable to fulfill his mission of resupplying the army by ferrying supplies from Wilmington to Cross Creek because Patriot militiamen infest the banks of the river, and control Heron's Bridge once more. The letter never makes it to Cornwallis.

3/1 - A skirmish is fought at Cole's Mill in Cumberland County.

3/4-3/5 - Militias skirmish at Clapp's Mill in Orange (modern Alamance) County.

3/9 - Craig leads troops in the second skirmish against Patriot militia at Heron's Bridge.

3/25 - A skirmish between Patriot and Loyalist militias is fought at Stewart's Creek, now part of Fort Liberty (formerly Fort Bragg).

3/27 - Cumberland County militia ambush Banastre Tarleton's dragoons at Barbeque Church in Harnett County.

3/30 - Cornwallis' army arrives at Cross Creek after the Battle of Guilford Courthouse and departs on **4/1** after finding no supplies waiting for him. The general heads towards Wilmington.

4/2 - Well-liked British officer Col. James Webster dies of wounds sustained at Guilford Courthouse and is buried along Cornwallis' route of march, most likely somewhere along modern Hwy 87. No one knows exactly where his remains are today.

4/3 - Cornwallis' column reaches Brown's Creek, two miles south of Elizabethtown.

4/7 - Cornwallis' army camps at Maclean's Bluff near modern Navassa.

4/9 - Alexander Lillington establishes a militia camp at Rutherford's Mill (near modern Burgaw).

4/9 - Cornwallis' badly wounded are ferried across the Cape Fear River to Wilmington.

4/10 - Skirmishes are fought at Drowning Creek (modern Fair Bluff) and at Rockfish Creek.

4/11 - Brunswick Town blacksmith William Cain is hanged from the yardarm of *H.M.S. Delight* for espionage. His body is dumped into the Cape Fear River.

4/13-4/19 - The rest of Cornwallis' army crosses the Cape Fear into Wilmington.

4/21-4/25 - Cornwallis, learning that a British army under General Phillips has landed in the Chesapeake, departs Wilmington for Virginia. He leaves behind his wounded under the supervision of Craig.

5/6 - Cornwallis' force skirmishes with Pitt County militia at Peacock's Bridge, south of Stantonsburg in modern Wayne County.

5/6-5/7 - Skirmishes occur between British troops and militia at Swift Creek, Fishing Creek, and at Halifax.

5/9 - Loyalist terror David Fanning narrowly escapes capture by Patriot militia at Deep Creek.

5/11 - Duplin County's Owen Kenan is killed in pursuit of Loyalists in Duplin County's Coharie Swamp (modern Sampson County, west of Clinton).

5/13-5/16 - Col. James Kenan's militia chase Middleton Mobley's Loyalists through Duplin County. The two sides clash at Myhand's Bridge before Mobley escapes.

5/16 - Col. James Kenan ambushes Loyalists fleeing from the fight at Myhand's Bridge at Portvent's Mill in Duplin County, northeast of Garland in modern Sampson County.

5/13 - David Fanning's Loyalists ambush a Patriot force at Legat's Bridge (a.k.a. Leggat's Bridge, Rockfish) in Bladen (modern Hoke) County, southeast of Rockfish.

June 1781 - Skirmishing occurs with increasing frequency across North Carolina. Craig establishes a British post at Rutherford's Mill, seven miles east of modern Burgaw.

6/20 & 6/27 - Craig and N.C. Governor Abner Nash exchange letters regarding the treatment of prisoners.

6/28 - Redcoats sortie from the camp at Rutherford's Mill with a combined force of regulars and militia.

7/4-7/10 - Col. Thomas Bloodworth snipes at British soldiers along the Wilmington waterfront from a cypress tree on Point Peter.

7/5 - David Fanning is commissioned a colonel of Loyalist militia by Maj. Craig at Wilmington.

7/6 - Craig issues a decree for Loyalists in Bladen and adjacent counties to be ready to march upon his order.

7/6 - N.C. Governor Thomas Burke is notified that roughly 250 Loyalists are assembled at Rutherford's Mill with the intention of taking Duplin and Onslow counties.

7/15 - Craig's men rebuild part of Heron's Bridge, joined by David Fanning's militiamen.

7/17 - Fanning captures 53 prisoners by ambush at Chatham County Courthouse. They are delivered to Maj. Craig at Wilmington.

7/26 - Militias skirmish at Stewart's Creek for a second time when irregulars under Hector McNeil interrupt Patriots commanded by Col. Thomas Robeson, Jr. from hanging a Loyalist in Cumberland County.

7/29 - Fanning's militia attack Col. Philip Alston's house (the House in the Horseshoe) in Cumberland (modern Moore) County, where he is barricaded with fellow Patriots.

8/2 - Craig departs Wilmington on a raid to the north, as far as New Bern.

8/2 - Redcoats under Craig defeat Col. James Kenan's militia at Rockfish Creek in modern Duplin County.

8/4-8/10 - The Piney Bottom Massacre on land that is now part of Fort Liberty (formerly Fort Bragg) and retaliation for it occurs.

8/14 - Loyalist militia under John Slingsby, Duncan Ray, Archibald McDugald, and Hector McNeil raid Cross Creek.

8/16 - Patriot militia try unsuccessfully to stop Maj. Craig's raiding force near Kingston (modern Kinston).

8/17 - Fanning burns the plantation homes of Whig officers Peter and Thomas Robeson in Bladen County, outside modern Tar Heel.

8/17 - Alexander Lillington's militia attempts to slow Craig's raiding

force with an attack on the redcoats at Webber's Bridge, in Craven County southwest of New Bern.
8/19 - Craig's redcoats reach New Bern, occupying it for two days and destroying Patriot property there.
8/21 - British forces skirmish with Patriot militia at Bryan's Mill on the Neuse River, seventeen miles outside New Bern (a.k.a. Battle of Kingston #2).
8/24 - Craig's raiding force arrives back in Wilmington.
8/27 - The Battle of Tory Hole is fought at Elizabethtown in Bladen County.
8/29-9/1 - Battle of McPhaul's Mill (a.k.a. Little Raft Swamp, Drowning Creek, and Beatti's Bridge, depending on the source) is fought in what is modern Hoke County, west of Antioch.
Mid-August - BGen. Griffith Rutherford receives orders to prepare his men to march to Wilmington.
Early September - Redcoats set an ambush for LtCol. Jacob Leonard's forces at Hood's Creek in Brunswick County, northeast of Sandy Creek.
9/12 - Fanning captures N.C. Governor Thomas Burke, along with several Continental officers, s in a successful raid on Hillsborough, N.C. He delivers the governor to Maj. Craig at Wilmington, who sends him by ship into captivity at Charleston, S.C.
9/13 - The Battle of Lindley's Mill (a.k.a. Cane Creek) is fought in Orange County (modern Alamance County) east of Snow Camp.
9/23 - Skirmish fought at Livingston's Creek in Bladen County, on modern Hwy 87, between Elizabethtown and Carvers.
9/28-10/1 - Battle of Brown Marsh is fought in Bladen County (modern northwest Brunswick County) southwest of Clarkton.
10/1 - Rutherford's force departs western N.C. to drive Craig's redcoats out of Wilmington.
10/15 - Battle of Little Raft Swamp fought near modern Red Springs, in Robeson County.
10/17 - MGen. Sir Charles Lord Cornwallis surrenders his army at the siege of Yorktown in Virginia.
10/23 - Griffith Rutherford marches his force from Cross Creek to Wilmington, splitting into two elements to attack the British there from the north and east.
11/14 - Patriot cavalry scatter Loyalists at Alfred Moore's Buchoi Plantation in Brunswick County (modern Belville).
11/15 - Troops of the N.C. Legion attack fifty redcoats garrisoning the "Brick House" on Eagles Island, across the river from Wilmington's Mar-

ket Street.

11/16 - Skirmishers fight at Seven Creeks in Brunswick County, southeast of modern Tabor City near the border with South Carolina.

11/17 - Henry "Lighthorse Harry" Lee brings word of Cornwallis' surrender at Yorktown. Patriot forces surrounding Wilmington fire celebratory shots into the air, alerting Craig that something important has happened.

11/17 - Patriot forces advance to Schaw's Plantation in Brunswick County, tightening the noose around Craig's occupiers.

11/18 - Maj. Craig orders the evacuation of Wilmington. Soldiers, civilian Loyalists, and escaped slaves all board British ships and make their way down the Cape Fear River to leave southeastern North Carolina for good.

12/10 - Violence continues between Patriot and Loyalist militias in N.C., including a large raid along the Deep River.

12/1781 - David Fanning catches Patriot Captain John Cox at his father's home on Big Juniper Creek in Cumberland (modern Moore) County. Cox escapes, but two other Patriots with him are killed.

1782

1/1 - The sale of confiscated Loyalist property begins in N.C.

1/7 - Loyalist Col. David Fanning seeks to negotiate his surrender.

9/1782 - N.C. Continental Line officer Capt. Robert Raiford leads thirty men into the courthouse at Elizabethtown and attacked lawyer Archibald MacLaine for defending a Loyalist in court.

Timeline of British Naval Activity at Cape Fear, 1775-1776

(Compiled and contributed by historian Jim McKee from ship's logs and naval records)

March 22, 1775 (Cruizer): Capt. Francis Parry arrives in CFR to take command of *Cruizer*.
Snow Point NWBN 1 mile

May 27 (Cruizer): Moved to Fort Johnston

June 2 (Cruizer): Off Ft. Johnston. Gov. Martin onboard that day. Martin saluted w/ 13 guns

June 9 (Cruizer): Sent Lt. & 7 men onboard a schooner called the *Royal Hunter*

July 4 (Scorpion): Charleston. Sailed for Cape Fear.

July 5 (Scorpion): AM off cape Fear bar. 4:30PM anchored, Cape Fear EbN1/2N 5 or 6 miles.

July 9 (Scorpion): Cape Fear NW 12 leagues. 8AM saw sail, gave chase & fired 2 6-pdrs.
July 16 (Cruizer): removed stores from Ft. Johnston
July 17-18 (Cruizer): Ibid
July 20 (Cruizer): recovered trucks taken into the woods and placed onboard *Sally*. *Sally* left for Boston with garrison and stores from Fort. Guns & carriages left behind.
July 21 (Cruizer): burned carriages in fort. A tender arrived from Adm. Graves
July 22 (Cruizer): spiked the guns. Ship from Glasgow arrived
July 26 (Cruizer): Parry's report to Adm. Graves reporting condition of *Cruizer*.
July 31 (Cruizer): Seized Snow *Fisher & Friendship*
August 22 (Cruizer): Orders drafted for *Cruizer* to return to Boston
Sept. 17 (Scorpion): Arrived Bermuda
Oct. 7 (Cruizer): seized Brig *Adventure*
Oct. 25 (Scorpion): Depart Bermuda
Nov. 11 (Scorpion): Off Cape Fear River bar.
Nov. 12 (Scorpion): anchored off Fort Johnston with *Palliser* transport & and a ship with Emigrants from Scotland. Too late to relieve *Cruizer*.
Nov. 13 (Scorpion): Moored off Fort Johnston WNW 2 cables length. Sent party of men to clear away for getting the guns off.
Nov. 14 (Scorpion): Onboard Gov. Martin. Saluted with 13 guns. 3PM fired 6-pdr with round and grape at rebels
Nov. 15 (Scorpion): *Cruizer* moved closer to shore to protect men removing guns.
Nov. 16 (Scorpion): AM sent gear to *Palliser* to receive guns from fort. Fired 2 6-pdrs at rebels. Sent Lt. and 15 marines to prevent rebels taking possession of fort.
Nov. 17 (Scorpion): Sent the fort 4 swivels & 2 musquettons. Punished Frank Duffy Marine w/ 12 lashes for drunkenness & neglect of duty. PM fired 2 6-pdrs with round and grape.
Nov. 17 (Cruizer): fired grape to keep rebels out of musket shot of the fort. Prepared guns for removal
Nov. 18 (Cruizer): moved guns out of fort & onto transport
Nov. 18 (Scorpion): Lt. & men still guarding fort.
Nov. 19 (Scorpion): Fort fired swivels and musquets at rebels. PM fired 9 6-pdrs (5 of which were grape) at rebels. Fort fired 12 swivels with round and grape at rebels.
Nov. 19 (Cruizer): fired grape at advancing rebels
Nov. 20 (Cruizer): at 11pm fired 5 guns to scower the woods
Nov. 21 (Scorpion): Officer and men brought off swivels and musquets from

fort
Nov. 22 (Scorpion): Blacked the sides & prepared to sail
Nov. 23 (Scorpion): received guns & provisions from *Palliser*
Nov. 24 (Scorpion): supplied *Cruizer* with 3 ½ barrels of powder, 2 bright musquets, & 2 cartouche boxes.
Nov. 25 (Scorpion): PM cutter returned having been detained by rebels who took 2 musquets.
Nov. 26 (Scorpion): 8AM weighed anchor sailed with *Palliser* to Charleston.
Dec. 18 (Scorpion): Depart Charleston with *Palliser* transport.
Dec. 19 (Scorpion): Off Cape Fear
Dec. 24 (Scorpion): 3:30 AM made for Cape Fear. 830AM touched on middle ground. 5PM anchored in river.
Dec. 24 (Cruizer): *Scorpion* grounded at mouth of river. *Scorpion* free at 4:30pm
Dec. 25 (Cruizer): anchored off fort
Dec. 25 (Scorpion): moored with *Cruizer*

1776
Jan. 26 (Scorpion): Moored in Cape Fear River
Jan. 27 (Scorpion): 9AM alarmed by waterers hailing the ship. 11AM fired 15 round & 11 grape at the rebels in the fort. Burned or taken by the rebels 6 hogsheads & 4 barrels of powder
Jan. 27 (Cruizer): AM Rebels about the fort. Fired great guns & small arms at rebels behind the walls. Rebels returned fire with small arms
Jan. 28 (Cruizer): 1AM fired grape @ rebels in fort. Rebels fired small arms
Feb. 10 (Cruizer): came in a sloop from Jamaica & a ship from Saultitudas and seized them. 3PM heard guns firing in disatance. 4 saw Man of War and brig near the bar.
Feb. 11 (Cruizer): 6AM weighed anchor, signaled all boats to run down as far as The Fingers, saw the ship and brig getting under way. Anchored off Bald Head. 1PM *Falcon* entered
Feb. 12 (Cruizer): 9AM anchored off Fort. Brig seized by *Falcon* entered
Feb 13 (Cruizer): Noon saw large ship in New Inlet. Fired gun and *Scorpion* answered
Feb 14 (Cruizer): 2AM schooner seized by *Syren* entered. 7AM sailed upstream with *Scorpion* and packet. Noon Gov. Martin aboard near Snow's Point, **Scorpion** grounded. 2PM passed Brunswick. 5:30 anchored at the Flats (Ferry House to the east)
Feb. 14 (Scorpion): Noon sailed with *Cruizer*. 2PM aground on McKnight's Shoal.
Feb. 15 (Scorpion): 2AM afloat. 3PM anchored off Brunswick.
Feb. 15 (Cruizer): AM employed filling water. Received fresh beef. Met by

schooner *Lady Wm*

Feb. 16 (Cruizer): *Scorpion* joined

Feb. 16 (Scorpion): 530PM anchored near the flats.

Feb. 17 (Scorpion): Watering and wooding

Feb. 17 (Cruizer): 7AM weighed anchor and sailed up river w/ *Lady Wm*. 11AM anchored at mouth of NW River. 4PM moved in NW river about 3 miles, grounded

Feb. 18 (Cruizer): 6AM floated and moved down river. 8AM anchored at mouth of NW River

Feb. 18 (Scorpion): Anchored near the Flats

Feb. 19 (Cruizer): Fired 5 3-pdrs for private signals

Feb. 20 (Scorpion): Anchored near the flats.

Feb. 20 (Cruizer): fired several guns for private signals. Joined by sloop Dispatch. 4PM sailed downstream. 7PM anchored abreast of Old Town.

Feb. 21 (Cruizer): 8AM sailed down river. 11AM anchored below the Flats

Feb. 21 (Scorpion): Anchored near the flats.

Feb. 22 (Scorpion): received 16 chests of arms from *Cruizer*.

Feb. 22 (Cruizer): 10AM sailed down with *Lady Wm*. Noon Negro Island bore SW about 1 ½ mile. 3 PM anchored abreast Brunswick, Church bearing WbN

Feb. 23 (Cruizer): *Scorpion* and *Terrible* (tender) anchored abreast Brunswick

Feb. 23 (Scorpion): 11AM unmoored. 5PM moored at Brunswick (WbN)

Feb. 24 (Scorpion): at Brunswick. Received 24 chests of arms & other gunner's stores. Supplied tender with water.

Feb. 24 (Cruizer): 9AM weighed anchor. 11AM anchored at 5 Fathom Hole, Snow's Point NNW, South point of Inlet EbN. 3PM sailed
4:30PM moored Fort SWbW, the point of Oak Island S1/2E. *Falcon* sailed.

Feb. 25 (Scorpion): Loosed sails to dry

Feb. 26 (Scorpion): received bread from *Cruizer*. Dispatched sundry gunners stores to Gov. Martin.

Feb. 26 (Cruizer): Received provisions from prizes. 7AM moved upriver with *Lady Wm*. Noon fired 2 guns as signal, Brunswick west about 2 cables length.

Feb. 27 (Scorpion): *Cruizer* and 2 armed tenders passed by to Wilmington.

Feb. 27 (Cruizer): 4AM anchored below Dram tree. Fired 9 3-pdrs as signals. 9PM run up and anchored ½ mile S of Wilmington with *Lady Wm* and sloop *Betsey* and pilot boat. Sent boat to Wilmington. Received 10 chests of arms & some powder from *Betsey*. PM fired 3 guns at different times as signals. At 2PM boat returned.

Feb. 28 (Cruizer): AM fired 2 guns as signals. Sailed downstream with *Pencicola Packet*.

Feb. 29 (**Cruizer**): received wood
Mar. 1 (**Cruizer**): AM fired 3 guns as signal.
Mar. 2 (**Cruizer**): Noon sailed down river with *Lady Wm, Pencicola Packet, & Delegate*. 3PM sent purser to Wilmington. 5PM boat returned without him and brought one of the Committee off
Mar. 3 (**Cruizer**): Below Wilmington. 11AM grounded
Mar. 4 (**Cruizer**): 8AM floated. 11AM anchored abreast old town. 5PM grounded on the Flats.
Mar. 5 (**Cruizer**): Floated sailed down to Brunswick. Joined by *Betsey* tender and sloop *General Gage*. 10PM grounded upon flats.
Mar. 5 (**Scorpion**): Moored off Brunswick. Sent gunners stores to Gov. Martin
Mar. 6 (**Scorpion**): Blacking Masts yards. Fired 2 guns as signal to *Cruizer*.
Mar. 6 (**Cruizer**): AM pumped water. Received from *Betsey* 10 chests of arms with 3 barrels & 5 half barrels of powder.
Mar. 7 (**Cruizer**): AM still not floated at high tide. Received 20 chests of arms from *Delegate* schooner. AM pumped water and finally floated. Got arms from schooner. 11AM grounded again. PM sent transports down with 6 chests of arms.
Mar. 8 (**Cruizer**): AM employed heaving over the flats. Noon free and anchored.
Mar. 8 (**Scorpion**): Fired 4 6-pdrs with round and grape at rebels. Scraped & cleaned between decks.
Mar. 9 (**Scorpion**): received gunners stores from Gov. Martin. Exercised great guns and small arms & target practice. *Cruizer* passed by. *General Gage* anchored here. Received some chests of arms from Martin. Fired 3 6-pdrs with round and grape at rebels
Mar. 9 (**Cruizer**): 9AM weighed anchor. 6PM anchored (Deep Water Point SW1/2W).
Mar. 10 (**Cruizer**): 8AM anchored abreast Fort (fort NW)
Mar. 10 (**Scorpion**): AM sent the boat on a secret mission. PM sent an officer & 11 men to reduce rebel breastworks.
Mar. 11 (**Scorpion**): Employed as before
Mar. 11 (**Cruizer**): PM heard guns in the distance, fired 8 guns in answer. Sent out *Comite Packett* and **Mercury's** tender with pilots.
Mar. 12 (**Scorpion**): Fired a 6-pdr with round and grape at rebels
Mar. 12 (**Cruizer**): came in sloop *Adventure* (Francis Boardman, master) from Winea seized by **Falcon**. 5AM entered brig *Glasgow Packett* with soldiers.
Mar. 13 (**Cruizer**): fired 4 guns as signals.
Mar. 14 (**Cruizer**): 3PM entered *Mercury* with Gen. Clinton
Mar. 15 (**Cruizer**): AM entered *Terrible* tender. Came in *Mercury* and *Falcon*

tenders & sloop *Hope* (Andrew Brown, master) seized by *Mercury*.
Mar. 16 (Cruizer): AM came in Fifty transport with troops.
Mar. 25 (Cruizer): Moored off Fort J. Went up river with *Kitty* transport and *Palliser* transport with Gen. Clinton.
Mar. 27 (Scorpion): Moored off Brunswick. Anchored *Palliser* transport and an Armed schooner
Mar. 28 (Scorpion): Saluted Gen. Clinton with 15 guns on his coming aboard. Noon sent the boat manned & armed on a secret mission.
Mar. 29 (Scorpion): 5AM boat returned. *Kitty* transport here.
Apr. 6 (St. Lawrence): 6PM anchored at Brunswick, church WbN ½ mile
Apr. 6 (Scorpion): Moored at Brunswick. AM fired 4 6-pdrs at rebels. PM fired 4 6-pdrs at rebels
Apr. 7 (Scorpion): PM fired 6 6-pdrs & 3 hand granadoes at rebels
Apr. 7 (St. Lawrence): 8AM weighed anchor and run upriver with watering sloop. Fired 7 4-pdrs and 12 swivels & small arms at rebels who fired from shore. 1PM anchored, Dram Tree NEbN, the Old Town House WSW.
Apr. 8 (St. Lawrence): 6AM weighed and got further downriver. 1PM got aground. 9PM got off.
Apr. 8 (Scorpion): Punished Thomas Doyle seaman with 12 lashes for neglect of duty
Apr. 9 (Scorpion): Fired 8 6-pdrs with round & 6 with round and grape at rebels
Apr. 9 (St. Lawrence): 4AM came onboard 4 refugees which escaped from rebels. 9AM sailed & kept firing at rebels who fired at us.
Apr. 10 (St. Lawrence): 5AM sailed downriver. 9AM Bald Head SSE Deepwater Point WSW. 4PM received 14 Highlanders, weighed and anchored at Brunswick, church W ½ mile.
Apr. 12 (Scorpion): Moored at Brunswick. Fired 3 6-pdrs at rebels
Apr. 13 (Scorpion): Fired 1 6-pdr with round & 1 with grape and cannister at rebels. Employed barricading the ship
Apr. 14 (Scorpion): Employed barricading. Fired several vollies of small arms at rebels
Apr. 16 (Scorpion): Fired at a Mark. Fired a 6-pdr & several musquets at rebels
Apr. 17 (Scorpion): Fired 2 6-pdrs at rebels
Apr. 18 (Scorpion): Fired a 6-pdr at rebels
April 19 (Cruizer): Moored off fort. AM entered transport with part of 57th Reg't. (1st transport of Parker's fleet).
Apr. 20 (Cruizer): Noon saw two ships in distance. Came in transport with part of 33d Reg't.
Apr. 21 (Cruizer): entered *Falcon*
Apr. 21 (Scorpion): Moored at Brunswick. Fired 3 6-pdrs with grape & can-

nister & several musquets at rebels
Apr. 22 (Scorpion): Fired 6 6-pdrs with grape & cannister & several musquets at rebels
Apr. 22 (Cruizer): AM sailed *Terrible* tender & *Committ Packett*. Received a hogshead of Mollasses.
Apr. 23 (Cruizer): AM Came in transports with troops, fired one gun.
Apr. 23 (Scorpion): Received water from watering sloop.
Apr. 24 (Cruizer): AM fired 2 guns in answer. Saw 2 ships in distance. Sent *Delegate* out with pilots. Came in *Earle of Oxford*, transport.
Apr. 25 (Cruizer): AM saw 2 ships in distance. Received on board some provisions.
Apr. 26 (Cruizer): entered *Clyburn* transport, saluted with 5 guns, answered with 3.
Apr. 26 (Scorpion): Fired 8 swivels with round & grape at rebels
Apr. 27 (Scorpion): Boat employed fishing. Fired several musquets at rebels
Apr. 27 (Cruizer): loosed sails to dry.
Apr. 28 (Cruizer): Entered one transport. Saluted with 5 guns, answered with 3
Apr. 29 (Cruizer): AM received one cask of Rice. PM sent tender out to assist with bringing in transport.
Apr. 30 (Cruizer): 4PM entered *Sphinx*, 3 transports, and 1 hospital ship.
May 1 (Cruizer): fired 5 guns at rebels ashore. Sailed upriver *Terrible* tender and *Glasgow Packet* transport.
May 2 (Cruizer): AM received water & provisions.
May 2 (Scorpion): Transport arrived (n)
May 3 (Cruizer): AM came in *HMS Solebay*. Fired at several rebels who fired back. 3PM *HMS Bristol* (Peter Parker) & transport anchored at mouth. Entered 14 sail of transports.
May 4 (Cruizer): entered *HMS Actaeon, Hinchinbrook*, and 2 small prizes taken by *Actaeon*. 9PM commodore's (Peter Parker) pennant hoisted on *Solebay*. Men of War saluted with 13 guns each.
May 8 (St. Lawrence): 11AM anchored below upper Flats, the old town House SbE & Dram Tree NbE 2 ½ miles. Kept all hands at quarters all night. Reports of a privateer and boats intending to attack.
May 9 (St. Lawrence): 1PM unable to cross lower Flats Barnet's Creek NbE old Town House WSW one mile.
May 10 (St. Lawrence): 1AM warped over the flats. 6AM old town house NNW1/2W and Newton's Ferry SE1/2S. 8AM came onboard 2 refugees.
May 11 (Scorpion): Seaman John Jefferies died (n)
May 12 (Scorpion): Moored at Brunswick. AM sent boat with officer manned & armed on secret expedition. Boat returned supplied the transports boats with rum & rice. Interred body of John Jefferies at Brunswick. PM fired

a 6-pdr & made signal for embarkation of the troops.

May 13 (Scorpion): AM received Beef & bread. Large cutter employed fishing. PM arrived *HM Sloop Falcon.*

May 15 (Falcon): Moored at Brunswick. Exercised small arms. PM supplied *St. Lawrence* with 105 galls of rum. Came on board 2 negro men from rebels.

May 16 (Falcon): Received water. Huld ship and hogg'd her both sides. Rebels fired at us, returned fire with round and grape.

May 16 (St. Lawrence): Fired 4 6-pdrs at a party of rebels who fired at us.

May 17 (St. Lawrence): 11PM sent the Master and 9 men to assist Capt. John Linzee in dislodging a party of rebels from Newtown Ferry House.

May 18 (St. Lawrence): AM Boats returned

May 19 (Scorpion): Snows Point NNW 1 ½ mile. 6AM weighed anchor. 630AM moored at Fort Johnston W ½ mile. Saluted Commodore Sir Peter Parker with 18 guns

May 20 (Falcon): Moored at Brunswick. Tarred the rigging "& taken by the rebels the latter end of March the Armed sloop *General Clinton* with pilots looking out for Sir Peter Parker & his fleet."

May 20 (St. Lawrence): Sent the boat to tow a fire raft the rebels had constructed to burn us and the *Glasgow Pacquett*. Towed it to edge of the marsh and set it on fire.

May 22 (St. Lawrence): Discharged the Highlanders to *Glasgow Packett* & 16 negro refugees by order of Sir Peter Parker. *Glasgow Pacquett* sailed down river w/ watering sloop

May 23 (St. Lawrence): Sent boat at 9 to Row guard

May 24 (St. Lawrence): 6PM fired 4 4-pdrs at Rebels who seemed to be very manny on shore. Kept hands at quarters. Sent the boat to row guard.

May 25 (St. Lawrence): 9PM sent boat to row guard

May 26 (St. Lawrence): 5PM weighed anchored and sailed down river. 8PM anchored off Brunswick near **Falcon**. Church WbN.

May 27 (St. Lawrence): 9AM fired 8 4-pdrs at a party of rebels who was firing from behind a breastwork.

May 30 (Cruizer): Sailed *Solebay, Thunder* bomb ketch, and all transports .

May 31 (Cruizer): sailed *Syren, St. Lawrence* schooner. 7AM sailed Comdr Peter Parker with the fleet. Remain on station *Cruizer, Falcon,* and *Scorpion.*

June 24 (Cruizer): 8AM saw flag of truce on shore. Made signal to *Scorpion* fired 3 guns to bring up prisoners for exchange.

July 15 (Cruizer): Off Snow's Point. 5AM came on 5 Negroes and 2 white men from shore. Received info rebels coming down in boats. Crew on alert all night.

August 20 (Cruizer): off Snow's Point. PM saw a great number of rebels on shore

Aug. 21 (Cruizer): 11AM joined by *Scorpion*. 3 PM weighed anchor & 7PM

anchored.
Aug. 22 (Cruizer): 5AM weighed anchor. 7AM anchored abreast fort.
Sept. 6 (Falcon): Moored off Bald Head. AM 20 men & 2 officers sent to shore to work on the fort. PM Rebels discovered on Bald Head & attacked Fort George with musquetry with 150 men commanded by Col. Poke [Col. Thomas Polk 4th NC]. Fired about 10 minutes rebels driven off by a party in the fort of about 25-30 men with only 12 musketts. The men in the fort belonged to different ships. Rebels had 1 killed & wounded. "Notwithstanding they had the opportunity of firing on the greater part for some minutes before they could get into the fort. 5 men belonging to *HM Sloop Cruizer* that was straggling in the woods was taken & carried off before the rebels came to the fort on the fort's firing made signal for all boats manned & armed sent arms & men from the ship to support the fort. Fired 6-pdrs through the woods at the rebels. 1PM we discovered 2 of the rebels boats in Buzzards Bay. Sent Lt. Dickerson with the command of Sloop *Defiance* manned & armed and 5 boats to block them in or destroy them."
Sept. 6 (Cruizer): abreast Fort Johnston. Noon battery on Bald Head fired upon by rebels. 1PM **Falcon** made signal for all boats to unmoor. 7PM entered schooner from West Indies.
Sept. 7 (Cruizer): 10AM small schooner into Bald Head. Put 4 3-pdrs onboard a sloop to go upriver to prevent rebels from getting by Bald Head. 6PM boats fired swivels at rebels in Buzzard's Bay, but obliged to retreat.
Sept. 7 (Falcon): AM fired 6-pdrs through the woods knowing the rebels to be there. PM Boats & sloop attacked the rebel boats in Buzzards Bay with swivels & musquetry the sloop fired some 3-pdrs with was returned by the rebels as was thought with either 2 or 3-pdrs. Our boats returned without being able to destroy them under cover of night got off."
Sept. 7 (Scorpion): AM rebels landed on Bald Head. Burned *Red* cutter which was hauled on shore to prevent falling into their hands. Boats employed with armed sloop in cutting off the retreat of rebels from Bald Head, they having been repulsed by the fort (Fort George) in the W part of the island.
Sept. 17 (Active): **Cruizer's** stores, ammo, & furniture transferred to *Active, Falcon, & Scorpion*.
Sept. 27 (Cruizer): [Continuously pumping water to keep afloat]
Sept. 28 (Cruizer): Moored abreast Fort Johnston. 8AM ran down to Bald Head with orders to for dismantling & destroying the sloop. PM sent some stores to other ships
Sept. 29 (Cruizer): sent to *Active, Falcon, & Scorpion* the Warrant officers stores
Sept. 29 (Falcon): Moored off Bald Head. Anchored here HM Sloop *Terrible*. Gunners stores received from **Cruizer**. PM "our men came on board from the

fort which was burnt.

Sept. 30 (Cruizer): Stripping the masts, sent remains of the stores & provisions to different ships.

Sept. 30 (Falcon): Employed occasionally

Oct. 1 (Falcon): received boatswn & carpenter stores from *Cruizer*

Oct. 2 (Falcon): 11AM weighed anchor and sailed in company with HM ships *Active*, *Scorpion*, & 2 tenders, with some merchant vessels. **HM Sloop Cruizer** burnt (along with some prizes (assumed)).

Oct. 2 (Active): **Cruizer** hauled near shore and burnt.

Oct. 18 (Falcon): (n) Fleet reached New York on Oct. 18

Introduction

Some historians have observed that the famous battles of the American Revolutionary War were fought in the North, but the decisive battles were fought in the South. That is largely true. Yet in southeastern North Carolina, it is the conflict of 1861-1865 that seems to grab the lion's share of the historical spotlight. This is puzzling to me, since the Revolutionary War history of North Carolina - including in the southeastern part of the state - is just as rich as that of the conflict that came a century later. With the coming 250th anniversary of the American Revolutionary War in 2026, it seems a perfect opportunity to make it more widely known just how deep and important that history is.

The Revolution was not something that just popped into consciousness among American colonials in 1776. For years prior to the Declaration of Independence, British subjects living in the thirteen North American colonies displayed growing dissatisfaction with their treatment by King George III's Ministers and Parliament. Some of this originated in the British policy of salutary neglect that left the American colonies largely to their own devices for most of Great Britain's colonial rule here. It was only after the French & Indian War that Great Britain tried to rein in the independence and relative autonomy enjoyed by the thirteen colonies, but by then it was largely too late. Like a teenager chaffing at the restrictions placed on them by their parents after being allowed to do as they please for a long time, Americans resented the efforts of the king to bring them more in line with Britain's imperial policy as practiced elsewhere in the world.

New taxes to recoup the debilitating costs of winning the French & Indian War met with staunch resistance in the American colonies. In the Cape Fear, outraged citizens showed solidarity with Boston's boycott of English tea by pledging to do the same. Before that, the Stamp Act, which taxed virtually every printed object used or produced in the colonies, created an even stronger uproar. Around 1,000 armed men from Brunswick Town and Wilmington lined the banks of the Cape Fear River when British authorities sought to land the hated stamp papers there - an act of armed rebellion against the Crown that happened eight years before the famed Boston Tea Party.

Abuses by Crown officials in the North Carolina piedmont led to a rebellion by farmers and tradesmen in 1770. Known to history as the Regulator Rebellion, it was such a threat to British authority in the colony that Royal Governor William Tryon called out the militia to put it down. When the two sides clashed in the climactic Battle of Alamance most of the men under Tryon's command were from the coast, led by monied elites from among the plantation class. The expedition to put down the Regulators caused a lasting resentment between the men of central North Carolina and their coastal brethren. It would also provide valuable training for the men who would assume the mantle of command a few years later when war with Great Britain erupted.

In 1776, at a time when the war was not going well for George Washington's men fighting in the North, a short but fierce clash at an unremarkable bridge 20 miles northwest of Wilmington gave a shot in the arm to Patriot hopes against what seemed a British juggernaut. The fight at Moores Creek Bridge only lasted a few short minutes, but it had the effect of chilling loyalist activity in the Carolinas for the next four years, until the fall of Charleston, S.C. in 1780. When Sir Peter Parker's British fleet dropped anchor off Smith Island (Bald Head Island), opposite what would later become Smithville (and later still, Southport), they had to content themselves with sending expeditions out to destroy plantations, sacking Brunswick Town, and skirmishing with Patriot forces arrayed against them in the woods along the river.

In 1781, Major General Charles Lord Cornwallis set out on an expedition to reclaim the Carolinas for his king. To do that, Major James Henry Craig and the 82nd Regiment of Foot - a Scots regiment - were dispatched to occupy and hold the port at Wilmington. Craig's mission was to supply Cornwallis' Southern Campaign by ferrying supplies up the Cape Fear to Cross Creek. Redcoats would remain in control of the town for most of the year, until evacuating in November as Griffith Rutherford's Continentals and militia closed a noose around them. To carry out his orders, Craig sent troops to secure Heron's Bridge, on the Northeast Cape Fear River, where militia under Alexander Lillington created a choke point that had to be reduced if supplies were to reach Cornwallis. While nominally successful in chasing off Col. Henry Young's men in the first attack, the American militia returned and proved more stubborn in two later clashes. Because of this and other factors, one might make the argument that it was Cape Fear men who won the Revolutionary War by thwarting Craig's resupply mission, causing Cornwallis to alter his plans for a campaign to bring the rebels to heel, which in turn led to his march into Virginia and surrender at the Yorktown. Wilmington provided a safe haven for loyalist guerrillas like David Fanning, who wreaked havoc throughout the countryside on behalf of his British masters. When the heat got to be too much, Fanning would withdraw to the safety of Craig's fortifications at Wilmington to rest and resupply.

    Several people who are experts on the Revolutionary War in North Carolina in their own right have generously helped me with this book by providing additional eyes to ferret out any obvious mistakes, by offering insights into the subject matter, and by being sounding boards for the thoughts and concepts that have gone into it. They include Dr. Chris E. Fonvielle, Jr., author and professor emeritus of the UNC Wilmington History Department; Robert M. Dunkerly, U.S. Park Ranger, author, and an expert on the role of the Cape Fear region in the Revolution whose own work was an integral source for my own; historian and mapmaker J.D. Lewis; Jason C. Howell, U.S. Park Ranger and historian at Moores Creek National Battlefield; U.S. Park Ranger Jason Collins, also of Moores Creek National Battlefield; Jim McKee, site manager and historian at Brunswick Town Fort Anderson State Historic Site, and Christine Jamet Lamberton, historian and director of the Burgwin-Wright House and Gardens in Wilmington, N.C. All of them are fine historians but even better friends, and this book is the better for their input. Any errors are my own.

I would also like to express my appreciation for the fine artwork of James C. Horton that graces the cover of this book and in other places within its pages. He is truly a great artist and a lover of history too. Spellings and quotations are presented as written in the source material, with some instances where I have made parenthetical corrections for clarity. I have tried to be as comprehensive as possible in this book in hopes that the story of the Cape Fear in the Revolution might become more widely known and appreciated by those of us who live here, and by those everywhere who study the conflict.

The Revolutionary War in North Carolina was a civil war, vicious, bloody, and with plenty of atrocities to go around on both sides. But the war that happened here helped pave the way for a new nation, one that changed the world. Southeastern North Carolina played a major role in that. Here is its story.

Jack E. Fryar, Jr.
Wilmington, N.C.
January, 2024

Origins

Cape Fear River Watershed

Origins

It begins as two streams in central North Carolina that grow into the Black and Haw Rivers, eventually coming together to create the Cape Fear River at Mermaid's Point near modern Sanford. It is North Carolina's greatest inland waterway, stretching for 500 miles across the state including all its tributaries, ever widening, before it spills into the Atlantic between Bald Head (called Smith Island in the colonial era) and Oak Islands. The Cape Fear River basin is the largest in North Carolina, encompassing over 9,000 square miles. It separates New Hanover and Brunswick counties. It is navigable as far inland as modern Fayetteville, and it is the single most important geographic feature influencing the founding of Brunswick Town, Wilmington, Smithville (modern Southport), and Cross Creek (modern Fayetteville, N.C.).

European settlement in what became North Carolina began with Juan Pardo's abortive expeditions of 1566, followed later by John White's ill-fated and legendary Lost Colony on Roanoke Island in 1585. Across the eastern half of North America, settlement by Old World peoples occurred from Canada to Florida over the course of a century or more. England's first successful settlement came at Jamestown in 1607, but Spain, the Netherlands and France also landed colonists to stake out claims to the continent's New World bounty. In the 1660s explorer William Hilton wrote two glowing reports about the Cape Fear - then known as the Charles River - that lured Englishmen from Barbados and Massachusetts to attempt a colony along its banks, the first such effort below the Albemarle. The Cape Fear River has been key to southeastern North Carolina's history from the start.

Over time, English settlers began to eclipse the colonial enclaves of other nations, until France and England were the two greatest powers in contention for control of North America. The French & Indian War (part of the larger global conflict known as the Seven Years War), inadvertently sparked by a young George Washington in the western Pennsylvania wilderness, settled the question of who would control the continent, at least east of the Mississippi River. But while American colonists were happy to have their king's help to thwart French ambitions, that effort resulted in frictions that later led the colonies to break from the crown.

Fighting a war is expensive, especially when it is happening more than 3,000 miles from home, and while troops and resources are needed for other priorities, as well. When King George III's banner eventually emerged victorious against France and its native allies, it was perhaps not an unreasonable expectation from the king's ministers that the colonists, whose liberty as Englishmen redcoat armies had just secured, might be expected to help pay off the costs of that effort. To that end, the king and parliament undertook a reassessment of their colonial policy when it came to the Americans.

In an age when it took weeks to pass communications between London and its colonies, across an ocean that separated the imperial seat of power from its North American possessions, strict oversight of those colonies was virtually impossible. American colonists, lacking prompt instructions from the mother country, began to develop their own institutions of government. In Virginia, delegates began meeting at Williamsburg in their own assembly, the House of Burgesses. Similar bodies convened in other colonies. As long as nodding acceptance of British authority was observed, a policy of self-determination developed under the nominal supervision of royal governors selected for the task. Basically, provided the mercantile trade that was Britain's chief reason for American colonization was not interfered with, and as long as American activities did not conflict with broader British global policy, the colonies were largely allowed to run their own affairs. This policy of salutary neglect was allowed to exist for decades. After the French & Indian War, British efforts to rein in the colonies sparked anger among the American colonials.[1]

North Carolina had a reputation for being difficult when it came to acknowledging royal authority. All five of its royal governors during the colonial period related in their letters and diaries how rebellious the locals could be when it suited them. That rebellious spirit would grow from spark to flame in the decade before the first shots rang out at Lexington and Concord, and spread into an all-consuming conflagration that became America's war for independence. Nowhere was the struggle more hard-fought than in North Carolina.[2]

Along the Cape Fear, those who longed for independence clashed in bloody battles with those whose loyalty, livelihoods, and identities were tied to Great Britain. Redcoats and loyalists roamed the countryside, raiding Whig homes and fighting neighbors who supported a free and independent America, and those same Whigs willingly returned the favor. Whigs raised regiments of Continentals at Wilmington to augment George Washington's army, seeing action both within and outside North Carolina. Pivotal battles and skirmishes in the Cape Fear region played a crucial role in the American Revolution that has been largely overlooked by historians up to this point. In our 1861 Civil War, the Cape Fear's geography made the port at Wilmington the single most important one in the Confederacy, but that civil war was not our first. That happened almost a century earlier. While the Cape Fear's part in the great civil war fought between 1861-1865 is well known, its role in the birth of our state and nation nearly a century before has only been told in bits and pieces. Between 1765 and 1782, the Cape Fear was at the epicenter of the fight for independence in North Carolina.[3]

King Charles II

At its founding, Carolina was unique in that it was not settled around a specific place. Jamestown, Plymouth, Providence, New Haven - all were colonial ventures built around a particular colonial settlement. In Carolina, the eight Lords Proprietors who were granted a 1660 patent by King Charles II in appreciation of their efforts to restore the monarchy were given virtual free rein over a vast territory that stretched from the southern boundary of Virginia to Spanish Florida. The first North Carolina settlers took up lands on the Outer Banks and in the Albemarle region below the Chesapeake. On the Cape Fear, enterprising adventurers from Barbados and a handful of Puritans from Massachusetts planted the first settlement in the south of the colony on the muddy riverbanks near Town Creek in 1664. That colony was doomed by a number of problems and was abandoned by 1667, but some of the settlers from John Vassall's Charles Towne colony went south to join Sir John Yeamans' Port Royal settlement. Port Royal eventually become the second - and more famous - Charles Town in Carolina. Fifty years after that first attempt to settle on the Cape Fear, men from the Goose Creek area of South Carolina returned. Those men, sons of a distinguished South Carolina family with ties to both England and Barbados, put down roots five miles below where Vassalls' Bajan settlers made their abortive attempt to colonize.[4]

The Cape Fear came to the attention of the Goose Creek men when, returning home from a war with the Tuscarora Indians around the Swiss colony of New Bern, Maurice Moore saw the potential of the place. He returned to Goose Creek, and spent the next decade convincing his relatives and friends that building a new town on the Cape Fear River was an ideal way to grow their plantations and secure their fortunes. The town that Moore and his companions established in 1726 was called Brunswick.[5]

Maurice Moore was the first permanent resident of Brunswick Town, but he was followed soon after by Cornelius Harnett, Sr. Harnett is said to have fled the Albemarle to avoid an arrest warrant on charges of riotous assault (his son and namesake, apparently a chip off the old block, would become a notable Revolutionary War patriot). Soon settlers began to flock to the Cape Fear, building plantations along the 397 named streams that feed the mighty waterway's basin and harvesting naval stores as their first cash crop. With no roads to make land travel convenient, the founding families of the Cape Fear used the river itself and its many tributaries as their highways, lashing rafts of longleaf pine and oak together to ride the tidal currents from upriver estates to the port at Brunswick. Brunswick became an official port of entry in 1731. There, British ships loaded their holds with Carolina tar, pitch, and turpentine destined for shipyards in New England, the Caribbean, and Great Britain. The nearly mile-wide expanse of river at the Brunswick waterfront was full of two-masted snows and three-masted sea-going brigs that collected the precious byproducts of the longleaf pine that kept England's merchant and naval fleets afloat. While sailors and slaves hefted cargoes onto waiting ship decks,

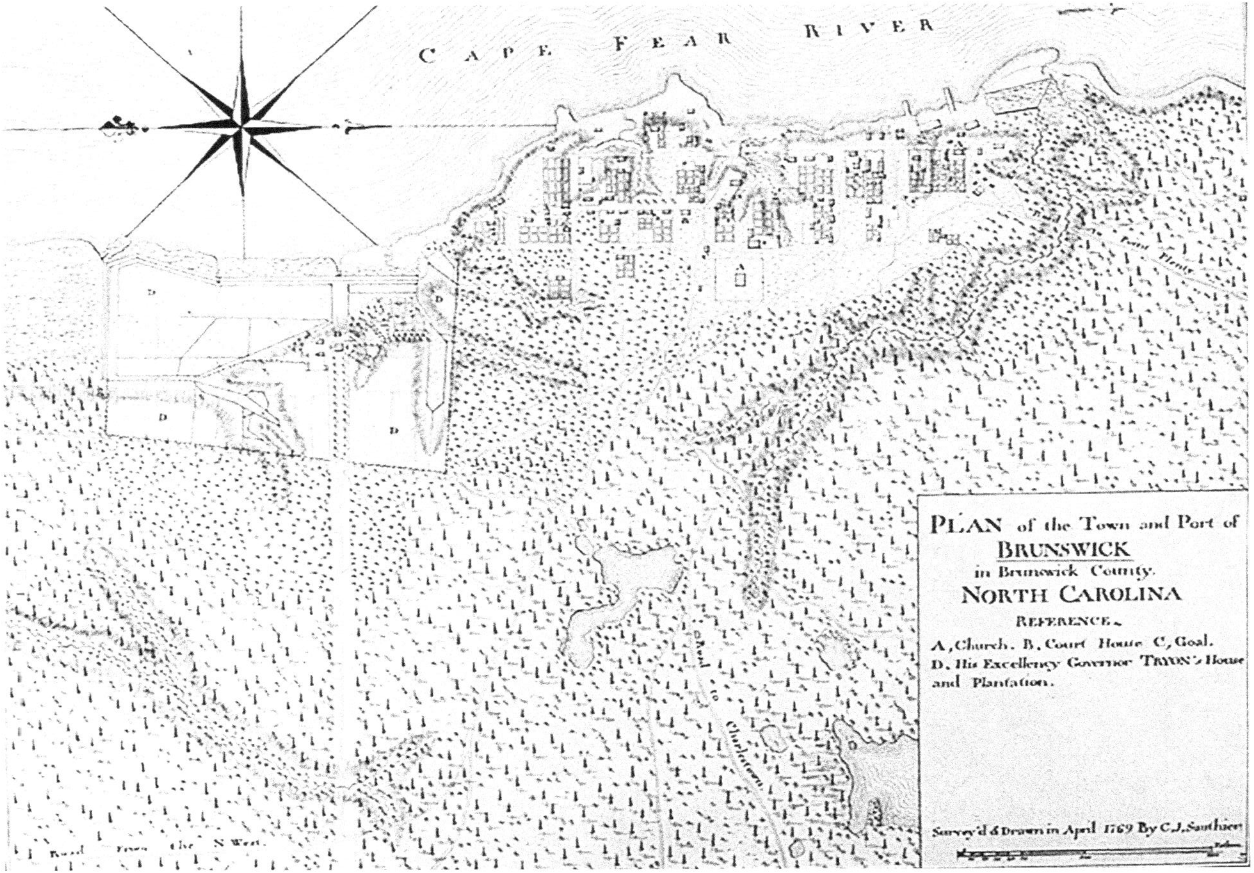

Claude Sauthier's 1769 map of Brunswick, the port of entry on the Cape Fear River.

In the 1700s Brunswick was a thriving port town on the Cape Fear River, as depicted in the painting Brunswick Rising by James C. Horton.

periaugers and cypress canoes ferried people from one place to another.[6]

Brunswick was situated on a high bluff overlooking the Cape Fear River roughly twelve miles above the bar at Old Inlet. The river was wide at that point, directly opposite the natural landmark locals called Sugarloaf, a huge sand dune on the east side of the river now encompassed by Carolina Beach State Park. Brunswick grew slowly, and only had a dozen or so houses by the time it secured official status as one of the colony's three ports where incoming ships had to stop and declare their cargoes. Its close proximity to the sea resulted in it being battered by hurricanes, especially in 1761 and 1769. Spanish privateers sacked the town in 1748, highlighting its vulnerability to attack. When a new town was created further upriver, it quickly surpassed and sealed the fate of Brunswick.[7]

Wilmington was founded thirteen years after Brunswick, and went through several name changes prior to its incorporation. Gov. George Burrington ran afoul of both his royal masters and the land-rich Moores when he began issuing blank land patents granting property to new settlers. Freely dispensing Carolina land did wonders for attracting newcomers, but did not win him any fans among the Cape Fear gentry. It was Burrington who first proposed a new town on the Cape Fear to the Assembly, but he was rebuffed by speaker Edward Moseley, a supporter of Brunswick, who observed that there was already a town on the river. Burrington was replaced by Gabriel Johnston in 1734, but by then property owned by John Watson, James Wimble, Michael Higgins, and Joshua

Grainger, Sr. was selected for the new town where the Cape Fear River forked into northeast and northwest branches. Originally identified as Watson on the first map of the town, James Wimble later produced a new map that called the town New Carthage. Later still, it was called New Liverpool, then New Town, which over time was shortened to Newton, before becoming Wilmington in 1739. The town received a boost at the expense of the Moores when Gabriel Johnston moved the collector of customs and the deputy naval officer of Port Brunswick to Wilmington that same year, after a real estate dispute with the Moores that did not go in the governor's favor. That, along with the 1748 raid by Spanish privateers on Brunswick Town, signaled the decline of the earlier settlement as the center of activity on the Cape Fear.[8]

New Town, as Wilmington was previously known, covered 300 acres bounded by modern Campbell, Wooster, and Fifth Streets. Town blocks were subdivided into five to six half-acre lots. Beginning at Front Street, roadways ran north to south, and were numbered. Crossing streets running east to west were named, commonly after trees or other significant geographic features (Chestnut, Walnut, Dock Streets). Such was the planning that went into the town that a 1757 visitor noted that "the Regularity of the Streets...[is] Equal to those of Philadelphia."[9]

Originally the town's footprint only occupied a portion of the land set aside for it. Homes were mostly framed buildings with a few brick structures interspersed among them. By the time of the Revolution, it was the most populous town in the colony, with most of its development centered around a corridor between Dock and Chestnut Streets, and running from the river to Third Street where Market Street turned into the post road to New Bern. In the 1750s Wilmington had 58 houses or taxable structures and a population of about 350. The population boom of the 1770s saw a huge influx of newcomers to North Carolina, and as a port of entry, Wilmington benefitted from that by seeing its size grow accordingly. By 1784, two years after the war ended in the Cape Fear, New Hanover County (including modern Pender County) had a population of over 2,000 white residents and 3,000 black residents. Economically and ethnically, it had much more in common with Barbados or the lowcountry around Charleston than it did with the largely rural rest of the state.[10]

Where St. James Episcopal Church is today was once occupied by the home of the widow of Benjamin Heron, whose drawbridge across the Northeast Cape Fear River would play a crucial role in the war to come.

This model in the collection of the Cape Fear Museum depicts Wilmington as it appeared in the 1760s.

The town cemetery was behind it, and still serves as the graveyard at St. James. Among the notables interred there is Revolutionary War patriot leader Cornelius Harnett, Jr., who died just one block away while in British custody in the Bullpen at the northeast corner of Second and Market Streets in 1781. The town jail was built across the street from Heron's home in 1769, using ballast stones jettisoned from merchant ships along the riverfront for its sturdy walls. The jail had a stocks and pillory, a whipping post, and a home for the jailor. Three years later, it would provide the foundation for merchant John Burgwin's new residence.[11]

In the middle of the intersection of Front and Market Streets stood the courthouse, the site of many gatherings of agitated Cape Fear men during the Stamp Act crisis and the growing calls for independence of the 1770s. Market Street itself was 99 feet wide, while other town thoroughfares were 66 feet in width. Homes along Market comingled with businesses, including a large bakery that provided ship's biscuits to vessels calling on the Wilmington port. Where the town boundary ended and the post road to New Bern began, in the intersection of what is now Market and Fourth Streets, sat the original St. James Anglican Church, a square, single story structure made of sturdy brick but lacking a bell tower. Funded by the salvage of the Spanish ship *La Fortuna* after the raid on Brunswick in 1748, the church was commandeered by British troops during the town's occupation in 1781.[12]

The towns along the Cape Fear River - Brunswick, Wilmington, and Cross Creek at the other end of the navigable part of the waterway - became centers of trade. As such, they were populated by a small but influential merchant class by the mid-eighteenth century. Further inland, merchants were fewer, and those that did exist often were satellite branches of businesses owned by Wilmington merchants. Society in colonial North Carolina was very hierarchical, with landed gentry at the top of the pyramid followed by small farmers and artisans, indentured servants and poor whites, and at the bottom, slaves. The families at the top made up only about five percent of the colony's population and were mostly moderately wealthy planters who owned fewer than 20 slaves that worked plantations of 500 acres or less. A smaller number of the landed class owned larger holdings and as many as 50 slaves. At the pinnacle of the social pyramid were the very few wealthy planters like Roger Moore, whose family owned hundreds of thousands of acres in the lower Cape Fear, and who personally owned more than 200 slaves.[13]

Wilmington's streets were lined with businesses catering to the seagoing trades and town residents, as well as acting as middlemen between the producers of raw materials for export in the interior and the carriers who would take them to far flung markets. There were shipwrights and millwrights, tailors, cordwainers (rope makers), blockmakers, carpenters, peruke (wig) makers, coppersmiths, saddlers, barbers, hatters, and medical men. Cornelius Harnett and partner William Wilkinson opened a turpentine distillery between Walnut and present Red Cross Streets, and John Lyon opened a tannery on Second Street.[14]

A large proportion of these merchants were Scots who took advantage of royal governor Gabriel Johnston's freewheeling dispensation of land patents to those willing to relocate to the Cape Fear region. For two decades before the Revolution began, more than 5,000 Highlanders, with a smaller number of Lowland Scots mixed in, immigrated to North Carolina and settled mostly in Anson, Scotland, and Cumberland Counties. Immigrants to the Cape Fear and the rest of the colony also included French Huguenots, Quakers, Welsh, Germans, and a smaller number of Jews. As each ship bearing hopeful newcomers dropped anchor in the Cape Fear off Fort Johnston, Crown officials boarded to require all males over age sixteen to swear an oath of allegiance to the king, promising to be "... faithful against all traitorous Conspiracies & attempts whatsoever...which shall be made against his [the King's] Person, Crown, and Dignity." The Scots who settled at Wilmington included men like Robert Hogg, who with partner Samuel Campbell and later, his brother James, opened the mercantile firm Hogg and Campbell with branches at Cross Creek and Hillsborough, as well as at the port town on the lower Cape Fear.[15]

The men of this merchant class depended on trade with Great Britain for their livelihoods. All other issues aside, their economic lifeblood relied on the mercantile system that Great Britain imposed on her American colonies. American colonial exports could go only to England, where raw materials from North Carolina were turned into finished goods like furniture, etc., and then sold back to the same colonies that had provided the raw materials in the first place. The mercantile system was the bedrock of British colonialism, providing not just much needed raw materials for domestic and international consumption, but also markets to sell those finished goods to. The merchants of the Cape Fear were almost entirely dependent on mercantilism. As a result, when the movement for independence emerged, many of them were inclined to remain loyal to the king and the system that put food on their tables. Southeastern North Carolina was the most loyalist-leaning section of the colony during the Revolutionary War, though the interior counties of Anson, Chatham, Cumberland, Forsyth, Guilford, Lincoln (then Tryon), Montgomery, Randolph, Robeson, Rowan, Rutherford (then also part of Tryon), Scotland, Surry, and northern Burke counties were the other places where loyalist sentiments were strongest. Wilmington, despite its large merchant community, was a notable exception in that it was also home to a large number of the men who led revolutionary efforts in the war.[16]

Many of those men carried arms as members of the militia. Most of the American colonies had militias as their first lines of defense. All North Carolina males between ages 16 and 60 were required to serve when called to duty by the governor. Exemptions were made for those who worked in critical professions such as doctors, millers, ferry owners, lawyers, and court officials. Clergy and Quakers could also opt out. Participation was enforced by fines and punishments levied by the courts. Militiamen did more than just fend off the occasional Spanish or Indian raid. They also built roads, fought fires, conducted slave patrols, and helped maintain law and order. The militia was expected to embody and train at least twice a year. Service was seen as a sort of taxation as well as a duty. Service times varied, but could range from a few days to two months.[17]

Slavery in the Colonial Cape Fear

The rising cost of indentured servants prompted North Carolina planters to turn to the more economical alternative of slavery. By 1775 North Carolina had a population that included an estimated 65,000 slaves. Roughly 50,000 of them lived east of the fall line and worked on the large coastal plantation estates there. The plantation system that operated in the Cape Fear depended on the availability of a large, free source of labor. Because of that, chattel slavery played an integral role in the development of the region. As one traveled further away from the large coastal estates, though, the number of slaves encountered was much smaller (though not nonexistent). During the Revolution, African Americans provided much of the manual labor for both sides of the conflict. Everything from the construction of fortifications to ditch digging, carpentry, sawyers (someone who saws timber from felled logs), smiths, teamsters, painters, and wheelers was done by enslaved and free blacks. As well, they often acted as orderlies and valets for officers of the opposing armies.[18]

On the Cape Fear, Wilmington ordinances sought to keep a tight rein on the slave population. The specter of slave uprisings loomed large in the nightmares of Southerners during the colonial era. Like the West Indies (where most North Carolina slaves were imported from) and the South Carolina lowcountry, the Lower Cape Fear was the only place in North Carolina with a majority black population. Several local merchants were active participants in the slave trade, including Robert Thresal, Dugald Thompson, and the firm of Alexander Hostler & Co. While the figures are not exact, records show New Hanover County with 1,476 blacks compared to 529 white men out of a total taxable population of 2,005 in 1765. Permits were required for enslaved people to travel alone at night. Whites were prohibited from supplying rum to slaves, while the slaves were themselves prohibited from selling anything without written permission from their owner.[19]

Fear of slave revolts led Wilmington officials to enact ever more stringent restrictions on the movement of bondsmen in the town that supplemented an already strict colony wide slave code. Nevertheless, slaves in Wilmington enjoyed more freedom than one might expect. They generally worked on a task system, in which slaves were assigned a job for the day. When that job was completed, they were free to indulge in their own pursuits, such as raising livestock, gardening, or hiring themselves out to other property owners in town to earn a little money for themselves. Often the bondsman's owner took a portion of their earnings, but it was still a way for an enterprising slave to generate income. Slaves in Wilmington frequently gathered in streets and alleys, vacant lots and empty houses, often disturbing white residents of the town. When the sun went down, slaves moved in shadows virtually unseen, posing a threat to whites and their property. At other times, slaves (and whites too) would hold impromptu horse races through the streets of Wilmington, sending pedestrians scrambling for safety. As a result, town fathers passed laws to restrict the unauthorized movement of area bondsmen.[20]

Anne Rutherford Schaw, Janet Schaw's mother, is said to bear a remarkable resemblance to her daughter.

Wilmington and the Lower Cape Fear was a simmering stew of tension in the summer of 1775. Traveler Janet Schaw claimed Cape Fear revolutionaries were saying that British authorities had promised "every Negro that would murder his Master and family that he should have his Master's plantation. This last Artifice they may for, as the Negroes have got it amongst them and believe it to be true. Tis ten to one they may try the experiment, and in that case friends and foes will be all one." The Stono Rebellion in 1739, when enslaved people made a lethal bid for freedom by escaping to Spanish Florida over the dead bodies of their owners and any whites who tried to stop them, was the example that spurred great terror among whites and restrictions on slaves afterwards. Schaw observed the danger during her 1775 stop in the Cape Fear. "I came to town yesterday with the intention of being in church this day," she wrote in her journal. "I found the whole town in an uproar, and the minute I landed, Mr. Rutherford's slaves were seized and taken into custody till I was ready to return with them...I found my short prophecy in regard to the Negroes was already fulfilled and that an insurrection was hourly expected. There had been a number of them discovered in the adjoining woods the night before, most of them with arms, and a fellow belonging to Dr. Cobham was actually killed. All parties are now united against the common enemies. Every man is in arms and the patrols going thro' all the town, and searching every Negro's house, to see they are all at home by nine at night."[21]

Despite the restrictions, Wilmington slaves were able to rent houses and tenements - another example of an independence granted them that slaves in other places did not enjoy. Slaves engaged in commerce (sometimes with, other times without their owners' permission) such as selling or bartering firewood, provisions, and various kinds of merchandise. Their customers were both black and white. They pursued such activities despite efforts by white leaders to stymie the "pernicious practice of dealing with Negroes." Even William Hooper, who would be one of three North Carolinians to sign the Declaration of Independence in the summer of 1776, lamented the relative freedom of local slaves, threatening to prosecute Wilmingtonians who bought things "from my Negroes whatever they pillage from my House in town or Plantation below."

William Hooper' signature

Regardless, in the Cape Fear slavery was still slavery. Too often masters paid little attention to the well-being of their bondsmen, neglecting to provide enough food to keep them healthy, or clothing fit to keep them warm in winter or covered in summer. Chattel slavery meant that slaves were not accorded the same rights as human beings that even the poorest white man could claim. Black slaves were property, and could be dispensed with as such. At a Wilmington slave auction in 1778, Elkanah Watson witnessed a "poor wench cling to a little daughter, who implored, with the most agonizing supplication, that they must not be separated." The daughter was sold nonetheless. In another account of a slave auction in Wilmington, Johann David Schoepf witnessed a slave father declare that his fifteen-year-old son, standing beside him on the auction block, was part of a package deal. "Who buys me must buy my son too," he said. In this case, the two were sold together.[22]

Slavery in the Cape Fear was both a visible sign of wealth (slaves were an investment and source of ready cash - the more one owned the wealthier one was), and also the engine that generated wealth for their owners through their labor. Most slave wealth in North Carolina was found along the coast, where great plantations demanded a large pool of slave laborers to harvest naval stores, rice, and indigo. Lieutenant governor William Tryon noted in 1765 that, "When a man marries his Daughters[,] he never talks of the fortune in Money[,] but 20[,] 30[,] or 40 slaves is her Portion..."[23]

North Carolina ended the official importation of slaves in 1774, mostly in solidarity with other measures banning imports as part of a campaign to wage economic warfare against the British. The import ban may also have been spurred by a reluctance of Carolina planters to deal with rebellious African or West Indian slave imports, preferring instead to work with more malleable homegrown bondsmen.[24]

By 1775, as war seemed imminent, North Carolina slave holders feared revolts spurred by British promises of freedom to any slave that took the king's side against their rebellious masters. Local Whigs feared their own royal governor, Josiah Martin, might follow the example set by Virginia's Lord Dunmore in his proclamation offering slave emancipation. Despite Martin's protests that he was not contemplating such a move, white slave owners in several eastern North Carolina counties claimed to have found evidence that just such a slave revolt was in the works. When rumors of an imminent revolt surfaced on the Cape Fear in June, Wilmington officials ordered all slaves to be disarmed, and whites patrolled the streets both night and day to squash any effort at rebellion before it could begin. Efforts were redoubled when rumor said that a band of armed blacks had been found in nearby swamps. Slaves arriving in town from elsewhere were sequestered until their business was completed and it was time for them to return home. Captain John Abraham Collett, commander of Fort Johnston at the mouth of the Cape Fear River, was accused of inciting slaves to "elope from their masters" to the protection of the British.[25]

As it turns out that Gov. Martin did entertain the idea of inciting slaves to revolt, at least briefly and under specific circumstances. In a letter to Lewis DeRossett made public after its capture by local Whigs, Martin confided that he had never actually advocated slave revolt, except in the event of "the actual and declared rebellion of the King's subjects, and the failure of all other means to maintain the King's Government." Rebel leaders scored a propaganda coup by publicizing the letter, lending credence to the rumors of slave insurrection at the urging of the British.[26]

The Cape Fear had its fair share of slaves who fled to the prof-

Thomas Peters was a slave of Wilmington merchant William Campbell. He escaped and joined with the British to earn his freedom, eventually helping to found a colony for escaped loyalist slaves in West Africa. This statue of him is in the Sierra Leone capital of Freetown.

fered freedom of the British. Violet, the slave of Whig militia officer Col. Henry Young, escaped from Wilmington to New York where the British held sway under Gen. Thomas Gage, and found her freedom. She married Boston King, another fugitive slave from South Carolina who ran in 1780, and they evacuated with the British to Nova Scotia before ending their journeys in Sierra Leone.[27]

Then there was Thomas and Sally Peters, and their daughter Clairy. Thomas Peters fled his master, Wilmington's William Campbell, in March 1776 to take the king's shilling and earn his freedom. Peters served well as a member of the Black Pioneers regiment of escaped slaves raised by the British. The regiment served as engineers and foragers for British forces operating in North America. When the British evacuated New York in 1783, Peters sailed with them to Nova Scotia and settled with his family in Digby. Thomas Peters became a leader of the community of expat former slaves who had been promised good lands there as payment for their services to King George III. But lands for the black loyalists never materialized, and Peters soon found former slaves to be just as unwelcome among the British as they had been in the American colonies. The Peters family relocated to St. John, New Brunswick. Soon Peters found himself once again at sea, this time among a group of former slaves who would found the African nation of Sierra Leone.[28]

Tempting as the offer of freedom might have been to many, not all slaves flocked to the king's colors. American forces in the Revolutionary War had their fair share of blacks who joined the ranks of the rebellious Whigs. Free blacks, especially, showed up in Continental Line units or in the ranks of state militias in greater numbers than seen for the British. Some even became celebrated heroes in their communities. Fayetteville's Isaac Hammond was a fifer during the war who served at least two years, including in action at the Battle of Eutaw Springs. Also from the Fayetteville area were Louie Revels, John Lomax, Thomas Bell, Charles Hood, and John Pettifort. African Americans made significant contributions to the war effort on both sides. The frigate *Randolph* captured four British vessels bound for New York from Jamaica in 1777. Among the Continental warship's crew was a black seaman from Wilmington identified as "Mr. M'Queen," along with several black friends and crewmates. Some blacks, like their white counterparts, had a fluid understanding of military enlistment obligations. Four "colored people" by the names of Gears, Billy, George, and Jack deserted from Gen. Francis Nash's regiment after the 1776 battle at Moores Creek.[29]

Nevertheless, militia units were not so scared of a black insurrection that the manpower needs of the war effort precluded African Americans from serving in their ranks. North Carolina permitted blacks to enlist in the militias before the Revolution, and continued to do so once war broke out with Great Britain. It was not something the General Assembly ever specifically endorsed, but the need for warm bodies in the ranks led those who might have objected to turn a blind eye to the practice.

Patriot forces in the Revolutionary War included roughly 5,000 African Americans, and North Carolina had its share. One Tar Heel brigade mustered 42 black men in its ranks, and in 1779 the General Assembly attempted to incentivize more to join them. While service by blacks was prohibited in some colonies (Georgia and South Carolina), other colonies welcomed men of color willing to fight for the cause of independence, and some (Maryland) incentivized them with offers of freedom in return. Black men from North Carolina, Virginia, and South Carolina all served in action at Charlestown and Savannah during the war, earning some of them their own independence. They would do their part - on one side or the other - in the Cape Fear, too.[30]

With the end of the French & Indian War, the relationship between Great Britain and its American colonies underwent a radical change. In 1763 Parliament imposed a ban on white settlement west of the Appalachian Mountains. The decree establishing the Proclamation Line was not intended to be permanent, but it still aroused anger among Americans who thought they had just fought a war to secure their claims to those lands. In fact, some whites had already moved across the Blue Ridge into those western territories. The act of Parliament was seen as a slap in the face.

Then there was the matter of protecting the colonies. The king's army had fought a very expensive war to keep the American colonies free from the French, and found it a good idea to keep some troops on hand in the colonies to secure King George III's claim to them. It seemed right and fair that those colonies should bear some of the burden of supporting that army. To do that, Parliament imposed a tax on sugar and molasses to raise the revenues needed. This was the first time the American colonies had been taxed to raise direct revenues. It was an internal tax and the Americans saw that as the sole prerogative of their own legislatures. Thanks to the British policy of salutary neglect, the days when the colonies would accept such a tax were past. More taxes and resistance would follow, until all-out war erupted between the thirteen colonies and the country that spawned them. North Carolina would be right in the middle of it. So would the Cape Fear.[31]

Endnotes

[1] Enoch Lawrence Lee. *The Lower Cape Fear in Colonial Days* (Chapel Hill, N.C.: University of North Carolina Press, 1965): 242. Hereafter cited as Lee.

[2] Lindley S. Butler. *North Carolina and the Coming of the Revolution, 1763-1776*. (Raleigh: N.C. Department of Cultural Resources Archives & History, 1976): 1. Defiance of authority in N.C. was characteristic from the very beginning. During the Proprietary Era (1663-1729) North Carolina politics were marked by episodes of disruptive violence. Five different governors were ousted during the time period, and Culpepper's Rebellion threatened the success of the colony. Weak leadership from the Lords Proprietors allowed and contributed to the instability. When the proprietors sold the colony back to the Crown in 1729, things stabilized somewhat, but not soon enough to eliminate the rebellious nature of North Carolina's people.

[3] Whigs is the term for those Americans who supported independence from Great Britain,

as opposed to the Tories, or loyalists, who supported remaining part of King George III's dominions.

[4] Alan D. Watson. *Wilmington, North Carolina, to 1861* (Jefferson, N.C.: McFarland, 2016). Hereafter cited as Watson 1861; Charles Christopher Crittendon. "The Seacoast in North Carolina History, 1763-1789." *The North Carolina Historical Review*. Vol. 7, No. 4 (1930): 433-442. Hereafter cited as Crittendon. There were as many as twenty-four inlets along the N.C. coast in the eighteenth century. The Cape Fear River inlet between Smith Island (a.k.a. Bald Head Island) and Oak Island was the best on the southern coast, capable of accepting ships of respectable tonnage despite the nearby presence of treacherous Frying Pan Shoals, making it the ideal place to establish a southern settlement.

[5] Watson 1861: 8; Franda D. Pedlow and Jack E. Fryar, Jr. *The Story of Brunswick Town & Fort Anderson* (Wilmington, N.C.: Dram Tree Books, 2005):3, hereafter cited as Pedlow. Maurice Moore was the grandson of Sir John Yeamans, the first governor of Carolina who established the Port Royal settlement in 1670. In April 1726 Moore was sent with militia to recover property stolen by Indians believed to be in the area of the Cape Fear.

[6] Malcolm Ross. *The Cape Fear* (New York: Holt, Rinehart and Winston, 1965): 65. Hereafter cited as Ross. Brunswick Town became the leading supplier of naval stores in the British colonies, exporting 50,000 barrels of tar, pitch, and turpentine annually. Wilmington, founded in 1739, produced the lion's share of lumber exports, and become the main market for deerskins and farm products in the colony. Its location at the forks of the river, further up from Brunswick, made it more convenient for settlers from inland.

[7] Robert M. Dunkerly, *Redcoats on the River: The Revolutionary War in Southeastern North Carolina* (Wilmington, N.C.: Dram Tree Books, 2008) 17. Hereafter cited as Dunkerly. Scottish visitor Janet Schaw, who visited the Cape Fear in 1775 as part of a tour of British colonial possessions, reported that Brunswick had "a few scattered houses on the edge of the woods, without streets or regularity."

[8] Watson 1861: 8-11; Dunkerly, 14-17; Donald R. Lennon and Ida Brooks Kellam, eds. *The Wilmington Town Book, 1743-1778.* (Raleigh, N.C.: Division of Archives and History) 1973: xxiii. Hereafter cited as Lennon. The rivalry between Brunswick and the upstart new town further upriver was fierce. As an example, in the summer of 1743, Roger Moore sold an island in the river to John Jean, who intended to use it as a convenient place to store cargo awaiting export aboard ships that could pull right up to it. One of the stipulations Moore included said that Jean "shall not permit any Inhabitant of the Town of Wilmington in New Hanover County or any persons who has a shop, Store or Warehouse in said Town of Wilmington, to Land or Store or put in Store any Rice, Tar, or Turpentine or Lumber of any kind whatsoever or any other goods or Commodities of North Carolina production for Exportation, on said Land." If Jean failed to abide by those terms, the entire agreement was void.

[9] Watson 1861: 10.

[10] Watson 1861:37-38; Dunkerly: 22; Lindley S. Butler, *North Carolina and the Coming of the Revolution, 1763-1776.* (Raleigh: N.C. Department of Cultural Resources Archives & History, 1976): 3. Hereafter cited as Butler. North Carolina contained a quarter million people by the time of the Revolution, many of them traveling south down the Great Wagon Road from northern colonies like Virginia, Pennsylvania and New Jersey, making it the fourth largest colony of the thirteen. These newcomers included large numbers of

Scotch-Irish Presbyterians and Germans. Scots Highlanders flowed into Cape Fear River ports as well, as the failed Jacobite Rebellion saw their future prospects at home in Scotland dim after 1748.

[11] Dunkerly, 19-20. John Burgwin came to the Cape Fear from England in the 1750s and quickly became one of the most successful merchants in the region. In addition to his fine house in town, he also owned the Hermitage plantation near modern Castle Hayne. He served the colony in the General Assembly and as a clerk of court and clerk to royal governor Arthur Dobbs. Burgwin was a loyalist, and as war between the colonies and Great Britain grew imminent he sailed for England, ostensibly to seek medical treatment. When the war broke out, he opted to remain in England until the conflict ended. When Burgwin returned, he was allowed to retain ownership of his property - something that rarely happened to loyalists who had been on the losing side of the war.

[12] Dunkerly, 19-20.

[13] Robert L. Ganyard. *The Emergence of North Carolina's Revolutionary State Government*. (Raleigh: N.C. Department of Cultural Resources Archives & History, 1978): 2-3. Hereafter cited as Ganyard. Roger Moore was one of the original founders of the Brunswick settlement, and built his grand Orton Plantation home just north of the town.

[14] Watson 1861, 63-64.

[15] Watson 1861, 63; Ross, 48-49; Flora Fraser, *Flora Macdonald: "Pretty Young Rebel."* (New York: Alfred A. Knopf, 2023): 134. Hereafter cited as Fraser. By the time Hogg and Campbell broke apart in 1778, it claimed assets of £18,330...James Innes, Hugh Campbell, and William Forbes were the first Scots to claim large land grants under Gabriel Johnston's invitation to settle in North Carolina. Campbell chose a section between Rockfish Creek and Cross Creek. Innes and Forbes selected plots twenty miles further upriver, near where the Lower Little River merges into the Cape Fear. Each patent was for hundreds of acres, so it is likely they brought family with them or expected them to follow soon afterwards.

[16] William Thomas Sherman. "Calendar and Record of the Revolutionary War in the South: 1780-1781." (2003). https://www.americanrevolution.org/warinthesouth.php (accessed 10/25/23): 647. Hereafter cited as Sherman.

[17] Dunkerly, 27; Sherman, 25. Militiamen were required to provide their own muskets, keep at least twelve cartridges of ammunition close to hand, and have two opposable teeth - so that they could bite the end off of the paper cartridges containing powder and ball to load their weapons. Capt. William Dry's company of militiamen were armed with 1748 dog lock muskets, an inexpensive smooth bore trade gun. Records exist of Dry purchasing some of the weapons out of his own pocket to arm his men.

[18] Watson 1861, 30; Ganyard, 3; Sherman, 32. Lord George Germain, the British Secretary of State for North America during the American Revolution, designed a plan to isolate coastal Southerners from those in the backcountry by drumming up the support of slaves on coastal estates and then using them to frighten whites there into submission with the threat of slave uprisings.

[19] Dunkerly, 11; Watson 1861, 30-31. In 1773 Thresal proposed to sell "20,000 seasoned slaves" imported from Grenada, while Thompson imported "a parcel of choice negroes" from Jamaica. A year later, Alexander Hostler & Co. advertised eighteen "prime Negroes from Jamaica for sale."

[20] Dunkerly, 11; Watson 1861, 31. In 1772, one such slave gathering may have contributed to a small fire, perhaps the other thing Wilmington residents feared most. The town has burned and been rebuilt several times over its history...One measure was to impose a curfew for slaves, requiring any who were out and about after a certain time to have a pass from their masters.

[21] Watson 1861, 30; Lennon, xxxi; Dunkerly, 11, 23; Jeffrey J. Crow, *The Black Experience in Revolutionary North Carolina.* (Raleigh: North Carolina Division of Archives, 1977): 56-57. Hereafter cited as Crow. Slavery arrived in the Cape Fear in the 1720s, with wealthy white settlers from Goose Creek, though it is likely the earlier settlers at Charles Towne also brought enslaved servants with them. Cape Fear slave ownership was concentrated in the hands of the wealthiest landowners. The top one percent of the richest planters held ten percent of all the slaves in the region, and the top one-half percent of property owners controlled ninety percent of the region's property. Wealth in the Cape Fear, like in the rest of the South, was measured in property and slaves...The Wilmington Committee of Safety implemented disarmament of blacks in June to keep "Negroes in order." Janet Schaw, a loyalist, believed the unrest was part of a plan to get uncommitted residents to take up arms on the side of the rebels after talking with a leader of the slave patrols.

[22] Watson 1861, 33-34

[23] Watson 1861, 31. In 1767, slaves in North Carolina accounted for only about twenty to twenty-five percent of the population, but in the Cape Fear slaves made up sixty-two percent of the population. The Lower Cape Fear had 2.49 bondsmen (slaves) for every square mile of land, as opposed to an average of one every .94 per square miles in the rest of the colony.

[24] Crow, 56. Evidence supporting this may be seen in the order of the Wilmington Committee of Safety in December 1774 that four West Indian slaves imported to the town be reshipped immediately. But a request by William Hooper to bring in a slave from Rhode Island met no resistance from the group.

[25] Watson 1861, 35. While the feared insurrection of 1775 never materialized, many North Carolina slaves did gain their independence during the war. Some earned freedom by fleeing to British forces. Others were seized by redcoats as they marched through the colony, and were freed in return for working for their new British masters. Such work included serving as guides, foragers, and laborers. Some slaves chose to remain with their masters, even after being drafted into service by redcoats. William Hooper, who lost three slaves to the British, noted that British offers of "clothes, money, freedom - everything that could captivate a youthful mind," did not deter his house slave, John, from returning to his household. According to Hooper, John pretended to support the British, but escaped during the night to return to Mrs. William Hooper, who in 1781 was forced to leave Wilmington by occupying British troops.

[26] Crow, 58. Such a slave revolt did, in fact occur, but not in the Cape Fear. Slaves from Beaufort, Pitt, and Craven Counties revolted that summer of 1775. On July 8, the Pitt County Safety Committee ordered patrollers out with instructions to "shoot one or any number of Negroes who are armed and doth not willingly surrender their arms, and that they have Discretionary Power, to shoot any Number of Negroes above four, who are off their Masters Plantations, and will not submit."

[27] Crow, 99. Violet and Boston arrived in Sierra Leone in 1792, but she died soon after.

[28] Crow, 82-83, 171. Even though the British government ordered land to be awarded to Peters and the other black loyalists in Nova Scotia, it never was. The British instead urged the former slaves to journey to Africa and form their own new colony there. Thomas Peters died in 1792, not long after arriving in Sierra Leone. Sally became a widow after birthing six more children.

[29] Crow, 66-67; John Alexander Oates, *The Story of Fayetteville and the Upper Cape Fear.* (Fayetteville, N.C.: Dowd Press, 1950): 695. Hereafter cited as Oates. In her application for a veteran's pension in 1849, Hammond's wife testified that Isaac "...was a fifer...& was also a good fiddler at weddings & other merry makings, and was too much given to making himself merry."

[30] Crow, 78; Michael Lee Lanning. *Defenders of Liberty: African Americans in the Revolutionary War* (New York: Citadel Press, 2000): 33, 63, 66. Hereafter cited as Lanning.

[31] Lee, 243.

1765-1766

1765-1766

Aboard *H.M.S. Viper*, assigned patrol duty on the Cape Fear River, there was trouble brewing. The sloop of war's captain and first officer had suffered deteriorating relations for weeks over a competition for the affections of a young woman who lived at Brunswick Town. It was a sticky situation for Lieutenant Thomas Whitehurst, as Capt. Alexander Simpson was not just his rival in affairs of the heart, but also his commanding officer. Yet the heart wants what the heart wants, and neither man would yield ground to the other in the race to win the fair maiden's favor.

Things reached a climax on March 18, 1765, when the two men decided to settle things on the dueling field. In a wooded thicket outside town boundaries close by St. Philip's Church, the naval officers primed their pistols, marched off the requisite ten paces, turned, and fired. Thomas Whitehurst scored first, his shot entering Simpson's right shoulder and exiting under his arm. Both shots expended, and no doubt enraged by his wounding, Simpson charged at Whitehurst and, according to one account, hit the junior officer so hard in the head that it broke the butt and pan of his pistol. Whitehurst, a relation of the royal governor's wife, died of his wounds. Simpson, aware of the prohibition against dueling in the King's Navy, immediately jumped ship and fled. Governor William Tryon offered a reward for his apprehension, and in due course the disgraced officer surrendered himself for judgement before the bar. At court, the outcomes differed according to which accounts you read. Benson J. Lossing claimed Chief Justice Charles Berry acquitted Simpson and set him free, provoking charges from Tryon of partiality that lead to Berry's suicide. But historian Louis Toomer Moore wrote that Simpson was convicted and branded with

The ruins of St. Philip's Church at Brunswick Town Fort Anderson State Historic Site, where the Simpson-Whitehurst duel took place, and the scene of much of the rebellion against British rule between 1765-1782.

the letter "M" on the ball of his thumb, identifying him as a murderer. Either way, the Simpson-Whitehurst duel was only the opening act of the discord on the Cape Fear that year.[1]

Salutary neglect was a big part of the troubles that developed between king and colonies. Had Great Britain taken a more active role in the development of the colonies, perhaps the evolution of the Americans' independent spirit may have been retarded somewhat. But hindsight is always 20/20, and what might have been is simply speculation. The fact is that after the French & Indian War, when Great Britain sought to recoup some of the war's costs and offset the expense of keeping British troops in America, the means chosen of accomplishing those ends hit a raw nerve with the colonials.[2]

At the same time that the Sugar Act was imposed in March 1764, the Grenville ministry announced that it would be followed by a stamp duty, as well. The British government estimated that such a tax in the colonies, not uncommon in Great Britain itself, would generate in the neighborhood of £60,000 per year for the king's treasury that was sorely needed to pay for the country's growing global commitments. The tax would impose new costs on virtually every paper product used in the colonies, everything from legal documents to newspapers, playing cards and dice, licenses, and more. Considering the sheer amount of paper people use on a daily basis, the relatively small tax on individual items soon added up to a sum that the colonists found appalling. Add in the fact that it was a tax enacted by Parliament and not their own elected colonial assemblies, and American outrage over the new revenue producer was manifest throughout all thirteen colonies.[3]

In a place where the people had been allowed to develop their own systems and traditions, the imposition of the Stamp Act was an alarming overreach by the British. Outside of the Navigation Acts, which mainly governed the mercantile trade between England and its colonies, Americans believed taxation was a function reserved for themselves. Great Britain's hands-off approach to its North American possessions led the colonies to assume powers that were never specifically granted to them. When Parliament tried to reassert its will after the war it was too late. By 1765 Americans, including those in North Carolina, had a long tradition of doing things their own way. While the colonials conceded that Great Britain was within its rights to impose duties for regulating trade, they reserved the right to impose revenue taxes for themselves.[4]

Parliament passed the Stamp Act overwhelmingly, despite French & Indian War veteran Col. Isaac Barre cautioning the lawmakers not to. Barre warned that the colonists, who he called "Sons of Liberty," would oppose it. Nevertheless, the act was passed on March 22, 1765, and scheduled to go into effect on the first day of November. It was a recipe for rebellion. Never before had the colonies been subject to such a direct tax. Add to that the fact that the money raised was largely to pay for a standing British army in the colonies, and colonial resistance was practically guaranteed.[5]

In fairness, even with the stamp tax American colonials were still paying less than the king's subjects in England. Interest alone on Great Britain's French & Indian War debt was crippling, so austerity measures were the order of the day in Parliament. Cutting costs and raising income became a priority, and Parliament insisted the Americans pay their fair share. Traditionally, the North Carolina government collected taxes via mechanisms like quitrents, poll taxes, shipping and import duties, and liquor taxes. Of the money collected, a portion was sent to the king's treasury. North Carolinians had never experienced a direct tax before the Stamp Act. They saw it as an infringement on their rights as Englishmen.

Distrust between the colonies and the Mother Country grew, made worse when Great Britain enacted stricter trade regulations. One such measure that greatly offended the colonists was a provision in the Stamp Act that declared that offenders would be tried in vice-admiralty courts in Nova Scotia, rather than in American courts, and without the benefit of juries. Additionally, the king's proclamation prohibiting settlement west of the Allegheny and Appalachian Mountains, to lessen the risk of clashes with Native peoples, was uniformly disliked by the Americans.[6]

On the Cape Fear, Judge Maurice Moore declared his disapproval of Parliament's actions. "The Stamp Duty is itself a burthen too great for the circumstances of the Colonies to bear," he wrote in 1765, "considering the many restrictions that have been put upon their trade, which are at present rigorously enforced throughout America." Moore pointed to the British constitutional principle that taxation could only come from the consent of the people through their elected representatives, and disputed Parliament's idea of virtual representation, arguing that "...it is a doctrine which only tends to allow the Colonists a shadow of that substance which they must ever be slaves without. It cannot surely be consistent with British Liberty, that any set of men should represent another, detached from them in situation and interest, without the privity and consent of the represented." The colonial view conflicted with Parliament's, whose concept of "virtual representation" asserted that Parliament as a whole represented the colonies.[7]

Delegates from nine colonies met in New York City in October to devise a response to the Stamp Act. North Carolina was not among them, as royal governor William Tryon successfully prevented the Assembly from selecting representatives to attend. The colonies that did go urged Parliament to rescind the Stamp Act, and resolved to resist any tax that did not come from their own elected legislatures. They issued what they called a "Declaration of Rights and Grievances," in which they claimed for all colonies the rights of Englishmen. For the first time, Americans decried "taxation without representation." To emphasize their resolve, the delegates implemented a plan of economic warfare, boycotting most imported European goods. As a result, many British merchants felt the pinch in their purses and joined American calls to repeal the stamp tax.[8]

The same month that the Stamp Act Congress was meeting in New York, tensions were ratcheting up on the Cape Fear River. On October 19, 500 citizens of Wilmington gathered in the crisp autumn air and hanged an effigy of Lord Bute near the courthouse at Front and Market Streets, before burning it in a bonfire made from barrels of tar. The gathering was spurred by a resident of the town who expressed at least mild support for the tax. The mob went door to door, rousting out the men of the town and urging them to join the protest. Liquor flowed freely around the bonfire, and around midnight toasts to "LIBERTY, PROPERTY, and NO STAMP DUTY" were made to proclaim the crowd's sentiments and keep the cool temperatures at bay.

North Carolina's objection to the Stamp Act was not just abstract political theory. The new law required that the stamps be paid for in specie (gold or silver), something Cape Fear's residents would find difficult to do. Bullion was scarce in the colony. Paying their taxes in hard coin was something most Cape Fear colonials found impossible. On October 31, the last day before the Stamp Act was

Stamp protesters burning Lord Bute in effigy.

due to go into effect, a crowd once again gathered in Wilmington. This time the group held a mock funeral for Liberty, represented by an effigy in a wooden coffin. The coffin was hoisted on the shoulders of pallbearers who led a procession to the town graveyard between modern Fourth and Fifth Streets, muffled drums tapping out a solemn beat. In the background, the town bell pealed the sad tidings. Under the flickering glow of torchlights, the coffin was lowered to the ground, and mourners prepared to bid goodbye to their freedom in the face of British tyranny. The coffin lid was removed before committing it to the grave, and a final check was made to be sure Liberty was no more. But Liberty, weak as she was, still lived! The crowd rejoiced and returned to the tar barrel bonfire burning near the courthouse, placed Liberty in an armchair, and paraded her around the Wilmington streets.[9]

The demonstrations continued over the next weeks. On November 15, a group of Wilmingtonians stole a ship's boat from *H.M.S. Diligence* on the occasion of Gov. Tryon's official posting as royal governor. Though he had assumed the governorship upon the death of the much-loved Arthur Dobbs in early 1765, his official commission did not arrive until almost the end of the year. It was in an environment of simmering tension due to issues surrounding the Stamp Act that Captain Phipps of the *Diligence* ferried Tryon from Brunswick to Wilmington aboard his ship's barge, "with all the parade peculiar to that kind of Gentry..." Tryon landed at the Market Street wharf, received by the mayor, town aldermen, and other distinguished citizens. New Hanover militiamen rendered military honors as the governor presented his credentials. As the boom of seventeen cannons echoed in salute, and vessels in the harbor unfurled their ensigns in tribute, Tryon introduced a sour note to the occasion by using his address to stress "the Necessity of America's helping her Mother" and ask the people to receive the stamps.

A hiss from the audience was the response, only to be replaced by a cheer as a ship in the harbor unfurled an Irish flag from its mast. Capt. Phipps, outraged at the offence to the British flag, made to seize the Irish banner, but demurred when some in the crowd threatened to burn the barge that had transported Tryon upriver if he did. With the Irish flag at its bow, the raiders paraded their prize through the streets of the town, with Mayor Moses John DeRossett leading the procession. Gov. Tryon gave the crowd a tongue lashing, and Phipps threatened to return to his ship and bring it upriver to shell the town for their insolence. At this, the people commandeered the barrels of ale and an ox that had been provided as refreshments, punctuating their displeasure by breaking open the casks and dumping the beverage to flow through the town streets. The ox head they strung up in a gallows. They gave the rest of the ox to watching slaves, but according to accounts even the "Negroes disdained to taste the Bait of Slaven' which was [la]id for their Masters..."

Mayor DeRossett tried to soothe things over with the governor later, asking Tryon to not "lay the whole Blame of every Transaction relative to the Opposition made to the Stamp-Act on this Borough when it is so well known that the whole country has been equally concerned in it." Tryon accepted DeRossett's apology on behalf of the citizens of Wilmington, saying that he was "willing to forget every Impropriety of Conduct" that the mayor, aldermen, and people of Wilmington "have shown personally towards me in the late Commotions."[10]

The next day, militia colonel John Ashe led a large crowd of between 300 and 400 hundred citizens, many of whom wore hats bearing the slogan "LIBERTY," to the lodgings of Dr. William Houston of Duplin County. Houston had been appointed as stamp receiver without his knowledge, and the mob wanted to impress upon him that they were in no mood to tolerate any efforts to enforce the stamp laws. Houston declared he had no intention of carrying out the duties of an office he neither sought nor knew he had been given, but the crowd was not inclined to take him at his word. Ashe and company escorted the doctor to the courthouse, where Houston signed a resignation as stamp receiver witnessed by Mayor DeRossett and several Wilmington aldermen. When the resignation was complete, the crowd hoisted Houston aloft in an armchair and paraded him around the town, ending up at a local tavern where cheers to his good health were enjoyed.

While Dr. Houston was promising not to "execute any Office disagreeable to the People of the province," newspaper publisher Alexander Steuart was ordered by the crowd to resume publishing his *North Carolina Gazette and Post Boy*. Steuart's paper, just the second in North Carolina, began in September 1764, and was filled with what Benson J. Lossing called "intelligence of current events." When the Stamp Act was passed, Steuart was forced to cease publication because of the added expense that burdened each copy of the Gazette after November 1. Steuart, fearing for his life and that the mob might destroy his press if he refused, agreed to begin publishing the *Gazette* again.[11]

Across the river, Governor William Tryon had been sidelined by illness to the comfortable confines of his home, Bellfont, just north of Brunswick Town. The spacious house with a wide porch and a grand view of the Cape Fear was a perfect place to recuperate, but too far off the beaten path for Tryon to have much influence on the disturbing activities upriver at Wilmington. On November 18, days after Dr. Houston was forced to resign as stamp receiver, Tryon tried to mollify the protestors. He invited 50 civic leaders from Wilmington and Brunswick to his home for a dinner, at which he hoped to sway them into accepting the stamp tax.

The next morning, a delegation of those who had attended the governor's parley returned to Bellfont to give Tryon their answer. The delegates expressed appreciation for Tryon's concern for the welfare of the colony, but insisted that the Stamp Act was a threat to their rights as British subjects, declaring that "submission to any part of so oppressive and... so unconstitutional an attempt, is opening a direct inlet for Slavery, which all Mankind will endeavor to avoid."

Governor Tryon went further to appease the men. He recognized that there was not enough specie in the entire province to meet the demands of the stamp duty for even one year. Tryon told them that while he would not debate the complexities of Parliament's right to tax its colonies, he did sympathize with the protestors. He told them that he hoped there would be no violence when the stamps finally arrived in the Cape Fear, and that there were none among them who desired "...destroying the Dependance [sic] on the Mother Country," by resisting British law.

Tryon confided that it was his intention to seek an exemption for North Carolina in the event that the stamp duty was not repealed, but asked the people's forbearance in the meantime. In a demonstration of his sincerity, the governor offered to pay the tax on all documents on which he collected a fee as governor, and to also personally pay for a number of wine licenses in some North Carolina towns. The delegation of protestors would not be swayed. Ten days later, the hated stamps arrived.[12]

When *H.M.S. Diligence*, carrying the Cape Fear's supply of stamps, dropped anchor off Wilmington on November 28, 1765, no one was there to take charge of them thanks to the resignation of Dr. William Houston. The failure to land the stamps was a problem for more than just the government's tax collection. Without the required stamps on ship's papers, business at the port came to a standstill, and the courts also shut down. No ships could enter or leave the Cape Fear until the issue of stamps was resolved. As a result, residents of Wilmington and Brunswick who depended on a functioning maritime trade began to suffer. By early 1766, Cape Fear anger at the Stamp Act reached a peak when news arrived that theirs was the only port still closed on the Atlantic seaboard. Officials in other places had bowed to local sentiment and economic necessity to keep their ports open by issuing certificates in the absence of stamps.

In mid-January 1766, the sloops *Dobbs* and *Patience* crossed the bar into the Cape Fear River and fell under the sway of local Crown authorities. As both ships put to sea before the act went into effect, their cargoes did not carry the required stamps that would let them be unloaded at Wilmington or Brunswick. Captain Jacob Lobb, of the sloop of war *H.M.S. Viper*, seized both ships and their papers; and when a third ship, the *Ruby*, entered the river, it was taken too. The seizures had an immediate economic impact on the Cape Fear. "The trade of this river is at present entirely ruined!" complained one report. "Besides the three vessels that have been seized by the man of war, seven others have, within the fortnight past, put into our capes; but on hearing of the above-mentioned seizures, made off for other ports. This is a stroke that must be sensibly felt by the people of Cape Fear, as these ten vessels would have carried off a vast deal of tar and turpentine, which, in a few weeks, will be running through our streets."[13]

Lobb turned the ship's papers of the *Dobbs* and *Patience* over to Port Collector William Dry, whose job it was to refer the ships for prosecution. Dry, knowing the circumstances of why the two ships did not carry the proper stamps, referred the case to North Carolina's attorney-general, Robert Jones. The reply from Jones declared that not only were both ships to be prosecuted, but that the lack of stamps for use by the local courts required that the *Dobbs* and *Patience* be taken to Halifax, Nova Scotia for condemnation and adjudication. The seizures ignited the anger that had been simmering among the people of the Cape Fear since the sloops arrived a month before. In retaliation, the residents of Wilmington refused to provide fresh provisions for Lobb's *Viper*, while forty leading citizens from across the Lower Cape Fear met in Wilmington to sign a letter to Dry, cautioning him that nothing good would come of any effort to send the *Dobbs, Patience*, and *Ruby* to Nova Scotia.[14]

In fact, William Dry was no more a fan of the Stamp Act than the men who warned him against enforcing it. Dry reasoned with the protestors that even if he resigned his office, the next port collector might view the tax more favorably and pursue enforcement of his duties more vigorously. Dry assured them that if his responsibilities as port collector did not restrain him, he would himself join them in protesting the tax. The people were not mollified. The "Sons of Liberty," as they had taken to calling themselves, met in Wilmington on February 18 to plot their next moves. Leading men from across southeastern North Carolina were among them, and swore to prevent "...entirely the operation of the Stamp Act."

On February 19, 1766, the men gathered into a force almost 1,000 strong, armed with muskets and fowling pieces, and marched to Brunswick Town. The mob included a wide cross section of Cape Fear people, from gentleman planters who owned great estates, to merchants and artisans of the middling classes, to yeoman farmers and craftsmen. They represented colonists from New Hanover, Brunswick, Duplin, and Bladen Counties. Ship's masters marched with wealthy merchants, alongside Mayor DeRossett of Wilmington, and also several town aldermen.

At Bellfont, the protestors arrayed themselves on the governor's lawn among the fruit trees, and waited as George Moore and Cornelius Harnett delivered a letter from Speaker John Ashe of the General Assembly, also signed by Thomas Lloyd and Alexander Lillington. The letter assured the governor of his safety, emphasizing that the armed men in the crowd were only there to protect him. Gov. Tryon insisted he had no need of their protection, but nevertheless, 150 men surrounded his home when Moore and Harnett departed. The group declared they only took issue with Jacob Lobb, the naval officer they believed to be sheltered by Tryon. Tryon replied that he did not recognize the mob's authority, and said that the naval officer was not there. The outraged governor dared the Cape Fear men to break into his house to look for themselves. Violence was averted when word arrived that Lobb was back aboard the *Viper*, but the crowd did not immediately disperse.[15]

Col. Hugh Waddell

As Tryon peeked through his curtains at the men arrayed around Bellfont, he worried that the protestors might try to seize Fort Johnston, at the mouth of the river, and make off with its powder and armaments. His worries proved prophetic. While armed protestors entered the home of Port Collector William Dry and rifled his desk to reclaim the ship's papers of the *Dobbs, Patience*, and *Ruby*, Col. Hugh Waddell led a force of 300 men to seize Fort Johnston. The governor sent orders to Capt. Constantine Phipps of *H.M.S. Diligence*, anchored opposite the fort, to be prepared to do whatever was necessary to defend it. If any sort of defense was to be mounted, it would have to come from the *Diligence* and her guns, as Captain John Dalrymple, commander of the fort, only had five men under his command. Hearing that the force of Cape Fear men he would likely face numbered about a thousand (an overestimation as it turned out), the captain determined that even with his ship's guns he would be sorely pressed to defend the fort. Phipps decided that without pilots to help navigate the shallow and hence dangerous Cape Fear River at night, the ship would be an easy target if the protestors

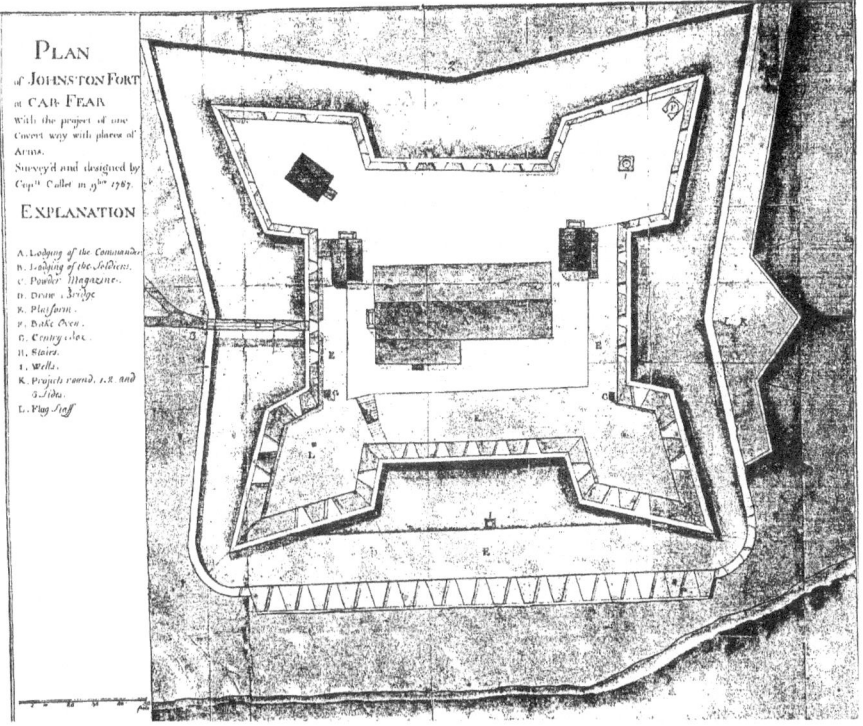

The 1767 plan of Fort Johnston at the mouth of the Cape Fear river. The fort never reached this final completed form, but was still functional. Much of the action that took place through 1776 occurred nearby.

took control of Fort Johnston's eight 18-pounderer and eight 9-pounder cannons, and 23 swivel guns. Phipps decided to interpret his orders from Tryon very loosely, and sent five men ashore to help Dalrymple spike Fort Johnston's guns.[16]

Governor Tryon was furious that Phipps ordered the disabling of the fort's cannons. He wrote that he was mortified that "his Majesty's ordnance at Fort Johnston" had been made inoperable, and demanded that Phipps and Lobb justify their decision to spike the cannons. Capt. Lobb replied in a letter that attempted to offer his reasoning.

"I received Your Excelleny's letter of the 23d inst. desiring me to give Your Excellency my reasons for ordering the guns at Fort Johnston to be spiked," Lobb wrote. "Pursuant to Your Excellency's letter of the 19th inst. signifying to me that as Fort Johnston had but one officer and five men in garrison and its standing in need of all the assistance the *Viper* and *Diligence* could give the commanding officer there should any insult be offered to His Majesty's fort or store and likewise Your Excellency's request to repel force with force, I, on information the same evening from Lieut. Calder, corroborated by that of several other gentlemen, that a party of men consisting of three or four hundred under the command of Col. [Hugh] Waddell were on their march to Fort Johnston in order to take possession of it, as there was no possibility of getting the ship down, being night and no pilots to be had, early enough to prevent their making their quarters good, sent Lieutenant Calder in a boat with Your Excellency's order address to Capt. Dalrymple, commanding that he should comply with any orders he should receive from myself or Capt. Phipps, with one to render the cannon unserviceable by spiking them up; to the end of facilitating our repossession as soon as the ships could arrive before it."[17]

On the morning of February 19, a delegation of protestors rowed out to *H.M.S. Viper* to demand that Capt. Lobb release the impounded ships. Lobb requested time to confer with other Crown officers, including Gov. Tryon, Port Collector Dry, Captain Constantine Phipps, and Vice-Judge of the Admiralty Thomas McGuire. Lobb and the other authorities agreed to release the *Ruby*, but the captain was adamant that the *Dobbs* and *Patience* be held. Although Gov. Tryon left believing that Lobb would be firm in defending the government's right to the ships, by later that evening he had been persuaded to let all three ships depart. At least until a new surveyor of general customs arrived, the Cape Fear River would join the rest of the American ports and be open to all maritime trade.[18]

Meanwhile William Pennington, virtually the only remaining officer charged with duties specific to the Stamp Act on the Cape Fear, knocked on the door at Bellfont on the evening of February 20. Pennington sought refuge with the governor from angry protestors who wanted the same concessions from him that they had extracted from William Houston and William Dry. Tryon provided Pennington with a bed, and the next morning around eight o'clock the two men saw Col. James Moore arrive at Bellfont leading a detachment of roughly 60 men.

Moore attempted to take Pennington into custody, but was prevented by Gov. Tryon, who told Moore that the comptroller of customs was engaged in government business and was unable to leave with the protestors. Moore bowed to Tryon's authority and left. Within minutes the lanes leading to Bellfont were again crammed with armed men. Moore sent a note to the governor declaring that while they only wished to speak with Pennington and that his safety was guaranteed if he cooperated, if Pennington failed to come out of the house no such guarantees could be made.

Two hours later, Cornelius Harnett led a body of armed men somewhere between 400 and 500 strong down the lane to Bellfont. Stopping three hundred yards from the house, Harnett and 60 followers approached the porch and again asked permission to speak with William Pennington. When Harnett was allowed into the house, he told Pennington he wished to have a conversation. Gov. Tryon interceded yet again, informing Harnett that Pennington was under his protection. Harnett replied that if the comptroller did not make himself available, the crowd might be inclined to take him by force. Pennington, listening as the two men discussed his fate, found it all unsettling. He told Tryon that perhaps in the interest of maintaining the peace he should go with Harnett. The governor finally agreed, but only after insisting on Pennington's resignation.

At Brunswick William Pennington, like Houston and Dry before him, was forced to sign a declaration that he would not directly or indirectly issue any stamped paper. Lesser officers of the court like clerks and lawyers were also required to make the same oath. Stamps were never landed in the Cape Fear thanks to the resistance of the men of the region who refused to allow it. It may have been the first act of armed resistance to British authority in the colonies, coming eight years before the famed Boston Tea Party.[19]

Although Governor Tryon was generally not vindictive in the wake of the stamp resistance, two Cape Fear men did suffer consequences. Judge Maurice Moore's opposition to the stamp tax earned him the enmity of Royal Governor Tryon, who viewed Moore's pamphlet and the position he took in it as an insult and betrayal. At the very least, Moore's writings made Tryon's job as an officer of the Crown more difficult. As a result, Tryon punished Moore by suspending him from his judgeship in early 1766. "He is a leading man in this river," Tryon wrote, "though he enjoys no great popularity in other parts of the province." Alexander Steuart was also suspended from his position as public printer because he allowed what Tryon termed an "inflammatory" letter to be published in his *North Carolina Gazette* newspaper.[20]

John Dalrymple, commander at Fort Johnston, survived the stamp crisis on the Cape Fear, but not much more. He passed away on July 13, 1766. His replacement was a local man whose plantation was located practically right next door to the fort. Robert Howe was confirmed as Fort Johnston's commander at the request of Gov. William Tryon. Until a royal commission could be secured, Howe was sworn in under Tryon's own local authority. Howe and Tryon knew each other well, as the Cape Fear man also held commissions as associate district judge and chief baron of the exchequer. Robert Howe was an incredibly good choice, bringing to the job local knowledge and standing, as well as political and military experience.

Howe was sworn in at Fort Johnston on November 3, 1766, and just days later was deep into his role as the fort's commander. Records show a reimbursement from the General Assembly for £69 paid out of Howe's own pocket to relocate "great guns from Wilmington to Fort Johnston, and sundry other charges." Despite his industrious embrace of his position, it did not last. On November 4, 1767, Capt. John Abraham Collet, a regular British officer, presented his commission as commander of the fort to Gov. Tryon. Howe found himself demoted to second in command.[21]

Endnotes

[1] Louis Toomer Moore. *Stories Old and New of the Cape Fear Region* (Wilmington, N.C.: Broadfoot Publishing, 1999): 31-35. Hereafter cited as Moore; Benson J. Lossing, *Lossing's Pictorial Field-Book of the Revolution in the Carolinas & Georgia* (Wilmington, N.C.: Dram Tree Books, 2005): n. 22. Hereafter cited as Lossing.. Gov. William Tryon issued a proclamation offering £50 reward for the apprehension of Simpson.

[2] William D. Brinkley. *Back to the Future: The British Southern Campaign, 1780-1781.* Army Command and General Staff College Fort Leavenworth KS School of Advanced Military Studies, 1998: 3. Hereafter cited as Brinkley. The British national debt in 1763 was £122,603,336. The ministry hoped to secure £200,000 per year from the American colonies to help retire that debt and support the British troops stationed there for defense.

[3] Watson 1861, 74-79. Also passed by Parliament in 1764 was the Currency Act denying North Carolina the right to emit paper money and called for the sinking of existing currency. Colonists objected to this measure because specie was hard to come by. So was paper. The combination, under the Currency Act, threatened to put a damper on trade.

[4] E. Lawrence Lee. "Days of Defiance: Resistance to the Stamp Act in the Lower Cape Fear." The North Carolina Historical Review 43.2 (1966): 186-202. Hereafter cited as Lee, Defiance; Lindley S. Butler. North Carolina and the Coming of the Revolution, 1763-1776. (Raleigh: N.C. Department of Cultural Resources Archives & History, 1976) 14. Hereafter cited as Butler 1776. Grenville suggested the colonists come up with alternative ways of raising revenues if they found the Stamp Act unpalatable, but by the time the ministry actually met with them in May the government was already committed to the stamp duty.

[5] Butler 1776, 15; William S. Price, Jr. *Not A Conquered People: Two Carolinians View Parliamentary Taxation.* (Raleigh: N.C. Department of Cultural Resources Archives & History, 1975): 1. Hereafter cited as Price.

⁶ Dunkerly, 30-31. Englishmen jealously guarded their historic right to be taxed only by their own elected representatives in Parliament, and the Americans - transplanted Englishmen though they were - did too. Since the colonies had no elected representatives in Parliament, they did not always recognize Parliament's power to tax them. For their part, Parliament took the view that all members of that body were de facto representatives of the king's overseas possessions, and they did not understand the Americans' outrage.

⁷ Butler 1776, 14-17. Judge Moore made his arguments in a pamphlet published in the summer of 1765, "Justice and Policy in Taxing the American Colonies in Great Britain Considered." Moore held that Great Britain had no right to tax the colonies, and also that direct colonial representation in Parliament was impossible.

⁸ Price, 5; Lee, 244. The pressure worked. Parliament lifted the stamp tax in March 1766, but not before the men of the Cape Fear committed what may have been the first act of armed resistance to British authority in the colonies.

⁹ Butler 1776, 18; Lee 244-245. New Hampshire, Virginia, and Georgia also failed to send delegates...The complete toast was to "LIBERTY, PROPERTY, and NO STAMP-DUTY, and Confusion to Lord B_te and all his adherents." Lord Bute was no longer Prime Minister in London, but Cape Fear enemies of the stamp tax held him responsible anyway.

¹⁰ Watson 1861, 74-79. The defiance on the Cape Fear likely happened largely because Gov. Tryon did not have a sufficient enforcement body at his disposal. Outside of the two sloops of war on station at Cape Fear, there was no other force he could use to compel compliance to the king's edicts...It was Tryon's intention to make Wilmington the colony's capital. He bought Bellfont with that goal in mind, but after his reception in Wilmington Tryon exacted a measure of revenge by moving the provincial seat of government ninety miles up the coast to New Bern.

¹¹ Butler 1776, 18; Watson 1861, 74-79. Adam Boyd, originally from New Bern, was an affirmed patriot. His *Cape Fear Mercury* is one of the only surviving Cape Fear newspapers from the Revolutionary period, though gaps in coverage due to scarcity of paper and British-ordered closings made its run sporadic...Houston related that upon arrival in Wilmington, "The Inhabitants immediately assembled about me & demanded a Categorical Answer whether I intended to put the Act relating [to] the Stamps in force. The Town Bell was rung[,] Drums [were] beating, Colours [were] flying and [a] great concourse of People [were] gathered together." At the courthouse he readily offered his resignation "to quiet the Minds of the inraged and furious Mobb ..."

¹² Butler 1776, 20; Lee, 245-246. Bellfont was originally known as Russllborough, after the ship captain owner who built it. The ruins of the house are now part of Brunswick Town Fort Anderson State Historic Site between Wilmington and Southport, N.C.

¹³ Lee, 246-247. The *Dobbs* sailed from St. Christopher in the Caribbean, and the *Patience* from Philadelphia.

¹⁴ Lee, 246-248; Butler 1776, 20-21. *H.M.S. Viper* was one of two ships stationed at Cape Fear. The other, *H.M.S. Diligence* under Captain Constantine Phipps, was the ship which actually brought the stamps to the Cape Fear...One unsigned letter in Alexander Steuart's *North Carolina Gazette* took locals to task, asking, "Where is your boasted Courage and Resolution? Have the Wilmingtonians, Brunswickers, and New Hanoverians lost their senses and souls, and are they determined to tamely submit to slavery?"...William

Dry was taken aback by the vehemence of his neighbors' letter, warning him that if he released the ships' papers to the British "...very ill Consequences...will attend this affair." As a result, Dry informed Gov. Tryon he would only release the papers if ordered to.

[15] Price, 246-248; Butler 1776, 23.

[16] Butler 1776, 23; Wilson Angley. *A History of Fort Johnston on the Lower Cape Fear.* (Southport, N.C.: 1996): 14. Hereafter cited as Angley. The custom of the time was to stock forts with munitions and other supplies and leave them in the care of a skeleton force of men to look after it all. When war clouds or emergency arose, the militia or regular troops would make up the rest of the fort's garrison... Hugh Waddell had seen previous service in the French & Indian War, and would later serve again as commander of Gov. Tryon's artillery in the Regulator Rebellion.

[17] Angley, 14. Capt. Dalrymple was able to report to Gov. Tryon later that all of the guns had been repaired and returned to service, mollifying him to some extent.

[18] Butler 1776, 23; Lee, 249. Lobb was uncertain if the seizure of the *Ruby* was entirely legal, so he was willing to relent in that instance...No doubt Lobb's later decision to release all three ships was influenced by the growing number of armed protestors that continued to filter into the area.

[19] Lee, 249-250.

[20] Price, 6-7; Butler 1776, 24.

[21] Angley, 15; Patrick O'Kelley, *Nothing But Blood and Slaughter: The Revolutionary War in the Carolinas-Volume One 1771-1779* (Booklocker.com Incorporated, 2005): 163. Hereafter cited as O'Kelley V1. Howe replaced Capt. John Dalrymple after the old commandant died...Collet's commission was dated six months earlier, and took precedence over Howe's claim by virtue of him being a regular army officer. Collet served in numerous capacities while at Fort Johnston, including as aid-de-camp to Tryon on his expedition against the Regulators in September of 1768. He also traveled to London in December 1768 with a detailed report on the colony entrusted to him by the governor. On that occasion, one of the things he took with him was a highly detailed map of North Carolina based on the work of William Churton, the surveyor of Granville District. It remains one of the best maps of N.C. during the colonial era. Collet did not return to the Cape Fear again until 1773. In his absence, Robert Howe assumed command of Fort Johnston.

1767-1773

An Impartial RELATION

OF THE

First Rise and Cause

OF THE

Recent DIFFERENCES,

IN

PUBLICK AFFAIRS,

In the Province of North-Carolina; and of the past Tumults and Riots that lately happened in that Province.

Containing most of the true and genuine Copies of Letters, Messages and Remonstrances, between the Parties contending:—— By which any impartial Man may easily find out the true Ground and Reasons of the Dissatisfaction that universally reigns all over the Province in a more or less Degree.

Printed for the Compiler, 1770.

1767-1773

While the Stamp Act and the discontent it caused in the American colonies seemed to have subsided, Parliament's determination to make the colonies pay their fair share did not. In 1766 they passed the American Colonies Act - more commonly known as the Declaratory Act - that reiterated Parliament's right to pass laws that the American colonies were compelled to obey. In 1767 the Townshend Act introduced tariffs on imported lead, glass, paint, paper, and tea. Like in 1765-1766, the colonies undertook non-importation pledges as a means of pressuring Parliament to rescind the act, but devotion to the effort did not reach the same levels as it did in the campaign against the hated stamps. Ambivalence in the Cape Fear towards the Townshend Act came from the fact that even though, like the Stamp Act, it concerned Parliament's right to tax its colonies, the burden of the tax fell less uniformly on North Carolina citizens.[1]

When Great Britain deployed four regiments of redcoats to Boston to enforce the Townshend Revenue Act, North Carolina's Assembly was in recess. As they met again in late October, North Carolina's representatives enthusiastically seconded the steps taken by Virginia's House of Burgesses. After reading the Assembly's resolves, Tryon told them that the representatives had "sapped the foundations of confidence and gratitude, ... [and] torn up by the roots every sanguine hope I entertained to render this Province further service ...."As a result, Gov. Tryon immediately dissolved the Assembly to head off any more rebellious activity. The governor's effort was unsuccessful. The released delegates gathered instead at the New Bern courthouse where they picked up right where they left off, and over two days put the finishing touches on a nonimportation agreement.[2]

The members of the General Assembly assured Tryon that their actions were aimed at Parliament, not him personally; but Tryon felt the actions of the representatives fatally damaged his ability to effectively govern North Carolina. In January 1770 he wrote his superiors in London that "the proceedings of the last Assembly have wounded my sensibility," and requested a transfer either to New York to become royal governor there, or to England for a rest. Not long after he received orders to New York.[3]

In the Cape Fear, disagreements with Parliament took a back seat to those within the colony between piedmont farmers and Crown officers appointed to govern them. Those disagreements would fester until breaking out in the violence of the Regulator Rebellion and the climactic Battle of Alamance. In the meantime, Lower Cape Fear leaders endorsed trade restrictions against Great Britain in September 1769, a year before the General Assembly, but as much as two years after other colonies. When South Carolina called for its sister colony to join them in non-importation efforts in 1770, James Moore called the Sons of Liberty of New Hanover, Onslow, Brunswick, Bladen, Cumberland, and Duplin Counties together at Wilmington on June 2 to get organized. The meeting produced plans for local committees to reaffirm the non-importation agreements and to enforce compliance. A month later, Sons of Liberty leader Cornelius Harnett, chosen to lead the enforcement committee, was able to write to his South Carolina counterparts that, "We beg leave to assure you, that the inhabitants...are convinced of the necessity of adhering strictly to their former resolutions, and you may depend, they are as tenacious of their just rights as any of their brethren on the continent, and firmly resolved to stand or fall with them in support of the common cause of American liberty."[4]

The moves of North Carolinians to join the resistance to the Townshend Act never amounted to much. The Cape Fear was the only place

The Great Wagon Road from Pennsylvania delivered large numbers of settlers to the North Carolina frontier.

where any real effort was made to enforce it, and even there it met with only middling success. Tryon was dismissive of the colony's efforts. In 1771 he wrote, "Notwithstanding the boasted associations of people who never were in trade, and the shallow Patriotism of a few merchants to the southward of the province, the several Ports of this province have been open ever since the repeal of the Stamp Act for every kind of British manufactures to the full extent of the credit of the country." Rumors that the Townshend Act was soon to be repealed probably contributed to the lack of serious resistance in North Carolina. Word was that Parliament would soon repeal the law with the exception of the duty on tea. Those rumors were borne out when, on March 5, 1770, the Townshend Act was repealed. It had only been four months since North Carolina joined the non-importation movement.[5]

In coastal North Carolina people were concerning themselves with the Townshend Act and the extent that Parliament's authority included the American colonies. Meanwhile, the people of the piedmont were dealing with their own troubles. In some senses, North Carolina was a tale of two peoples. The development of the central part of the colony was accomplished by different people than those who populated the coastal plain.

On the coast the population was primarily English and Anglican, colonists who made their living from naval stores, lumber, tobacco, and rice plantations worked by hundreds of enslaved Africans. That was not the case in the piedmont. The western parts of North Carolina were a melting pot of diversity, made up of Scots, Englishmen, Germans, Quakers, Presbyterians, and Baptists. The Great Wagon Road from Pennsylvania was a thoroughfare used by countless individuals and families seeking new starts in southern climes. Geography tended to isolate these people from their fellow citizens along the coast. The two regions were also separated by great rivers like the Yadkin and Catawba.

That isolation from the seat of power contributed to the events leading to the War of the Regulation, or the Regulator Rebellion, but it was only one cause. Westerners felt that the government was dominated by coastal elites who ignored their interests and installed officials who treated them unfairly. It was the ruling class of wealthy coastal planters and their placemen, the piedmont colonists believed, who dominated North Carolina to the detriment of the farmers who made up the bulk of the population in the west. High taxes also contributed to their discontent. North Carolina taxes were generated by quitrents, poll taxes, tonnage duties, import duties on liquor, and other lesser taxes. It was the poll taxes that raised the greatest objection from the people of the west, as it burdened small farmers with large families more than it did the wealthy along the coast. In fact, studies by modern scholars have shown that 90 percent of North Carolina's tax revenues came from the poll tax and the duty on alcoholic beverages. The tax burden facing North Carolinians was also higher than in other colonies, too.[6]

The assessing of taxes was rife with corruption. Local sheriffs acted as tax collectors, and were the chief offenders in the eyes of the westerners. A typical scheme involved sheriffs showing up unannounced to collect the tax. When the farmer was unable to pay, the sheriff placed a lien on property with a value in excess of what was owed. The sheriff would then conduct an auction of the property to pay the tax bill, selling it cheap to confederates working with him on the sly. Another area of abuse was the fees charged for licenses and legal services. Benson J. Lossing gives the example of Thomas Frohock, who as clerk of Superior Court in Salisbury, extorted people by charging as much as fifteen dollars for a marriage license (equal to about fifty dollars in the early 1830s of Lossing's time). The fee was so exorbitant that many people took to entering

The "palace" that William Tryon built in New Bern was an affront to the farmers of central North Carolina, who resented their taxes being used to construct such a building while they were losing their farms to unscrupulous tax men.

unofficial common law unions to avoid it.[7]

The people of the piedmont also took exception to Tryon's surveying of the western boundary of the colony, raising a militia to help keep order, and imposing taxes to fund a new seat of government at New Bern. Tryon did not have much say in these matters as all were tasks required by his superiors, but it is true that the new seat of government could have been something less ostentatious than the "palace" that the governor constructed by the waterfront at the junction of the Trent and Neuse Rivers. Regulator William Butler declared for the people of the backcountry that, "We are determined not to pay the Tax for the next three years, for the Edifice of Governor's House, nor will we pay for it."[8]

The War of the Regulation came in two acts. The abuses suffered by the backcountry folk were nothing new. What became the Regulator Rebellion sprouted from malpractice by government agents like Thomas Child and Francis Corbin in Granville, Edgecombe, and Halifax Counties as much as two decades before the climactic battle in Alamance. In 1758, their unfair and illegal practices prompted the attorney general to urge the colonists to petition the General Assembly for redress of their grievances. That was symbolic of the first phase, when those who felt they had been abused by unscrupulous officials sought justice through legal means such as petition, negotiation, and political action. The second phase saw backcountry men take matters into their own hands using violence and threats of rebellion as their chief tools.

When angry westerners began to organize, they called themselves Regulators, because in their view they could manage county affairs as well or better than the men in charge who were only driven by greed and avarice. Sandy Creek planter Herman Husband, late of Pennsylvania, became a chief spokesman for the disgruntled backcountry farmers. Husband was an extended relative of Benjamin Franklin, who helped him publish a series of pamphlets or small-sheet "advertisements" that trumpeted what the Regulators saw as abuse at the hands of government officials. Husband was joined by Rednap Howell, William Butler, James Hunter, Ninian Bell Hamilton, and others in castigating Col. Edmund Fanning, who they saw as a main culprit in the affair. Fanning, who referred to the backcountry colonists as "the ignorant people with their shallow understanding of the law," did little to endear himself with them.[9]

Edmund Fanning

Early protests included one by George Sims, of Nutbush (later Williamsboro), N.C. Sims wrote a protest against corrupt and extortionist public officials in a pamphlet published on June 1, 1765. The title of the protest was "An Address to the People of Granville County." School master Sims used the protest to accuse county clerk Samuel Benton of charging excessive fees to record legal transactions, calling the clerks, lawyers, and sheriff "these cursed hungry caterpillars, that are eating and will eat out the bowels of our Commonwealth." For his trouble, Sims was arrested, tried, and sentenced to jail for publishing what came to be known as the Nutbush Address.[10]

The Regulators made their objections public in the 1766 session of the Hillsborough court, when they widely circulated a broadside that has come to be known as the Regulator Advertisement #1. The document spotlighted what the Regulators called the "unjust Oppression in our own Province," and declared that "while Liberty prevails we must mutter and grumble under any abuses of power until such a noble spirit prevails in our posterity..." They called for representatives to attend a meeting to determine their next course of action. On October 10, a dozen delegates met at Maddock's Mill to enumerate their grievances, prompting Edmund Fanning to label them insurrectionists.[11]

A year and a half later, Orange County sheriff Tyree Harris announced that he would no longer go door to door to collect taxes. Citizens would now be required to travel to one of five collection points to pay their tax debts. The Regulators, not for the first time, requested that the sheriff account for the taxes already collected over the previous two years, and also that he provide a copy of the fees taxpayers were liable for. Rather than do that, the sheriff instead went after a delinquent debtor, confiscating his horse, bridle, and saddle. Outraged spread among the Regulators, and a band of men rode into town to retrieve what the sheriff had taken. The men also whipped the sheriff and damaged Fanning's house while they were at it. It was the spark that touched off a rebellion.[12]

Fanning was out of town when the raid happened, but when he returned he ordered the men responsible arrested. Herman Husband was chosen by the Regulators to go to Hillsborough to lower the temperature of the situation. Before he could Fanning, accompanied by the sheriff and a posse, arrived to arrest him, too. William Butler, who had been in the band that conducted the raid, was also arrested. The men were tossed into jail in Hillsborough, more a roofless stockade than a true gaol, on charges of inciting to riot. By sunrise on May 3, 700 men rode into Hillsborough to secure the release of Husband and Butler. Fanning ordered the two men released upon hearing of the Regulators' approach. As they reached the

Gov. Tryon confronted the Regulators in Hillsborough and ordered them to disperse. In return, he pardoned all but five men he considered ringleaders of the rebellion.

Eno River and surrounded the town, Rev. George Micklejohn pleaded with the band to not act in haste. Despite his cajoling, the Regulators would not be dissuaded. It took a promise that the Regulators' complaints would be heard from Gov. Tryon's secretary, Isaac Edwards, to convince the backcountry men to ride off, Husband and Butler along with them. At Thomas Lindley's mill the Regulators drew up a petition, signed by 500 men, and selected Rednap Howell and James Hunter to deliver it to Gov. Tryon at Brunswick. In late May the men made the journey, but despite his secretary's assurances, Tryon dismissed them. The governor warned them to stop holding meetings, disband the Regulators, and pay their taxes. In the meantime, pending his own investigation into the Regulators' claims, he ordered county officials to post a list of fees for services.[13]

The rebellion spread throughout central North Carolina. In Anson County, protestors offered military assistance to Orange County Regulators after a mob forced their own court officers to flee out of concern for their safety. In Rowan County, 300 Regulators burned down the Salisbury jail. In August an all-out brawl erupted in Johnston County between Regulators and court officers when the former tried to stop legal proceedings at the courthouse there. By September 22, 1768, some 3,700 Regulators had gathered around Hillsborough. When Tryon arrived with a force of militia, he ordered them to disperse in return for pardons for everyone except five men he identified as ringleaders. By the next morning, the Regulators had left, clearing the way for the governor to conduct his inquiry into what was going on in the backcountry. As a result, Herman Husband was acquitted. William Butler and two others were fined and sentenced to short terms in prison. Col. Edmund Fanning, whose imperious and impetuous actions precipitated much of the turmoil that summer, was convicted on six counts of extortion. Despite the verdict, Fanning was only fined one penny plus the costs of court.[14]

Maurice Moore was at Fanning's trial. Gov. Tryon restored his judgeship in March 1768, after the tensions of the Stamp Act rebellion were well behind them. Moore had behaved himself in the interim, and worked his way back into the governor's good graces. When Tryon traveled into the interior to deal with the Regulators, Moore led a troop of Gentlemen Volunteer Light Dragoons along with him. Over the next months, Moore spent a good deal of time in the backcountry serving on the bench as a circuit judge. By March 13, 1770, Moore was reporting to

Judge Richard Henderson (right) and Samuel Johnston (left)

Tryon that sheriffs in the western part of the province were unable in many cases to either collect taxes or serve writs due to Regulator agitation.[15]

Two years to the day later, yet another petition was drawn up by the Regulators, this time to be presented at the opening of the September 22, 1770 session of the court at Hillsborough. When the doors opened at the courthouse, Associate Justice Richard Henderson was the only judge on hand to receive the backcountry men's petition from James Hunter. The courtroom was packed to overflowing with Regulators, lawyers, and others. As Henderson began to speak, backcountry men outside began to harass attorneys with business before the court. William Hooper, a future North Carolina signer of the Declaration of Independence, was among several lawyers who were assaulted by the mob. The much-hated Edmund Fanning was beaten and dragged from his home, which the Regulators then destroyed. Judge Henderson said that Fanning was beaten so badly that "one of his eyes was almost beaten out." When the violence erupted, Henderson and other officials of the court fled in fear. The next day, the Regulators smeared feces on the judge's seat, and placed the body of an executed black man in Henderson's chair to preside over mock trials they held, complete with a profanity-laced set of court minutes. Stores and homes were looted, and the church bell cracked. Judge Henderson may have escaped with his life, but his property back in Granville County did not fare as well. His home, barn, and stables were burned by Regulators. Rumors spread that the Regulators intended to march on the provincial capital at New Bern, prompting Gov. Tryon to call out the Pitt and Craven County militias to counter any attack.

The new province house in New Bern hosted the Assembly that

convened on December 5, 1770, and opened with a speech from the governor in which he called on the body to deal with irregularities in the use of public funds, as well as misconduct by public officials and the Regulators. Maurice Moore chaired a committee of the legislature tasked with dealing with the Regulator problem. Moore's committee called for an aggressive response from Gov. Tryon to put a lid on the unrest. Based on the recommendation, Assembly member Samuel Johnston introduced to the legislators the Riot Act, providing a legal basis for the expedition against the Regulators to come later. According to the act, after February 1, 1771, any group of ten or more people gathered for the purpose of riot who refused to disperse would be declared felons and subject to the death penalty. The Assembly expelled Herman Husband from the body a week before Christmas after he was accused of publishing (and maybe writing) a libelous letter in the *North Carolina Gazette* on December 14. When Husband left, it was not long before violence spiked in the backcountry again.

Judge Martin Howard

The rest of the session was taken up with passing various acts to regulate attorney's fees, establish a fee list for public officials, and acts to create four new backcountry counties. Many of the complaints of the Regulators would have been resolved had the legislation had time to be put into effect, but Gov. Tryon and the Assembly were not inclined to patience. Not when a military answer to the Regulator problem was available to put them in their place.[16]

On the first day of February the Riot Act went into effect, and the Assembly tried but failed to secure an indictment of Herman Husband. They went back to the drawing board, and by the time the General Assembly met again in March, there was enough evidence presented to secure multiple charges against the Regulator leader. By March 18, the Assembly had given its consent for the governor to call out the militia to quell the Regulator rebellion in the western part of North Carolina. Tryon issued orders the next day for the commanders of the 2,550 volunteers he called up to muster their men for an expedition into the backcountry. Gen. Thomas Gage, commander of all British troops in the American colonies, sent two field guns to New Bern by ship. Nevertheless, there was sympathy for the Regulator cause even in the east, and the governor had trouble assembling the men he needed until he offered a bounty of forty shillings for their service. Even then, some counties had to resort to a forced draft to fill their quotas.[17]

Moore lobbied the governor for permission to join the Salisbury court session that met in March, 1771. By mid-month, it became apparent that attempting to hold the Hillsborough session of the Superior Court would be unwise, given the prevailing sentiments among the backcountry men of the area. The Regulators were willing to allow Martin Howard to hold court, but the other judges, Richard Henderson and Maurice Moore, were unwelcome. Moore seems to have been especially hated, with several Regulators expressing a fervent desire to flog him.[18]

As spring flowers began to open in mid-April, Tryon had gathered enough militia to begin his march

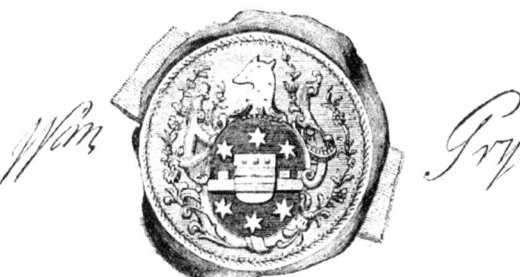

Tryon's signature and seal

against the Regulators. With him was Col. Joseph Leech in command of the infantry, Capt. James Moore in command of the artillery, and a Capt. Neale commanding a company of rangers. Moore also had an artillery company of sailors from Wilmington under the command of Robert Schaw to work the guns. Dr. Thomas Cobham of Wilmington was along to provide medical services. By April 23, a column a thousand men long departed the east and slowly made their way west. On the way to the Eno River near Hillsborough, Tryon's main body was joined by more militia from New Hanover under Col. John Ashe, from Carteret County led by a Col. Craig, from Johnston County under William Thompson, and from Beaufort and Wake under Colonels Needham Bryant and Johnson Hinton respectively. Once reaching the Eno, Edmund Fanning and various government officials joined the force, as well.

At Salisbury, Col. Hugh Waddell finally gathered fewer than 300 men to join Tryon, but almost immediately suffered a setback when

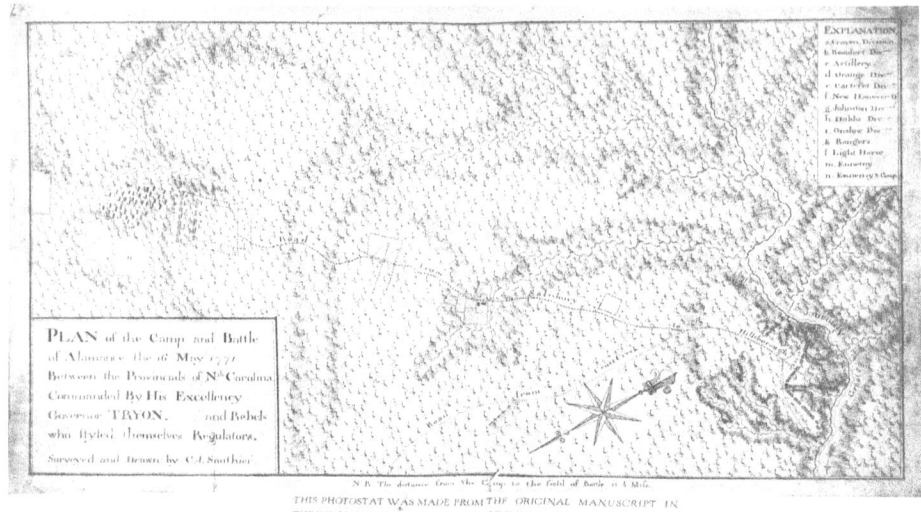

A contemporary map of the Battle of Alamance by C.J. Sauthier.

Regulators disguised as "black boys" exploded a powder wagon sent from South Carolina. Waddell's column reached the Yadkin River on May 5, but found his way blocked by more than 2,000 Regulators. Waddell was forced to return to Salisbury until such time as Gov. Tryon's main body could relieve him.[19]

Tryon's force forded the Haw River and set up a camp on Great Alamance Creek on May 14. When word reached him of Waddell's predicament, he resolved to march for Salisbury as soon as he could. While encamped, intelligence reached him that caused Tryon to put off the rescue mission. Scouts reported that a large Regulator force was nearby, and the governor altered his plans to deal with them first. The next day, the militia prepared for the engagement to come, and on May 16, 1771, Tryon and his army marched to meet the rebellious backcountry men five miles away. By mid-morning, the two forces came within sight of each other. Tryon commanded roughly 1,100 men, while the Regulators milling about across from him numbered between 2,000 and 3,000. Each side formed battle lines as Tryon tried one final time to get the Regulators to avoid bloodshed and return to lawfulness. According to Benson J. Lossing, it was Donald Malcolm who carried a white flag of parley across the field to deliver Tryon's message to submit.[20]

As negotiations went on, the two sides edged ever closer to each other, until only about 30 yards separated the lines of armed men. Taunts from the Regulators flew across the same field where lead ball would soon follow, daring Tryon's militia force to fire. "Never did I see men so daring & desperate as they were during the expiration of the hour," remembered participating militiaman Samuel Cornell, "...they would run up to the mouths of our Cannon & make use of the most aggrieving language that could be expressed to induce the Governor to fire on them..."

When an hour had passed and no progress was made towards a peaceful resolution, Tryon's artillery barked out to signal the end of negotiations. As the noon sun lit the field, the governor ordered the infantry to fire, but they hesitated. Tryon angrily ordered the militia to fire a second time, either at the Regulators or at him. Pans flashed and balls flew as musketry added to the din that continued for the next two and a half hours. The lines surged back and forth, and men fell on both sides. Herman Husband, the Regulator at the center of much of the rebellion, declared that his Quaker beliefs would not permit him to join the fray and left before the shooting started. The steady fire of the militia began to take its toll, and the Regulators, their ammunition running short, fell back to a rocky ledge at a ravine to their rear. As the Regulators fled the field, the militia took 30 prisoners and a substantial amount of supplies. When the shooting stopped, nine militiamen lay dead and another 61 wounded. At least as many Regulators lay on the field, and by some accounts the casualties among the backcountry men was as high as 300. Among them was a Captain Montgomery, commander of a company of what Lossing termed "Mountain Boys." Montgomery fell in the second round of cannon fire that put many of the Regulators to flight from the battlefield. The example of the retreating men notwithstanding, Hillsborough Regulator James Pugh was said to have done great damage to the militiamen facing him from the cover of a nearby rock. Pugh, a gunsmith and excellent shot, fired his rifles while companions reloaded for him. He was responsible for several militia casualties.[21]

The next day both sides took time to care for the wounded and bury the dead. Tryon took part of his force and marched to relieve Waddell's outnumbered troops entrenched at Salisbury. The two groups linked east of the Yadkin River, and on May 17, 1771, Tryon began issuing pardons to Regulators who would lay down their arms and become law abiding citizens again. By the end of July, 6,000 Regulators took the governor up on his offer. The only people excluded from Tryon's amnesty were the men perceived as leaders of the rebellion - Herman Husband, James Hunter, Rednap Howell, and William Butler.

Judge Maurice Moore and his two fellow judges were summoned to Hillsborough on May 30, 1771 for a special session of the court of oyer and terminer to decide the fates of the Regulators under the terms of the Riot Act. Moore and his fellow jurists found 12 men guilty and sentenced them to be executed, but Gov. Tryon commuted the sentences of half of them at the urging of his militia officers. The remaining condemned were taken to a hill and hanged on June 19, 1771.[22]

Herman Husband abandoned North Carolina and returned to Pennsylvania, settling near Pittsburgh and eventually serving several years in the Pennsylvania legislature. He returned to North Carolina on business once after the Revolutionary War, but it was a short visit. In 1794, he was once again embroiled in controversy in the Whiskey Rebellion. Captured and pardoned after the intercession of friends (including some from North Carolina), he died on his way home from Philadelphia.[23]

Signature of John Ashe

When the battle was over, Tryon turned command of the army over to Col. John Ashe near the Johnston County Courthouse. Ashe was ordered to return to Wilmington, taking oaths of allegiance from the populace in the places he marched through. Despite posting broadsides instructing citizens to come and swear their allegiance at every populated place he came to in Duplin County, no one did. At Wilmington, Ashe dismissed the troops with the governor's thanks and returned to his Rocky Point plantation 14 miles to the northeast. Like Ashe, assistant commissary officer Lieutenant Colonel Alexander Lillington returned to his plantation four miles southeast of Ashe's estate. James Moore and Robert Howe returned to their own plantations on the west side of the Cape Fear River in Brunswick County, Moore's near Brunswick Town and Howe's below the former port of entry.[24]

The Regulator Rebellion is widely recognized as one of the first - if not *the* first - acts of open rebellion that ended in violence against Great Britain in the American colonies. Studies of Regulator allegiances after the Regulator Rebellion show that more of them joined the Whigs than the Tories in the Revolutionary War that came four years later. When war clouds gathered in 1775, both sides went to lengths to get the backcountry men on their side. For many Regulators, it was ironic that the same men who had marched against them in 1771 wanted them to sign on to their own new rebellion in 1775. The residue of the Regulator Rebellion left a bad taste in the mouths of the men who rose up to protest their treatment at the hands of Crown officials, only to be cut down at Alamance. That the men who served in Tryon's army sought their aid in their own fight against British oppression a decade later was a hypocrisy they found hard to ignore. The men who fought on both sides of the Regulator Rebellion learned valuable lessons that would come into play in the next war, the one for American independence.[25]

Days after the battle at Alamance, William Tryon received word that his request for transfer to New York had been approved. His replacement was Josiah Martin, an ambitious young man who came to his appointment through the aid of his brother, Henry.

Josiah Martin was 36 when he came to the Cape Fear, handsome and full of the energy of a man out to make his reputation and fortune. Born on the Caribbean island of Antigua in 1737, he entered military service at age 17 with the Fourth Regiment of Foot in the regular British Army. His family helped him purchase a lieutenant colonel's post in the Twenty-Second Regiment in 1764, but he was later transferred to the Sixty-Eighth Regiment in his native Antigua. Martin managed to get selected to serve on the Governor's Council. While on a visit to his namesake uncle in New York, he met and married his cousin, Elizabeth. They would have eight children together.

Royal Governor Josiah Martin

Martin sold his commission in 1769 after five years' service, pleading bad health. Historians and biographers say it was more likely money troubles that led him to seek more lucrative employment. His brother Henry helped him find it when, using his connections in government, he secured the royal governorship of North Carolina for his sibling. Martin's commission is dated from December 14, 1770. News of Martin's appointment was greeted with cautious optimism in the colony after the antagonism of William Tryon's administration. Before he had ever met him, Samuel Johnston wrote that, "As we hear a very amiable Character of

Josiah Quincy, Jr.

him [we] are not uneasy of the approaching Change."

It was not until the summer of 1771 that Martin arrived in New Bern to officially assume his office as royal governor. The former army officer took the oath of office in the splendid new governor's residence that had caused so much resentment among the tax paying public in North Carolina. Martin and Tryon shared notes about the situation in the colony before the old governor left for his new post in New York. With the smoldering resentments of the Regulator Rebellion still fresh in the minds of the people, Tryon likely suggested Martin venture into the backcountry to see for himself the situation among his new charges. Loading his family into a carriage, Martin did just that in 1772. Traveling through Regulator country, he seemed to believe that he had found common ground with the backcountry folk. He made some changes to how government business was conducted based on what he saw and heard on the tour, and returned to New Bern feeling that his effort had borne fruit. But the honeymoon period between the new royal governor and the people was a short one, and his prickly colonists soon put an end to his hopes of continued amity.

In August, only a month after assuming his post, Martin issued a proclamation warning that anyone who attacked Fort Johnston at the mouth of the Cape Fear River would be put to death. The new royal governor's attempt to exert his authority did not impress or cow the king's subjects in the region. The local Committee of Safety answered him by declaring, "His Excellency Josiah

Cornelius Harnett's Hilton Plantation.

Martin, Esq., hath by the said proclamation discovered himself to be an enemy to the happiness of this Colony in particular, and to the freedom, rights, and privileges of America in general." Indeed, there was a faction in the Assembly that had chafed at recognizing Parliament's supremacy in the colony for more than a decade. These included John Harvey, Samuel Johnston, and Joseph Hewes in the Albemarle; New Bern's Isaac Edwards and Richard Cogdell, and Cornelius Harnett, Robert Howe, William Hooper, and John Ashe of the lower Cape Fear. Massachusetts patriot Josiah Quincy, Jr. noted the faction as "a select number who had mutually agreed and solemnly promised each other to keep each a regular journal not only of the public occurrences, but of the conduct of every public character."

Joseph Hewes

Josiah Quincy, Jr. was in North Carolina in March and April 1773. He spent the evening conversing with local patriots at Cornelius Harnett's Hilton plantation on Smith Creek. Of local patriots he noted, "Dined with about twenty at Mr. William Hooper's - find him apparently in the Whig interest, - has taken their side in the House - is caressed by the Whigs, and is now passing his election through the influence of that party. Spent the night at Mr. Harnett's, the Samuel Adams of North Carolina (except in point of fortune). Robert Howe, Esq., Harnett, and myself made the social triumvirate of the evening. The plan of continental correspondence highly relished, much wished for, and resolved upon, as proper to be pursued."[26]

When Boston sent its Circular Letter to Massachusetts' sister colonies in the face of British embargos in 1773, the North Carolina General Assembly appointed 9 men to form a Committee of Safety to establish

The Cape Fear Mercury newspaper

communications with the other 12 provinces and support the people of Massachusetts. Speaker of the House John Harvey, of Perquimans County, was selected to be a member. Planter and lawyer Samuel Johnston of Chowan was also selected. Richard Caswell, soldier, planter, lawyer, and speculator from Dobbs County, joined them. Planter, merchant, and ship owner Cornelius Harnett of Wilmington was on the committee. Joseph Hewes, shipping magnate and future signer of the Declaration of Independence represented the colony from Edenton. Wilmington Harvard graduate and lawyer William Hooper lent his talents to the committee, too. Wealthy planter and former Speaker of the House John Ashe was one of the nine representing New Hanover County, as was militia colonel Robert Howe of Brunswick County.[27]

The proclamations of the Committees of Safety in the Lower Cape Fear were announced in the pages of the *Cape Fear Mercury* newspaper. Printer Adam Boyd had purchased Alexander Steuart's press and by January 30, 1773 was firmly on the side of the rebellious Whigs. The *Cape Fear Mercury* is said by some historians to have been the first patriotic Whig newspaper funded solely by subscriptions. Martin was not a fan of the paper's coverage, and condemned it in the most forceful terms.[28]

At the very first meeting of the General Assembly during Martin's tenure, the new royal governor discovered how difficult the members of the legislative body could be. One of his first acts was to veto the legislature's repeal of a 1748 tax law because Martin felt it should remain in effect. In response, Speaker of the House of Commons Richard Caswell instructed county sheriffs to not enforce it. Martin was irritated that the sheriffs obeyed instructions from Caswell rather than from their governor. His ire led him to refuse to call another session of the Assembly until January 1773. In that session, the Assembly again exceeded its authority in the eyes of the royal governor by attaching a rider to a routine bill that would allow the confiscation of property in North Carolina owned by indebted non-residents. Martin refused to allow the measure. Since it was attached to a bill authorizing the province's courts to operate, Martin suddenly found himself having to use executive authority to create emergency courts in the regular courts' absence.

Then there was the issue of Robert Howe. From the outset, Howe rubbed Josiah Martin the wrong way. Installed as baron of the exchequer by William Tryon, Martin rescinded that position as being incompatible with Howe's commission as commander of Fort Johnston. When the opportunity to relieve him of command at Fort Johnston presented itself with the return of John Abraham Collet, Martin took advantage of it. Howe found himself a man frozen out of the official power structure in the Cape Fear, something that did not enhance his loyalty to the Crown.

Having only been in North Carolina less than a year, the governor surmised - correctly - that shepherding the people of the colony could be a difficult task. With that realization, he sought a way to get out of the colony - unsuccessfully, as it turned out.[29]

Endnotes

[1] Watson 1861, 74-79; Ganyard, 12; Lee 250-251. The difference between measures, perhaps explaining the differing resistance to the two, lay in the fact that the Stamp Act was felt by all citizens of the colony. The Townshend Act really only directly impacted merchants. If regular citizens were impacted, it would only be indirectly when they purchased taxed items like tea...The chief objection to the Townshend Act for the colonials was that even though it was not an internal tax, the act was designed as a revenue tax. The colonies objected to the Townshend Act tax because of what it was for - raising revenue.
[2] Ganyard, 19-20. In Virginia, the House of Burgesses enacted a non-importation agreement in response to Massachusetts' Circular Letter that went to each of the other 12 colonies. It sought unanimity in resistance to the Townshend Act and the implementation of a non-importation agreement among all 13 colonies. The burgesses produced resolutions that denounced taxation without representation, asserted the right of Virginians charged with treason to be tried in Virginia, and in an address to King George III they decried the transportation of colonials to England for trial as being unconstitutional.
[3] Butler 1776, 26-27.
[4] Watson 1861, 74-79; Ganyard, 19-20; Lee, 251-252; Butler 1776, 27-28. If the Townshend Revenue Act did not excite much outrage in North Carolina or the other mainly agrarian colonies, in the Northern colonies it was a different matter. Non-importation protests started there by August 1768. Virginia was prompted to greater efforts against the act when British redcoats were stationed in Boston to enforce the Townshend duties...The Cape Fear Sons of Liberty agreed to meet again on July 5, 1770 "to consult upon such measures, as may appear most eligible, for evincing their patriotism and Loyalty in the present critical Situation of affairs."
[5] Ganyard, 20-21; Butler 1776, 27. North Carolina's non-importation agreement went into effect on the first day of 1770, banning the importation of slaves, wines, and goods of British manufacture...The non-importation agreements resulted in the loss of £700,000 to the British treasury, so Parliament was quick to rescind it by March 1770.
[6] Butler 1776, 29-30, 12-13, 32-33. All five royal governors made their homes in the east, as did most other provincial officials, regardless of whether they were in the executive,

legislative, or judicial branches of government. Appointed justices of the peace and county courts ran local county governments, and those appointments came from the governor in the east...The primary offender was the poll tax, which applied to white males 16 or older, and all blacks over 12 years of age. The tax was not a burden to wealthy easterners, but for poorer western colonists, in a province where specie was scarce, it was exceedingly difficult to meet the burden. In 1769, westerners petitioned the governor for a tax in proportion to the size of the estate, but Tryon dismissed it.

[7] Butler 1776, 33; Lossing, n. 23; Peter R. Johnston, *Poorest of the Thirteen: North Carolina and the Southern Department in the American Revolution* (Haverford, PA: Infinity Publishing, 2001): 7. Hereafter cited as Johnston. The inefficiency and embezzlement was so rampant in the tax system that Gov. Tryon ordered an audit by Secretary of the Council John Burgwin. The governor was astounded when Burgwin reported to him that sheriffs were in arears to the tune of £64,013 for the period between 1754-1770. The Regulators declared that they had paid as much as £30,000 in excess of what was required to sink (retire) the currency from the French & Indian War, yet as much as £60,000 in currency was still in use...While a lawyer could legally charge a fee of 15s to represent a client in court, many charged double that. The fee for recording a deed set by the assembly was 8s, but Hillsborough's Edmund Fanning, who became quite notorious to the Regulators, charged 32s. If a farmer could not pay in specie, he was required to work it off at the rate of 1s 6d per day, despite the rate for day labor being 2s 8d.

[8] Butler 1776, 32-33. The General Assembly, at Tryon's recommendation, selected New Bern as the North Carolina capital in 1766. The body allocated £15,000 for the construction, and imposed an increased poll tax and additional taxes on liquor to pay for it. The house that noted English architect John Hawke began in 1767 and finished in 1770 became a symbol of government excess and oppression to the Regulators.

[9] Johnston, 8-11; Butler 1776, 36. Rednap Howell is credited with authoring several devastatingly satirical songs and poems featuring officials he believed to be responsible for the abuses of the backcountry people...Edmund Fanning came to North Carolina from New York. A Yale graduate, he was a close friend of royal governor Tryon, and held the offices of assemblyman, Superior Court judge, and country registrar in addition to his commission in the Orange County militia.

[10] Butler 1776, 31. Henry Eustace McCulloh, North Carolina's agent in London, commented in 1762 that "our little country now up in arms indicates that unrest continued in the backcountry because the major source of trouble - extortion by public officials - never ceased and no official action was taken to end the malpractices."

[11] Butler 1776, 36. The Regulator Rebellion was most virulent in Rowan, Anson, Orange, Granville, Cumberland, and Dobbs Counties.

[12] Johnston, 9-11; Butler 1776, 36-37. The sheriff made his seizure on April 8, 1768... Fanning's house stood where the Masonic Lodge is today in Hillsborough, across from the Colonial Inn...After the raid, the county militia was called in to protect Hillsborough, but officials were alarmed when as many as 120 of them declared neutrality...In addition to Husband and Butler, Fanning also secured warrants for the arrest of Peter Craven and Ninian Hamilton.

[13] Lossing, 7; Johnston, 11-12; Butler 1776, 36-37. Tryon criticized the Regulator movement, but promised to come to Hillsborough to investigate their claims for himself.

[14] Butler 1776, 38. Tryon's clemency extended to most of the prisoners taken in the episode. As well, he suspended their fines for six months. The only persons excluded from his pardon were James Hunter, Herman Husband, Ninian Hamilton, Peter Craven, and nine others.

[15] Price, 7.

[16] Butler 1776, 38-40; Price, 8. In the court session held on September 24, 1770, the packed audience included Regulator leaders James Hunter, Herman Husband, Peter Craven, Rednap Howell, William Butler, Ninian Hamilton, Samuel Devinney, and Jeremiah Fields...The letter that ran in the *Gazette* was purportedly from James Hunter to Maurice Moore, in answer to an earlier letter from Moore that named Hunter and Herman Husband as the instigators of the backcountry troubles. The original letter no longer exists.

[17] Butler 1776, 39-42. Charges included 62 counts of riot and felony against not just Husband, but the rest of the Regulator leaders too...The field pieces arrived the day before Tryon's expedition departed New Bern.

[18] Price, 8. Some of the animus for Henderson and Moore probably stemmed from the fact that the two were commissioned by Gov. Tryon, who by that point was widely despised by the backcountry men. The commission for Howard came from King George III, so he was not as tainted in the eyes of the Regulators.

[19] Butler 1776, 41-42; Lossing, 55; Johnston, 23-24. In addition to the officers listed, Tryon's army also had 9 colonels, 2 lieutenant colonels, 2 majors, 22 captains, 44 junior officers, 18 drummers, 1 chaplain of the Church of England, 2 surgeons, 22 clerks, 16 servants, 11 wagons, and 2 women...James Moore and his brother, "King" Roger Moore, led five Goose Creek families and 200 slaves from South Carolina to settle on the Cape Fear River.

[20] Butler 1776, 42; Lossing, 55. When word arrived that the Regulators were near, Col. John Ashe and Capt. John Walker were dispatched to reconnoiter the enemy's positions. The two militiamen were caught and flogged, according to Lossing.

[21] Butler 1776, 42-43. In his report on the Alamance battle, Tryon said, "The loss of our army in killed, wounded, and missing, amounted to about sixty men."...James Pugh was among the captured, and was sentenced to hang for his actions.

[22] Butler 1776, 43; Price, 8; Watson 1861, 79. The men hanged were Capt. Benjamin Merrill, Capt. Robert Messer, Capt. Robert Matear, James Pugh, and two others whose names have been lost to history...Not knowing that Tryon's victory at Alamance was so successful, Wilmington's Archibald Maclaine, William Hooper, and Robert Hogg sent the royal governor a message that they were raising money to enlist a body of men to reinforce him should it be necessary. Tryon offered his thanks, but told them there was no need.

[23] Lossing, 10.

[24] Johnston, 40-41.

[25] Butler 1776, 44. Author John S. Bassett said the Regulators had a "...distrust for the men who led the Revolution. The same men who had oppressed them, whom they had tried to turn out of office, whom they had fought, by whom they had been defeated, and who still kept the offices through which they had received their wrongs. These men now came to the Regulators asking aid in a movement which, to say the least, was of doubtful issue."

[26] Ross, 105; Ganyard, 25; Hugh F. Rankin. *The North Carolina Continentals* (Chapel

Hill: UNC Press, 1971): 3-6. Hereafter cited as Rankin; Andrew Jackson Howell, *The Book of Wilmington*. (Wilmington, N.C: A.J. Howell, 1979):46. Hereafter cited as Howell. There were other missteps by Martin that turned his colonists against him. In 1771 he declared a measure by the assembly to discontinue the sinking fund tax illegal. A year later he ordered a boundary survey between North and South Carolina on orders from his bosses in London. The result of the survey saw North Carolina lose several thousand acres of land. This so angered the Assembly that they refused to pay for the survey... Hilton sat at the place in Wilmington where the Sutton Water Treatment Plant is today. Andrew J. Howell says that based on the talks and the actions that followed from them, Hilton might fairly be called the "birthplace and cradle of American liberty."

[27] Ganyard, 26-27.

[28] Howell, 49.

[29] Rankin, 7; Angley, 20. According to Rankin, Martin always felt that the world was unkind to him in that he never seemed to acquire the wealth and perks that went to other men...Being royal governor of North Carolina was unlikely to solve Martin's financial woes, but it would serve nicely as a stepping stone to something better, namely serving as the agent for Lord Granville's North Carolina grant, which comprised almost half the colony... Hearing that William Tryon, now at his post in New York, was tiring of colonial service and thinking of giving up the governorship, Martin confided that, "the Climate of that Province [New York] is genial to my constitution & its vast emoluments would soon improve my future to the height of my wishes."

1774-1775

Excerpt of the map drawn by John Abraham Collet showing the Lower Cape Fear.

1774-1775

"The Ministry from the time of passing the Declaratory Act, on the repeal of the Stamp Act, seem to have used every opportunity of teizing and fretting the people here as if on purpose to draw them into Rebellion," wrote Samuel Johnston in a 1774 letter to Alexander Elmsley. "They have now brought things to a crisis and God only knows where it will end...for when once the Sword is drawn all nice distinctions fall to the Ground..."[1]

On the Cape Fear, distrust of the British was rising. Tensions spiked when Capt. John Abraham Collet began making improvements to the fortifications at Fort Johnston, which commanded access to the Cape Fear River. Local committees of safety kept a watchful eye on the improvements, which had been approved by Governor Martin. By February 1775, the fort still had a long way to go to be very intimidating. When Janet Schaw arrived in the Cape Fear on the next stop of her tour of the British colonies, she was disparaging in her description of the installation.

"We are now opposite to the fort which guards this coast," she recorded in her journal, "and the Capt. has gone to it to show his credentials and pay certain fees which constitute the salary of an officer [Collet]...In figure and size this fort resembles a Leith timberbush, but does not appear quite so tremendous, tho' I see guns peeping thro' the sticks. If these are our fortresses and castles, no wonder the natives rebel; for I would be bound to take this fort with a regiment of black-guard Edinburgh boys without any artillery, but their own pop-guns."[2]

The General Assembly met again on March 2, 1774, and once again the subject of the courts reared its head. Martin and the Assembly were still at loggerheads over the inclusion of a proposed measure allowing the confiscation of property in North Carolina owned by foreign debtors. On orders from the Crown, Martin explicitly forbade the inclusion of the measure in the bill to reauthorize courts for the province. The Assembly seemed equally determined to make the bill law with the foreign debtor attachment. The deadlock was overcome at least temporarily when a separate bill was written that established a court of oyer and terminer for the colony. The impasse prompted Martin to dismiss the Assembly until May. Martin was dumbfounded when three days later he learned of a request from the Assembly to the colony's treasurers that the poll tax for 1774 not be collected. He immediately issued a proclamation telling the treasurers to disregard the request and collect the taxes as usual. Martin asserted that the Assembly had "assumed to themselves a power repugnant to the Laws, and derogatory to the honour and good faith of this Province..." Despite this the treasurers obeyed the Assembly instead.[3]

The 1773 Tea Act resulted in "tea parties" throughout the colonies, in which people pledged to not drink the beverage that had become a staple of the American diet to show their displeasure with Parliament. North Carolinians joined the protest with their own tea parties, notably in Edenton and Wilmington. With the protests, Wilmington and the Cape Fear rose to the forefront of the growing rebellion in the province.[4]

Great Britain responded to rebellious Boston with the Coercive Acts of 1774, a series of moves designed to bring the Massachusetts Whigs to heel and teach them proper respect for the Crown. As a result of the Boston Port Bill, the colony's customhouse was moved from Boston to Salem, and the Boston port was declared closed as of June 1, 1774. On August 22, 1774 Boston sent out a letter pointing out that they were "suffering in the common cause" and asked their fellow colonies for aid and support. On the Cape Fear, people responded by loading one of Parker Quince's ships full of supplies for Boston and dispatching it to Massachusetts. Quince volunteered the vessel "without fee, freight, or reward."

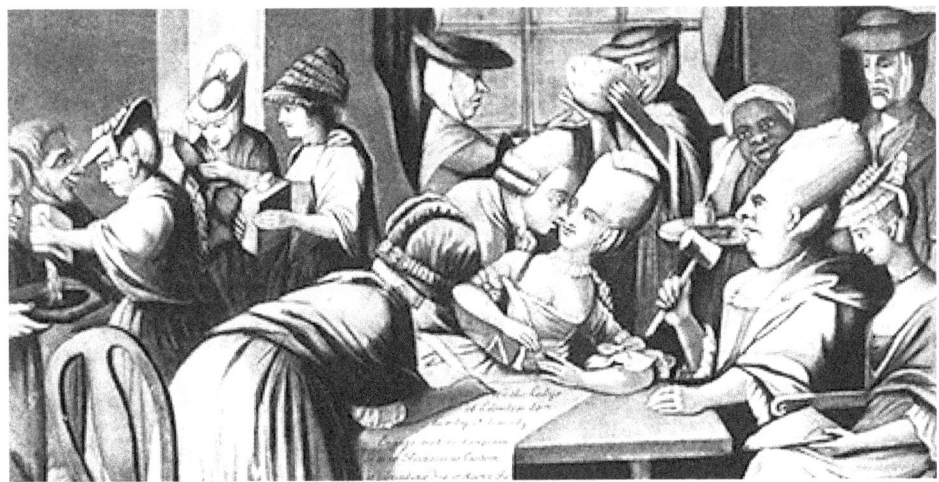

Penelope Barker led the ladies of Edenton in a boycott of English tea, as did women in Wilmington and other North Carolina towns.

Quince volunteered his ship, the *Penelope*, to ferry the aid raised for the blockaded city, and its master, a Captain Budd, and his crew agreed to sail her to Massachusetts. The committee formed to spearhead the relief effort, including James Moore, George Hooper, Robert Howe, Archibald Maclaine, William Howe, John Ancrum, Robert Hogg, and Francis Clayton, raised a very respectable amount of donations. All told, they collected 2,096 bushels of corn, 22 barrels of flour, and 17 barrels of pork that the *Penelope* eventually saw unloaded at Marblehead, Massachusetts.[5]

By May 1774, the Virginia House of Burgesses extended an invitation to the other twelve colonies to attend a Congress in response to the punitive measures taken by the British against Boston. Scheduled for the following September in Philadelphia, the gathering hoped to formulate a unified course of action to counter the British actions. In North Carolina, Royal Governor Josiah Martin had already experienced more than a little friction between himself and the elected representatives of the province in the General Assembly. When word of the proposed Congress reached Martin he decided to nip in the bud any chance of his colony's participation by not calling for a new session of the Assembly until after the event in Philadelphia was over. It might have worked, except Martin's secretary leaked his plan to Speaker of the House John Harvey.

Harvey met with Whig leaders Edward Buncombe and Samuel Johnston on April 4 to decide what their next move should be. The speaker was in no mood for conciliatory gestures. "[Harvey] was in a very violent mood," wrote Johnston, "and declared he was for assembling a convention independent of the Governor, and urged us to cooperate with him. He says he will lead the way, and will issue handbills under his own name, and that the committee of correspondence should go to work at once." Johnston relayed the outcome of the meeting to Wilmington's William Hooper, and asked that he notify Cornelius Harnett and John Ashe of the plan.

James Iredell

In a letter to Judge James Iredell, Hooper expressed the Whigs' thoughts on the state of affairs in the American colonies. "With you I anticipate the important share which the Colonies must soon have in regulating the political balance," he wrote. "They are striding fast to independence, and ere long will build an empire upon the ruins of Great Britain..."

Cape Fear Whigs called for North Carolina to hold its own Provincial Congress at a gathering in Wilmington on July 21, 1774. In attendance were Whig leaders James Moore, Robert Howe, and Samuel Ashe. Other counties were invited to attend by Wilmington Committee of Safety chair William Hooper. The purpose of the gathering, he told them, was to select their own delegates for the Philadelphia Congress. Notably, the letter resolved that, "we consider the cause of the Town of Boston as the common cause of British America and as suffering in defence of the Rights of the Colonies in general..." Another resolution called for the dispatch of provisions to aid the besieged Bostonians. Governor Martin called the Cape Fear freeholder meeting's resolves "inflammatory, disloyal and indecent" and intended to "excite clamour and discontent." Nevertheless, he was powerless to stop county committees of safety from putting forward a slate of delegates to the provincial congress.

The First Provincial Congress met at New Bern on August 25, 1774, and over the course of three days debated what actions should be taken. Moderator John Harvey led the discussions, and finally William Hooper, Joseph Hewes, and Richard Caswell were selected by their peers to attend the First Continental Congress in Philadelphia in a few weeks' time. The deliberations of the Provincial Congress took place within walking distance of the governor's mansion, something that must have been especially galling to Josiah Martin. The New Bern delegates also approved resolutions to enact a trade boycott of British goods, and to emphasize their loyalty to King George, claiming that they sought "... no more than the rights of Englishmen..." The Provincial Congress also addressed their position on taxation, reiterating that it was solely within the purview of the Assembly, as the king and his ministers constituted a wholly separate branch of government.[6]

Among the measures adopted by the First Continental Congress was a restriction of imports from Great Britain. After December 1, 1774, British tea and manufactured goods were banned in the American colonies. East India tea, especially - no matter when it had arrived in America - was banned as of March 1, 1775. Additionally, the Congress declared that if Parliament did not meet their demands, no goods from America would be shipped to Great Britain or the West Indies.

William Hooper

If any of the American colonies failed to abide by the embargoes, the Congress declared that they would find their own products boycotted, too.

When Parliament banned exports from the colonies to Great Britain and the West Indies as punishment for the rebellious American provinces in April 1775, North Carolina and a few others were exempted. William Hooper and other Whigs were worried that the exemption might lead their fellow North Carolinians into a false sense of security, and warned their neighbors not to weaken their resolve.

"Do you ask why then you are exempted from the Penalties of the Bill restraining Trade?" they asked. "The reason is obvious - Britain cannot keep up its Naval Force without you; you supply the very sinews of her strength. Restrain your Naval Stores and all the Powers of Europe can scarcely supply her; restrain them and you strengthen the hands of America in the glorious contention for her liberty. Through you the Minister wishes to disunite the whole Colonial Link; we know Your virtue too well to dread his success."[7]

For the most part, Cape Fear merchants happily abided by the restrictions set out by the Congress. Brunswick merchant William Hill refused to accept a shipment of tea that arrived for his shop in October 1774, saying in a letter to his London suppliers, "If I was ever so willing to take it, the people here would not suffer it be landed. Poison would now be as acceptable." Another merchant, this time upriver at Wilmington, showed his support for the ban by holding his own personal tea party, dumping the stocks of tea in his store into the Cape Fear rather than keep it in betrayal of the American cause. Writing in the spring of 1775, a correspondent to the *South Carolina Gazette* noted that "all the Tea in this Town and Brunswick is locked up, never to be offered for sale, 'till all American measures are changed." He went on, "It would be injustice to the Ladies not to add that they have entirely declined the use of Tea. Such a sacrifice by the fair sex, should inspire [us]."[8]

The First Continental Congress also adopted resolutions that in practice would eliminate pretty much all of the favorite pastimes enjoyed by the people of the American colonies. Horse racing, cockfighting, billiards, card games, public dancing, plays and every other extravagance and activity leading to dissipation - the Congress called on colonists to abstain from all frivolities in order to emphasize to Parliament the seriousness of British actions in their eyes. The Wilmington Committee of Safety took the resolution as marching orders. Led by Cornelius Harnett, the Committee set about locking down the amusements of the town. More than one man in Wilmington thinking of wagering on the races received the warning that they would be held to account for disregarding what the Committee considered the patriotic duty of all citizens. "Nothing will so effectively convince the British Parliament that we are in earnest in our opposition to their measures as a voluntary relinquishment of our favorite amusements," the Committee reasoned. Adhering to the pledge to abstain from fun pastimes was mandatory, even though the Committee did not come out and say so. But the ban was clear anyhow. One Wilmington woman received this message when the Committee learned of a party she intended to host: "Mrs. Austin, Madame: The ball intended to be given at your house, this evening, is contrary to the Resolves of Congress. We warn you that your house cannot be at this service, consistent with the good of your country."

North Carolina's Second Provincial Congress convened at New Bern on April 7, 1775, where it endorsed the Continental Association that drew the 13 colonies closer together in resistance to the British. Hooper, Hewes, and Caswell were again appointed to represent the colony at the Second Continental Congress. At the same time, the General Assembly approved the measures called for by the First Continental Congress. Martin could not abide the insult to the Crown, and dissolved the body on April 8. It was the last time that the General Assembly met in North Carolina under Crown authority.[9]

To better coordinate resistance efforts in the Cape Fear, Wilmington Whigs formed one of North Carolina's first Committees of Safety on November 23, 1774. New Hanover County followed suit with a committee of their own a few weeks later, on January 1, 1775. The two merged briefly before separating again, but both remained focused on coordinating the enforcement of the resolves of the Continental and Provincial Congresses. With the emergence of the Committees of Safety, royal authority on the Cape Fear was eradicated for all intents and purposes by March 1775. The committees undertook many of the functions that previously had been the purview of the Crown, such as conducting censuses, tax collection, road maintenance, fiscal policy, and conducting slave patrols.

Generally speaking, every function of government that had belonged to the king's ministers and the royal governor, was adopted by the Committees of Safety. That included enforcing price regulation. Merchant Jonathan Dunbibin drew the ire of the New Hanover Committee of Safety by charging exorbitant prices for salt. That necessary article was so important that the Continental Congress anticipated the lack of it might weaken the Whig cause. The New Hanover Committee censured Dunbibin, and forced him to reduce his inflated prices.

The two committees undertook to reinforce the military spirit among the other committees and various militias, and to respond to British military threats when they happened. The Wilmington-New Hanover Committee issued a warning to Brunswick County that a ship from Scotland anchored near Fort Johnston violated the non-importation agreement. On another occasion they thanked Bladen Whigs for the capture of two men suspected of being British spies. When Cumberland County formed their own committee of safety, the Wilmington-New Hanover Committee wrote them a letter congratulating them "on the favourable disposition of their Committee & County to support the Common cause of America."

Violations of the non-importation agreement were dealt with by the committees of safety in port towns like Wilmington and Brunswick. Ships arriving in the Cape Fear after the ban went into effect had their cargoes seized and auctioned off, with the money raised earmarked for Boston relief. Several of the violations handled by the Committees involved the importation of slaves, who were ordered to be reshipped back to where they had come from. The committee also required proof that the reshipment had been carried out. An exportation ban went into effect in September 1775, and after that only the ships which had already loaded their cargoes were allowed to leave the river. One other exception was made for a Captain Magill, master of the sloop *Ranger*, who was allowed to sail for New York with a cargo hold full of deerskins.[10]

Despite the occasional violation, on the whole the people of the Cape Fear supported non-importation measures just as they did the boycotts on commodities such as tea. The importation ban went into effect on December 1, 1774. It was only two weeks before merchant ships dropped anchor in the river carrying full cargoes of imported goods and merchandise that area merchants " ...most readily and cheerfully gave them up to be sold under the direction of the Committee there, in terms of the Continental Association."[11]

The committee also turned its hand to preparing Wilmington for another unpleasant possibility - British military action. As North Carolina's largest town, and the key to controlling the vital Cape Fear River, it did not take a genius to foresee the likelihood that at some point British forces would make a move on the port. When the British issued a royal proclamation forbidding the shipment of gunpowder to America, the Wilmington Committee of Safety took an inventory of powder already available in the town and undertook to raise money to buy it. Flints, lead, muskets, swords, and other small arms were collected in case they were needed to turn back a potential tide of redcoats. Small cannons were collected, and men were put to shaping molten lead into musket balls, all to prepare for "the worst Contingency."[12]

When British redcoats opened fire on Massachusetts Minute Men at Lexington Green in April, 1775, the die was cast. News of the clash hit

North Carolina like a bolt of lightning, and throughout the province people were called on to choose a side. Cornelius Harnett read a letter with the news, delivered at 3:00 in the afternoon of May 8, 1775 by an express rider. He scribbled his own note, then sent the rider on to deliver it to Richard Quince in Brunswick County.

For a while, colonial committees of safety had compelled people to declare their allegiances through the use of loyalty oaths. Using intimidation and public ridicule as a cudgel against the undecided, Whigs pressured their fellow citizens to join the cause against the British, and be vigilant against any perfidy. One such rumor was that Gov. Martin intended to free area slaves and arm them against their masters. After the bloodshed at Lexington and Concord, their efforts took on an added urgency.[13]

Militias turned out to drill and practice marksmanship, preparing for the day when they might be mustered to fend off a British invasion. Robert Howe assumed unofficial command of the units, putting them through their paces accompanied by drummers and fiddlers to keep the march tempo. None of their efforts impressed Janet Schaw, who found them more hillbillies than Hannibals. Yet even she saw something in them that the redcoats should be wary of, writing that "...the worst figure there can shoot from behind a bush and kill even a General Wolfe."[14]

Robert Howe

Whigs used something called the "association test" to compel people to show where their allegiances lay. Citizens were required to sign the test publicly, to make their sentiments known to everyone. The test was a statement of principle that declared support for American rights, and denounced British tyranny in general and taxation specifically. The association test also pledged support for the Continental Congress and North Carolina Provincial Congress. Wilmington's first association test was based on the resolutions of the Continental Congress of 1774. Cumberland County adopted the same test, as well.

Lexington and Concord introduced a new element to the association tests. No longer was it enough to proclaim support of American rights and denounce the King's tyranny. Now the tests had an added bit, proclaiming the colonists' right to resist force with force. The tests called on the people to pledge their lives and fortunes in support of the American cause. Wilmington created two additional versions of the association test in March and June 1775. The new tests included language that accused the British of an evil tyranny that was being unleashed on the land. The June test labeled King George III's government as "Wicked and despotic," and by its actions "to drive an Oppress'd people to the Use of Arms." The Wilmington Committee of Safety declared that "the Duty of Good Citizens" was to resist "force by Force..." and stated that the people were "Ready to sacrifice [their] Lives and fortunes to secure...[the] freedom and Safety [of their country]."

Saying no to the test was not much of an option. According to Janet Schaw, a committeeman or member of the militia would travel to a Cape Fear area plantation to invite the owner to sign the pledge, an offer they likely found hard to resist. Failure to comply could result in destroyed crops and livestock, sometimes destruction of the home, too. Slaves might be seized, and the reluctant could suffer a beating to make them more receptive. "Not to chuse the first requires more courage than they are possessed of," Schaw wrote, "and I believe this method has seldom failed with the lower sort [of people]."

Schaw witnessed an episode of intimidation by the militia in Wilmington when a number of loyalists were surrounded by Whig soldiers. The loyalists asked the officer by what authority he compelled their signing of the test. The officer pointed to the armed men with him and replied, "There is my authority, dispute it if you can." Schaw said the loyalists were held by the militia until 2:00 am, before finally being released without signing. While the soldiers failed in that instance to get the signatures they sought, their intimidation did have an effect. Schaw was back in Wilmington a few days later, and noted in her journal that the town was "entirely deserted by the Tories, some of whom are out of the country, and others gone out of the way...."

Mandatory militia membership was another way the Committees of Safety were able to coerce the reluctant into signing the test. In the colonial era, all males between ages 16 and 60 were required to be members of the militia. By 1775, militia musters were occasions to pressure the men to sign the association test proclaiming their loyalty to the Whigs. In Wilmington, all white men able to bear arms were required to join one of two local militia companies in July 1775. Militiamen were required to sign the association or risk being labeled as enemies of the cause of liberty. According to the Committee, failure to sign could only be interpreted "as a Declaration of Intention inimicable to the Common cause of America."

Some people remained loyal to their king despite the pressure put upon them to sign the associations. Dr. James Fallon of Wilmington is one example. Fallon had the temerity to write a two-page critique of the American cause that drew the ire of Col. James Moore, who ordered his arrest. Fallon was unrepentant even after he found himself tossed into the militia guardhouse. It did not take long before Moore reported to the Committee of Safety that Fallon was proving to be a "dangerous Person among the Soldiers." The colonel recommended that Fallon be released before he could poison the revolutionary fervor of the rest of the militia with his arguments on behalf of the king. In any event, Fallon's incarceration was not much of an inconvenience. The doctor was allowed to come and go as he pleased, entertain visitors, and correspond with whomever he wished without restric-

Abner Nash

tion. On Moore's advice, Fallon was moved to the public jail, where the liberties he enjoyed under the militia's supervision were sharply curtailed. After two weeks in that less hospitable accommodation, Fallon relented and promised to behave himself from that point on. Others were more circumspect in their support for King George III. Wilmington's Farquahard Campbell served on the Committee of Safety and in the Provincial Congress, but used his access to feed information to the British.[15]

Governor Josiah Martin was well aware of the discord in the provincial capital. From the windows of his palatial home in New Bern, he could see watchers, no doubt from the local Committee of Safety, keeping an eye on his movements. The news from the north was bad, and the simmering tensions in his own colony seemed ready to overflow. Martin decided to take steps to prepare for what he now believed was inevitable.

Martin had seen it coming. On May 23, 1775, Abner Nash of the New Bern Committee of Safety called on the governor to request that the cannon Martin had dismounted from their carriages be returned to their normal places. In letters Martin disparagingly referred to Nash as the Whigs' "Oracle," and considered him a "principle promoter of sedition" in North Carolina. The governor took the request as a thinly veiled insult, but replied that the guns had been removed so that new carriages could be built in anticipation of the upcoming king's birthday celebration. Mollified for the moment, Nash and his delegation left; but Martin saw the whole episode as further evidence of the erosion of royal authority in the colony. Josiah Martin, destined to become North Carolina's last royal governor, concluded that he could no longer govern from the house William Tryon built.

The next day, Martin put his pregnant wife and six other children aboard a small sloop for transport to her father's home in New York. With the help of house servants, the governor spiked the dismounted cannons and buried the powder supply stored at the mansion in the vegetable garden. Word had reached him that a ship loaded with weapons was enroute to him, but Martin doubted he would ever see any of it, given the way the local rebels kept watch on him and the port. He believed he stood a better chance if the shipment was rerouted to Fort Johnston on the Cape Fear River. Martin did not think much of the installation, first constructed in the wake of a Spanish raid on Brunswick in 1748, describing it as "a little wretched place." But there was a British sloop of war on station there, and thus it was the best option open to him. Making an announcement that he was traveling to see Chief Justice Hand, Martin left New Bern and fled south. He arrived at Fort Johnston on June 2. For all intents and purposes, royal government in the colony was at an end. To punctuate its demise, John Ashe marched into Wilmington in June at the head of several hundred militiamen to demand that all the town's merchants take the Test of Allegiance.[16]

As Martin unpacked at the fort, the Wilmington and Brunswick Committees of Safety jumped into action to put a lid on the governor's ability to cause mischief. Calls for gunpower from surrounding counties

A model of H.M.S. Cruizer

went out, but stocks were so meager that efforts were made to make it locally to remedy the deficit. Rumors of a plot to arm slaves created a stir, too. Any blacks having weapons were disarmed, and roving slave patrols were organized to keep a watchful eye on them. New recruits - meaning any male of military age - were quickly drafted into the militias and sent through a hurried boot camp to train them up. In Wilmington, the Committee also erected batteries of artillery, including one of 9-pound guns, another consisting of 5 and 12-pound guns, and the mounting of one of two field guns in the Committee of Safety's arsenal.

In early June, the Continental Congress selected George Washington as commander-in-chief of the new Continental Army. In August, the Provincial Congress authorized the raising of 1,000 troops in North Carolina. With the arrival of Martin on the Cape Fear River, 300 of them were assigned to New Hanover County and an additional 100 to Brunswick County to keep an eye on him.[17]

The Wilmington Committee of Safety forbade correspondence with Governor Martin on July 10 in an attempt to isolate him and impede his plans. At Fort Johnston, the governor felt equal parts outrage and impotence. The growing belligerence of rebel forces in the province offended his sense of duty and loyalty to King George III and his ministers. At the same time, under the circumstances, he felt powerless to stop the slide towards open rebellion. A week later Martin shifted from the fort and its

The site at Bow and Person Streets in Fayetteville, N.C. where the Liberty Point Declaration was made.

dubious defenses to *H.M.S. Cruizer*. The governor ordered Capt. Collet to remove the fort's guns, men, powder and shot to the safekeeping of ships in the river. The guns too heavy and large to be taken aboard one of the ships were dismounted and rolled down onto the beach in front of the fort. Josiah Martin was now truly isolated. News of Lexington and Concord did not reach him until two months after the shots heard 'round the world were fired, but the governor was already formulating a plan to reclaim North Carolina for his king.[18]

    The governor continued planning his operation to return the colony to Crown control at Fort Johnston. Concerned about the militia watching the fort from the wood line, Martin moved aboard *H.M.S. Cruizer* on July 15. The first order of business was to beef up the fort so that it could reliably be a base of operations for the coming actions. Captain John Abraham Collet had already begun strengthening the fort's defenses, but there was still much to do. Collet recognized how weak the fort was. In May, two weeks before Gov. Martin arrived, Collet had written Capt. Francis Parry of *H.M.S. Cruizer* for aid in the event his small garrison was attacked.

    "I am credibly informed that a body of militia in this province have actually taken arms against the government and are determined to attack

His Majesty's fort and garrison under my command," Collet wrote, "in order to enable themselves to oppose and keep off His Majesty's ships and troops that may be ordered here. In this fort the King has a very valuable sett of artillery, but a very inconsiderable number of men to defend it; &, above all my store of powder is just exhausted... It is my duty to lay my situation before you & crave Your assistance and protection, with which I am conscious I can repulse any force, and answer the trust reposed in me; any quantity of powder you can spare me will be received most thankfully (for I have not [enough] to load again after the first firing) & the proximity of your ship will answer all my wishes."[19]

Collet was right to be worried. On June 16, 1775 Governor Martin issued a proclamation stating, "Whereas...ill disposed persons have been...industriously propagating false, seditious and scandalous reports, derogatory to the honor and justice of the king and his Government...I do most earnestly exhort and advise all His Majesty's...Subjects within this Province, firmly and steadfastly to withstand and resist all attempts of the seditious to seduce them from the duty and allegiance they owe to His Majesty." It was too late in the Lower Cape Fear. Even as Martin's proclamation was going out, in Cumberland County patriots were signing the Liberty Point Declaration on the corner of Bow and Person Streets. On the Cape Fear below Wilmington, preparations were being made to neutralize Fort Johnston.[20]

The Whigs were hesitant at first to make such a bold move. On July 13 the Wilmington Committee of Safety wrote Edenton's Samuel Johnston that they had men willing to undertake an assault, but they were unsure if such a move would meet with approval by the Provincial Congress. "Our situation here is truly alarming," they wrote, "the governor collecting men, provisions, warlike stores of every kind, spiriting up the back country, and perhaps the slaves, finally strengthening the fort with new works, in such a manner as may make the capture of it extremely difficult...We have a number of enterprising young fellows that would attempt to take the fort, but are much afraid of having their conduct disavowed by the convention." Two days later, the Wilmington Committee of Safety gave the go ahead for a move against the fort.[21]

Gov. Martin received a note from the Wilmington Committee of Safety on July 16, warning him that the Whig militia was intent on taking Fort Johnston, and not to interfere.

"As the establishment of Fort Johnston was intended to protect the inhabitants of Cape Fear River from all invasions of a foreign enemy in times of war," the note from "The People" related, "and during peace has been supported at very great expence to this province, and not only to prevent contagious and infectious disorders, but to aid and support the trade and navigation thereof ... by the conduct of the captain [Collet] of the said fort most of these salutary ends have been entirely defeated...

"These circumstances Sir, and many others too tedious to enumerate, could not but excite the indignation and resentment of the publick... but upon being informed of Captain Collet's intention of dismantling the fort, erected and supported at the real expence of this colony, for its protection and defence, we collected ourselves together in order to prevent it, but finding upon enquiry that he had already dismantled it nothing more is left than to recover the cannon thrown over the walls and left in a situation which must entirely ruin them, to a place where attention and care shall preserve them for His Majesty when his service shall require them, because with that we conceive the safety of the province is intimately connected, with this intention we shall proceed to Fort Johnston and that our conduct may not be misunderstood by your Excellency we have thought proper to give you this information and persuade ourselves we shall not meet obstruction from any person or persons whatsoever in the execution of a design so essential to His Majesty's service and the publick utility."[22]

John Ashe, Robert Howe, Cornelius Harnett, and James Moore planned the assault on Fort Johnston on July 17, 1775, and Gov. Martin learned of it soon after. He immediately ordered the fort's armaments and ammunition removed to the two British sloops of war anchored offshore. The governor advised Lord Dartmouth of his actions in a letter that downplayed the fort's significance. In Wilmington, the Committee of Safety assembled 800 militiamen for the effort. The Whigs used alleged misbehavior and malfeasance by Fort Johnston's commander, Capt. John Abraham Collet, to justify the action they were about to take. As the militia were making preparations upriver, on July 17 sailors and Marines from *H.M.S. Scorpion* and *H.M.S. Cruizer* joined Collet's five-man garrison and carried out Martin's orders to dismantle the fort.[23]

The militia marched from Wilmington to Brunswick on July 18, where plans were finalized. Howe and his men learned on arrival that one of their main objectives was already a moot point, as Martin had removed the arms and ammunition from the fort to the warships offshore. In the darkness, men shouldered muskets and set out to cover the four miles to the fort. It was after midnight when the attack finally came, sometime between two and three o'clock on the morning of July 19. Whig troops approaching the fort carried torches into the compound and set fire to the undefended buildings. An officer aboard the *Cruizer* shook Gov. Martin awake and escorted him up on deck to watch the spectacle. One of the first targets Howe chose for the torch was Capt. Collet's quarters. Flames licked the walls of barracks and storage buildings, lighting the night and providing a humiliating spectacle for Martin, Collet, and *Scorpion*'s Capt. Parry, watching from the safety of the sloop's decks. At least the great guns, too heavy to shift aboard the sloops before the rebels attacked, were nominally safe. Their impotent tubes lay scattered along the beach beneath the fort's river wall, well within range of the guns of the *Scorpion* and *Viper*. Martin had written to Gen. Thomas Gage in March that Fort Johnston was in sad shape, a "most contemptible thing, fit neither for a place of Arms, or an Asylum for the friends of Government." Even so, it flew the British flag, and colonists in open rebellion had set it alight. Worse, there was nothing Josiah Martin could do about it. *H.M.S. Cruizer* became, the governor wrote, "my best asylum in the present time of Confusion in this Country."[24]

    Militiamen returned the next day to finish burning any buildings that might have escaped the night before. Aboard *Scorpion*, crews trained ship's guns on the fort but did not fire. Their main goal was to prevent the rebels from retrieving the heavy ordnance from the ballast stone covered beach below the fort. Martin retired to his quarters to pen a letter to Lord Dartmouth with his account of the evening's attack:

    "I have embrassed the moment only that the immediate departure of a vessel affords me to acquaint your Lordship that I received about 9 o'clock at night on the 18th inst. a letter signed 'The People,' Martin wrote. "...At between 2 and 3 o'clock the next morning an officer of the *Cruizer* came down to the cabin where I was to inform Captain Parry that Captain Collet's house was on fire. The necessary preparations were immediately made for the security of His Majesty's ship and covering the artillery on shore in case the people should attempt to possess themselves of it, during which no creature was seen, and all the buildings in the fort, which being of wood burnt like tinders, were entirely consumed. Early in the morning of yesterday a body of men with three stands of colours were seen in motion on a point of land about 2 miles above the ship, which soon afterwards entered the woods and disappeared until between 7 and 8 o'clock when we discovered a large party at some distance, and some lesser parties about the fort which a few of the people soon afterwards entered and with a degree of wanton malice not to be described set fire to everything that had escaped the flames the preceding night, which indeed was nothing but a sentry box, and some of the parapets of wood work that Captain Collet had newly raised upon the defenses of the place. These proceedings however to the last degree violent, extravagant and provoking, I did not think My Lord of consequence sufficient to justify me in commencing hostilities against the people so long as they forebore to touch the King's artillery, as I had no men to land I could do it with so little effect and as all the material damage that the fort could sustain had been effected in the night by persons yet undiscovered. Some of the trucks of the gun carriages, which owing to Captain Collet's oversight, were not embarked as I directed with the shot and other small stores, the rabble removed four or five hundred yards from where they lay and left them. These I hope to recover to day and get them on board ship.

"After sauntering about the fort, and its neighborhood till between 2 and 3 o'clock in the afternoon, this rabble which amounted as nearly as I can learn to about 300 men, with a savage and barbarian wantonness, disgraceful to humanity, set fire to a large barn, stable and coach house, and a new small dwelling house together with several outhouses that Captain Collet had built for his own convenience on the king's land belonging to the fort, without the works, and immediately after completing this desolation retired by the route they came."[25]

The Whigs may have destroyed Fort Johnston's usefulness to Gov. Martin and the British, but it did not end their machinations around Wilmington and Brunswick. Martin continued to denigrate the rebels in public proclamations and private correspondence. At the same time, efforts went on to rally the Highlanders of the interior to the king's cause. Martin planned to journey into the Upper Cape Fear River Valley to personally recruit Scotsmen to carry out his campaign, or so the rumors said. Another rumor that came in November from Brunswick County said that a British

 *Flora MacDonald (left), and her husband Allan (right), sailed for North Carolina to start a new life after the failed Jacobite Rebellion in Scotland.*

warship and troop transports had anchored in the river, awaiting the summons of the governor to land their redcoats. Yet another rumor claimed Capt. Collet, in command at Fort Johnston, had a plan to incite insurrection among local slaves.

All of these whisperings spurred the Committees of Safety to redouble their efforts to prepare the Lower Cape Fear to defend itself against an invasion by British soldiers. Carriage guns were sent to Brunswick to defend the town against an attack. The Wilmington Committee of Safety authorized the sinking of boats in the river channel below town near The Flats at the south end of Eagles Island to barricade access by water. Booms were stretched across the northwest branch of the Cape Fear between Eagles Island and Point Peter. Breastworks were built using slave and militia labor south of Wilmington to protect it from an army approaching from downriver. Urgent requests were sent to the New Bern Committee of Safety for gunpowder and ammunition, and for troops from the western counties to augment local militia numbers.

The Committees of Safety had cause to think that such preparations were necessary. In Martin's plan, he thought he could conceivably raise as many as 20,000 men from among the loyalist population in North Carolina. If North and South Carolina returned to the fold under the British banner, then Virginia ought to be easy to subdue. Martin speculated that if he was successful, it would frighten Virginia enough that they would keep all of their soldiers at home to repel any southern invasion from North Carolina, rather than dispatching troops north to assist Washington's efforts there. The people the governor targeted for this grand army were the oath-bound Highland Scots of the North Carolina piedmont, and the remnants of the Regulator force defeated at Alamance back in 1771.[26]

Martin's schemes found support among the large community of expat Highlanders. After the 1748 Battle of Culloden spelled the end of the Jacobite Rebellion in Scotland, many Highlanders who gambled and lost in the effort to place a Stuart king on the English throne realized their prospects in the land of their birth were poor. Many of them looked to the west and America as a place where they could start anew, away from the heavy hand of England's Hanoverian king. North Carolina became a preferred place to emigrate to, with thousands of Scots arriving at Brunswick and Wilmington over the next few decades.

Among the Highlander newcomers were Allan and Flora MacDonald, famous among their people for their efforts on behalf of Charles Stuart in the failed rebellion. Flora famously hid "Bonnie Prince Charlie" from English searchers bent on capturing the pretender to the throne in the wake of the Scots' defeat at Culloden. The native of the Isle of Skye and her husband boarded the *Baliol* sailing from Campbelton, Scotland with their five children in August 1774, and made their way to North America. The North Carolina piedmont promised a future for the family that it was evident could not be had in Scotland. Allan and Flora were both middle aged when they arrived in North Carolina, Flora in her fifties. The MacDonalds landed on the Cape Fear to much celebration from the people of the Cape Fear.

The MacDonald family settled first along the banks of Cross Creek, before moving to Cameron Hill, 22 miles from modern Fayetteville. They also lived in Montgomery County on Cheek's Creek, near their daughter, who had married into the McLeod clan. The last thing Flora wanted was more turmoil and fighting. Her husband, however, proved a different story. Allan MacDonald was eager to profess his loyalty and offer his services to the beleaguered royal governor at the mouth of the river.

Josiah Martin was convinced that there was an untapped pool of supporters for the king's cause in North Carolina. For years, when newcomers came ashore, they were required to swear a loyalty oath to King George III before they could claim land in the interior on which to start their new lives. Many of them no doubt meant it, but many others probably considered it a perfunctory promise. This led Martin - and truth be told, virtually all the other royal governors in America - to believe thousands of loyalists were just waiting for the call to rally around the king's banner. His meeting with Allan MacDonald could only have reinforced that belief.

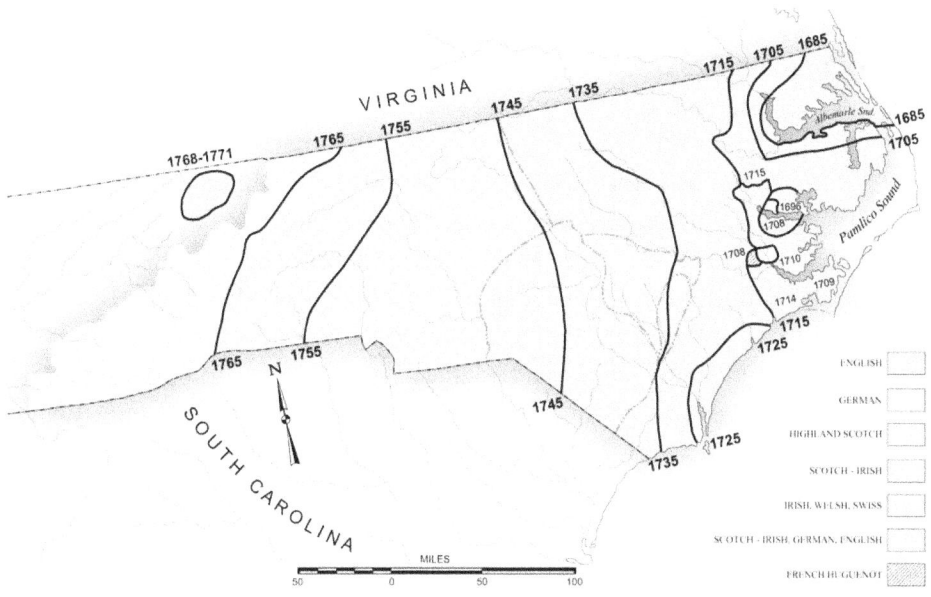

A map showing the settlement of North Carolina. (Map by Mark Moore)

MacDonald and his wife attended a ball thrown in their honor in Wilmington soon after their arrival. Shortly after that, Allan and his kinsman by marriage, Alexander McLeod, made their way to Fort Johnston to seek an audience with the governor. MacDonald greeted Martin with the proposition that he could raise "a battalion of good and faithful Highlanders," made up of men from the MacDonald and McLeod clans already in the province. The offer aligned nicely with Martin's thoughts. He had already written to Lord Dartmouth saying much the same thing, and requested that his military commission be reinstated to lead a campaign to reclaim North Carolina for the king. MacDonald's declaration, coming from "one whose principles were always steady to his King and country," just served to confirm it.

The meeting came about after a gathering of Highlanders chose MacDonald to meet with Martin. Traveling incognito, he carried with him a letter confirming the readiness of the clans to rise up and carry out the governor's orders. The two men took an instant liking to each other. Martin wrote in a letter to Highlander leaders that, "I part with him [MacDonald] more reluctantly than I can tell you,"[27]

Flora, on the other hand, was not so enamored of the scheme. Flora had seen plenty of ups and downs in her life, including grand plans that more often than not ended up going sideways. All she wanted at her stage of life was to live a peacefully in North Carolina with her husband and family, minding her own business and keeping well away from imperial intrigues and danger. If it were up to her, Allan would have stayed at home to tend their farm and cattle. But it was not up to her.[28]

It was not as if the Whigs did not know something was afoot. In June 1775, Highlander emissaries visited Gov. Martin to seek commissions and arms to raise a force from among their kinsmen in the piedmont. In fact, the Wilmington Committee of Safety wrote to Allan MacDonald in early July to ask if it was his intention to raise troops for the governor. Then there was the case of loyalist James Hepburn of Cumberland County, accused of derogatory speech regarding the Committees of Safety and spreading the rumor that King George III had hired 50,000 Russians to cow his unruly American subjects. This is the same James Hepburn who applied to the Cumberland County Committee of Safety for permission to raise a company of militia, but who then declared he intended to use them against the Whigs and their cause. The Wilmington Committee, unsure how much they could count on their Cumberland counterparts, took steps of their own to mitigate Hepburn's royal leanings. A resolution issued by the Wilmingtonians described him as "inimical to the liberties of his country and the common cause of America..." Despite this, Hepburn actually was elected as a delegate to the Provincial Congress that met in August. Yet his true colors soon emerged again. When the Highlanders rose up in February 1776, James Hepburn was among them.[29]

The Wilmington Committee received a message from New Bern on July 21, 1775, alerting them that two British officers were in the area with the intent of recruiting for the British in the North Carolina backcountry. Gen. Thomas Gage had dispatched the two, Bunker Hill veterans Major Donald MacDonald and Capt. Donald MacLeod, from Boston to organize loyalist Highlanders for military action. MacDonald had the added credibility of having also been at the Battle of Culloden in 1748. Their orders were to recruit enough men to form a Royal Highland Emigrant Regiment from among the piedmont Scots, and to enlist additional support from the remnants of the Regulator movement as well. "There is reason to suspect their errand of base nature," the New Bern Committee of Safety warned.[30]

The two soldiers' presence was noted even before they reached New Bern. Edenton's Samuel Johnston penned a letter warning the Committee in the capital of their arrival and the suspicious nature of their activities. He recommended they be taken into custody, but if they got away, at the very least the New Bern Committee should write to Wilmington and make them aware of MacDonald and MacLeod. "They pretend they are on a visit to some of their countrymen on your river but I think there is reason to suspect their errand...," Johnston confided. "...I doubt not the prudence of the Gentlemen with you will have suggested the necessity of securing the Highlanders and that proper measures have been adopted for that purpose."[31]

As the Cape Fear entered the dog days of summer in August, Josiah Martin took up his pen to express his anger and frustration. He bemoaned his quarantine aboard *H.M.S. Cruizer*, "reduced to the deplorable state of being a tame Spectator of Rebellion spreading over this Country." In a fit of pique, he wrote what has come to be known as his Fiery Declaration, a litany of offenses against the Crown and himself as its representative in North Carolina. At the top of his list was the destruction of Fort Johnston, which Martin termed "a degree of wanton barbarity that would disgrace human nature in the most savage state." He also condemned the Mecklenburg Resolves, and the upcoming Provincial Congress, all of which he labeled as "subversive of the whole Constitution of the Country." The governor challenged those loyal to King George III to rebuke those who were trying to "erect among them the standard of rebellion under the cloak and pretense of meeting for solemn deliberations on the public welfare." He called those Whigs "evil minded Conspirators," and their actions a "most unprincipled and unnatural Rebellion." The Whigs read Martin's proclamation and dismissed it as "false, Scandalous, Scurrilous, malicious, and sedicious Libel, tending to disunite the good people of this province," and had it publicly burned.

Martin also continued his correspondence with Lord North in London. In July he had asked the Ministry for "Ten Thousand Stand of Arms at least with proper Accoutrements...six light brass field pieces... and a good store of ammunition," with drums, colors and other military materiel. From his isolation aboard *H.M.S. Cruizer*, the governor assured North that, "The people are in general well affected and much attached to" the government and king. The governor was still convinced of an untapped pool of loyalists in the backcountry just waiting for the opportunity to rise up for their sovereign.[32]

The governor's plan was approved by the Secretary of State for the American Colonies, Lord Dartmouth, on November 7, 1775. Martin's request to have his commission reinstated was denied, but the government did find his assertion that he could raise an army of loyalists intriguing. King George himself ventured to dispatch MGen. Charles Lord Cornwallis with seven regiments and accompanying artillery from Ireland to support Martin's plan. Fifty-three British warships were assigned to ferry Cornwallis's troops across the Atlantic, and another 2,000 men under Sir Henry Clinton from Boston, to the Cape Fear. Admiral Sir Peter Parker immediately began preparing his ships to transport Clinton's troops. If Martin's plan reached fruition, the British would be able to cleave the American colonies in half, separating the Northern from the Southern, then destroy the rebellion in detail. It was more than a simple raid. It was a major operation, and it all hinged on the ability of an army of loyalist Highlanders and former Regulators to rise up and march to the coast, where they would link up with British regulars to reclaim North Carolina for the Crown.[33]

A soldier of the N.C. Continental Line in the white hunting frock and trousers that were common uniform for them early on. The N.C. units did not get the distinctive blue coats until later in the war.

At the Third Provincial Congress that convened on August 20, 1775, delegates authorized anti-British actions despite Martin's condemnations. One move was another economic boycott proposed by the Continental Congress. Another was the passage of a test oath, and the creation of committees to meet with the Highlanders to sway them to the American cause. Another was to provide for the defense of the colony, and yet another to maintain communications with the other colonies. The Congress also took steps to create a Whig government, complete with a fiscal system and an army. A Provincial Council comprised of 13 members of the Congress was created to direct the use of military force and handle the colony's business when the Provincial Congress was not in session. James Moore and Robert Howe were commissioned colonels to command the first two (of a hoped for ten) new provincial regiments that would eventually be absorbed into the Continental Army. Each regiment would be made up of 500 men. The Provincial Congress designated that 400 men of the First North Carolina Regiment be stationed in the Wilmington District. The rest, along with the entirety of the Second Regiment, were dispatched to Salisbury, New Bern, and Edenton.[34]

The Wilmington District consisted of New Hanover, Onslow, Brunswick, Bladen, Duplin, and Cumberland Counties. Whigs belonging to it began organizing in much the same way it was being done at the province level and in the other colonies. Samuel Johnston and Samuel Ashe were chosen to represent the district on the Provincial Council. Frederick Jones, Sampson Moseley, Archibald Maclaine, Richard Quince, Thomas Davis, William Cray, Henry Rhodes, Thomas Routledge, James Kenan, Alexander McAlister, George Mylne, John Smith, and Benjamin Stone made up the District Committee of Safety. Alexander Lillington took command of the battalion of Minute Men authorized for the district. Lillington was commissioned as colonel, supported by Lieutenant Colonel Robert Ellis and Major Samuel Swann. The district called on Brunswick County and Cumberland County to supply one company each to the battalion, while the remaining counties supplied two each. Other assorted officers included William Purviance of New Hanover, William Cray of Onslow, John Davis of Brunswick, Thomas Robeson of Bladen, James Kenan of Duplin, and Thomas Rutherford of Cumberland Counties.[35]

Janet Schaw seemed to believe Robert Howe was eager to gain overall command of all North Carolina forces, and she wished him well in the attempt. Schaw believed Howe to be much less dangerous to British plans than his fellow colonel, James Moore, would be.

"I wish he may get the command with all my heart," Schaw recorded in her journal, "for he does not appear to me half so dangerous as another candidate, a Coll Moor, whom I am compelled at once to dread and esteem. He is a man of free property and a most unblemished character, has amiable manners, and a virtuous life has gained him the love of everybody, and his popularity is such that I am assured he will have more followers than any other man in the province. He acts from a steady tho' mistaken principle, and I am certain has no view or design, but what he thinks right and for the good of the country. He urges not a war of words, and when my brother told him he would not join him, for he did not approve the cause, 'Then do not,' said he, 'let every man be directed by his own ideas of right or wrong,' If this man commands, be assured, he will find his enemies work. His name is James Moor. Should you ever here him mentioned, think of the character I gave him."

Like Moore, Howe was also a veteran of the French & Indian War, though his tour was brief. Howe was related to Moore (as many of the notable families in the Lower Cape Fear were through blood and intermarriage), and described by many as having a devil-may-care outlook, a keen mind, and a vigorous appreciation for the ladies and a good drink. In her journal Schaw described Robert, "or as he is called here Bob Howe. This Gentleman has the worst character You ever heard thro' the whole province. He is however very like a Gentleman, much so indeed than anything I have seen in the Country. He is deemed a horrid animal, a sort of woman-eater that devours everything that comes in his way, and that no woman can withstand him...I do assure you they overrate his merits and as I am certain it would be in the power of mortal woman to withstand him, so I am convinced he is not so voracious as he is represented. But he has that general polite gallantry, which every man of good breeding ought to have..."

John Murray, Lord Dunmore, Royal Governor of Virginia

Not everyone shared Schaw's opinion. Josiah Quincy, Jr. found Robert Howe to be an exemplary sort of man. He was, Quincy wrote, a "most happy compound of the man of sense, the sword, the senate, and the buck. A truly surprising character....He was formed by nature and his education to shine in the senate and the field - in the company of the philosopher and the libertine - a favorite of the man of sense and the female world. He has faults and vice - but alas who is without them."[36]

By October, Cornelius Harnett had been elected the president of the provincial government. A month later, Virginia's Lord Dunmore issued his proclamation offering freedom to any slaves who would abandon their masters and join with the British against the rebels. Dunmore (actual name John Murray) announced that "all indented servants, Negroes, or others, (appertaining to Rebels.) [are] free, that are able and willing to bear arms, they joining His Majesty's Troops, as soon as may be, for the more speedily reducing the Colony to a proper sense of their duty, to His Majesty's crown and dignity." Almost before the ink had dried on the proclamation, 300 slaves had abandoned their servitude to join the British from around the Norfolk area. Still more came from farther afield to earn their freedom with service to the king.

Pennsylvania Loyalist Joseph Galloway, in a letter to the Earl of Dartmouth observed that, "The Negroes may be all deemed so many Intestine Enemies, being all slaves and desirous of freedom." Now Dunmore, who like Josiah Martin had been run off from his capital to the safety of the *H.M.S. William* in Norfolk harbor, had a force of 2,000 men, half of whom were black. The presence of such a force to the north of the Carolinas spurred orders to take action.[37]

During the first weeks of November, Whig militia and the British ships in the Cape Fear River exchanged shots that were more annoying than impactful. Rebel soldiers fired musket balls at the sloops, hoping for a lucky hit, and the British crews answered with cannon fire. On November 11, *H.M.S. Scorpion* returned to relieve the *Cruizer* on station in the Cape Fear, but Gov. Martin refused to release Capt. Parry's ship. Martin's excuse was that extended duty on the river had rendered the sloop of war unseaworthy for the journey back to Boston. More likely, Martin simply wanted as many weapons close to hand as possible, and *Cruizer*'s guns were valuable ordnance. Col. James Moore responded to the presence of the newcomer and her guns by erecting a battery at Brunswick armed with field guns sent down from Wilmington. The Wilmington Committee of Safety was so worried about the two sloops sailing upriver to shell Brunswick and Wilmington that a delegation was sent to put a value on properties that might be destroyed if they did.[38]

A day later, the guns that had lain dormant since the July attack on Fort Johnston were finally reclaimed by the British. When the transport *Palliser* dropped anchor in the Cape Fear, along with the *Scorpion* and another civilian vessel carrying more Highland immigrants, on November 12, 1775, it gave Martin the manpower he needed to recover the cannons. Seamen from the *Palliser*, led by their captain, landed on the fourteenth to get the guns, but Whig militia intercepted them and captured the transport's commander. The *Cruizer* saw what was happening and fired on the

Tarring and feathering was a vicious treatment imposed on those who drew the anger of the side in power.

militia with their swivel guns. *H.M.S. Cruizer's* log recorded that "the rebbels retir'd quickly to the woods." Captain Parry went on to record that two days later, when the seamen were able to return and actually get ahold of the gun tubes, that "Some rebbels appeared in the woods, but retired on our fireing grape." He noted also that as a precaution, he "sent 40 men to keep possession of the fort." The guns were retrieved, packed aboard the *Palliser*, and sent back to Boston.[39]

The growing potential for serious combat on the Cape Fear River prompted the Continental Congress to absorb the First and Second North Carolina Regiments into the national army under George Washington on November 28, 1775. The Congressional resolution read, "Resolved that the two Battalions which Congress directed to be raised in the Province of North Carolina be increased to the Continental Establishment, and kept in pay at the expense of the United Colonies for one year from this time, or until the further order of Congress, as well as for the purpose of defending the good people of that Colony against the attacks of Ministerial oppression, as assisting the adjacent Colonies."[40]

Tensions continued to rise along the river in Wilmington and Brunswick. In November, the Wilmington Committee of Safety ordered militiamen to go door to door and confiscate any weapons they found except for one musket per white man. The militia were careful to issue a receipt for the muskets, powder, and shot they took, but the need for arms was too great to not take them. After a month of trading lead with British ships and soldiers, Whigs were in no mood to tolerate loyalist activity. Some Tories abandoned the Cape Fear for Virginia. Mobs took out their anger and frustrations on those who did not flee. Abraham Pollock was a case in point. According to Samuel Johnston, the Wilmington Committee of Safety questioned Pollock, whose answers seemed to satisfy the interrogators. But a mob broke into his home, confiscated his liquor, and forced money from him to add insult to injury. The mob dragged Pollock to the courthouse in the intersection of Market and Front Streets, and tarred and feathered him while his half-naked wife stood nearby. Johnston recalled that Mrs. Pollock "...rent the Air with the most affecting Shrieks and Cries imaginable. At last quite exhausted, she fainted and was carried home more dead than alive."[41]

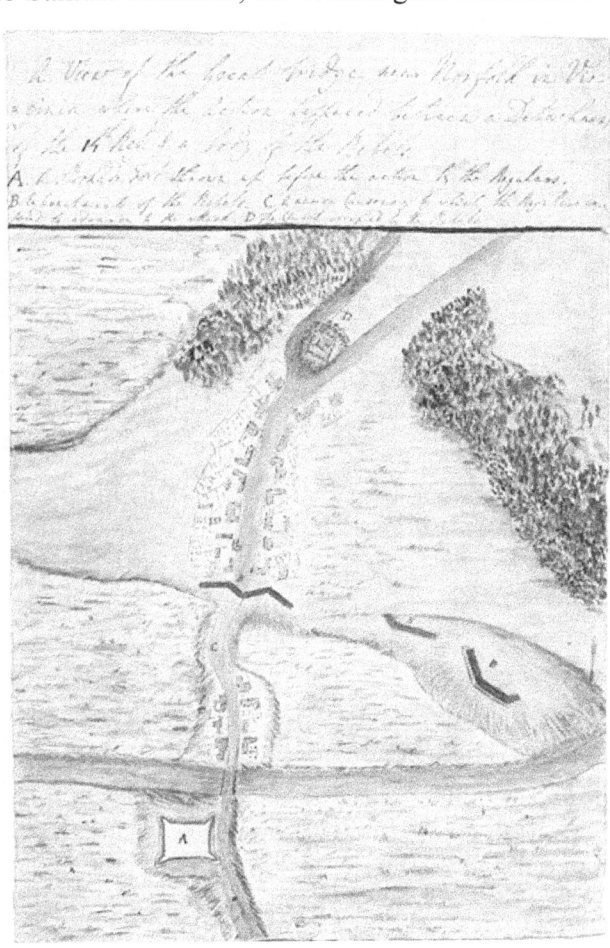

Lord Rawdon's map of the Battle of Great Bridge

In December 1775, Royal Governor John Murray, Lord Dunmore, decided to attack Col. William Woodford's 2nd Virginia Regiment at the Great Bridge leading into the port of Norfolk. Halifax, North Carolina's Minute Men under Col. Nicholas Long arrived in Virginia to lend their support to Woodford, and Col. Robert Howe led another 250 men to Norfolk as well. Roughly the same number of the Second North Carolina Regiment had already joined

Civilians flee the British burning of Norfolk, Virginia.

the defense from Edenton, where they had been stationed by order of the Provincial Council.

The bridge itself was nothing special, but long causeways on either side that spanned thick swamp made it a key to controlling the town on the Chesapeake Bay. The bridge and the small village west of it both went by the same name. On the Norfolk side, north of the bridge, a windmill made for a recognizable landmark, where Gov. Dunmore's forces dug in. On December 9, 1775, Dunmore's army surged out of their entrenchments to try to race across the bridge and wrest control of it from Woodford's Virginia Continentals and volunteer militia. The attack was crushed, and Dunmore did not attempt it again. The weight of numbers rallying to the rebels' defense convinced Dunmore that there was little to be gained from pressing the issue further.[42]

Five days later, Woodford rode into Norfolk accompanied by Robert Howe and more than 400 men of the Second North Carolina, including several cannon. Halifax's Minute Men and other volunteers had been discharged to return to their homes. According to Woodford, Howe assumed command of the town by right of rank and commission date. The Virginian said Howe "mentioned to me in a very genteel manner his appointment by the Congress, & his Right of precedence by that appointment." Woodford consented, but retained command of the Virginia troops in the army. Howe proved to have a knack for command in the negotiations with Dunmore over the exchange of prisoners after the battle, including five British regulars held by Howe who were part of Lord Dunmore's personal guard.[43]

Any satisfaction the Americans might have felt over the outcome at Great Bridge was soured somewhat when on New Year's Day 1776, Lord Dunmore decided to shell Norfolk after Howe declined to allow the British ships to replenish their supplies there. Cannon balls fired by Royal Navy gunners destroyed Norfolk, helped in the task by Whig looting and the burning of the former Tory stronghold in retaliation. Robert Howe, still in town with half of the Second North Carolina Regiment, related the British bombardment to the Virginia Convention in a letter.

"The cannonade of the town began around a quarter after three, yesterday, from upwards of one hundred pieces of cannon," Howe wrote, "and continued till near ten, at night, without intermission; it then abated a little, and continued till two, this morning. Under cover of their guns they landed, and set fire to the town in several places near the water, though our men strove to prevent them all in their power; but the houses near the water being chiefly wood, they took fire immediately, and the fire spread with amazing rapidity. It is now become general, and the whole town will, I doubt not, be consumed in a day or two. Expecting that the fire would throw us into confusion, they frequently landed; and were every time repulsed, I imagine with loss, but with what loss, I cannot tell; the burning of the town has made several avenues, which yesterday they had not, so that they may now fire with greater effect; the tide is now rising, and we expect at high water another cannonade." Three days later, Howe reported that there were no Americans killed in the action, but five or six suffered wounds. He went on to say nine-tenths of Norfolk was destroyed, but at least the fire was out.[44]

It had been a busy year, 1775. The Americans and British had grown farther apart than ever. In North Carolina and Virginia, the king's men in charge of the colonies had been reduced to living in the cramped confines of ship's quarters while rebels took over running their provinces. Armed rebellion against the king had taken place. Shots had been fired, blood had been shed. And in the Cape Fear, the friction between the Whigs and Tories would soon reach a boiling point, ending in a sharp, fierce clash at a small creek twenty miles northwest of Wilmington.

Endnotes

[1] Butler 1776, 46; Rankin, 1.
[2] Angley, 21.
[3] Butler 1776, 50-51.
[4] Watson 1861, 81.
[5] Lee, 254-255; Rankin, 7. The Boston Port Bill was Great Britain's response to the Boston Tea Party, in which the Sons of Liberty disguised themselves as Native Americans and dumped 300 chests of tea into the Charles River to protest the East India Company's

monopoly on the tea trade in the American colonies...Parker Quince was a resident of Brunswick Town.

[6] Butler 1776, 52-53; Flora Fraser. Flora Macdonald: "Pretty Young Rebel." (New York: Alfred A. Knopf, 2023): 144-145. Hereafter cited as Fraser; John R. Maass. "A Complicated Scene of Difficulties": North Carolina and the Revolutionary Settlement, 1776-1789. PhD. dissertation, Ohio State University, 2007: 27. Hereafter cited as Maass; Lee, 255-256. Governor Martin had already castigated the North Carolina General Assembly who, according to him, in their March 1774 session had "assumed to themselves a power unconstitutional, repugnant to the Laws, and derogatory to the honor and good faith of this Province."

[7] Lee, 262-263. On July 1, 1775, the Committees of Safety from around the Cape Fear region pledged "that we will not accept the advantages insidiously thrown out by the said act, but will adhere strictly to such plans as have been, and shall be, entered into by the honorable continental Congress; so as to keep up a perfect unanimity with our sister colonies."

[8] Lee, 261. Janet Schaw, visiting the Cape Fear region at the time, noted that "The Ladies have burnt their tea in a solemn procession."

[9] Lee, 256-257; Watson 1861, 81-82; Ross, 101-102. North Carolina held five Provincial Congresses between August 1774 and November 1776. Wilmington was not represented in the first Congress thanks to Gov. Martin's outmaneuvering the Assembly to prevent them from choosing delegates. But Cornelius Harnett represented the town in the next three, and William Hooper in the last. Lawyer and town commissioner Archibald Maclaine served with Harnett in the third Provincial Congress. William Hooper also served as a delegate for New Hanover County in the first four congresses.

[10] Isabell M. Williams and Leora H. McEachern. Salt, That Necessary Article. (Wilmington N.C. 1973): 6 Hereafter cited as Salt; Watson 1861, 83-84.; Dunkerly, 58. Two exceptions to the reshipment of slaves rule were made, one of them for Cornelius Harnett... Salt was incredibly essential. In the last half of 1774, Brunswick Town imported over 33,000 bushels of salt, with some ships bringing in 5,000 bushels at a time. Used to preserve meat in a time before refrigeration, no home, farm, or business could operate without it.

[11] Lee, 261.

[12] Watson 1861, 86-87. Wilmington's importance stemmed from three factors: it was deep enough to allow access by fairly large seagoing vessels, the Cape Fear River ran far enough into the interior to reach the large number of loyalists living in the Upper Cape Fear River Valley, and Gov. Josiah Martin was taking refuge aboard *H.M.S. Cruizer* off Fort Johnston.

[13] Dunkerly, 60; Lee, 257.

[14] Rankin, 11; Ross, 103.

[15] Watson 1861, 84-86; Kristen M. Seielstad, "Upon secrecy, success depends" intelligence operations during the southern campaign of the American Revolution." PhD diss., College of Charleston, 2010: 59-60. Hereafter cited as Seielstad. Militiamen were required to muster with their musket, twelve rounds of ammunition, and two opposable teeth (needed to bite off the end of the paper cartridges holding the powder and ball)... Many of the militiamen compelled to swear allegiance to the Whigs may have been reluctant to do so, but most served loyally in spite of their reservations...Royal Governor Mar-

tin admitted that the Whig tactic was working. "Scotch Merchants at Wilmington who so long maintained their loyalty have lately been compelled ostensibly to join in sedition by appearing under Arms at the Musters appointed by the Committees," he wrote....The militia officer was John Ashe, according to author Robert M. Dunkerly.

[16] Rankin, 11-12; Dunkerly, 61-62.

[17] Lee, 265.; Dunkerly, 70; Patrick O'Kelley, Nothing But Blood and Slaughter: The Revolutionary War in the Carolinas-Volume One 1771-1779 (Booklocker.com Incorporated, 2005): 204. Hereafter cited as O'Kelley, V1; Butler 1776, 59. The troops in New Hanover County were posted to Barnard's Creek (where Greenfield Park is today), three miles below Wilmington. A small fort was constructed near modern Northern Boulevard. The men sent to Brunswick set up camp roughly four miles above Fort Johnston...A July 8, 1775 slave revolt in Beaufort and Pitt Counties fanned the fears of something similar on the Cape Fear. The uprising was put down by local county slave patrols, who arrested forty blacks after confiscating an alarming amount of ammunition from them. The revolt was blamed on incitement by a British seaman. For his part, Martin always swore he never advocated slave revolts.

[18] Dunkerly, 65. Isolated or not, Martin was still able to communicate. He had regular correspondence with loyalists like Alex McLean, Samuel Campbell, Robert Hogg, William McTier, and John Slingsby. Campbell and Hogg were secretly providing supplies to the *Cruizer*, while McTier acted as a go between relaying messages for Martin.

[19] Angley, 23; Rankin, 15. The Wilmington Committee of Safety also accused Collet and Martin of wantonly detaining merchant vessels when they applied for bills of health (required to leave a port), of ignoring local mgistrates, and embezzling government property. Collet, when the sheriff served him with papers to collect a debt, is said to have replied "with the shameful contempt of wiping his b-k s-de with them."

20 Angley, 23; Oates, 129-131. The Liberty Point Declaration came on June 20, 1775, just one month after the Mecklenburg Declaration.

[21] Angley, 26. Their proclamation read, "Resolved unanimously that a reinforcement of as many men as will voluntarily turn out, be immediately dispatched to join Colonel Howe, who is now on his way to Fort Johnston and that it be recommended to the captains of the independent and artillery companies in Wilmington and the officers of the several companies in the county to muster their men and immediately equip those who are willing to go to that service."

[22] Angley, 26-27. River pilot Nathan Adams delivered the message to Martin aboard *H.M.S. Cruizer* on the evening of July 1, 1775. Adams told the governor that Col. John Ashe had given him the note at Brunswick and told him to deliver it. Martin wrote a reply that angrily told the rebels that any move against the fort would be vigorously resisted as an affront to "lawful authority."

[23] Ross, 106-107; Butler 1776, 59-60; Lee, 265; Angley, 26. James Moore was selected over John Ashe as colonel of the first Continental Regiment raised in Wilmington, winning the election by one vote. At roughly the same time, Alexander Lillington was chosen to lead one of several companies of Minute Men raised in the region, paying from his own pocket a bounty of 25 shillings per man to outfit them with a uniform consisting of a hunting shirt, spatterdashes, and black garters...Martin was tipped off about the impending attack by the captains of four British merchant ships doing business at Wilmington.

The captains had been approached by Wilmington Whigs who wanted them to join them in the move against the fort.

[24] Rankin, 15.

[25] Angley, 27-28.

[26] Dunkerly, 71-74.

[27] Fraser, 146-149; Dunkerly, 62-63; Oates, 58. The meeting took place in the summer of 1775...Flora confirmed Allan's mission in her writings, when she recorded that her husband was to "settle the plan of rising [raising] the Highlanders in arms."...The disguised journey to Fort Johnston was prudent. Whig Committees of Safety dispatched at least two parties to find MacDonald before he could reach the governor.

[28] Fraser, 153.

[29] Laura Page Frech, "The Wilmington Committee of Public Safety and the Loyalist Rising of February, 1776." The North Carolina Historical Review, Vol. No.1 (1964): 21-33. Hereafter cited as Frech; Dunkerly, 61. Where the loyalties of the Cumberland County Committee of Safety lay was open to debate. The area around Cross Creek had more than its share of Tories. Farquahard Campbell joined the loyalists at Cross Creek in February 1776...The Committee of Safety called Hepburn a "...false Scandalous Incendiary...who...favors tyranny and oppression." They advised citizens to avoid "such a wicked and detestable Character." Within a month of being publicly castigated by the Wilmington Committee of Safety, Hepburn wrote them begging to be "restored again to the favor of the public."

[30] Dunkerly, 66; Rankin 33. At Bunker Hill, Donald MacDonald suffered a wound for his efforts. MacDonald began his British military career as a colonel of Marines in 1763. He and MacLeod both had relatives living among the Scots in the North Carolina piedmont.

[31] Frech, 21-33.

[32] Angley, 30; Rankin, 15; Butler 1776, 61. The Fiery Proclamation was issued on August 8, 1775.

[33] Ross, 115-117; Maass, 27.; Dunkerly, 73. Clinton's rosters included sixty female camp followers for each regiment, and twelve servants. These people did routine tasks like laundry, etc.

[34] Butler 1776, 61-62.; Rankin, 16-17; Lee 260. The Provincial Congress authorized £125,000 to fund the military...Moore took command of the First Regiment at the rank of colonel; Howe took command of the Second Regiment at the same rank. The other officers of the First Regiment included Lieutenant Colonels Francis Nash and Major Thomas Clark. Howe's officers included Lieutenant Colonel Alexander Martin and Major John Patten.

[35] Lee, 260-261.

[36] Rankin, 17-18. There is some evidence that Moore may have been a veteran of the French & Indian War according to Rankin, though he was certainly a veteran of the Regulator Rebellion, where he commanded "all the artillery and artillery company of volunteers." Moore was well regarded enough that by age 28 he was a colonel in the local militia...Gov. Martin said Howe's name was originally "Howes" but that he changed it to create the impression that he was somehow related to a distinguished British family of that name. Janet Schaw was one who noted Howe's proclivity for feminine companionship.

[37] Jeffrey J. Crow, *The Black Experience in Revolutionary North Carolina, Vol. 16.* (Raleigh, N.C.: North Carolina Division of Archives, 1977): 59. Hereafter cited as Crow. Dunmore's Proclamation came on November 7, 1775. Murray called the black men he enlisted "Lord Dunmore's Ethiopian Regiment," and they wore a uniform with the slogan "Liberty to Slaves" across their chests.

[38] Rankin, 21. Martin had been begging for more ships at Cape Fear to prevent the rebels from getting smuggled shipments of armaments, even though it was his belief that the time for preventative measures to stem the coming storm had passed...The British ships in the Cape Fear in November 1775 had crews of the following sizes: *H.M.S. Cruizer* - 60 men, *H.M.S. Scorpion* - 100 men.

[39] Angley, 29. Between November 16-20, *Cruizer* fired at rebels on the shore every day while the Fort Johnston guns were being recovered.

[40] Rankin, 21.

[41] Dunkerly, 73; Rankin, 22.

[42] Rankin, 24; Lossing, n. 212; Charles E. Bennett and Donald R. Lennon. *A Quest for Glory: Major General Robert Howe and the American Revolution.* (Chapel Hill: University of North Carolina Press, 1991): 2-4. Hereafter cited as Bennett and Lennon; Crow, 61. The heavy reinforcements for Woodford were also intended to prevent slaves in Pasquotank, Currituck, and other northeastern North Carolina counties from escaping to the British...The British forces suffered 100 killed, the Americans just one man wounded.

[43] Rankin, 24; J.D. Lewis, *NC Patriots 1775-1783: Their Own Words, Volume 1, The NC Continental Line, Second Edition* (Stocksdale, N.C.: Carla G. Harper, 2021): 143. Hereafter cited as Lewis V1. Known N.C. Continental troops at Great Bridge from Howe's Second Regiment include five battalions led by Captains James Blount, Simon Bright, Charles Crawford, Hardy Murfree, and Henry Irwin Toole.

[44] Lewis V1, 6.

1776

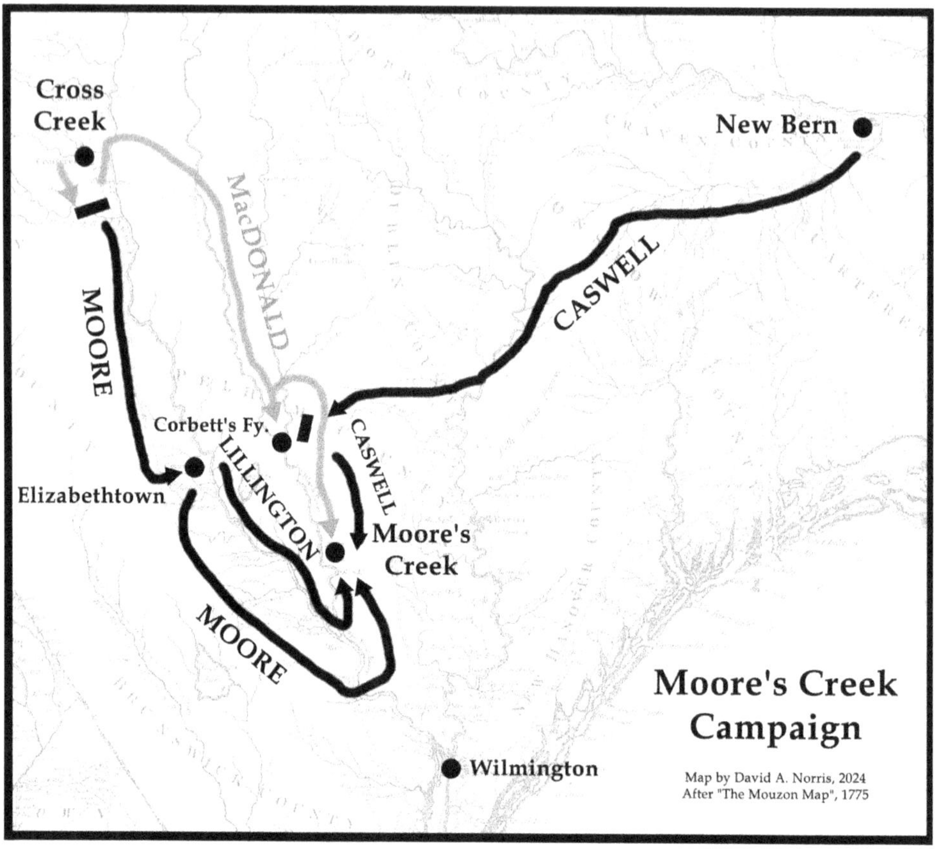

Movements of Whig and Loyalist forces in the Moores Creek Campaign of February 1776. (Map by David A. Norris)

1776

In King George III's Privy Council, his ministers debated the merits of Josiah Martin's plan to wrest control of North Carolina back from the Whigs who had, for all intents and purposes, ousted the royal governor. To their way of thinking, Charlestown should be the target of any combined force of redcoats coming from Boston and Ireland, but Alexander Schaw, Martin's emissary in London, made the case that the Cape Fear was key to any expeditionary planning. Charlestown's importance was obvious. Being the largest port in the South, it was the entry point through which most of the rebel supplies in the Southern Theater flowed. Losing it would be a serious, perhaps insurmountable, blow to the Whigs. But Schaw argued that taking the Cape Fear first, embodying the large number of loyalists he and the governor were confident resided in the North Carolina backcountry, would make taking the South Carolina port much easier. Schaw convinced the ministers to include a strike at Cape Fear in the plans for seizing Charlestown.

    Orders went to Gen. William Howe, Thomas Gage's successor at Boston, and to recently promoted Lieutenant General Charles Lord Cornwallis in Ireland, who would command seven regiments dispatched to form a junction with the troops being ferried south from Massachusetts. Among the final acts of Lord Dartmouth as secretary for the American Department was to voice some concerns for the likelihood of the expedition's success. Replaced by Lord George Germain, the plan went forward anyway. On December 6, 1775, Cornwallis' transports departed Cork for North Carolina.[1]

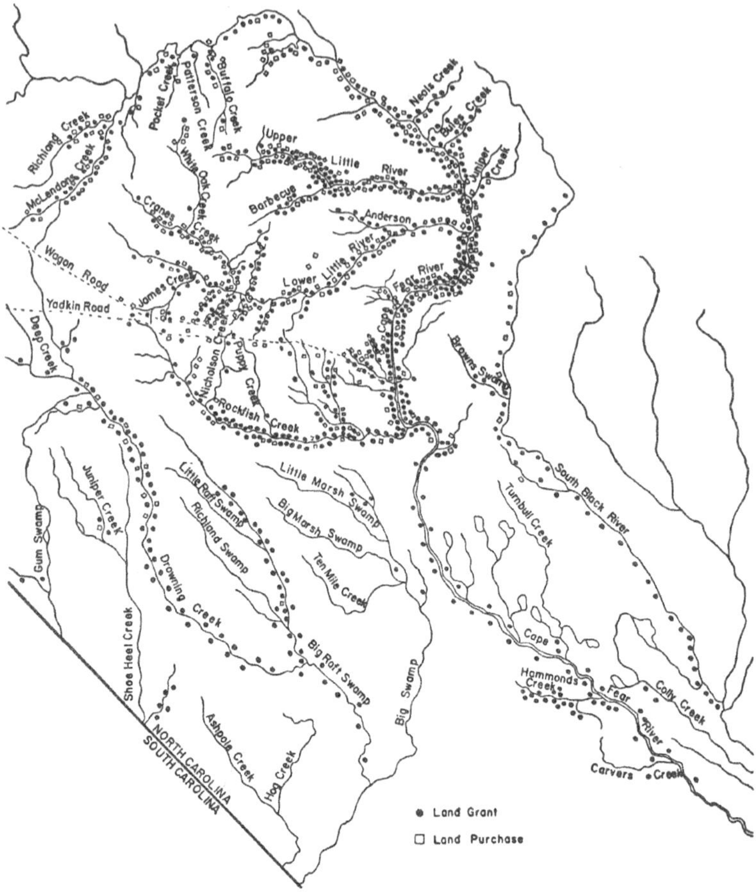

A map showing Highlander settlement patterns in the North Carolina piedmont, around Cross Creek and in adjacent counties.

The Highlanders were key to the success of Martin's plans. For decades, newly arrived Scots had been required to swear a loyalty oath to King George III before they could claim land in the interior. The pledge required them to swear "their readiness to lay down their lives in the defence of his Majesty's Government." Both sides courted the Highlanders for their fearsome fighting skills. As early as 1775 the Whigs dispatched two Presbyterian ministers into the backcountry to present their side of the argument between the colonies and Great Britain. They failed, according to one historian, largely because they did not speak Gaelic.[2]

Martin's conviction that the Highlanders were in his corner was solid, at least in public. There were occasions, however, when that certitude waivered. The Highlanders had been no friends to the king during the Stamp Act rebellion in 1765-1766; nor in the fall of 1775, when they declared themselves neutral. Farquard Campbell, a man Martin had come to rely on as an intermediary with the Scots, also served on a committee of the North Carolina Provincial Congress, prompting Martin to call him "ignorant." The doubts passed however, because by November 1775 the governor was again emphatic that the Highlanders were steadfast allies to the royal cause.[3]

As the winds carried Cornwallis west, North Carolina was awash in rumor. One said that former governor William Tryon had arrived offshore with 700 men to join an equal number of Scots led by current governor Josiah Martin. The rumor claimed that the combined force threatened Mecklenburg and Rowan Counties in western North Carolina. This rumor was easily disproved (Martin was still ensconced aboard *H.M.S. Cruizer*), but was replaced with one that claimed loyalists under Capt. William Fields in Guilford County had been ordered to be ready to march. Meanwhile, the refusal of Cross Creek merchants to buy surplus produce, or to sell iron, sugar, and salt unless the farmers took a loyalty oath to the king, proved to be yet another rumor. Rumors or not, all of the claims created anxiety and tension among the people. As it turned out, the rumor mill had one positive aspect. Fear of loyalists marching through the colony led to troop mobilizations on the part of Whig militias, so when Tory troops actually did rally to the king's colors, the Whigs were ready for them.[4]

In Wilmington, the Committee of Safety ordered Ralph Millar to begin making gunpowder in anticipation of a coming fight. North Carolina's Provincial Council, fearing that "this Province may soon be invaded by British troops," took steps to further isolate Gov. Martin on the Cape Fear River. Gunsmiths and others shifted into overdrive to procure the weapons, ammunition, and other supplies that would be needed to stave off a redcoat incursion. On December 20, the Provincial Council told Richard Quince, Samuel Ashe, Robert Ellis, and John Forster to arm a ship on the Cape Fear to answer any threat coming by water. By December 29, 500 soldiers were at Wilmington, busily building defenses.[5]

In North Carolina, the loyalists that would play such a key role in deciding who controlled the province were a people that would have chaffed under any master. Fiercely independent, the people of the backcountry that Josiah Martin called on to fight for the British sovereign were notoriously hard to govern. Historian Isaac S. Harrell, describing them in a

1926 article, said "Turmoil, fighting, disregard of social and civil responsibility were as characteristic of the settlers in the 'hill country' as was their hunger after land. The coming of the Revolution removed any check that government and law had ever placed on their passions." Largely originating somewhere else, these immigrants to North Carolina were relative latecomers to the colony. A lack of time to assimilate may have been a big factor in determining the side they chose to support when the revolution began.[6]

As January brought a new year, Josiah Martin kept in contact with loyalist sympathizers in Wilmington. Alexander McLean became his main intermediary with Wilmington Tories. McLean, who arrived in Wilmington as a half-pay British army officer, married a local woman and became Martin's helping hand when the governor arrived on the Cape Fear after fleeing New Bern. Among his duties was delivering Martin's instructions to other Wilmington loyalists like Samuel Campbell, Robert Hogg, William McTier, and Bladen County's John Slingsby. McLean masterminded the intelligence network that coordinated the formation of the governor's loyalist army in the interior. John Burgwin, who left the Cape Fear for England in 1775, was kept abreast of developments at home by Mrs. Elizabeth Catherine DeRossett. She wrote that Alexander McLean spoke "such things as are disagreeable to the people" and that his friends wished he would leave. DeRossett said that McLean and his wife were going to the backcountry.

John Burgwin

McLean did go into the backcountry, and he was gone so long that Governor Martin feared he may have met with some mishap that could derail his plans. In the interim, the governor was encouraged by a secret approach from some Brunswick County residents, who assured him of their loyalty to the king and their diminishing patience with the tyranny of the Committees of Safety. The Brunswick delegation was confident that they could raise as many as 3,000 men for Martin's command. Anxious over McLean's absence, the governor chose one of the Brunswick County emissaries as his new agent. Martin was mortified to later find that the new man betrayed him to the rebels, and that he may have provided the Whigs with a list of names of his men in the interior.

The governor received the news that his plan had been approved on January 3, 1776. He immediately penned orders to loyalist commanders in the backcountry, ordering that "...you are hereby required immediately & with all possible secrecy to concert a general place of rende-vous thence to march in a body to Brunswick by such route as you judge proper..."[7]

A week later, Josiah Martin wrote orders to Alexander McLean to begin raising men and assigning officers to every group of fifty. McLean resurfaced when he met with Martin aboard the *Cruizer* to confirm their plans, but was captured by the militia when he departed. The Whigs tossed McLean in jail and fined him for breaking the governor's quarantine, but McLean swore he was only meeting on personal business and doing nothing that would put him at odds with the Committee of Safety. The Committee let him go free on his promise of good behavior. Instead, McLean immediately set about carrying out Gov. Martin's orders.[8]

Martin's timetable called for the loyalists to link with British regulars at Brunswick no later than February 15, but that would prove to be wishful thinking. Alexander McLean's reports from around Cross Creek had been unequivocally positive, but now there was a new danger. Afraid that a betrayal by the Brunswick messenger might lead to the loyal Highlanders and Regulators being rounded up by rebel militias, Martin felt he must raise the king's standard earlier than he had planned, on January 10, 1776.[9]

Highlander and Regulator leaders met in a raucous meeting at David Shane's home on McLendon's Creek (near modern Carthage, N.C.) on February 5, where Alexander McLean conveyed Gov. Martin's orders. The Scots were alarmed that Martin expected to see them at Brunswick in only ten days time. The fact that the ships carrying the British regulars had not yet arrived at Cape Fear added to their misgivings. They proposed a deadline almost a month later than the one in the governor's orders, on March 1. Regulators at the gathering dismissed the Highlanders' concerns, insisting that they and the 3,000 men they claimed to have mustered were ready to march immediately. For their part, the Highlanders said given the short timeline of Martin's orders, they could only be confident of raising about 700 men. Regulators waived that away too, saying instead of bringing 3,000 men, they would bring 5,000 to make up the difference. To see just how truthful the Regulator claims were, Capt. Donald McLeod was sent into Regulator country to see for himself.[10]

In Wilmington, all river pilots were taken into protective custody on January 5, to prevent them from being used by any British ships that might arrive in the Cape Fear. To distract from the loyalists mobilizing in the interior, Gov. Martin ordered *H.M.S. Cruizer* and her sister sloop of war *H.M.S Scorpion* to attack Fort Johnston, where rebel militia of the New Hanover County Regiment were still in control. On January 27, 1776 *Scorpion* came close to the fort and fired 26 rounds from her cannons before withdrawing. *Cruizer* tried to get close enough to fire with good effect, but was unsuccessful in the attempt.

BGen. Donald MacDonald

John Stuart

Maurice Moore had pleaded with Gov. Martin to try to reconcile the differences between the two sides in the Assembly, but by January 10 that ship had sailed. In the interior, Bunker Hill veteran Donald MacDonald was commissioned brigadier general of the loyalist army. By February 5, 1776, MacDonald raised the king's standard in Cross Creek and issued a call for the loyal to mobilize. A few days later, MacDonald's call to arms was read at former Regulator William Fields' camp, but the response from the people there was lukewarm. The last time Regulators rose up in rebellion ended badly for them, and they were reluctant to repeat that history again.

Martin and the ministers in London were hoping that the Regulators would side with them, or at the very least, remain neutral. The British considered North Carolina and Georgia the weakest colonies in North America, and thought the people there "steed in perpetual awe of the Regulators." One of London's men on the ground, Superintendent of Indian Affairs John Stuart, shared the opinion that most of the backcountry men were Tories who would support King George III. The British were not alone in their assessment of North Carolina's willingness and capabilities. A Pennsylvania loyalist described the colony as "...in general the poorest country on the Continent, Nova Scotia excepted, and one of the Floridas. With a few very honourable exceptions, much of the same character must be given of the people. The bulk of them are renegades from other Colonies." Renegades or not, the people of the Cape Fear recognized the threat they faced.[11]

The Committees of Safety knew of the governor's call to arms almost as soon as the loyalists did. Richard Caswell and James Moore both already commanded substantial forces embodied to thwart a Tory uprising. On February 10, Col. Alexander Lillington alerted the Wilmington militia to be ready to stand to. In New Bern, Col. Richard Caswell was ordered by the New Bern Committee of Safety to muster the militia. Caswell's command had artillery, and he was empowered to purchase such provisions and equipment as he might need on his march to reinforce Moore's Continentals. Whig units were ordered to stand ready in Dobbs, Johnston, Pitt, and Craven Counties, too. The militias moved to block the former Regulators from joining the Highlander army forming at Cross Creek. Whigs had been busy trying to make sure the backcountry men never reached the rendezvous. One unit, from Guilford County, was decapitated when the Committee of Safety ordered the arrest of seven of its leaders who were then jailed at Halifax. The rest of the rank and file turned around and went home. Nevertheless, 200 of the backcountry men managed to rendezvous with MacDonald by February 15. The loyalist force MacDonald was able to muster at the point was roughly 1,400 men.[12]

Not everything was coming up roses for the Whigs. By June 1776, Cornelius Harnett related some of the troubles they had endured in the first six months of the year. "The great want of Fire Arms, Ammunition and other Warlike Stores, render our situation truly alarming," he wrote, "...an Army hourly expected to land on our Coasts and apprehensions well founded of an immediate War with the Southern Tribes of Indians, and a large body of people disaffected to the American Cause residing in the very heart of our Country ready (altho' once subdued) to make use of a more favorable opportunity to throw this Colony into a scene of Blood and Confusion."

While men and militias were mobilizing in the Cape Fear, the merchant ship *America* sailed over the bar between Old Inlet and Oak Island, only to be captured by *H.M.S. Cruzer*. The *America* carried a cargo of rum and salt that would fetch a nice purse at an admiralty court, but Capt. Francis Parry did not have enough seamen to make up a prize crew. When the British left the Cape Fear River in the spring of 1776, Parry ordered the *America* burned.[13]

To meet the challenges they faced, North Carolina's Whigs were constantly trying to enlist soldiers by whatever means necessary. The colony raised ten Continental regiments and several other militia units, but doing so was burdensome. Most of the regiments were understrength, and none had a full complement of the things they needed to fully outfit themselves. In addition to raising Continentals to serve with Washington's army outside North Carolina, the Committees of Safety were also responsible for arming, supplying, and feeding them and the militias that held the line against the loyalists at home. Answering the call for battalions of regulars to serve in the national army in the winter and spring of 1776 nearly bankrupted North Carolina.

In the Continental Congress, North Carolina's representatives were embarrassed by their colony's lukewarm support of the American cause when compared to that of other provinces. "North Carolina alone remains an inactive Spectator of this general defensive Armament," complained William Hooper, Joseph Hewes, and Richard Caswell. "Supine and careless, she seems to forget even the Duty she owes to her own local Circumstances and Situations." The situation on the Cape Fear was about to become front and center in the minds of both sides.[14]

The waiting was nerve wracking. Where was the British fleet? How was the mobilization of loyalists in the interior going? Had the Committees of Safety and the Provincial Council done all they could to prepare the colony, especially in the Cape Fear, for attack? While waiting for the answers to those and myriad other questions, the two sides passed the time with what amounted to trash talk - written communications between Gov. Martin and the Whigs that took sarcastic jabs at each other and their causes. Couriers carried letters between Wilmington and *H.M.S. Cruzer*, where the governor was headquartered, on a daily basis. Cornelius Harnett complained to Martin that the British were using Fort Johnston improperly, saying the fort was "... built by the People at a great expense for the Protection of their Trade and made use of for a purpose the very reverse; and to crown all, you Sir, have brought up the *Cruizer* to cover the landing of an army composed of highland banditti; none of whom you will ever see unless as fugitives imploring protection." Gov. Martin replied, expressing surprise at being addressed in such a way by "a little arbitrary Junto (stiling itself a Committee) under the Traitorous Guise of a combination unknown to the laws of this Country: the Revilings of Rebellion, and the gasconadings of Rebels are below the contempt of the Loyal and faithful People [the Scots] whom I have justly stiled Friends of Government."[15]

Col. James Moore

The force the Regulators feared was coming for them was Col. James Moore's men of the recently formed First Regiment of the North Carolina Continental Line. Moore received word of the loyalists gathering in Cumberland County and marched his men towards Cross Creek to thwart their ambitions. The rank and file of the regiment was heavily salted with veterans of the Regulator Rebellion who had fought at Alamance years before. Over the preceding twelve months, John Ashe and Alexander Lillington had trained them hard, sharpening the edge of any man whose skills may have dulled since 1771. Cornelius Harnett had seen to it they were properly uniformed. Donald MacDonald's Highlander Emigrant Regiment would be going against the best the colony had to offer.[16]

Meanwhile Donald McLeod was having his own troubles in the backcountry. The British officer, made a lieutenant colonel at the same time Donald MacDonald received his commission, had gone to see how much support they could count on from Highlanders and Regulators beyond Cross Creek. What he saw did not instill him with confidence. He found the prospective recruits unrefined and definitely ungovernable, unless a great deal of effort was exerted to impose something resembling military discipline. For their part, the backcountry men did not take to having a spit and polish regular soldier as their commander. McLeod instructed that a hogshead of rum be brought out to slake their thirst and ease the concerns of the men. According to McLeod, they availed themselves of the elixir it contained most "industriously." The Regulators had talked a good game at Cross Creek, but when word arrived that Whig troops were on the way to counter them, the 500 men McLeod had gathered melted into the countryside. Others abandoned the loyalists because a rumor said that they would be taken to Nova Scotia to be enlisted in the regular British army. The lieutenant colonel sent a message to the leaders who had claimed to have 3,000 men ready and waiting for the call to arms to meet with him, but none did. Their neighbors told McLeod that the Regulator captains were "...Sculking & hiding themselves through Swamps & such concealed places." McLeod had no choice but to return to MacDonald empty handed.

Scottish Claymore Sword

At the loyalist's Cross Hill encampment outside Cross Creek, everything was a bustle. Recruiters were signing up men as fast as they could, while the Scots took advantage of very generous enlistment bonuses offered for their service. The biggest problem facing Donald MacDonald after his arrival on February 12 was that he had more men than muskets. The brigadier was confident that the Highlanders could muster as many as 3,000 men, but there were only firearms for a fraction of that number. Inventories revealed only 520 muskets for the entire army. Many of the Scots would carry only their dirks and claymore swords on the march, with a few civilian muskets and fowling pieces mixed in. For his force to be truly effective, it was imperative that they reach Brunswick to link up with the coming British regulars, who would remedy the loyalists' lack of firepower. In the meantime, MacDonald ordered detachments to scour the area and confiscate the firearms of civilians for use by the loyalists. They also confiscated 1,000 pounds of gunpowder from the Cumberland County Committee of Safety.[17]

Another complication was the lack of the seasoned Highlander leaders MacDonald had hoped would help direct the energies of the younger loyalists into useful channels. Those older men refused to commit themselves to the cause. For better or worse, MacDonald's army was shaping up to be largely young and poor. Outside of a few Highlander leaders, not a man in the army owned property worth as much as £100.[18]

Logistics was a tricky proposition for the loyalists, who theoretically were under an embargo by the Committees of Safety. Despite the ban, the Tories still managed to acquire the materials they needed to keep an army on the march. After the war, loyalist William McTier told the British Loyalist Claims Commission that he furnished supplies to MacDonald's army at Cross Creek. So did John and James Cruden. At the request of "a Gentleman high in office for the Royal cause," John Cruden and Donald Downie ferried a boatload of rum, sugar, coffee, and salt intended for the loyalists upriver. The boat was captured, but Downie managed to escape and make his way to Cross Creek, where he joined the ranks of the Tories. Not long after, he was among the dead at Moores Creek.

The ability of loyalist agents to supply MacDonald and Governor Martin despite prohibitions dictated by the Wilmington Committee of Safety and others speaks to the division of loyalties in the Lower Cape Fear, especially in the port town itself. In 1775, the white population of Wilmington was around 250 people. Between 60 and 100 of those were adult males. Planters living outside the town were able to vote in local elections so long as they also owned property within town boundaries. There were 44 merchants in Wilmington, making up a large portion of the business in the small town. More than half of those were demonstrably sympathetic to the loyalist cause, and only six remained true to the Americans fighting for independence. Of the rest, ten appeared before the Loyalist Claims Commission after the war, a dozen others abandoned North Carolina for England or the British army, and two others were killed in battle against the rebels. While merchants like Cornelius Harnett, John Ashe, Robert Howe, and James Moore were among the most vigorous supporters of the American cause, they often overshadow the fact that most of their fellow businessmen in Wilmington were decidedly on the side of the king.[19]

Wilmington got a startling surprise on February 14 when *H.M.S. Cruizer* sailed upriver to attack the town, or so the people believed. Actually, the sloop of war was trying to position itself to lend support to MacDonald's expected loyalist army. As the sloop approached, its lookouts identified breastworks that seemed to bristle with cannon. The *Cruizer*'s

Captain Francis Parry aborted the mission, turned the ship down the channel on the west side of Eagles Island (the modern Brunswick River) and back down below The Flats, south of Wilmington. Whig militia peppered the ship with small arms fire for the remainder of the time it spent there.

Col. William Purviance had taken charge of preparing Wilmington for the possibility of a British attack, a move that paid off. In a letter to the Provincial Council dated February 24, 1776, he gave an account of his efforts.

"On Wednesday the 14th instant in the evening the committee received repeated expresses from Brunswick that the *Cruizer* Sloop of War with a Tender had passed that Town, and was on her way up,» Purviance wrote. "We had then, in the general Confusion, no doubt but that the intention was to destroy Wilmington, unless we Should submit to ignominious Terms. This opinion had such an instantaneous effect upon the Inhabitants, who had a number of enemies among them, that they, as if by concert, immediately began to remove their effects. The Town is now almost cleared of all kinds of Goods, and of the women & Children. Since that time I have been reinforced by Captain Clinton's Company of minute Men from Duplin, a minute company from Onslow, and part of the Militia of this last County, under the Command of Col. Cray. I have also had between 50 & 60 Men under Major Quince from Brunswick County, and with all those forces I have been almost constantly employed, in throwing up Breastworks on the principal Streets & Wharfs and the hills above & below the Town, these I shall soon have Compleated, so as to prevent the landing of any men from the Ships—I am making the necessary preparations for fire rafts and shall be able to make use of what swivels are mounted, and of a number of blunderbusses. But I am now assured the Ships never will venture to Wilmington. They too much dread the rifle men to approach us. The *Cruizer* and her tender attempted to go up the North West River, on the West side of the great Island, opposite to Town, but found there was not sufficient Water all the Way, and they returned. It is thought the intention was to favor the Regulators & the highland banditti, whom they expected in Triumph, and to protect the Provision Boats which would Consequently come from Cross Creek for their Army and Ships. After the *Cruizer* Had fallen down below the Island, her people went several times on Shore at Mr Ancrums Plantation, Carried off his live Stock and vegetables, and attempted to seize his Negroes, who fled to the Woods. They have even taken away a parcel of printed Books, Old Clothes &c.

and threatened to burn the house. I therefore thought it necessary to dispatch Major Quince with his detachment to protect the inhabitants on the West Side of the River, as I found that the more necessary, as Col. Davis of Brunswick County informed me yesterday, that there were 50 men from the Ships at the fort, pillaging the Inhabitants. Captn Dupre with only 15 Men arrived at Mr. Ancrum's plantation just as the *Cruizers* Boat was coming ashore the third time, fired upon them, which was returned, and kept up about a minute, when the Sailors pushed off with precipitation. We certainly did some execution, tho' they carried off their Men. The *Cruizer* fired three Guns without effect, since this the ship is gone down below the flats.

On Wednesday last, I rece'd Intelligence that a boats crew from the *Scorpion*, which is also below the flats, went ashore on the East side of the river, and killed some hogs, steer, &c. Captain Clinton's minute-men are gone down and I make no doubt but with prudence they will be able to seize the next party that presumes to come on shore, as they are to remain there three days. I have got in confinement several Tories and suspected Tories. Many of those still here had inrolled themselves with Col. Ashe, in order, as is believed, to skreen themselves from duty; but when the day of trial came they shrunk back. That Gentleman went so far as to inlist an open Enemy who had been disarmed by the Committee and even presumed to require his arms. It was not however thought proper to comply with this preposterous requisition. On the contrary the Committee disarmed every man who would not take the Test of the Congress in form of an Oath. The neutrals, as they call themselves, have been forced greatly against their inclinations to work at the breastworks."[20]

The bustle of military construction in the town resulted in defensive works at Smith Creek, Burnt Mill Run, and Jumping Run to the south (near modern Greenfield Lake). Col. James Moore and half his regiment on the Cape Fear were busy monitoring Martin's communications with the backcountry in and around Cross Creek. Militiamen were required to take the Test Oath to cement their loyalty to the Committee of Safety. The Whigs were ready.[21]

BGen. MacDonald organized his loyalist force into four divisions. Col. Thomas Rutherford commanded the Cumberland County militia, plus some small numbers of men from Bladen County and Cross Creek.

Col. Hugh MacDonald led the Anson County men. Donald McLeod was commander of the former Regulators from around Hillsborough, and Col. James Cotton commanded a body of loyalist militia. Each division was further divided into companies of roughly 30 men each. MacDonald's division had two battalions of 12 companies each, about 720 men. McLeod had between 130-160 men under him, while Cotton's 500 men were divided into 15 companies. Flora MacDonald, whose husband Allan was an officer in the loyalist army, witnessed their preparations and was both unimpressed and worried. She noted that of the roughly 1,600 men gathered at Cross Creek, they had "no arms but 600 old, bad firelocks and about 40 broadswords."[22]

Even so, when the army marched out of Cross Creek on February 18, Flora watched from beneath an old oak tree, waving goodbye to the loyalists from under its canopy. Mounting a white charger, she rode up and down the ranks, doing what she could to cheer and inspire the men. Drums beat, and pipes played beneath swirling banners. Among them, her husband Allan, commissioned a major; her son Alexander, a captain; and her son-in-law. Accounts say she addressed the men before they departed, giving a rousing speech from horseback. "I remember seeing her riding along the line of troops on a large white horse, and encouraging her countrymen to be faithful to the king," one witness told Benson J. Lossing. "Why, she looked like a queen."[23]

The loyalists stopped at Haymount, near the site of the old Fayetteville Arsenal and the current (2024) Museum of the Cape Fear Historical Complex, and camped for the night. Couriers brought word that Col. James Moore with 2,000 men had arrived at Rockfish Creek, six miles from Cross Creek, to block MacDonald's march. The actual number was 650, but they also had artillery and, unlike the Tories, all of them were armed. Moore established a defensive position at the bridge crossing Rockfish Creek. Over the next few days, as many as 60 people brought intelligence into Moore's camp, keeping him apprised of MacDonald's activity. The Continentals were outnumbered by the Highlander army, but Moore's five cannon gave him an advantage in firepower that made him confident. The regulars were augmented by a small number of militiamen and Minutemen. By February 15, the Whigs were in position. The next move was MacDonald's.

On February 18, MacDonald paraded his troops and made a final check of their equipment. Even as the bagpipes swirled and units passed in review under homemade British colors, the brigadier was mindful of his primary mission, to get the men he had gathered to the coast to link with the redcoats coming to the Cape Fear by ship. Engaging in a fight with Whig forces more than a hundred miles from his final destination was not something he wanted to do. Buying time, MacDonald dispatched a messenger under a flag of truce to Col. Moore at Rockfish Creek. In the message, he pretended to give Moore the benefit of the doubt, furnishing him a copy of Gov. Martin's proclamation calling on all loyalists to rally to the king's banner, as well as his own manifesto. The old general observed that Moore must have been unaware of the documents, or else he would not have been engaged in an action such as interfering with the king's forces under order from the lawful authority in the colony. MacDonald's note went on to say that if the Whig troops had not come over to the loyalist side by noon the next day, he would be forced to consider them enemies and take "the necessary steps for the support of royal authority."[24]

Col. Moore's reply was designed to buy time as well. So vague as to almost be no reply at all, Moore said that before he could consider MacDonald's terms he must first consult with the other officers in his command. He assured the loyalist commander that he would have his reply by noon on February 20. When it came, Moore said his officers were unanimous in their support for "the defense of the liberties of mankind." The Continental commander enclosed a copy of the Continental Congress test oath for MacDonald's consideration. Moore's ploy worked better than MacDonald's. In the interim, the Anson County men in the Highlander army decided their best interests lay elsewhere and went home. Meanwhile, Farquard Campbell brought word to MacDonald that Richard Caswell and 600 more men were fast approaching Rockfish Creek. The loyalists decide to fall back to Cross Creek and ford the Cape Fear River at Campbellton. Once across, the general plan was to follow the river to the coast. MacDonald addressed his troops, calling them the instrument by which order would be restored to the king's dominions. He chastised the Anson County men who abandoned the Highlander camp the night before as "base rascals," and challenged the fainthearted among them to decide then and there if they were the king's men or not. Declaring that "their Courage was not Warproof," 20 men from Cotton's regiment lay down their arms and faded into the woods, the cheers and jeers of their former comrades ringing in their ears. That night, the Tories marched out.

Despite the people bringing information on MacDonald's force into Moore's camp, the movement of the Highlanders went unnoticed by the Whigs. Once Moore realized MacDonald had stolen a march on him, he sent dispatches out to other commanders. Col. Richard Caswell was instructed to make his way to Corbett's Ferry on Black River to block the loyalists. Colonels James Thackston and James Martin were ordered to occupy Cross Creek to head off any loyalist retreat. Others were ordered to destroy all bridge crossings between Cross Creek and the coast in order deny MacDonald any route of march except the one the Whigs wanted him to take. Alexander Lillington and John Ashe were detached from Moore's command to reinforce Caswell. If the two bodies of Whig troops were not able to link up, Lillington was ordered to secure the crossing at Moores Creek Bridge. Moore broke camp and made for Elizabethtown. If MacDonald managed to cross the Black River before the Whigs could stop him, Moore and the Continentals would give chase and hopefully be able to engage the Tories from their rear.

With his orders in hand, Richard Caswell made for Corbett's Ferry, with two artillery pieces in tow. "Old Mother Covington" was a 3-pound Dutch cannon, while her "Daughter," was a swivel gun. Both were deployed to cover the approaches to the ferry crossing over the Black River. Details were sent to cover narrow spots along the river on either side of Caswell's position to prevent MacDonald from fording the river someplace else. Moore's orders to destroy any bridges except the one at Moores Creek were only partially carried out. Bridges were luxuries the people of the region were reluctant to part with, so not all of the spans were

"Old Mother Covington" (left) and her swivel gun Daughter (right).

The modern recreation of Moores Creek Bridge in Currie, N.C.

destroyed. Nevertheless, most of the crossings were not strong enough to support the weight of the loyalists' baggage train. A rider was captured who related that Caswell had changed his route of march, prompting MacDonald to move with more caution than his original plan called for.[25]

On February 23, four miles from the Black River, scouts brought news that Caswell had entrenched his men at Corbett's Ferry. Macdonald deployed his men to do battle. Claymore broadswords were collected and reissued to a vanguard under John Campbell who would lead the charge against the Whig militia. Meanwhile, Donald McLeod's cavalry explored four miles further upstream. They came across a black man who told them of a sunken "flat" on the far side of the river that could be raised to provide a means of fording. A rider was quickly sent to inform BGen. MacDonald, while McLeod hired the local man to raise the flat and help build a bridge the loyalists could use. MacDonald, already reluctant to close with the better armed militiamen, considered McLeod's news a lucky break. He halted the planned assault, and pointed his column upriver to find McLeod. Before marching, he detached a body of men to keep Caswell occupied and believing that the Highlander army still intended to cross at the ferry. MacDonald's luck got even better when his men came across two wagons of supplies and 21 steers intended for the Whig force, taking 22 Whig prisoners at the same time. The loyalists camped at James Rogers' sawmill the night of February 25, and McLeod's horsemen rejoined the main body there. By eight in the evening on Monday, February

26, the loyalists were across the Black River and again marching for the coast.

Richard Caswell soon realized MacDonald's ruse and set about moving his men to get ahead of the Highlanders again. At the same time, James Moore was trying to get his Continentals in position to close with the Highlanders. The only way to do so in time would be to load his men aboard small boats and float down the river for about 60 miles. Moore reached Dollison's Landing on the afternoon of February 26, and waited for the rest of his men to catch up before leaving the next morning at first light. During the night, a rider brought word that Caswell had effected a link with Alexander Lillington at Moores Creek Bridge.

Moores Creek is a tributary of the Black River, which itself empties into the Cape Fear River about ten miles above it. Lillington's Minute Men were the first to reach the black creek that snakes through low lying pine forest and cypress bog 22 miles northwest of Wilmington. Lillington immediately recognized what a superb piece of ground it was for a defensive action. The bridge was wide enough to accommodate most wagons. Its span stretched across the tannin-rich water, surrounded on either side by swamp and thick underbrush. At the bridge Moores Creek is 50 feet across in some places, and five feet deep, with a tidal variation of three feet. The only easy way to get across was the bridge itself, made of pine planks laid across three runners that supported them. On the east side, the bridge emptied onto a causeway of 120 yards that climbs up a slight rise. The causeway enters a gentle curve to the left then terminates in a bowl-shaped depression before reaching level ground again. The curve obscures the view of the high ground from the bridge. It was here that Alexander Lillington chose to make a stand.

In a move as old as the Roman Legions, the Minute Men did what infantry have always done when on the defensive, and started digging earthworks on the rise above the depression. The chest-high walls of earth provided good cover for the militia that soon would face down the Highlander army. At either end, Old Mother Covington and her Daughter anchored a line that in the coming hours would be filled with muskets. Richard Caswell arrived a short time later with 800 additional men to bolster Lillington's force. The colonel from New Bern, by virtue of leading

The view of Moores Creek Bridge from the curve in the causeway looking west.

more men, assumed overall command from Lillington and directed more earthworks be built on the west side of the creek.

The loyalists camped at Colvin's Creek, seven miles from Moores Creek Bridge and about three miles from modern Atkinson, on the night of February 26. The Colvin family was absent, away on a visit to relatives, but their servants were still on hand. Upon arrival after a rainy, wet march, an ill Donald MacDonald sought refuge in the house with its fireplace and hot food. MacDonald, according to one who knew him, was "near seventy years of age" when he led the loyalist army on its march to the coast. The younger officers gathered around campfires to hold a war council, which MacDonald did not attend "by reason of his having contracted a cold brought on by sleeping in the damp night air." The general did not want to attack the Americans at Moores Creek, but his subordinates disagreed. These young Highlanders, with fire in their blood and perhaps anxious to live up to their ancestors' distinguished military exploits, were eager to close with the Whigs. They did take the precaution of sending James Hepburn with a message for Col. Caswell, urging him to surrender and join the Crown's forces. Failure to do so would leave MacDonald no choice but "to conquer and subdue you." Caswell refused, as was expected; but Hepburn's real mission was to gather intelligence on the Americans that could be used in formulating battle plans for the next day.

Hepburn met Caswell on the west side of Moores Creek. He noted no artillery, and not many soldiers. He did not realize that almost a thousand men were busy on the other side of the bridge, rolling ammunition cartridges and emplacing their two small cannons. The loyalist did recognize one thing - the Americans were encamped with the black waters of the creek at their backs. If the Highlanders could engage them swiftly, they would be trapped there. Hepburn took Caswell's polite but firm reply and returned to the Tory camp to report what he saw.

James Hepburn was not the only spy out and about that chilly February evening. Felix Kenan, one-time sheriff of Duplin County now enlisted in MacDonald's army, deserted the Highlander encampment and reported to the Whigs that the loyalist war council had decided to attack at dawn. Caswell and Lillington were forewarned of the coming action, and had their men ready to meet it.

The Whig force spent the rest of the day preparing. Most of the men were between ages 17 and 36, with the majority of them between 21 and 27 years old. Virtually all of them were locals who knew the terrain. Their campsite was enclosed within stout earthworks. The side facing the bridge was the strongest, as that was the direction everyone expected the attack to come from. There the earthwork wall was five feet high and seven feet wide, complimented by a ditch two feet deep. Caswell ordered the men on the west bank of the creek to abandon their positions and pull back into the main encampment. They left fires burning to deceive the attacking foe. A trench that Lillington's men began digging close to the bridge was abandoned, too, perhaps because of the wet ground. Drummers and fifers practiced their calls, used to send signals across noisy battlefields. Old Mother Covington and her swivel gun Daughter were assigned to Capt. John Vance, who positioned the two guns so that they could fire on the bridge at the end of the causeway. One last detail was to pull up the planks of the bridge itself and grease the sleepers with soft soap and tallow to make it slippery. Guards were placed to observe the bridge and sound the alarm when the Highlanders tried to cross it. Preparations made, the men spent the evening eating a meal of pork, bacon, and cornmeal. They rolled cartridges, checked their flints, and tidied up any last-minute preparations for the coming battle. Militiaman James Isaac and his friends shook hands and promised one another to defend the bridge or die in the attempt.[26]

The Battle at Moores Creek Bridge
Forces Engaged:
American Forces: Overall Commanding Officer Colonel Richard Caswell (Capt. John Vance - New Berne militia: 800 men; 3lb.- Dutch cannon [Old Mother Covington], swivel gun [Her Daughter]; Colonel Alexander Lillington (Capt. Robert Roman - Wilmington Battalion of Minutemen: 150 men); Lieutenant Colonel William Cray (Onslow and Craven County Militia - 200 men); Lieutenant Colonel Thomas Robeson (Halifax District Militia - 200 men); Lieutenant Colonel Thomas Brown (Bladen Co. Militia - 200 men; Col. James Kenan (Duplin Co. Militia - 200 men); Maj. Joseph Winston (Surry Co. Militia - numbers unknown); Col. John Ashe, Sr. (New Hanover County Militia Volunteer Independent Rangers under Capt. Thomas Wade - 100 men). Historian J.D. Lewis also identified N.C. Continentals who participated at Moores Creek: *1st NC Regiment detachment of seven (7) known companies, led by*: Capt. Thomas Allen (little evidence), Capt. George Lee Davidson (little evidence), Capt. William Davis (boated from Cross Creek), Capt. Henry "Hal" Dixon (possibly), Capt. Alfred Moore (marched from Brunswick), Capt. Robert Rowan (marched 'from Cross Creek), Capt. John Walker (marched from Wilmington). *2nd NC Regiment detachment of two (2) known companies supporting Militia, led by:* Capt. James Armstrong with the New Bern District Minutemen under Col. Caswell, Capt. William Knox with the Guilford County Regiment of Militia under Lt Col. James Martin. Total America forces engaged: 1100 (1 wounded, 1 killed).

Loyalist Forces: Overall Commanding: BG Donald MacDonald. Captain Donald Macleod (2nd in command - Royal Highland Emigrants detachment); NC Provincials: 300 men (Col. Allan MacDonald, Maj. Alexander Stewart); Cumberland Militia: 500 men (Col. Thomas Rutherford); Bladen Co. Militia: Unknown number (Capt. John Leggett, Capt. John Slingsby); Regulator Militia: (Col. Alexander McLeod of Glendale, Capt. James Mews); Highlander Light Horse: 100 men (Capt. John Pyle, Jr.); Regulators: 130 men (Capt. David Jackson, Capt. John Campbell); Anson Highlanders: Unknown number (Capts. Alexander McLeod, Alexander McRae, Murdock Caskill, Samuel Williams, James McDonald, Kingsborough McDonald); Chatham Co. Militia: 130 men (Col. John Pyle, Sr.); Light Horse: Unknown number (Capt. Donald McLeod); Cotton's Corps of the

Moore County Militia: Unknown number (LCol. James Cotton, Capts. John McLeod, Alexander Morrison, Angus McDonald). Total Loyalist Forces engaged: 1800 (30 KIA, 20 WIA, 850 POW)

A lot happened on February 27, 1776. At Wilmington, Captain Francis Parry moved *H.M.S. Cruizer* up to the town and sent ashore an ultimatum that he expected a thousand barrels of flour "to be supplied by six this evening. If His Majesty's ships are in the least annoyed it will be my duty to oppose it." Neither Parry, nor the residents of Wilmington, knew that a momentous battle was soon to come a short distance away, one that would have an outsized impact on the course of the war.[27]

Modern Moores Creek Bridge in the morning fog, presenting an image similar to what the Highlanders saw on February 27, 1776.

At one o'clock in the morning, 800 loyalists marched the six miles to the bridge. It was not an easy march, taking five hours. One man reported that they had to make their way through "a very bad swamp which took us a good deal of time to pass, so that it was within an hour of daylight before we could get to their camp." The creek was swollen thanks to heavy rains over the preceding days. Capt. Donald McLeod took the right wing of the divided force, while Thomas Rutherford and Capt. Alexander McLean took the left. A reconnaissance by McLeod's men discovered that Caswell's positions before the bridge were now abandoned, leading the Highlander officers to believe the Whigs had fled. The new development prompted McLeod and his officers to march their men back to a nearby house (possibly that of James Rogers) to await the return of the other wing and devise a new plan. The loyalists held a war council, where it was decided that a dawn attack was the best maneuver. McLean, unaware that the right wing of their army had withdrawn, continued forward with the left. Darkness, fog-shrouded woods and swamp, no means of communication, and unfamiliarity with the terrain sowed confusion between the two Highlander elements. One loyalist recalled that the "left wing did not know that the right wing had marched back." The loyalist plan was literally confused by the fog of war.

Approaching the bridge, fog rose off the creek and clouded the chilly air in a white mist that obscured everything beyond a few yards in front of them. Mclean and Rutherford entered Caswell's old camp from the left. The 300 Highlanders armed with firelocks were moved to the rear as follow-on troops. Seventy-five handpicked broadswordsmen were in the vanguard as they made their way through the Americans' abandoned camp and down to the bridge, unsure of its exact location. Tradition says the signal to begin the attack was the shouted phrase "Three cheers, the Drum to beat, the Pipers to play." The phrase for rallying was "For King George and broadswords!" The two have often been conflated according to differing accounts. Both conjure the image of kilts swirling as bagpipes rent the morning air in what some have called the last Highland charge in North America. The truth was something different.

McLean's scouting party reached the bridge first. One account said that "Mr. McLean with a party of about 40 men came accidentally to the bridge. He being a stranger and it still being dark, he was challenged by the enemy's sentinels, they observing him sooner than he observed them. He [McLean] answered that he was a friend. The figure on the other side of the creek asked, 'a friend to who?' McLean replied, 'To the King.' Upon making this reply, they squatted down upon their faces to the ground. Mr. McLean, uncertain but they might be some of our own people that had crossed the bridge, challenged them in Gaelic, to which they made no answer, upon which he fired his own piece and ordered his party to fire."

At the house, McLeod heard the musket fire. Not knowing what had happened, he quickly ordered his men to march to where the shots had come from. The gunfire also woke the Whigs behind their earthworks a short distance away. Men rolled out from their blankets to grab muskets and man their positions. In the dim light a sentry raced to report contact with the enemy to Col. Caswell. Across the creek, the Highlanders shouted their war cries and pipes stirred the morning stillness.

Donald McLeod's loyalist Highlanders charge the bridge, only to find it dismantled. (Art courtesy of the National Park Service).

Capt. Donald McLeod charged to the bridge with the handpicked swordsmen in two columns under Capt. Angus (another account says John) Campbell, only to find the spanners gone and the sleepers slick with grease and tallow. What had started as a gallant rush to glory devolved into a humiliating logjam of Highland warriors, as fierce claymore swords were used to try and find purchase on the slippery timbers. After a tense time that for many seemed longer than it actually was, Capt. McLeod had between 50 and 80 swordsmen on the east side of the bridge, including Donald Morrison who carried the loyalist's battle colors. Gathering their strength, they began running down the causeway towards the American positions. In the heat of the moment, it never occurred to the loyalists that the Whigs had built strong defensive positions. Behind them more men tried to make it across the skeleton of the bridge. Bagpipes played Highland military music, and muskets rang out trying to provide some small bit of cover for the brave Scots racing up the causeway.

When McLeod and his men were within 20 or 30 yards of the Whig earthworks, Richard Caswell gave the order to fire. At least one account says Old Mother Covington failed to fire when the match was applied, so Caswell himself fired it by sparking his pistol above the touch hole. Thirteen-year-old Hugh McDonald witnessed the charge. "In our Tory party was a Captain, John Campbell...who commanded Broad-swordsmen," he remembered, "consisting principally of McRae's strong, resolute men, ignorant untutored and untrained to the use of arms, but every one of that company had his broad-sword drawn and marched in front..."

The oncoming Scots disappeared in a wall of gray smoke from the muzzles of Old Mother Covington and her Daughter. Between them, nearly 1,000 muskets belched flame and iron ball to add to the din. One witness described what happened when the Whigs opened fire. "Come on my boys, the day is our own," the witness recalled McLeod shouting, "when he was instantly shot down, and all those on the sleepers coming over were fired upon and shot, falling off into the creek...they attempted three times to come over, but all being killed who came on the sleepers, they did not attempt it a fourth time."

When the smoke cleared, Donald McLeod lay in a tumbled, bloody heap in front of the earthworks. Most of the men following him met similar fates. McLeod's body was riddled with nine musket balls and 24 pieces of swan shot. Two of those balls came from Militiamen Ben Lanier and Abraham Newkirk, friends who fought side by side at the earthworks and clearly hit the Highlander leader. Highlanders caught on the bridge were swept off and into the icy waters of Moores Creek, sinking under the weight of their water-soaked clothes and arms to drown in the dark waters.

The Highlander charge was shattered by a hail of lead delivered by Caswell's militia. (Art courtesy of the National Park Service).

The other men, witnessing what happened to their vanguard, turned and ran. Col. Cotton went into a headlong retreat as soon as the first blast tore the morning air. Thomas Rutherford, said one witness, "ran like a lusty fellow." One loyalist who witnessed the rout said, "the country-born army began to run away and could not be made to stand their ground." The fight had lasted about three minutes.

Richard Harrell was among the militiamen at the earthworks, and witnessed the carnage. Writing in the third person, he recalled, "When they first came in sight, advancing through the open pine woods on the long slope of descending ground, their officers well dressed in gay regimentals, banners and plumes waving in the breeze, and all marching in good order, but with quick step, to the sound of their pibrochs [bagpipes], while the thrilling notes of the bugle were heard in the distance, they made quite a formidable appearance and he felt a good deal of trepidation. He had never before heard the din of war, nor seen an army ready to engage in the work of wholesale destruction. He had never been called to shoot down his fellow men, some of them his neighbors and acquaintances, nor had he ever seen them shot down by scores at a time; and no wonder if his nerves were a little excited. The firing commenced with the small arms, and continued for a round or two; but...he could neither load nor fire with a very steady hand. They had two pieces of artillery, one of which had by some means or other, got the sobriquet of MOTHER COVINGTON and for that or some other reason, was rather a favorite with the men. Not wishing to act cowardly, or be suspect of doing so, he kept trying to do his part, but was all the time wishing most heartily he could hear what Old Mother Covington had to say. At last she let out, and with terrible effect. From that moment, he said, his fear was all gone, and he could load and fire with as much composure, as if he had been shooting squirrels."

When the massed fire of the militia broke the Highlander charge, the rest of their army began to flee. The Whig troops, their blood up in the heat of the action, leaped the earthwork walls to give pursuit. The few loyalists still alive on the east side of the bridge were scrambling to get back across when the militiamen caught up to them. Loyalist Neil Colbreath suddenly found himself in hand to hand combat with a militiaman named Little. Colbreath, fighting for his life, held his own until Little bit him on his lips and leg. The loyalist surrendered and was taken prisoner.

Col. James Moore and his force reached Caswell's camp hours after the battle, but he immediately organized a pursuit of the fleeing loyal-

Pvt. John Grady was the only Patriot soldier killed at Moores Creek, shot as he fired from behind the Whig earthworks. (Art courtesy of the National Park Service).

ists. A rider was dispatched to Wilmington with orders for the Wilmington garrison to march out and join the chase. Likely avenues to the coast were covered by patrols, and all Highlanders and Regulators were to be disarmed regardless of their political allegiances.[28]

An accounting of captured loyalist materials included 350 muskets, 1,500 "excellent" muskets, 150 swords and dirks, two English medicine chests - one of which was valued at £300, 13 wagons and their horses, and $75,000 in gold - £15,000 sterling, a huge sum in those days. The butcher's bill for the loyalists was 30 dead, 20 wounded, and 850 captured. On the bloody field were the bodies of McLeod, Capt. John Campbell, Privates Duncan McCrary, William Stewart, Kenneth Murchison, Laughlin Bethune, Murdock McRae, Alexander Campbell, and John McArthur, all felled on the east side of the bridge. McArthur, Campbell, and McRae were captured and taken to Wilmington. A few others, though wounded, managed to make it back over the bridge to join the retreat. Bethune, Murchison, and William Stewart all later died of their wounds. Private John Grady of Duplin County was the only Whig fatality. Modern evidence suggests Grady was possibly the victim of friendly fire, as accounts say he was shot in the back of the head. One other man, James Foy, was wounded in the wrist. Grady was buried on the battlefield with full military honors. Capt. Love, also of Duplin County, placed his sword on Grady's chest as he was lowered into the earth.

Tradition tells one more story of the fight at Moores Creek Bridge, though its veracity stands on much shakier ground. Mary Slocumb of Duplin County had a bad feeling when her husband, Ezekiel, marched off to join the militia at the bridge. That night she had a nightmare, seeing a body wrapped in Ezekiel's cloak. The next morning she saddled her horse and rode for the bridge, gunfire echoing in the distance doing nothing to calm her fears. She found a terribly wounded man in her husband's cloak and tended him, washing away blood from a gash across the face until she was able to see it was not Ezekiel. Not long after, she found her husband alive but covered in blood from tending to the wounded. Mary Slocumb is commemorated with a monument at Moores Creek National Battlefield in Currie, N.C.[29]

James Martin

BGen. MacDonald did not know of the loyalists defeat until he was captured by Whig militia in his sick bed at Colvin's house. Wagon master Longfield Cox took MacDonald's horse, saddle, pistols, and sword as trophies. Col. James Moore accepted MacDonald's official surrender, then sent him into captivity first at Halifax, then in Philadelphia. A large number of the fugitive soldiers were rounded up at Smith's Ferry on the Cape Fear River near Averasboro (also known as Devo's Ferry). The rest of the Highlander army retreated to Cross Creek, though some skirted the militia patrols trying to round them up and made their way to Fort Johnston to report the defeat to a dismayed Governor Johnston. Others left North Carolina completely, traveling as far as Florida or New York to escape the vengeance of the Americans. Loyalist James Cotton went into hiding for the next six months. Joseph Mercer managed to make it to one of the British warships in the Cape Fear River for refuge. Another, Daniel Ray, hid himself for four years before emerging to join the British when they took Charlestown, S.C. in 1780. The loyalists who did make it back to Cross Creek were crestfallen to find LtCol. James Martin with the Guilford County Militia waiting for them.[30]

Now that they had them, the Whigs were not entirely sure what to do with their prisoners. No formal declaration of war existed yet, nothing that defined a break from Great Britain. The majority of the prisoners were paroled to their own homes, but the ones who were retained in custody, mostly officers, did not enjoy their captivity. At first they were held at the temporary provincial capital of Halifax. Then they were transferred to Philadelphia to be dealt with by the Continental Congress. The prisoners of Moores Creek were "robbed of all our horses and strictly searched for secreted arms powder (gunpowder) or any papers," wrote one. He went on to claim they were fed tainted pork, bad water, and crammed into overcrowded rooms with no beds or necessaries. The prisoners were marched through the Whig encampment to the jeers and epithets of the victorious Americans, delivered to guards who "seemed to feel as little for us as carters commonly do for the unfortunate animals they become masters of."[31]

A great deal of looting took place by both sides in the wake of the battle. In Cross Creek, Scottish merchants suffered through their association with their kinsmen who had marched out a week earlier with MacDonald, and many were painted with the same brush of Toryism whether they were loyalists or not. The victorious Whig militia in Cross Creek decided each man was entitled to one bushel of Tory salt as long as they could transport it home themselves. Some of the merchants who had supplied the loyalist army were jailed at Halifax too, until released soon after to return to their mercantile pursuits. Some Whigs passing through the Moravian towns on their way back home after the battle were noted by residents to be wearing "Scottish clothe." The Whigs were not the only ones taking advantage of the social chaos that war brings to help themselves to their neighbors' belongings. The Regulators who had deserted MacDonald's army before the battle broke into smaller bands to make their way home. One such band had as many as 180 people. They were not shy about raiding the farms and homes of Whigs whose property was on their route into the backcountry. The retaliation of the Whigs was swift and in many cases final. When the militiamen of the Upper Yadkin Valley got home and learned of the looting, they immediately scoured the surrounding Wake County countryside to find several Tories in their wooded hiding places. The militia promptly hanged them.

Josiah Martin continued to maintain that North Carolina was ripe for a return to Crown rule, though he conceded that a future attempt at it might be better done by linking regulars and loyalists somewhere in the interior. Though Martin kept the threat of *Cruizer*'s guns in his tool box to try and coerce cooperation from the people of the Cape Fear, the threat was much diluted by the outcome of the Moores Creek fight and the people of Wilmington calling his bluff when they tried to extort supplies from the town earlier. Just to be safe, though, Col. Moore moved his regiment of Continentals into Wilmington before dismissing the militia and Minutemen to return to their homes.

In November 1776, the state passed an act confiscating loyalist property. Five months later, in April 1777, another new law ordered the death penalty for certain enumerated crimes against the state by loyalists. The writing was on the wall for many loyalists, and many of them whose allegiance to King George III made them targets of the new Whig authorities sailed for friendlier ports like England or Nova Scotia. The outcome of the battle at a little creek in the woods 20 miles north of the port at Wilmington cost them dearly. One other thing the clash at Moores Creek did was ease the fear of a slave rebellion instigated by the British. One Cape Fear planter observed that, ''The Negroes at Cape Fear were never known to behave so well as they have lately.''

In the North, where the war effort was going badly, Moores Creek was hailed as a great victory. It was the first decisive victory by American arms against British forces at least in the South, if not the entire country. To listen to people from above the Chesapeake, North Carolina's generals and colonels were all Caesars, more than equal to the task of vanquishing the hated redcoats from American shores. New Englander Ezra Stiles recorded in his diary that, "The Colonels *Moore, Martin, Caswell, Polk, Thockston, Lillington & Long,* have great Merit; any one of these Gent. in this Country would be an over match for a Howe, Burgoyne, or a Clinton. Their knowledge of the Country and necessary Modes of Attack would frustrate any Attempt fallen upon by the Characters last mentioned. The Whole Province in general consider Regulars in the Woods an easy Conquest."[32]

Moores Creek illustrated difficulties that would come to characterize the Revolutionary War in North Carolina that persisted until the end. Campaigning in the southern provinces was hard and continued to be so. The British reliance on loyalists to bolster their army and be dependable partners in the support of King George III was also problematic. The crucial role of militia in governing and fighting in the southern colonies was often underappreciated. The vicious civil war between Whigs and Tories that developed among Southern neighbors caused rifts and scars that continued for years after the war actually ended. Moores Creek prompted loyalists to lay low in the Carolinas for the next four years, until the British took Charlestown in 1780; but it also proved to war planners in London that provincial forces could be a potent force multiplier in campaigns to come.[33]

Even after the British finally left the Cape Fear in the spring, the Whigs were never able to completely stamp out loyalist sentiments in and around Wilmington. Much of that loyalty was found among North Carolinians who had been born elsewhere then migrated to the colony, like the Highland Scots. Support for the Church of England (the Anglican Church in America), being involved with the mercantile trade with England, and/or having a job working for the royal government were all factors that impacted one's willingness to break from Great Britain. For instance, in 1779 North Carolina passed a Confiscation Act to take the property of those still in the colony who were active loyalists. Out of a list of 68 men, 45 were merchants whose Tory proclivities made them targets of sequestration. In 1777, John Ashe wrote to Gov. Richard Caswell that so many Wilmington residents were "disaffected" that he had ordered out the militia to keep an eye on them. William Hooper echoed the sentiment in 1778, when he observed that Wilmington loyalists were making "observations... painful to men who love our cause." Even as late as 1780, 20 men still had not taken the oath of allegiance to the state.[34]

The Moores Creek victory led to North Carolina instructing its delegates to the Continental Congress "to concur with the delegates of the other colonies in declaring "Independency..." As early as April 5, Samuel Johnston had suggested this, writing from Halifax that "all our people here are up for Independence." For the Whigs, Moores Creek boosted their belief in their ability to stand and fight against the world's most accomplished military. That would dampen the recruitment of men to join the Continental Line units raised in North Carolina, with consequences to be paid a few years down the road. Nevertheless, Joseph Hewes, who that summer joined William Hooper and John Penn in signing the Declaration of Independence that officially proclaimed the American break from Great Britain, wrote of their new confidence.

"All accounts from England seem to agree that we shall have a dreadfull storm bursting on our heads thro all America in the Spring," he wrote. "We must not shrink from it; we ought not to shew any simptoms of fear; the nearer it approaches and the greater the sound the more fortitude and calm, steady firmness we ought to possess...Altho the storm thickens I feel myself quite composed. I have furnished myself with a good musket & Bayonet, and when I can no longer be usefull in Council I hope I shall be willing to take the field."[35]

LtGen. Charles Lord Cornwallis (above), and Admiral Sir Peter Parker (below)

The Continental Congress had been warning since January 1776 that the British were planning an invasion of the Carolinas and Virginia, but people in North Carolina seemed to dismiss it. Even after the fight at Moores Creek Bridge, there did not seem to be an urgency to be ready in the face of a possible tidal wave of redcoats that could come into the river at any time. Joseph Hewes' "dreadfull storm," loomed large in his mind. Rumors of possible peace talks led him to ask what kind of terms would the Americans be able to get, when the British would be negotiating with the weight of a "...mighty Fleet & Army" at their backs. "[W]hat are we to expect from the mouth of a Cannon or the point of a Bayonet?" he asked. Hewes' rhetorical question was resolved, at least in his own mind. He determined that "nothing is left but to fight it out." Fighting against the greatest military power on Earth was something that North Carolina (and the entire country) was woefully unprepared to do.[36]

The British fleet that Josiah Martin had been expecting in January finally dropped anchor in the Cape Fear River on March 12, 1776. Their tardiness was due in part to bureaucratic red tape slowing things down, and in part to bad weather. It took eight months from the time Martin's plan was approved to the day LtGen. Cornwallis and his seven regiments of redcoat regulars sailed from Cork, Ireland aboard Royal Navy transports under the command of Admiral Sir Peter Parker. General Sir Henry Clinton was selected for overall command of the combined British forces once everyone linked up at Cape Fear. Now Clinton, aboard *H.M.S. Mercury*, waited with 20 British warships and transports for the arrival of Cornwallis and his men.[37]

Loyalist activity waned in the Cape Fear as those sympathetic to the king kept a low profile in the immediate aftermath of Moores Creek, but both sides still conducted operations. Militia units were guarding key places in the region. Camps were manned at Swan's Point, Captain's Mills, Brunswick Town, Orton Mill, and Lockwood's Folly. At the same time, Wilmington recruiters were trying to man up the third, fourth, and fifth regiments of the North Carolina Continental Line. Quartermasters were busy stockpiling arms, ammunition, and the sundry other things needed to raise and supply an army. Ralph Millar, who had been ordered to manufacture gunpowder by the Wilmington Committee of Safety the previous December, continued to do so. Gunsmith Timothy Bloodworth was ordered to continue making weapons to arm the

Gen. Sir Henry Clinton

new American regulars and militias. Barracks were built to house several thousand men, including one on modern Front Street in Wilmington between Orange and Ann Streets. A new magazine was built to store several tons of powder and shot, barrels of pork, beef, flour, and corn. It still was not enough. One officer observed that the new regiments were "badly Armed and many of the soldiers without Arms." That was concerning, because a letter aboard a captured British packet ship in the Chesapeake alerted the Whigs that the British were on their way.[38]

Days before the British fleet under Clinton arrived, Capt. Francis Parry of *H.M.S. Cruizer* decided to harass the men of Capt. Alfred Moore's company of the First Regiment of the N.C. Continental Line and a handful of men from the Brunswick County Militia occupying Fort Johnston. Parry brought *Cruizer* abreast of the fort, a mere 200 yards away, and used his cannons and swivel guns to fire round and grape shot at the Americans whenever they exposed themselves. The rebel troops were using the remains of the burned fort to deliver harassing fire on the British. On March 10, Parry sent a landing party of one officer and 11 men to destroy the fort, but musket fire from Moore's Continentals drove them off. Two days later, Clinton's redcoats arrived.[39]

Clinton's fleet looked more dangerous than it actually was. Of the ships anchored between Smith Island, Oak Island, and Fort Johnston, roughly a dozen of them were vessels captured as prizes on the trip south from New England. Whig spies estimated that Clinton's force comprised somewhere between 400 and 700 men. The general met with Gov. Martin and learned of the loyalist defeat at Moores Creek. With Cornwallis' men still enroute, Clinton decided against landing his men on the mainland. The presence of so many rebel troops made it too dangerous given the number of men he had. Instead, he ordered them landed on Smith Island and Battery Islands. His reasons were two-fold. Clinton knew the ultimate objective of the British force was Charlestown, so he took the opportunity to train his men in the house to house fighting he expected to encounter there; he also realized that after a long voyage, his men needed to feel solid ground under their feet again.[40]

Gen. Charles Lee

Gen. Charles Lee took command of the Southern Department by order of the Continental Congress, arriving at Williamsburg, Virginia on March 26, 1776. At the same time that Lee was elevated to command of the American war effort in the Southern states, six other officers were promoted to the rank of brigadier general, James Moore and Robert Howe among them. Robert Howe was one of two newly minted generals ordered to take command of Continental troops in Virginia, while Moore was given command of North Carolina.

Brigadier General James Moore arrived in Wilmington wearing the pink ribbon denoting his new rank. His first priority was preparing the Lower Cape Fear for an imminent British invasion. Moore deployed the 1,847 men at his disposal at key locations between Eagles Island and the mouth of the river, and ordered the fortification of Wilmington, to include two batteries of artillery that were used to sink hulks in the river to thwart any British effort to assault the town by water. Additionally, noncombatants were evacuated from Wilmington to protect them from the looming British attack.

While Moore fortified the state's largest town on the Cape Fear River, Richard Caswell was on the march with an additional 600 men from Craven County. According to Moore's estimate, Clinton had "no less than 7,000 men," so he was desperate to get as many troops as he could. He was certain the redcoats would land and march inland and that he would have too few men to counter them, they "being at this season engaged in the farming business." All available militia were ordered to Wilmington to serve under the command of John Ashe to reinforce Moore's Continentals. Lacking any real artillery, there was little BGen.

Col. Richard Caswell

Moore could do to take the fight to the British, so he confined himself to defensive and retaliatory actions. But with the arrival of Ashe's militia, the Whigs deployed on the Cape Fear were a formidable force. At no other time in the war would so many North Carolina men be gathered under arms together at the same time.[41]

It was humiliating to Capt. John Abraham Collet when the rebels burned his home and destroyed his command in the summer of 1775. Collet left the Cape Fear then, but he returned aboard the armed vessel *H.M.S. General Gage*. Clinton dispatched troops to help Capt. Collet, who one Whig described as a "pert audacious little scoundrel," exact a measure of revenge for the destruction of Fort Johnston. Raiding parties landed to burn Bellfont, the home of Col. William Dry at Brunswick Town, and

William Hooper's new home three miles below Wilmington. Dry, who had been a member of Gov. Martin's council, had his property destroyed "for no other crime than being a friend to his country." Hooper remarked, "That hopeful Youth made a Bonfire of a country house of mine...I suffered little more than the mortification of having given Martin an opportunity to triumph at my expense." Another party landed on Smith Island to forage for livestock to feed the navy's messes. Cattle ranged free on the island, owned by the descendants of Landgrave Thomas Smith, its first owner.[42]

On March 29, Captains Thomas Reid and Walter Cunningham marched into Cross Creek with 100 men they had raised for MacDonald's army, only to learn that the loyalists had been handed a definitive defeat at Moores Creek a month before. Reid, Cunningham, and 14 of the men resolved to continue on to the Cape Fear to offer what services they could to the king's representatives there. While at Cross Creek, someone informed the loyalists that Whig militia from Tryon County under Col. William Graham were laid up at Cochrane's Mill as they made their way back home from the Moores Creek campaign. Graham and his men were exhausted from the march and thought there were no loyalists about after the victory at the creek. In a security lapse, the Tryon men posted no sentries. Capt. Reid boldly marched up to the door of the mill and made out that he commanded many more men than the 14 he actually had, convincing Graham to surrender. The loyalists disarmed the Whigs and sent them off, then resumed their march to the coast, boarding a British warship some days later.[43]

The first page of the Halifax Resolves

Two months after the rout at Moores Creek, the repercussions were still influencing events in North Carolina. On April 4 the Fourth Provincial Congress met at Halifax and adopted the Halifax Resolves eight days after that. The resolves instructed North Carolina's delegates in the Continental

Congress to vote for independence, declaring "That the delegates for this Colony in the Continental Congress be impowered to concur with the delegates of the other Colonies in declaring lndependency." Meanwhile, British shells crashed into Brunswick Town on April 6, as warships including *H.M.S. Cruizer* sailed up and down the river looking for loyalist survivors of Moores Creek and any escaped slaves, petulantly taking shots at anyone else who might show themselves.[44]

Clinton, annoyed at the incessant sniping coming from Fort Johnston, ordered the fort destroyed. Capt. Francis Parry had tried to use his *Cruizer* to eliminate the American snipers several weeks earlier with no success. Clinton resolved to do better. Between May 1-3, 1776, ships of the Royal Navy again moved close in and peppered the fort with shot as a landing party went ashore to destroy the fort's usefulness as a sniper's position. It did little good. American riflemen continued to fill the air above the redcoats' heads with lead balls. Even after moving 200 yards away from the fort, five shots hit the armed transport *H.M.S. Sovereign*. Some shots missed their mark on the *Sovereign*, but hit men aboard the transport *Glasgow Packet* behind her. The *Glasgow Packet* suffered two men killed and two more wounded. *H.M.S. Cruizer* and the *Sovereign* returned fire with their cannon, but no American casualties were recorded.

Ten companies of redcoats went ashore near Fort Johnston on May 2 to eliminate the rebel snipers but they were gone, the only sign they had been there the tracks of their wagons left in the sandy soil. The British searched across four miles trying to locate them with no luck, but when the sun rose on May 3, the snipers were back again. *H.M.S. Cruizer* fired on them with her guns, and that seemed to run them off for the time being.

The British moved another 200 yards further off from the fort, but the Americans continued to snipe at them from Johnston's remains. One British report said there were "between fifty and sixty of the Rebels well-armed, and draped in caps and hunting frocks" who were doing the shooting. The distances involved meant the rebels were not doing too much damage, but it was annoying nonetheless. The schooner *St. Lawrence* joined the *Cruizer* and *Sovereign* in returning fire, but her guns were no more successful than those of the other two British vessels.[45]

Aboard Sir Peter Parker's ships sailing from Cork, it had been two months of dreadful weather that started five days after leaving Ireland and continuing for most of the way across the Atlantic. When the first ships limped into the Cape Fear River on April 18, everyone was grateful to escape the tossing seas. The rest of the 14 ships in the flotilla did not arrive in southeastern North Carolina until May 3, but at long last the entire British expedition was reunited. Two days later, aboard the sloop of war *Pallas*, MGen. Sir Henry Clinton issued a proclamation declaring North Carolina in rebellion against King George III and his government.

    Cornelius Harnett and Robert Howe were both high on the British most wanted list, and one of the landing parties dispatched by Clinton sought to capture or at least inconvenience the new brigadier general leading the rebel war effort in Virginia. On May 7, about 600 redcoats led by escaped slaves acting as guides made an attack on Howe's Kendal Plantation home (now part of Military Ocean Terminal Sunny Point) in Brunswick County. The soldiers managed to get away with £1,500 worth of valuables, but the quick response of American troops prevented them from burning the house down.

    With the arrival of Cornwallis' regiments, Clinton began deploying his men. Clinton sent more men to Fort Johnston and Smith Island on May 15, when soldiers from the British 15th, 28th, 33rd, 37th, and 54th regiments went ashore. American forces were just two miles away to keep an eye on British activity, though most of the rebel troops were at Wilmington. The redcoats "encamped near a demolished post opposite to our shipping," wrote one soldier sent to the fort. Others went to Smith Island to build an earthen encampment that became Fort George, giving the British a commanding position at the mouth of the Cape Fear River. Among them was the young Francis Lord Rawdon, who complained of the "miserable thin-topped pine, which springs from white sand."

    Using the fort as a base of operations, Clinton determined to give the men, who had been cooped up aboard ships for weeks, something to do to work off some of their excess energy. Tasked for the job were four battalions of foot and two companies of light infantry. MGen. Clinton himself joined Cornwallis and led them on a raid against the Brunswick base camp of the Americans.

The Skirmish at Orton Mill and Kendal Plantation
The Raid Against Brunswick Town
Forces Engaged:
American Forces: Maj. William Davis (1st NC Regt: 90 men, 2 swivel

guns). Outcome: 5 POW.
British Forces: MGen. Sir Henry Clinton CO, British Regulars); MGen. Charles Lord Cornwallis, 33rd Regt. of Foot; LtCol. Robert Abercromby, 37th Regt. of Foot, Capt. Primrose Kennedy, 44th Regt. of Foot - Light Infantry (3 Battalions). Outcome: 2 KIA, several WIA, 1 POW.

On May 16, the sloop of war *H.M.S. Falcon* took its turn as the target of American snipers. While British seamen aboard the *Falcon* were dodging American riflemen, LtGen. Cornwallis was planning a mission against Brunswick Town "in the most secret manner imaginable and left in the dead of the night." The men chosen for the attack were 900 redcoat regulars of Cornwallis' 33rd, 37th, and 44th Regiments. Coming ashore at Robert Howe's Kendal Plantation between 2am and 3am on May 17, their muffled oars were not enough to mask the noise of so many troops disembarking onto the beach. British scouts found the guard posted at the bridge crossing near the mill, located on Orton Pond, a short distance from the Orton Plantation house built by Roger Moore in 1726. Alerted to the incursion, militia sentries shot down one British soldier, Private George McIntosh, after giving the alarm. With surprise gone, Clinton halted to form up his men, ordering them to fix bayonets.

Orton Plantation house in 1890.

As drums beat a tattoo calling the militia to arms, Major William Davis of the First Regiment of the N.C. Continental Line, took advantage of the British pause to order his 90 men to retire from their camp at Brunswick Town, carrying most of their baggage and two swivel guns with them. The redcoats did not pursue the retreating Americans, but did linger long enough to burn the mill and several homes in Brunswick.

Cornwallis and Clinton discovered Brunswick had long since been abandoned save for its use by the rebels as a base camp. The British burned Bellfont, the former home of two royal governors, then owned by William Dry, and sacked the rest of the Cape Fear's first port of entry. Brunswick Town would never recover. Withdrawing back to their boats, the British plundered the homes of Cape Fear residents on the way. The redcoats sacked and burned Robert Howe's home, apparently treating several women in residence so badly that Cornwallis and Clinton later issued a formal apology for their men's behavior, and compensated them for damages done. "A few Women, who lived in the House, were treated with great Barbarity," one account relates, "one of which was Shot through the Hips, another stabbed with a Bayonet, and a third knocked down with the Butt of a musket." The redcoat raiders suffered two killed and several wounded in the action. A sergeant of the 33rd was captured by the Whigs. The Americans had five men taken prisoner.

As May progressed, MGen. Clinton was deciding what his next move should be. British troops were almost all consolidated within the confines of Fort Johnston, where their diet consisted of what one redcoat called rice and "cabbage trees." When darkness fell, the British set pine trees on fire as torches to illuminate the area around the fort and help keep lurking Americans at arm's length. The rebels continued to harass the British clustered near the mouth of the river. On the night of May 20, the Americans sent a fire raft downriver in hopes of setting the transport *Glasgow Packet* alight. The British redirected the raft before it came in contact with the transport, letting it burn itself out in a nearby marsh without causing any damage.

Two days later, American horsemen approached the British encampment at Fort Johnston, but were turned back by a company of redcoat light infantry who surprised them. No one was harmed on either side. American rebels were not the only thing British soldiers had to contend with. The weather was often as much an enemy to Clinton's forces as Whig marksmen. On May 23, British surgeon Dr. Forster described a fearful storm that crashed down on the redcoats and provided cover for an attack by the Americans.

It was "a Thunder Storm by much the most dreadful one I ever saw in my Life," he said, "it terminated in a most violent storm of Rain and Wind, several Tents were thrown down and others blown some distance from the spot where they were pitched and many of the highest Trees shiver'd to threads by Lightning and others torn up by the roots by the violence of the Wind, it was a most shocking night to pass in Camp."

While the storm was raging, three Whigs crept up to the British sentry on duty, Private James Wilcox, and fired on him. Wilcox, though wounded in the hand, returned fire and killed one of his assailants. As Wilcox sounded the alarm, the other two Americans left their companion where he fell and fled the scene.

Sniping from the shadowy woods lining the Cape Fear continued for the rest of the month. On May 24 and 27, the armed schooner *St. Lawrence* returned fire with her guns against the hidden Whigs whose well-aimed shots were an annoyance and made moving on the river a gamble. The British crews could find no evidence that they hit anyone. By the end of the month, Clinton decided there was nothing more to be accomplished at Cape Fear. He recalled all of his deployed troops and the nearly 70 ships of the combined British force set sail for Charlestown. With him went Josiah Martin, North Carolina's last royal governor.

The British left behind a small garrison of about 30 men to man Fort George, and three ships to provide support. Not long after the British sailed for Charlestown, 15 empty troop transports joined the three ships already on station at Cape Fear. The tiny garrison manning the redoubt was not much of a threat, having only a dozen muskets between them, but it was hoped the guns of the three warships in the river channel off Smith Island would make up the difference. That hope would be put to the test before the year was out.

Clinton's decision was easy to make. Despite rumors bandied about the region regarding the true aim of the British, the truth is that the actions conducted by the redcoats on the Cape Fear were of little consequence. Sending raiding parties up and down the river only served to keep the men busy while the major general decided what to do next. After the defeat at Moores Creek eliminated a loyalist army from the equation, Clinton dismissed thoughts of beginning a serious land campaign. It was getting late in the season, and the British had an aversion to campaigning in the heat of Southern summers. One regiment of British regulars, the 46th, was already a casualty of an illness that decimated its ranks. With all of that in mind, Clinton seemed inclined to sail north, to the Chesapeake, but Admiral Sir Peter Parker remained fixated on Charlestown.

With Royal Governor William Campbell of South Carolina lobbying for the British to make an attack on Charlestown to wrest it away from rebel control, a sloop was sent to reconnoiter the port 185 miles south of Cape Fear. The British scout found rebels hard at work constructing a palmetto log fortification on Sullivan's Island at the mouth of the harbor. It seemed there would be little difficulty sailing past the incomplete fort to shell the city and land troops if needed. On May 30, 1776, the British fleet on the Cape Fear weighed anchor and turned their rudders south.

When the British departed Cape Fear, they carried more than just redcoats and jack tars with them. A goodly number of escaped slaves from area plantations joined up with the British in return for freedom after their service was complete. *H.M.S. Scorpion* alone carried 36 blacks with them when they left, a dozen of them women. Fifteen of them - including one woman - joined the Royal Navy.

Thomas Burke

Rumors of war were rampant in North Carolina in the spring of 1776. Gen. Charles Lee, new commander of the Southern Department, was urged to make haste in traveling into the Carolinas to be ready when the British hammer fell. Robert Howe picked up information from deserters that all the British were waiting for was a supply of bombs before they sailed up the Cape Fear and reduced the town of Wilmington to smoking rubble. Thomas Burke, in Halifax, reported hearsay that said the British had landed redcoats at Little River, 30 miles south of Cape Fear, with the intent of meeting Highlanders and Regulators at Lake Waccamaw. Burke urged true patriots to do "every thing [that] may be expected from our people which a generous warmth and active enterprising disposition and an invincible love of liberty can impel men to perform." Yet Lee showed no urgency, remaining in Virginia. He assured impatient Carolinians that as soon as his "important" business was settled, he would

Peter Muhlenberg

venture south, "both for the public service, and my own gratification in making the acquaintance of Mr. Howe."

While Lee dallied, the British soon had about 70 ships at anchor in the Cape Fear. Suddenly Lee being in North Carolina had a new urgency. The general convinced the Virginia Assembly to send aid to their sister colony to the south to complement the battalion of riflemen he had already ordered to Halifax. Lee himself joined them there by May 19. Traveling by way of Tarboro and New Bern, Lee arrived in Wilmington on June 1, 1776, just a day after the British had sailed. Locals told Lee that the British had set their eyes on Charlestown, but he was not convinced. Nevertheless, he ordered Continentals under Col. Peter Muhlenberg and detachments from the North Carolina regiments to the South Carolina port city. Confident that he was correct that Clinton was not going to Charlestown, Lee sent a messenger telling the Virginia regiment on the way to bolster the Carolinians to stand down and return to their own province.

The North Carolinians and Virginia Continentals who did make it to Charlestown were held in reserve, most of the North Carolinians positioned on the south side of the harbor at Fort Johnston on James Island. Another 200 were combined with an equal number of Virginians and stationed at Haddrell's Point, a mile west of Fort Sullivan. South Carolina militia were also there.

The British attempt at taking Charlestown failed miserably, and caused the king's ministers to re-evaluate their plan for the South. When the shooting was done at Fort Sullivan, Whig control of North and South Carolina was stronger than ever. But the loyalist sentiment in the Carolinas was still strong, if more subdued than before Moores Creek and Charlestown. It would rise again. In the meantime, the war did not stop.

The summer of 1776 saw the Council of Safety beset by a number of concerns, none of which got better with time. Military supplies were still difficult to get, making the raising of Continental Line units problematic. The Toryism of the Carolina backcountry and the mercantile class was still strong. Finally, the Cherokees were taking advantage of the distraction offered by war with Great Britain to create trouble in the western part of the colony. The trouble could be traced back in large measure to the presence of British traders among the tribe, who used their positions to instigate things. By July 1776, the tribes were attacking frontier settlements in North Carolina and Virginia. This compelled the committee to launch four different expeditions against the Cherokee to quieten things in the west.

In June, the pressure was building for those with loyalist sympathies to either join the Whigs in the cause of independence, or to leave Wilmington altogether. Isaac DuBois owned a store on Market Street, plus mills, wharves, and a large bakehouse in Wilmington. His loyalty to King George III made him a marked man in the eyes of the Whigs, who ordered "Mrs. Jean DuBois and Mrs. McNeill and their Families remove from the Town of Wilmington" and remain at least 12 miles from it. DuBois lost all of his property, which was put to use in the service of the Americans.

For Robert Howe, the time from the summer of 1776 until the end of 1778 was occupied to a large degree with trying to stop British raids coming from Florida. Small bands of British regulars, Indians, and Tories would sneak across the border into Georgia, wreak havoc, then retreat to the safety of British outposts in Florida before the Americans could catch them. Howe had too few troops to make a real effort at ending the raids, and he had even less when in February 1777 James Moore and his North Carolina Continentals were ordered to strengthen George Washington's army in the North. Moore's departure was held up for a bit after a large raid led BGen. Howe to believe something was afoot. He kept Moore and his men until he was sure the threat was past.

The veterans of Moores Creek received a bonus of an extra salt ration in July, after the Committee of Safety ordered it distributed. Salt was very much essential in the days before refrigeration, and historically was used as a bartering mainstay. Several weeks later, the committee issued orders for a new distribution to the Moores Creek veterans, this time to be sold "to the Whigs, who bore arms on the late Expedition against the Tories at Moores Creek, at ten Shillings per Bushel, not selling more than half a Bushel to each man." The veterans were likely glad to have it, because by September salt was in short supply. The Committee of Safety tried to get more from the West Indies as North Carolinians became increasingly desperate to find it, salt being a key ingredient in the meat curing that took place in the fall. That desperation sometimes translated into ugly actions. The Committee wrote its congressional delegates in Philadelphia that "...a certain James Love, of Duplin County, aided with a party of armed men, came to the House of Samuel Portevent, of New Hanover County, and violently broke open an outhouse, and took from thence

Mutiny among Continental Line regiments was rare but did happen, at Wilmington and among Connecticut Continental Line soldiers as depicted in this painting.

a Quantity of salt." The report by the Council of State blamed the incident on the men's eagerness to get into the fight against the British, "... and not from any dislike or Aversion to the Services of their Country." Within ten days a committee formed to address the salt problem ordered that no salted meat be exported from the state. Not long after, the governor "...issue[d] a proclamation forbidding all riots, routs and unlawful assembling of the inhabitants of the State on any pretense whatever, and to assure them that Congress have taken the most effectual measures to procure a sufficient quantity of salt for the inhabitants."

Salt was produced by using wind-driven pumps to feed salt water into clay-bottomed, wood-sided vats or ponds. Here the sand and other debris was sifted out as the clean water flowed into ever smaller tanks. As the water evaporated, salt fell to the bottom of the last tanks. The operation only worked on sunny days, and not many men had the foresight to make the investment in tanks and windmills to produce the commodity. For them, it was easier to just import salt from the West Indies in trade for homegrown things like tobacco, foodstuffs, barrel staves, and lumber.

No amount of salt could ease the restlessness of the Continental Line units stationed at Wilmington during that hot summer. On July 14, 1776 the simmering dissatisfaction burst forth in the form of what was called an "unhappy Mutiny" that required Brigadier General John Ashe to call out the militia to quell it before it could spread.

Unimpressed with the fighting zeal of Gen. Charles Lee, the Continental Congress recalled him in September 1776 and replaced him with Robert Howe as commander of the Southern Department. While Lee had been in command, he allowed North Carolina Continentals to change regiments to those of Virginia units offering better bonuses. By the time Lee was recalled and ordered to help Washington repel an invasion of New York, Robert Howe was left with a skeletal core of an army, thanks to Lee allowing men to go to the highest bidder, and to a sickness that brought low many of the men he did still have. On October 20, 1777, Howe received a bit of sweetness to go with the sour, when he was promoted to Major General. He would be the only North Carolinian to reach that rank.

As Lee was packing his bags to leave the South, Continentals on the Cape Fear were planning what would be one of America's first amphibious assaults. Recognizing that when Clinton's fleet left in May the force left behind to man Fort George was woefully inadequate to the job, Col. Thomas Polk of the Fourth Regiment of the North Carolina Continental Line devised a plan to take Smith Island back by eliminating the redcoats there.

The Battle of Fort George, September 6-7, 1776
Forces Engaged:
American Forces: Col. Thomas Polk, 4th NC Continentals (150 men), artillery: Two 3lb.-cannons. Outcome: 1 KIA, 1 WIA.
British Forces: Capt. John Linzee (H.M.S. sloop of war *Falcon*), Capt. Francis Parry (H.M.S. sloop of war *Cruizer*), Lt. Dickerson (H.M.S. sloop *Defiance*), Fort George garrison (30 men). Outcome: 5 POW.

BGen. Robert Howe had stationed Col. Thomas Polk and his Fourth Regiment at Fort Johnston as spies to watch the diminished British force still on the Cape Fear at Smith Island and in the river nearby it. Observation and a little snooping exposed to Polk just how weak the redoubt named after King George III really was. Polk, with Howe's blessing, decided to capture it.

On the night of September 6, 150 men led by Polk loaded into boats and set out for the island at the mouth of the Cape Fear River. Muffled oars kept their approach silent, and the Americans beached their boats in Buzzard's Bay on the north side of Smith Island without incident. Once ashore, they threaded through the woods with Polk in the lead. Before any-

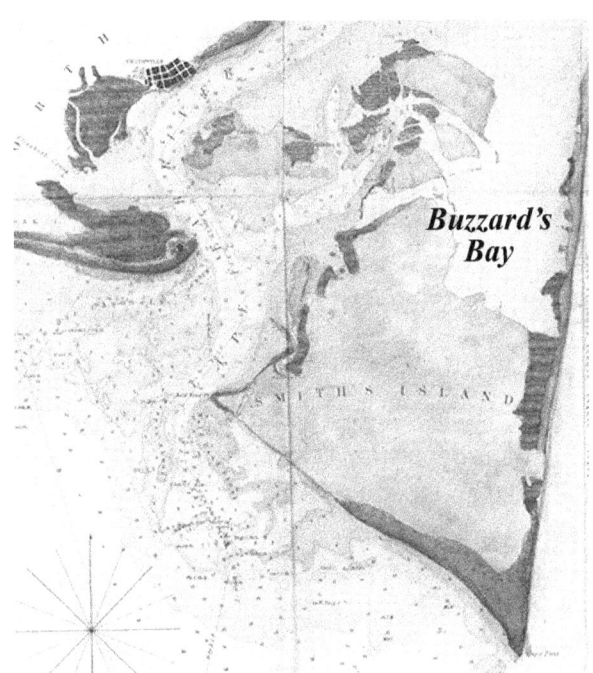

Col. Thomas Polk led soldiers of the Fourth Regiment of the N.C. Continental Line by boat in one of the first amphibious assaults conducted by Americans. They landed at Buzzard's Bay on the north side of Smith Island (modern Bald Head).

one realized it, they stumbled across five British seamen from the *H.M.S. Cruizer*. The Continentals managed to capture them, but not before the alarm was sounded.

The remaining 25 redcoats that made up the Fort George garrison quickly took cover behind its earthen walls and put their 12 muskets to use. Hearing the gunshots, *H.M.S. Falcon* fired her 6-pounders into the woods hoping to make the Americans keep their heads down until a relief force could reach them from the ships in the river. Polk's Continentals kept the ship at a distance with return fire from their own 3-pounders. The shots from the sloop of war drew first blood, killing one Continental and wounding another. Given they had lost the element of surprise, and that the ships firing in aid of the fort's garrison outclassed the Americans' two 3-pounder field pieces, Polk made the decision to abandon the attack and withdraw.

The Americans retraced their steps back to the beach to retrieve their boats. In the river, *H.M.S. Cruizer* loaded four 3-pound cannons into the sloop *Defiance*. Capt. Parry of the *Cruizer* and Lt. Dickerson commanding the *Defiance* hoped to cut off Polk's retreat back across the river and marshes. Polk loaded his men into the boats, pausing only long enough to torch a British cutter on the beach to prevent pursuit by the Fort George garrison. The Americans made their escape relatively unscathed, but were also unsuccessful in their attempt to erase the British presence on Smith Island.

One month later, on October 8, the last British warships departed the Cape Fear, leaving three burned out vessels behind. One of them was *H.M.S. Cruizer*, whose long duty at Cape Fear had left her so badly deteriorated that she was deemed unfit for further service and set alight to prevent her from being scavenged by the rebels left behind. Samuel Ashe, the brother of BGen. John Ashe, sent the news to the North Carolina Council of Safety.

"Dear Sir," he wrote. "Te Deum Laudamus: We here at present joyfully chant forth. The Vessels of War lately here, I am Just informed, took their departure a few days since, first burning two of their Tenders. We have an Open Port, tho' I fear it will not long be one, unless ye honble Board will hurry down some Balls....

The Humor of Salt boiling seems to be taking place here, I have seen some boiled here, the cleanest & whitest (I think) I ever saw in my life - every Old Wife is now scouring her pint pot for the necessary operation.

Pray tender my respectfull compts to every member of ye Board, & believe me Dear Sir, wth Esteem, Ye Obt Servt

SAML ASHE

P. S. Just as I finished this, I was told, the *Cruizer*, too long the Terror of Cape Fear, was likewise burnt."

North Carolina issued a Declaration of Rights on November 12, 1776 that spelled out protections for trial by jury, the right to face an accuser in court, freedom of the press, the right to bear arms, and that no hereditary emoluments, privileges, or honors were to be granted (meaning no hereditary titles or aristocracy). None of these rights included African Americans. Bondage was the foundation on which so much of colonial North Carolina was built that to contemplate doing away with the institution was apostasy to most. The "freeman" that the North Carolina Declaration of Rights spoke of were white men of property. It guaranteed that "no freeman shall be deprived of life, liberty, or property, but by the law of the land." The writers of the declaration let the laws in force under the royal government remain in effect so long as they were "not destructive of, repugnant to, or inconsistent with the freedom and independence of this

State." The slave holders in Congress and in North Carolina definitely did not find slavery repugnant.

As frost dusted winter gardens in December and 1776 drew to a close, the people of the Cape Fear had much to reflect on. In the short span of a year they had gone from disgruntled subjects of the English king, to a people in open rebellion, to an independent people willing to fight and die to make their freedom from what they saw as the tyranny of kings a reality. The had defeated a British army of loyalists, and kept an invading fleet bottled up in the lower reaches of the Cape Fear River. Cape Fear men had proven their mettle on battlefields inside and outside their home territories, and that the revolutionary spirit in North Carolina was as stout as any to be found in the American colonies.

Yet there were still battles to be fought, problems to be resolved, and a new government to be built. The Fourth Provincial Congress gathered in Halifax in April 1777 to chart a path forward. Military matters were at the top of their agenda, as the threat to independence did not end when Admiral Sir Peter Parker's fleet slipped over the Cape Fear River bar. The delegates authorized the printing of $250,000 in paper money to fund the war effort. They paroled some Tories and issued new regulations on the purchase of gunpowder and weapons. Officers were appointed and promoted, and an eye was given to defensive preparations. Finally, before adjourning in mid-May, the delegates voted to remove all "insurgents" who had fought on the loyalist side at Moores Creek, and their families, from their settlements. Those who did not support the American cause were to find a cold welcome in North Carolina.[64]

Endnotes

[1] Rankin, 30-31; Maass, 40; Dunkerly, 75. Dartmouth's reservations were centered around the difficulty of getting large warships over the bar at Old Inlet, thus depriving the invasion force of the benefit of the heavy guns they could provide...According to Maass, historians Hugh Lefler and William S. Powell also suggested that North Carolina's production of naval stores was also a big motivator for including the Cape Fear in plans for Charlestown.

[2] Rankin, 32. The British sent loyalist minister John McLeod into the Carolina backcountry to court the support of the Highlanders, and the two men of the cloth sent by the Congress were supposed to counter his efforts.

³ Rankin, 32-33. Highlander neutrality might have been more about giving the impression that they remained aloof to British ministrations. Committees of Safety had begun implementing restrictions on what people who were loyalists could buy. For instance, one restriction prohibited the sale of salt unless the buyer could produce a certificate identifying him as a "Liberty Man."

⁴ Rankin, 38-39. Whig militia units were supposed to march with six week's provisions, but some chose not to. That led to some hard feelings when they seized lead and other goods from several Moravian towns they passed through on the march.

⁵ Dunkerly, 75. James Kenan, Samuel Ashe, and William Campbell were authorized to make purchases to be used in preparing the town for war.

⁶ Isaac S. Harrell, "North Carolina Loyalists." The North Carolina Historical Review 3.4 (1926): 575-590. Of 2,560 loyalist claims filed in Nova Scotia and London, 139 claimed to be North Carolinians of the following occupations: Merchants - 48, Farmers - 25 (eight of which operated grist mills), Public Officials under the Crown - 8, Ministers - 2, Physicians - 2, Miscellaneous Trades - 5, No Occupation Given - 11. Only ten were native North Carolinians. Nine came from other colonies. Sixty-eight came from the British Isles. Four never resided in the colony, and eleven more did not say where they were from originally. Almost half arrived in North Carolina between 1760 and 1775.

⁷ Dunkerly, 78; Rankin, 32. Martin's proclamation authorized loyalist leaders in Anson, Cumberland, Chatham, Guilford, Mecklenburg, Rowan, Surry, and Bute Counties to begin raising and arming men.

⁸ Dunkerly, 78-79. Martin issued his orders to McLean on January 10, 1776. At the same time, the governor issued a proclamation condemning the rebellion.

⁹ Donald R. Lennon, John Burgwin biography, NCPedia (1979), https://www.ncpedia.org/biography/burgwin-john (accessed 12/9/2023); Frech, 21-33. Samuel and William Campbell and their partner, Robert Hogg, were the primary victualers of the Cruizer while Gov. Martin was aboard...Burgwin was in England seeking medical treatment after he broke his leg playing Blind Man's Bluff during a party at his Hermitage Plantation in January 1775. He remained there until 1777, before returning via New York to Wilmington and seeking state citizenship. When the British occupied Wilmington in 1781, Burgwin again left town, traveling through Europe and remarrying. After the war, he and his new family returned to North Carolina...Though Alexander McLean moved into the backcountry, he would later find himself in trouble with the Wilmington Committee of Safety again.

¹⁰ Rankin, 35.

¹¹ Rankin, 29-30. Stuart also advanced the possibility of using Native American tribes in support of the British cause.

¹² Butler 1776, 63; Rankin, 37-39; Clayton Brown Alexander, "The Training of Richard Caswell." The North Carolina Historical Review 23, No. 1 (January 1946): 13-31. Hereafter cited as Alexander NCHR 23. Richard Caswell had served in the militia since 1754, with service at the Battle of Alamance, rising through the ranks until he commanded the New Bern men.

¹³ O'Kelley V1, 77. It was ten days after the capture of the America that seamen from the Cruizer went upriver to raid John Ancrum's plantation.

¹⁴ Maass, 404. Measures adopted by the Whigs included impressment, issuing paper

money, and drafting men into the military ranks...Supporting the North Carolina military effort put a heavy burden on the citizens of the colony.

[15] Oates, 119. Martin upped the ante by declaring, "It is expected & hereby required that the Inhabitants of the Town of Wilmington do furnish for His Majesty's service one thousand barrels of good flour on or before Saturday next." When the deadline came on February 28, the battle at Moores Creek Bridge had taken place and Martin's loyalists had been soundly defeated. Capt. Parry, aboard *H.M.S. Cruizer,* ignored Gov. Martin's ultimatum and sent a message ashore politely asking the people of Wilmington for a couple of sides of beef for his hungry crew.

[16] Ross, 124.

[17] Dunkerly, 85.

[18] Rankin, 36-37; Lewis V1, 7; Ross, 117. The British offered two hundred acres to all Highlanders who would fight for the Crown, plus arms and pay equal to that of British regulars. They would receive good money for any personal equipment or livestock used in the campaign, and were promised they would only be used in North Carolina. All quitrents were to be forgiven as well, with an exemption extending for an additional twenty years...The Scots at Cross Creek told Martin they only had 1,000 stand of arms for their loyalist army...Samuel Williams, James Colson, Dr. John Pyle, and Thomas Rutherford - who had been a member of the Provincial Congress but now was termed a "poor creature" by his former associates - were among the leaders of the loyalist force... As Alexander McLean said later about the fear of impressment into the British ranks, "Suspecting that such a project was in view, one Captain Snead with two companies of Colonel Cottons corps ran off with their arms that very night."

[19] Frech, 21-33. Merchants were not the only loyalists in Wilmington. The list of confirmed Tories includes doctors, lawyers, Crown officials, planters, and others of more meager means. Some loyalists, like Robert Hogg, even served on the Wilmington Committee of Safety until resigning after the burning of Fort Johnston. Another, Samuel Marshall, was removed from the committee in July 1775. Others, including Samuel and William Campbell, refused to serve on the committee, but James Walker and John Slingsby were still members late into 1775. Slingsby would later be killed leading loyalist militia at the Battle of Elizabethtown in 1781.

[20] O'Kelley V1, 98; Documenting the American South: Colonial and State Records of North Carolina, https://docsouth.unc.edu/csr/index.php/document/csr10-0232 (accessed 12/11/23); Dunkerly, 87; Lee, 269-270. Purviance only had a small force with which to defend Wilmington, and little military experience to direct them. It was lucky that reinforcements from Duplin, Onslow, and Brunswick Counties came to bolster his ranks. He dispatched some of those men to defend Heron's Bridge on the Northeast Cape Fear River, and to Mount Misery, west of Point Peter, to stretch a boom across the waterway bordering the north side of Eagles Island.

[21] Dunkerly, 80; Lewis V1, 6.

[22] Dunkerly, 85, 107-108. Most accounts inaccurately say MacDonald had 1,600 men at Moores Creek, but the actual number is closer to 900. Desertions, low supplies, bad weather, a scarcity of weapons, and doubts about the mission they were on all contributed to the loyalist army whittling away to half its original size when the clash came. A company at full strength would have 50 men instead of the 30 that MacDonald's army had.

[23] Fraser, 156. The tree is said to still stand on Cool Spring Street.
[24] Rankin, 40-41
[25] Lewis V1, 9.; Rankin, 42-45. Cross Creek and Campbellton later combined to form what is today modern Fayetteville...Farquard Campbell suggested falling back to Cross Creek and then crossing the Cape Fear at Campbellton. Once across, the loyalists would march east for Negro Head Point across from Wilmington before the Whigs could respond...Richard Caswell gets the lion's share of the accolades for the victory at Moores Creek, but it was really Alexander Lillington who deserves most of the credit. While Caswell assembled a large force to add to the men Lillington deployed at Moores Creek Bridge, he had no knowledge of the terrain. It was Alexander Lillington who chose the spot to make the stand against MacDonald's Highlanders.
[26] Lewis V1, 9-10; Dunkerly, 90-94. Caswell never gave a reason why he ordered the earthworks built on the west side of the creek...Colvin was active in area politics and had served on the Wilmington Committee of Safety.
[27] Lewis V1, 13. Historian J.D. Lewis elaborates on the size of the Whig forces that were at Moores Creek. Many more men answered the call to arms to meet the loyalist threat than many historians relate; but according to troop rosters and other accounts, militia and Minutemen from five of North Carolina's six military districts participated in the fight. That includes 11 companies of New Bern District Minutemen, 5 companies of Wilmington District Minutemen, 5 companies of Halifax District Minutemen, 7 companies of Hillsborough District Minutemen, 1 company of the First Battalion of the Salisbury District Minutemen, 11 companies of the Second Battalion of the Salisbury District Minutemen, 21 companies of the New Bern District Militia, 26 companies of the Wilmington District Militia, 2 companies of the Halifax District Militia, 10 companies of the Hillsborough District Militia, 25 companies of the Salisbury District Militia, 7 companies of the First Regiment of the N.C. Continental Line, and 1 company (under Col. Richard Caswell) and another company (under LtCol. James Martin of Guilford County) from the Second Regiment of the N.C. Continental Line. A significant number of units were marching to Cross Creek when they received word that the battle was over. While none of these units were at full strength (and many may have been represented by only a handful of men), the roster does speak to how seriously the Whigs considered the threat Martin's plan posed.
[28] Ross, 119-120. Cornelius Harnett answered Parry's threat with one of his own. He wrote that he found it difficult to conceive of what the king needed a thousand barrels of flour for, and that should Parry destroy Wilmington, its people would "have one consolation left, that their friends will in a few days make ample retaliation upon those whom your Excellency thinks to dignify with the epithet of friends of government."
[29] Rankin, 49.
[30] O'Kelley V1, 77-86; Dunkerly, 94-100; Rankin, 48-49. The house the Highlanders retreated to after finding Caswell's camp empty may have been that of James Rogers. Rogers claimed that McLeod stopped at his house the night before the battle...Duncan McCrary was hit seven times in the charge. Wounded, he was made prisoner. McRary took two years to recover, and was never able to work again. He eventually moved to England. His is the only account of the bridge crossing given by someone who participated in it...Kenneth Stewart was at Moores Creek with his father and a brother, both of

whom were killed. Kenneth was captured and imprisoned in Philadelphia before escaping to British-held New York...Recalling the death of John Grady, one witness said, "There was but one of our men killed and he was unfortunately shot in the back of the head." Grady likely picked the wrong time to raise his head over the earthworks to fire... James Foy was a wealthy planter who owned land that is now Poplar Grove Plantation near Hampstead, N.C. ...Newkirk and Lanier both raced to claim a prize from McLeod's body. Newkirk, whose sword is on display at Moores Creek National Battlefield, claimed the Highlander's watch.

[31] Dunkerly, 107-108. Duncan McNicol made it to the banks of the Cape Fear and managed to flag down *H.M.S. Scorpion*. McNicol delivered the bad news about Moores Creek to Gov. Josiah Martin, who tried to mask his disappointment in letters to London which described the defeat as a "little check" that he doubted "will have any extensive ill consequences."...The majority of the loyalists were captured at Black Mingo Creek, then marched to Smith's Ferry. Capt. Nicholas Long brought in 500 men to help herd the remaining prisoners to Halifax after paroles were given.

[32] Dunkerly, 103; Oates, 146. One of the prisoners taken at Smith's Ferry was Nathaniel Rochester, namesake and founder of Rochester, N.Y. Rochester said of the capture, "In disarming the prisoners at Devo's Ferry, the Scotch gave up their dirks with much reluctance. these having as they said been handed down from father to son for many generations."...The prisoners sent to Halifax were divided into four categories: Prisoners who had served in Congress; prisoners who had signed Tests or Associations; prisoners who had been in arms without such circumstances; and prisoners under suspicious circumstances.

[33] Rankin, 53-54. There was debate about who should get the lion's share of credit for the Moores Creek victory. The issue was even set to poetry, where after the battle it was written that, "Moores Creek field, the bloody story/ Where Lillington fought for Caswell's glory." Historian Hugh Rankin points out that there is no doubt Caswell had command at the actual battle, but goes on to nominate another candidate, Col. James Moore, who orchestrated the campaign that forced the loyalists into battle at the perfect place to ensure their defeat.

[34] Maass, 32.

[35] Alan D. Watson, *Wilmington: Port of North Carolina* (Columbia: University of South Carolina Press, 1992): 90. Hereafter cited as Watson Port. One visitor to Wilmington in 1775 observed that most of the merchants in the town were sympathetic to the British, who "disapproved of the present proceedings. Many of them intend quitting the country as fast as their affairs will permit them...." Ten Wilmington merchants appeared before the Loyalist Claims Commission after the war, 12 fled to England, and two died fighting against the Americans.

[36] Butler 1776, 65.

[37] Rankin, 56. Hewes noted that the Americans, "having but little ammunition, no Arms, no money, nor are we unanimous in our Councils, we do not treat each other with that decency and respect that was observed heretofore, Jealousies, ill-natured observations and recriminations take the place of reason and Argument, our Tempers are soared ..."

[38] Rankin, 56.

[39] Dunkerly, 110-111. The men of the Third N.C. came from Wilmington, Halifax, Eden-

ton, and Hillsborough. The Fourth came from Wilmington with a sprinkle of men from Salisbury and Edenton. The Fifth was made up of soldiers from New Hanover County, New Bern, Edenton, and Hillsborough...Timothy Bloodworth was a prominent politician who represented the upper part of New Hanover County (modern Pender County) in the General Assembly. In addition to serving in the Continental Congress, Bloodworth also was on the Wilmington Committee of Safety, at one time was port collector at Wilmington, and was Commissioner of Confiscated Property in 1783.

[40] O'Kelley V1, 137; Lewis V1, 16. Col. James Moore had 449 men of his First Regiment of the N.C. Continental Line, 120 men from the Second Regiment of the N.C. Continental Line, and 1,278 militiamen deployed between Wilmington and Smith Island to face what then was an unknown number of British troops coming to the Cape Fear by ship.

[41] Lewis V1, 16.

[42] Rankin, 57-59; Lewis V1, 16.; Johnston, 92-93. Moore's artillery included 6 and 9-pounder cannons...No militia were sent from the Western part of North Carolina, but they were told to be ready in case they were needed.

[43] Dunkerly, 109; David Stick, *Bald Head: A History of Smith Island and Cape Fear* (Bald Head Island, 1985): 29. Hereafter cited as Stick; Rankin, 58. William Hooper barely escaped capture when a boat loaded with British soldiers went unnoticed until they were almost upon him at Finian, his house on Masonboro Sound.

[44] O'Kelley V1, 97-98.

[45] Dunkerly, 113.

[46] Lewis V1, 17.

[47] Lossing, 228; Crow, 61. With the entire British fleet together at Cape Fear, the Wilmington Committee of Safety believed an invasion could come at any time. To prevent the redcoats from getting help from enslaved persons as had happened at Corbett's Ferry on the loyalist march to Moores Creek, the committee recommended that all male slaves capable of bearing arms or being of assistance to the British be removed into the interior.

[48] Rankin, 59; Johnston, 93. Harnett and Howe were especially wanted by the British because they had formed the first militias to act against British rule. When the British came to the Cape Fear in 1776, they offered blanket pardons for any citizen who abandoned the cause of independence and returned to the royal fold - except for two people: Cornelius Harnett and Robert Howe.

[49] Dunkerly, 117.

[50] Rankin, 60; Lewis V1, 22; Dunkerly, 116-117. Four companies were deployed to Battery Island, and another four to Smith Island...The bayonets the British and Americans used in the eighteenth century bear no resemblance to modern bayonets. These were 18 inches long and designed to rend flesh in such a way as to make it difficult for physicians to mend the wound.

[51] Lewis V1, 18. "Cabbage trees" are what the British called the palmettos found in the southern coastal regions.

[52] Rankin, 61; Lewis V1, 29.

[53] Dunkerly, 118. N.C. royal governor Josiah Martin influenced what was happening in Charlestown by convincing Captain Tallemache of *H.M.S. Scorpion* to abandon his post off the South Carolina port and join *H.M.S. Cruizer* on the Cape Fear. Construction of the

fort on Sullivan's Island began after the watchful eyes of the Scorpion had sailed away.
54 Johnston, 94.
55 Rankin, 67-69; Johnston, 94-95. Arms were so scarce that the 700 men Lee sent to Charlestown had to take muskets from local militia to make sure every man had a weapon.
56 Maass, 54.
57 Dunkerly, 119.
58 L. Van Loan Naisawald, "Major General Robert Howe's Activities In South Carolina and Georgia, 1776-1779", The Georgia Historical Quarterly, Vol. 35, No. 1 (March, 1951), pp. 23-30. Hereafter cited as Naisawald.
59 Isabell M. Williams and Leora H. McEachern, *Salt, That Necessary Article* (Wilmington N.C. 1973): 7-8. Hereafter cited as Salt.
60 Johnston, 113.
61 Rankin, 68. Understandably, news of the uprising was swept under the rug to prevent any wavering supporters from question the Whigs' resolve.
62 Johnston, 103; Dunkerly, 120-121; Lewis V1, 29-30. The Continental Marines conducted their first amphibious landing at Nassau, Bahamas in February 1776.
63 Johnston, 112-113.
64 Johnston, 115-117. In North Carolina, slaves were prohibited from attending church, or any gathering. Husbands, wives, and children could be separated. Children born of a female slave and a freeman was a slave. A slave could gain freedom through heroic acts or good deeds, but if freedom was granted they had to leave the county and state; and if a slave owner wanted to grant freedom to a bondsman, it could only be granted with a court's permission.

1777-1780

American troops retreated from a British flanking movement that spelled disaster for MGen. Robert Howe's position outside Savannah, Georgia in 1778.

1777-1780

In the summer of 1776, North Carolina's delegates to the Continental Congress begged leaders back home to waste no time recruiting for the Continental Army. "We must most earnestly importune you to compleat the Continental Battalions," they wrote to the Council of Safety in August, followed by another plea in September. Congressman William Hooper urged a correspondent in the state to "pray hasten by every means in your power the recruiting Service amongst you [,] we shall have difficulty enough this way to encounter." It was a problem that would persist. At the end of 1777, Continental Congressman Cornelius Harnett anxiously wrote home about the requirement for troops. Philadelphia had fallen to the British, and George Washington suffered defeats twice that fall. "For God's sake fill up your Battalions, Lay Taxes, put a stop to the sordid and avaricious Spirit which infected all ranks and conditions of men," Harnett implored fellow North Carolinian Thomas Burke. "If we have Virtue, we certainly have power, to work out our own salvation, I hope without fear or trembling."[1]

Off the Cape Fear, the Royal Navy continued to blockade the state's most vital maritime artery. The British frigate *H.M.S. Solebay* patrolled off Cape Fear's Frying Pan Shoals between February 6-9, and bagged four vessels. The merchant sloop *Speedwell* bound for Philadelphia carrying rice and indigo from Charlestown, S.C. was forced to heave to on February 6, 1777. A prize crew from the *Solebay* boarded the

Speedwell and sailed her to the admiralty prize court in Jamaica. The next day, *Solebay*'s very good cruise got even better when she took two prizes, the schooner *Hope* and the brig *Fortune*. On the ninth *Solebay* captured the *Little Dick*, another schooner that, like all the other prizes, was sent to Jamaica. But unlike the other three vessels, *Little Dick* was lost on the Nassau Bar.[2]

The American military effort in North Carolina suffered another blow when BGen. James Moore died on April 15, 1777. For the Moore family, it was a double loss, as James' brother and fellow patriot, Maurice, passed away on the same day and in the same house. Widely considered North Carolina's best tactical mind, James Moore died of what one contemporary source called "gout of the stomach." Others attributed his demise to lingering effects of malaria. When Moore died, no other American general had been as successful as a strategist, at organizing a hodge-podge collection of militias, regulars, and Minutemen into an effective army, and at coordinating with civilian leaders and governments to advance the American cause. Janet Schaw's 1775 description of Moore was common to both his friends and enemies. He was, Schaw wrote, "a man of...most unblemished character...and a virtuous life...his popularity is such that I am assured he will have more followers than any other man in the province."[3]

The Americans could have used James Moore at Brandywine in September 1777. North Carolina's Continental Line regiments were sent north to bolster Washington's army under the command of Brigadier General Francis Nash. The need for troops was so urgent that the North Carolina men were hurried to join the main American army despite none of the regiments being at full strength. The North Carolinians did not make the difference for Washington, as the British under General William Howe won the day. The North Carolina regiments involved included the 1st, 2nd, 3rd, 4th, 5th, 6th, 7th, 8th, and 9th, with a total strength of just over 500 men. Francis Nash, whose brother Abner would become North Carolina's governor in the not too distant future, was mortally wounded two months later at Germantown, in November.[4]

If the North Carolina men at Brandywine were understrength, it may not have mattered much. Officials in the state had a devil of a time arming the men they did manage to recruit. The N.C. Continental Line's Major Griffith McCree complained to Gen. Jethro Sumner that finding weapons for his men was extremely difficult. To remedy the situation,

This recently discovered and authenticated sketch that depicts North Carolina Continentals as they passed through Philadelphia on the way to join Washington's army was drawn by Swiss artist and eyewitness Pierre Eugène Du Simitièrein in 1777. It is now in the collection of the Museum of the American Revolution. The sketch is one of only about a dozen such works, and the only one showing North Carolina troops and women camp followers.

N.C. Continental quartermaster Nicholas Long sought permission to borrow weapons from the state and issue them to the 180 new Continental recruits from the Wilmington area in need of them. The plan hit a roadblock when Gen. Allen Jones of the state militia objected, asserting that the muskets were "procured for the use of the militia they should be reserved for that purpose." McCree bitterly responded that ""I will be obliged to march thro' a disaffected country among inhabitants who still bid defiance to our power, without Arms sufficient for a Sergeant's Guard."[5]

The disaffected inhabitants McCree spoke of were loyalists who never left North Carolina, even after the setbacks of Moores Creek and the abandonment of the Cape Fear by the British fleet in the spring of 1776. Civil war was a very real thing in North Carolina, even if the threat after 1776 was more of a low simmer than a boiling pot. Records from 1777 show plenty of incidents in which Whigs and Tories clashed in the state. Loyalist activity was so out in the open that in July 1777, BGen. John Ashe of the Wilmington militia suspected they intended to make a move against the local armory. Ashe wrote that there were "so many of the inhabitants here disaffected, and such a number of Tories from other Counties here...occasions me to suspect they intend seizing the magazine by surprise." Ashe called out the Whig militia from surrounding counties to counter the threat.[6]

In East Florida the British, under nominal command of Gen. Augustine Prevost, were a growing threat. The situation in Georgia was so bad by February 1778 that it demanded Congress take action to correct it. British raids coming from Florida strongholds on the St. Mary's and St. John's Rivers, and at Pensacola, were a constant nuisance that took away from the larger war effort. MGen. Robert Howe, commander of the Southern Department, was dispatched to reorganize Georgia military units and meet with officials to devise a plan to deal with Florida. Howe was authorized to use what Continental military stores there might be in Georgia and South Carolina, and to borrow from the states any additional materials he might need. Congress authorized Howe to lead the Florida expedition himself, or to delegate it to the senior Georgian, Col. Samuel Elbert. Though Howe did not hold out much hope for success, he shifted his headquarters from Charlestown to Savannah and began to plan.[7]

Privateers pounced on American shipping off North Carolina with increasing frequency in the spring of 1778. In May, privateers took several prizes off Ocracoke, prompting Congress to order the Continental frigate *Raleigh* and the brigantine *Resistance* to patrol from Cape Henlopen to the Outer Banks to stop it. One of the best (or worst, depending on your point of view) privateers, Tory Capt. John Goodrich, Sr. of Virginia. He had actually been in custody at Ocracoke in 1777, but he returned to sea with a vengeance a year later. Goodrich made it a special point to terrorize shipping around the Outer Banks. The Continental warships' main target was Goodrich. On May 12, Goodrich teamed with two other captains, a McFarling and Neale, to take several ships off Ocracoke. The privateers were lured into Topsail Inlet and managed to burn a brig captured by the *Raleigh* down to her waterline. Onboard was 1,200 bushels of hard-to-come-by salt. The incident spurred the North Carolina legislature to fund the construction of a new fort, Fort Hancock, on Ocracoke Island to protect the shipping lanes.[8]

From Georgia, Robert Howe wrote to keep Congress informed of events in the Florida campaign. It was not going well. Congress considered his letter of June 1778 and came to the conclusion that the military forces devoted to curbing the British and Indian incursions coming from south of the Georgia border would be required to stay for the time being. That meant paying them in Continental currency because the Georgia notes were so inflated as to be worthless. Congress thought it necessary because "the paper currency now in circulation in said State greatly exceeds any medium on which the value of paper currency can support any credit."

Later that week, Congress passed a resolution recalling Robert Howe to the North, replacing him with Major General Benjamin Lincoln. Howe did not learn of the change until October, and the news hurt him deeply. He dispatched a letter to South Carolina's Henry Laurens in the Continental Congress, asking him to intercede on his behalf. Dated October 9, 1778, Howe's letter implored Laurens, "Think, Sir, the undeserved mortification I must feel upon an occasion like this...How, Sir, have I deserved this disgrace...?"[9]

Robert Howe's time in Georgia was not yet complete, however. The same month that he wrote Henry Laurens for help retaining his command, the British decided to attempt re-taking Savannah. It was the first part of a plan to capture Charlestown, South Carolina, and parts of North Carolina, returning the region to royal authority and splitting the colonies between North and South. When redcoats landed off Tybee Island at the end of December, Howe had already done all he could to secure the main roads into Savannah. The

MGen. Benjamin Lincoln

main line of defense was southeast of the city, near the Sea Island Road on the town side of a small creek. "The situation I chose was the most defensible I could find;" Howe wrote, "the left flank covered by the river and a long extent of marsh, a morass in my front not easily passable which extended so far beyond my right flank, that I hoped would secure me from being turned, at least from it being done so suddenly as to prevent my retreat."

Good as the terrain may have been, nothing else was in Howe's favor. He only commanded about 650 Continentals in two brigades. Campaigns in Florida had badly weakened the Georgia contingent of Continentals, whose weapons according to Samuel Ebert consisted of a "medley of Rifles, old muskets & fowling pieces." There were about 100 Georgia mi-

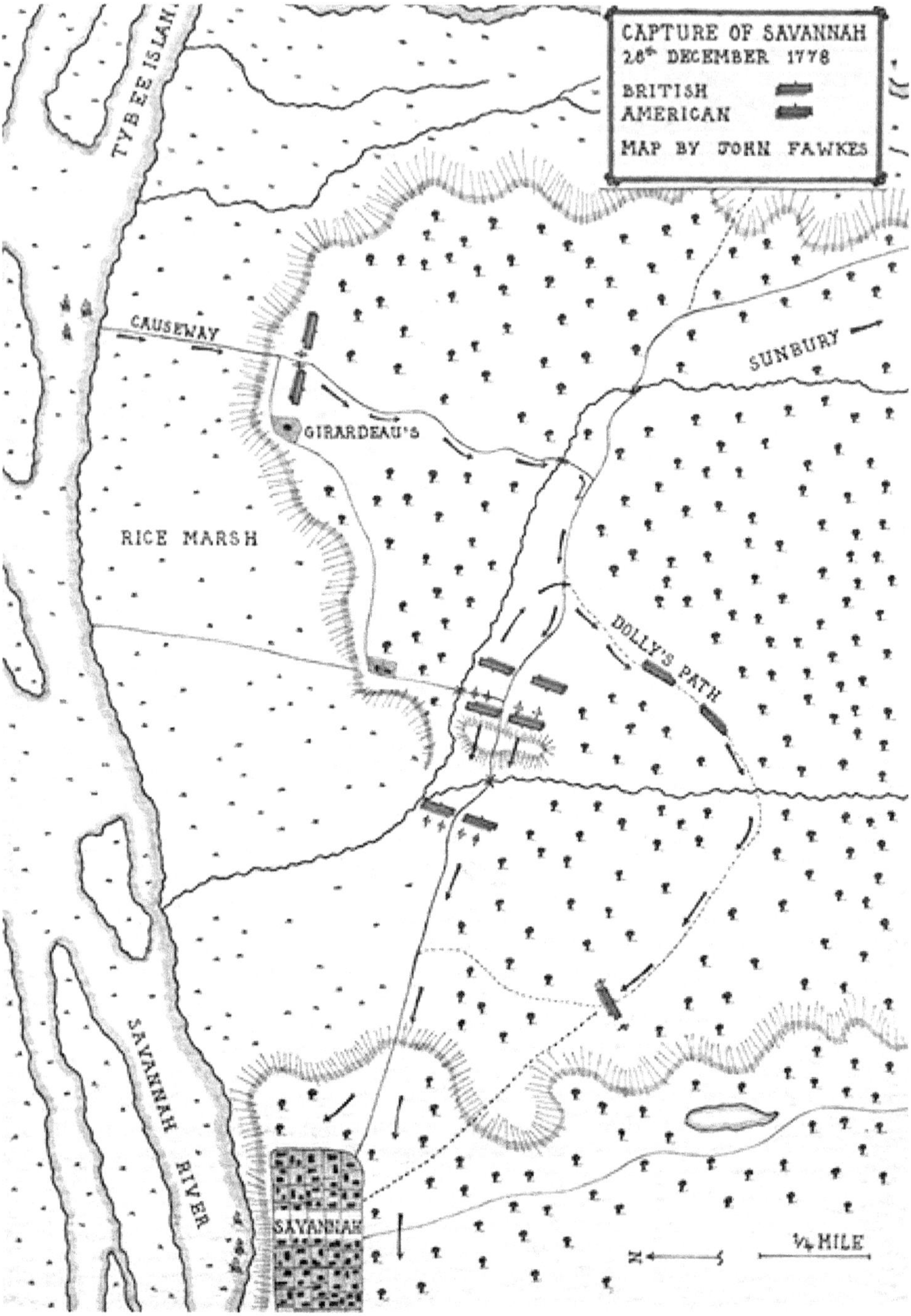

John Fawkes' map of the capture of Savannah, Georgia. Robert Howe did the best he could with what resources he had, but treachery led the British to victory.

litiamen who answered to their governor, not Robert Howe, and a small artillery unit. It was with this meager army that Howe intended to face down 3,000 well-disciplined British troops. Add in betrayal by a slave belonging to a loyalist Savannah planter, and the Americans' defeat was assured.

British Lieutenant Colonel Archibald Campbell wrote, "A confidential Slave [named Quash, who must have been extremely loyal to his master] from Sir James Wright's Plantation informed me, that the Carolina Brigade was commanded by Colonel Eugee [Huger], the Georgia Brigade by Colonel Elbert [Ebert] and the whole under General Robert Howe... that 600 militia were posted at Ogichee Road near to the New Barracks, and after many Questions, I found that he could lead the Troops without Artillery through the Swamp upon the Enemy's right."

Led by Quash, Campbell's troops threaded their way into the swamps through Milledge Pass to come out on Howe's flank. With another British force engaging from the front, Campbell's assault from the swamp was too much for the much smaller American force to withstand. The British captured Savannah without much in the way of losses. Robert Howe was recalled from Georgia and court martialed for the disaster on the south Georgia coast. In his testimony he defended his actions, asserting "that had the enemy attacked us there, I think there was every probability that the events of that day had been determined in our favour." Even British LtCol. Campbell himself described Howe's position as "advantageous." Howe was acquitted, and reassigned to West Point in February 1780.[10]

LtCol. Archibald Campbell

Howe was not the only Cape Fear soldier who found disappointment in Georgia. Gen. John Baptiste Ashe also suffered defeat at the hands of the British at Brier Creek in 1779. After the British took Augusta, Georgia, the Americans ambushed a large party of loyalists on the way to reinforce LtCol. Archibald Campbell there. The resulting battle at Kettle Creek led Campbell to order the evacuation of Augusta. As the British withdrew, Ashe's forces followed. Campbell ordered the destruction of the

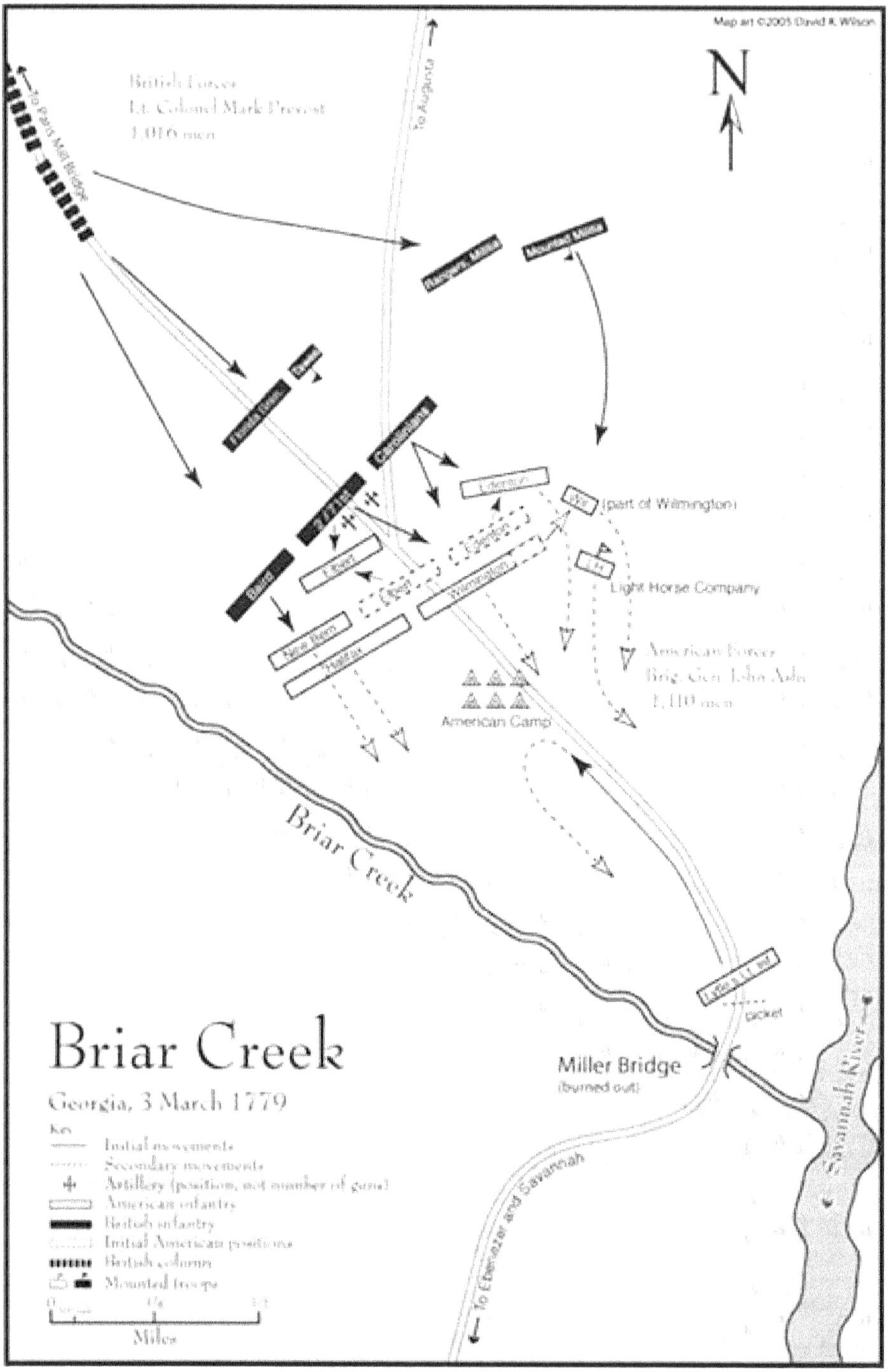

The Whig loss at the Battle of Brier Creek, Georgia represented another bad day for generals from the Cape Fear.

bridge at Brier Creek. The Americans camped by the creek while trying to rebuild the bridge and resume their pursuit. It was then that the British attacked. Campbell, taking his men in a wide flanking movement, re-crossed the creek and hit Ashe's men before they realized the danger. It turned into a rout.

John Fergus, who was in the right wing of Ashe's army at the battle, painted an unflattering picture of the general's performance. "We rode close along the rear of the line," he said, "when the first general fire was made; as we were on lower ground than the enemy, it passed chiefly over our heads. We had got to the extremity of the right wing where General Ashe commanded by the time the second fire was made. This was our post, but we had not time to give more than one fire, when the general wheeled and fled and the whole wing with him. He was gone 150 yards or more before our little party followed. The British left wing was advancing rapidly, and, as Colonel Elbert afterwards informed me, he knew not that the right wing was gone till he found the enemy in his rear, killing his men. Of course he and all his men that escaped death were made prisoners. (It was after Colonel Elbert was released that I met him in Virginia, and he gave this account and added that he fully believed General Ashe betrayed us to the British, and declared that if he ever met with him, one of them should die before they parted).[11]

John Baptiste Ashe asked for a court martial to clear his name. In a trial presided over by General William Moultrie, Ashe was acquitted on charges of cowardice and poor generalship. Nevertheless, the court found he did not take all precautions he should have, leading to the capture of a large number of Whig forces.[12]

Great Britain and its former colonies were essentially stalemated by 1780. Redcoats were spread from Canada to the Caribbean. While Lieutenant General Sir Henry Clinton controlled most major population centers, much of the countryside remained in rebellion. Under Washington, what was once a ragtag collection of would-be soldiers had been trained into a well-honed and blooded army capable of taking on the British Lion. The grumblings in England to end the rebellion in America and pressure from Parliament to bring the redcoats home led Clinton to propose a campaign to end the war by isolating the South. New England the British could lose, but not the South, with its agricultural production.

Washington recognized that the war was shifting from the North to the South, and sent the best of his troops there to meet the threat. The Maryland and Delaware Continentals were the finest in the American army, and their deployment was a strong indication of the seriousness that Washington assigned to the development.[13]

    In North Carolina, the impact of the loyalist defeat at Moores Creek was fading, and Tories began to feel emboldened again after the setbacks suffered by the Americans in Georgia. Josiah Martin still maintained there was a large number of people loyal to the king in the state. "I have great reason to believe," wrote Martin, "that all my representations of the fidelity of His Majesty's subjects there, at the beginning of the Rebellion will be fully justified in their zeal and numbers, whenever the army enters their country."[14]

    As it became more and more apparent that the British had set their sights on Charlestown, North Carolina Whigs had a difficult time raising militia to send to their sister state's aid. With the unrest caused by loyalists at home, not many men felt comfortable leaving their farms and families unprotected. One Whig general wrote to the North Carolina governor that, "You will see, Sir, by the return how backward the Colonels have been in turning out the men and providing for them. The Duplin men have at this time neither Cart, pot or any other necessary for marching."[15]

    The British, too, were experiencing recruiting troubles. Clinton knew that loyalists in the Carolinas were cautious of throwing in with the British after what happened at Moores Creek and other setbacks elsewhere. "The good will of the inhabitants is absolutely requisite to retain a country after we have conquered it," Clinton asserted. "I fear it will be some time before we can recover the confidence of those in Carolina, as their past sufferings will of course make them cautious of forwarding the King's interests before there is the strongest certainty of his army being in a condition to support them."[16]

    BGen. James Hogun reached Wilmington on February 19, 1780 with 700 North Carolina Continentals on the way to reinforce Benjamin Lincoln in Charlestown. The men had marched from Philadelphia as the danger to the South Carolina port city mounted. British and loyalist activity in South Carolina was on the rise. In Berkeley County, a Whig raid on loyalists at Wambaw's Plantation prodded LtCol. Banastre Tarleton and his dragoons of the British Legion to pursue LtCol. Anthony White as he

South Carolina's Peter Horry (left), and George Washington's cousin, William Washington (right). William Washington recuperated at Wilmington after British dragoons smashed the Americans at Lenud's Ferry on the Santee River.

retreated to link up with between 200 and 300 American cavalry under LtCol. William Washington, Major John Jameson, and Col. Peter Horry. Tarleton caught up with them on the Santee River at Lenud's Ferry and engaged them in a complete rout. Those Americans not killed or captured were scattered to the four winds. William Washington, a second cousin of George Washington, only avoided being killed or captured because he had the good sense to abandon his horse in the middle of crossing the Santee and fleeing on foot. He joined White, Horry, and Jameson in making it to the safety of the other side of the river. The Americans lost 41 killed and 67 taken prisoner. The British also captured 100 badly needed horses, arms, and other supplies that would be put to good use by the British. The British light infantry captured at Wambaw's Plantation, of course, were all set free. William Washington and about 75 men, most unfit for combat, eventually made their way to Wilmington to rest and recuperate.[17]

The British siege of Charlestown resulted in the destruction of the American Southern army. North Carolinians serving there by the end of April included James Hogun's brigade made up of the First, Second, and Third Regiments of the N.C. Continental Line. North Carolina militia under James Lachlan helped man the Charlestown city batteries. More N.C. militia and dragoons were stationed at Mount Pleasant, while Isaac Huger had North Carolina men under his command east of the Cooper River. When Benjamin Lincoln surrendered the city on May 12, 1780, the British captured seven generals, 93 officers of other ranks, 5,175 men, and over

300 guns and mortars. Eighteen Continental Line regiments were among those laying down their arms, including one third of the total number of North Carolina regiments. British authorities allowed militia and armed civilians to be paroled to their homes, and even allowed Gen. Lincoln to send along his dispatches to George Washington advising him of the catastrophe.

Capturing Charlestown allowed LtGen. Charles Lord Cornwallis to accomplish several things. It permitted royal authority to be re-established in South Carolina, and the reorganization of the loyalist militias there to act as garrison troops when Cornwallis ventured into the interior. He was also, in his words, able to "deal with the disaffected," settling scores with those who chose to stand for independence from Great Britain. More importantly, it allowed the British to establish a string of backcountry posts to quell Whig influence and operations there, secure his supply lines, and get ready for any counterattack that the Americans might muster.

Major Patrick Ferguson

Gen. Clinton was more cautious than Cornwallis. He was dubious of an expedition into North Carolina until South Carolina was well and truly under British control. He rightly pointed out to Cornwallis that his most important duty was to protect Charlestown and South Carolina for the British. Any move into North Carolina that jeopardized Cornwallis' army was to be avoided, and a move into North Carolina could do just that. Still, Cornwallis' persistence eventually earned him permission to fight the Southern Campaign as he saw fit.

Let off the leash, Cornwallis planned the second part of his campaign to subjugate the Carolinas. It would come in the form of a three-pronged attack originating in Charlestown and advancing into the South Carolina backcountry, moving north into North Carolina, and eventually, Virginia. Maj. Patrick Ferguson would lead the westernmost column north through the Carolina mountains. His force would consist of newly raised loyalist South Carolina militia. Ferguson's orders were to pacify the frontier and protect Cornwallis' western flank. Cornwallis would move with his main army through the central part of the Carolinas, while a third force would be dispatched to Wilmington on the coast to function as a logistical base for the main army, ferrying supplies up the Cape Fear River to Cross Creek where Cornwallis could replenish his stores on the march.

The man chosen to command the seizure and occupation of Wilmington was Major James Henry Craig, leading the 82nd Regiment of Foot, comprised of Highland Scots. A detachment of the 82nd was among the British troops occupying Charlestown, and was selected to go to Wilmington with Craig. The bulk of the detachment would evacuate from Wilmington in November 1781. Writing from Camden, S.C., Governor John Rutledge warned North Carolina Governor Abner Nash that Cornwallis had his eye set on his state, and that Wilmington might be next to fall to the redcoats.[18]

"We have no certain account what the force above mentioned is, or by whom commanded," Rutledge said, "but it is said to be considerable, and under Lord Cornwallis. It is evident that the conquest of North as well as South Carolina is the enemy's plan. The time for which they endeavour to enlist men is until those countries can be conquered, and a junction with them at Cross Creek will probably be attempted with the body above mentioned, who have with them a large Highland regiment. I have good reason to believe that they will send vessels (some perhaps with troops) to possess your rivers, and the towns on them, and it is probable that they will establish at Brunswick and Wilmington magazines of provisions. They may send hither great quantities of rice from the lower part of our State. They can hardly expect, I apprehend, to penetrate far into your back country unless they depend more than I hope they can with good grounds on the disaffection of your people, but I presume they will extend their camp along, and at some distance from the sea."[19]

Col. Francis Marion, the Whig guerilla fighter also known as the Swamp Fox by his South Carolina neighbors, laid an ambush at Great Savannah on August 20, 1780. His target was Sumter's Plantation on the north side of Nelson's Ferry. Marion had 150 men with him, including fellow guerilla fighter Major Peter Horry. After midnight, a convoy of prisoners taken at the Battle of Camden four days earlier came into Marion's trap. The Swamp Fox managed to free 147 Maryland and Delaware Continentals in the action, catching most of the escort asleep in a home along the road. The Whig guerillas killed or captured 22 loyalists out of 38 in the unit, made up of men from the 63rd and Prince of Wales Regiments and some loyalist militia. Marion suffered one killed and another wounded. On August 26, Marion crossed Lynch's River at Witherspoon's Ferry. The Continentals split off there and made their way to Wilmington. Just over a month later, Col. Otho Williams wrote South Carolina Governor John Rutledge that, "Of the 150 men retaken by Marion only about 60 rejoined their corps - some were sick but most of them just departed." In Wilmington, Col. James Read wrote to BGen. Jethro Sumner of the North Carolina militia, "Col. Marion retook one hundred and forty-seven soldiers of the Maryland and Delaware line, fifty-seven of whom have arrived in town [Wilmington] and committed to my care."[20]

Col. James Read

Marion had returned to his South Carolina camp by September 8, when he got word that loyalist forces were about to encircle him. One force marched from Kingstree through Indiantown, and had crossed Lynch's Creek to approach from the west. Tory Militia from Georgetown led by John Coming Ball and John Wigfall were approaching from the south in the direction of Black River. More loyalists were coming from the east. There was only one escape route left to him, to the north. Most of his men had been let loose to return to their homes to check on their families, so Marion only had about 60 men with him at the time. The Swamp Fox led them, along with two pieces of field artillery, towards North Carolina.

Marion was not the sort of man that Hollywood would pick as a hero. "He was rather below the middle stature of men, lean and swarthy," recalled William Dobein James, who served with him as a young teen during the war. "His body was well set, but his knees and ankles were badly formed and he still limped upon one leg." He had an eagle's beak of a nose over a jutting chin and a large forehead. But he also had "a countenance remarkably steady," on a wiry frame "capable of enduring fatigue and every privation necessary for a partisan."

A nonstop forced march took Marion's guerilla fighters to Ami's

Mill on the border between North and South Carolina. The two field artillery pieces were abandoned in the swamps along their route, in order to more quickly flee their pursuers. A week after escaping the Tory ambush, Marion was safely ensconced in the Great White Marsh in Bladen County (outside modern Whiteville in Columbus County). On September 15 Marion wrote to Gen. Horatio Gates, commander of the Southern American army, that he intended to remain in North Carolina "until I hear from you or l have an opportunity of doing something."

The guerilas' stay in Great White Marsh was not pleasant. There was never enough food, and southeastern North Carolina's mosquitos were a constant nuisance. With the mosquitos came malaria, and Marion's men started coming down with the tropical disease. The summer and early fall was wetter than usual, and among those who were brought low by the fever was Peter Horry.

William Dobein James, the son of one of Marion's officers, was another that became feverish with malaria. James later related an account of the forced march to North Carolina and their stay in Great White Swamp.

Col. Francis Marion

"The general's march, was, for some time, much impeded by the two field pieces, which he attempted to take along; but, after crossing the little Pedee, he wheeled them off to the right. and deposited them in a swamp; where they may since have amused the wondering deer hunter. This was the last instance of military parade evinced by the general. By marching day and night, he arrived at Amy's mill, on Drowning Creek west of Aberdeen, N.C.; whence he detached Maj. James, with a small party of volunteers, back to South Carolina, to gain intelligence, and to rouse the militia. Considering the distance back, and the British and Tories in the rear, this was a perilous undertaking. The general continued his march, and pitched his camp for some time, on the east side of the White Marsh, near the head of the Waccamaw.

"At this place, the author had, (in the absence of his father,) the honour to be invited to dine with the general," James wrote. "The dinner was set before the company by the general's servant, Oscar, partly on a pine log, and partly on the ground; it was lean beef, without salt, and sweet potatoes. The author had left a small pot of boiled homminy in his camp, and requested leave of his host to send for it; and the proposal was acquiesced in, gladly. The homminy had salt in it, and proved, although eaten out of the pot, a most acceptable repast. The general said but little, and that was chiefly what a son would be most likely to be gratified by, in the praise of his father. They had nothing to drink but bad water; and all the company appeared to be rather grave.

"At length Maj. James arrived. The news was, that the country through which Wemyss had marched, for seventy miles in length, and at places for fifteen miles in width, exhibited one continued scene of desolation. On most of the plantations every house was burnt to the ground, the negroes were carried off, the inhabitants plundered, the stock, especially sheep, wantonly killed; and all the provisions, which could be come at, destroyed. Fortunately, the corn was not generally housed, and much of that was saved. Capt. James had fired upon a party at McGill's plantation; but it only increased the rage of the enemy. Adam Cusan had shot at the black servant of a Tory officer, John Brockington, whom he knew, across Black Creek. He was taken prisoner soon after, and for his offence, tried by a court martial, and, on the evidence of the negro, hanged. His wife and children prostrated themselves before Wemyss, on horseback, for a pardon; and he would have rode over them, had not one of his own officers prevented the foul deed; from this scene he proceeded on to superintend the execution. But these acts of wantonness and cruelty had roused the militia; and Major James reported they were ready to join the general Marion, a few days after, returned to South Carolina by a forced march."[21]

Maj. Patrick Ferguson, leading the westernmost prong of Cornwallis' army over the North Carolina mountains, had two missions. One was to recruit as many men to the loyalist cause as possible. The other was to protect the main body of the British army from any attack coming from that direction. On October 7, 1780, Ferguson's column was trapped atop Kings Mountain, not far from and southwest of Charlotte, just across the North Carolina/South Carolina border. Col. Isaac Shelby of Tennessee and militia leader William Campbell's "Overmountain Men" pinned the British force down on Kings Mountain's plateaued top and decimated them. After the defeats at Charlestown and Camden, it was a sorely needed victory for the Americans.[22]

Whig and Tory militias clashed at Myhand's Bridge, west of Clinton, N.C.

West of Clinton, half way between there and the modern town of Concord in Duplin County (modern Sampson County), loyalist and Whig forces clashed at Myhand's Bridge. As Cornwallis moved closer to an invasion of North Carolina, loyalists in the state became emboldened. Captain John C. "Shay" Williams formed a militia company to deal with the growing danger the loyalists posed. Williams had served previously as an enlisted man in the militia, and as a lieutenant in the N.C. Continental Line from 1776-1778.

Williams' men were a rowdy bunch, as often fighting among themselves as with the king's faithful. According to historian J.D. Lewis, they often settled disputes with hunting knives and fists, fueled by a love of whiskey. They might have been a handful, but Williams claimed they could march and drill "as neatly as any militia could hope for, afoot or mounted, and fight like savages when needed."

Anticipating the British arrival in the state, loyalist Middleton Mobley organized his own band in Duplin County. Hoping to disrupt Whig activity in the area, Mobley and his men set up an ambush at Myhand's Bridge. Williams and his men rode into it before they realized the danger. Mobley's men fired on Williams' column, killing one man and badly wounding several others. Williams' Duplin County Militia were thrown into confusion at the sudden attack. Luckily for them, Mobley did not press the advantage surprise had given him. Abandoning some wagons the loyalists captured just before Williams arrived, Mobley and his men retired in good order through the swamps and down Cross Creek Road.

Thinking he was a loyalist, Williams challenged the surviving Whig teamster to surrender his cargo of meal and cloth that the captain thought had been stolen by Mobley's men. The wagon driver refused and threatened Williams with a musket and sword. So Williams shot him. Tearing a piece of striped cloth from the cargo in the wagon bed, Williams wiped his face off and tucked the cloth into his belt. Several of his men did similarly, some pinning a square of the cloth to their hats, others turning the cloth into striped sashes. Those striped pieces of cloth became Williams' men's version of a cockade from that point on.

In November 1780, Bladen County loyalists at Great Swamp suffered an attack by Camden County Whig militia under Engineer Col. John Senf. The Camden men, 90 strong, killed two of the Bladen County Tories at the cost of just one of their own wounded.

While Williams and Mobley were fighting in the east, and as Cornwallis drew closer to the North Carolina border, the Bladen and Caswell County regiments of the N.C. militia joined those of Guilford, Orange, and Rowan Counties in another clash at Shallow Ford on the Yadkin River (near modern Highway 421). The violence in the state would only increase in the coming year - the year the redcoats came.[23]

Endnotes

[1] Maass, 59.
[2] O'Kelley V1, 170.
[3] Price, 9; NCPedia, https://www.ncpedia.org/biography/moore-james (accessed 12/20/2023). Some accounts say the Moore brothers died in January, but there is no disputing that both James and Maurice died on the same day at the same place...The home in which the Moore brothers died is located a few yards south of the site of Charles Towne, the first attempt at settlement on the Cape Fear River, just north of the mouth of Town Creek. Maurice's house at Brunswick was destroyed in the Cornwallis raid on Brunswick in 1776...Maurice's son, Alfred Moore, became an Associate Justice of the Supreme Court of the United States in 1799, the only North Carolinian to ever hold a place on that bench.
[4] Maass, 62.
[5] Maass, 67.
[6] Maass, 160.
[7] Naisawald, 23-30. Part of Howe's doubts came from the fact that he only commanded

the Continentals in Georgia, while state militia units were commanded by Governor John Houstoun. The two men squabbled over how best to meet the threat.

[8] O'Kelley V1, 101.

[9] Naisawald, 23-30.

[10] Seielstad, 22; Alexander A. Lawrence, "General Robert Howe and the British Capture of Savannah in 1778." The Georgia Historical Quarterly 36.4 (1952): 303-327. Hereafter cited as Lawrence. Howe's position lies just east of the modern intersection of Randolph and Wheaton Streets, roughly where the Savanna Planing Mill was located in 2010.

[11] John C. Dann, ed. *The Revolution Remembered: Eyewitness Accounts of the War for Independence.* (Chicago: University of Chicago Press, 1980):179-180. Hereafter cited as Dann. John Baptiste Ashe was the son of Samuel Ashe, born on his father's plantation, The Neck, in Rocky Point, N.C. He later moved to Halifax, and represented the state in the U.S. House of Representatives. He was also elected governor of North Carolina, but died before taking office.

[12] Lossing, n. 65.

[13] Brinkley, 7.

[14] Isaac S. Harrell, "North Carolina Loyalists." The North Carolina Historical Review 3.4 (1926): 575-590. Hereafter cited as Harrell.

[15] Maass, 266.

[16] Lawrence Edward Babits, and Joshua B. Howard. *Long, Obstinate, and Bloody: the Battle of Guilford Courthouse.* (Chapel Hill: University of North Carolina Press, 2009): 6. Hereafter cited as Babits-Howard.

[17] Sherman, 117, 148.

[18] Brinkley, 24; O'Kelley V2, 105-106. Cornwallis' main target was Charlotte, N.C., where a large portion of the remnants of the southern Continental Army was gathered to reorganize.

[19] Sherman, 166.

[20] Sherman, 243-244. The Battle of Camden, another disaster for the Americans, was fought on August 16, 1780.

[21] John Oller, *The Swamp Fox: How Francis Marion Saved the American Revolution* (Da Capo Press, 2016): 6, 62-66. Hereafter cited as Oller; William Dobein James, A Sketch of the Life of Brigadier General Francis Marion (Wilmington, N.C.: Dram Tree Books, 2008). Hereafter cited as W.D. James; Ann Courtney Ward Little, Columbus County, North Carolina: Recollections and Records (Whiteville, N.C.: Bicentennial Commission, 1980): 11-12, 16. Hereafter cited as Little. Great White Marsh is where the N.C. city of Whiteville was founded, on land owned by Wilmington planter and merchant John Burgwin. Burgwin bought the land from John Burgwin Waddell in 1804.

[22] Brinkley, 8. Shelby's drubbing of Ferguson at Kings Mountain dealt a setback to British efforts to recruit loyalists to Cornwallis' campaign.

[23] J.D. Lewis, "The American Revolution in North Carolina." https://www.carolana.com/NC/Revolution/revolution_myhands_bridge.html (accessed 12/23/23).Hereafter cited as Carolana; O'Kelley V2, 353. Williams' claim about his men's abilities was made to Richard Richard Clinton after the war.

1781

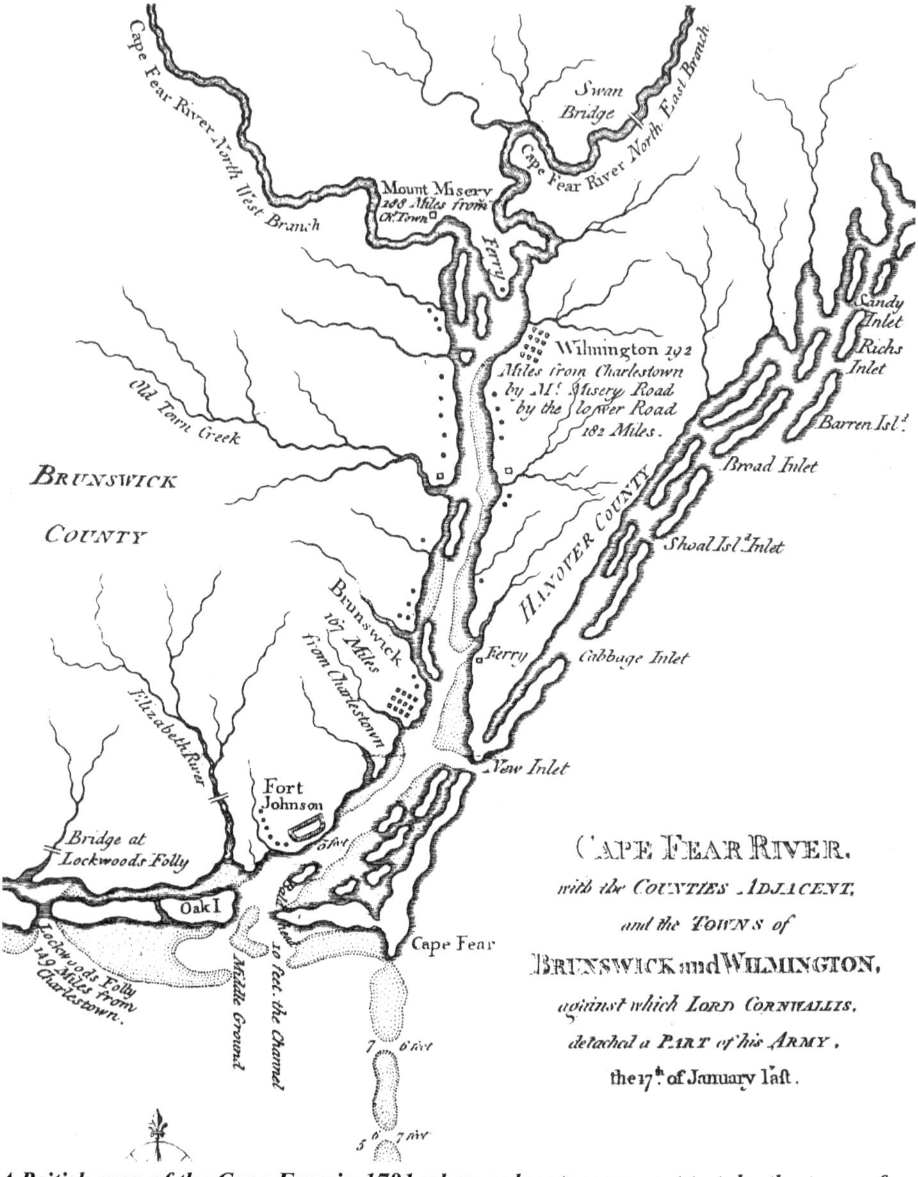

A British map of the Cape Fear in 1781 when redcoats were sent to take the town of Wilmington.

1781

Between 1775 and 1781, the British army blossomed from a total of 48,000 men to 48,647 in North America alone. Yet in the South, Gen. Clinton could only muster 8,500 troops due to commitments in other places like Canada, the West Indies, New York, New Jersey, Rhode Island, Georgia, and West Florida. Professionalism made up for a lot when it came to numbers, but by 1781 the American Continentals were a much more professional force themselves, compared to earlier in the war.[1]

After capturing Charlestown, the British undertook a campaign to bring North and South Carolina back under the control of the king and his ministers. The main obstacle to that goal was Gen. Nathaniel Greene's American army of Continentals and Carolina militia. At Winnsborough, S.C., Lord Cornwallis prepared for his invasion of North Carolina in pursuit of Greene by sending an order to Lieutenant Colonel Nisbet Balfour at Charlestown to dispatch an expedition to take Wilmington, N.C. The port town 28 miles upriver from the mouth of the Cape Fear was perfectly situated to provide control of the state's largest internal waterway, giving Cornwallis a means of resupplying his army from stores sent upriver to Cross Creek. From Cross Creek, roads stretched west into the interior. The ability of British ships to reinforce or evacuate the army if necessary made it equally attractive. A third consideration that favored Wilmington was the fact that if the British controlled it, the town could provide a base of operations for loyalist militias active in the state.

 *Gerrit Schipper's painting of a young Maj. James Henry Craig, as he would have looked when he occupied Wilmington in 1781 (left), and an older Craig when he served as Governor General of Canada (right).*

Cornwallis marched north from Winnsborough in early January and reached North Carolina just over a week later. The march was slow, covering just 25 miles in eight days, due to bad weather, a large baggage train, and the need to wait for Gen. Leslie's troops to join the earl. Emboldened by the imminent arrival of British regulars, North Carolina loyalists engaged American forces in a series of skirmishes in the new year. The clashes reached a crescendo when Col. James Kenan defeated a band of loyalists at Drowning Creek. Describing another fight, S.C. governor John Rutledge wrote the state delegates in Congress that, "Some Tories embodied here last week, on Little Pedee [Pee Dee]-- Colo. Kolb has dispersed 'em as he could find collected, but I fear a Storm is gathering in that Quarter, & will burst, if the Enemey [sic] should advance, in force, this Way, for I am well informed, that they have several British Officers, in disguise, & other Emissaries, recruiting in No. Carolina, and on the Borders of this and that State."[2]

By mid-January, Balfour had assigned the capture of Wilmington to Major James Henry Craig and the 82nd Regiment of Foot. The Highland regiment embarked on Royal Navy transports on January 21, accompanied by Isaac DuBois, whose family had been banished from the Wilmington area earlier in the war. The 82nd had been raised in Scotland and initially sent to Nova Scotia in 1778. As far as combat was concerned, they were a relatively untested unit. They would get their first real taste of action in southeastern North Carolina. As Craig watched, his men, their red coats trimmed with black on collars and cuffs, boarded the ships that would take them north. Six companies - 300 men - and two brass 3-pounder cannon, headed off to play their part in LtGen. Cornwallis' grand plan.[3]

On January 28, 1781, a frigate, two sloops of war, and 18 other vessels crossed the bar at Smith Island to enter the Cape Fear River. The British ensign at their mast tops flickered in the breeze from offshore. Ghosting upriver, past the remains of Fort Johnston and Brunswick, Capt. John Barclay and a contingent of 26 Royal Marines landed at Ellis Plantation in New Hanover County, roughly nine miles south of Wilmington. Barclay's naval detachment marched ahead of Craig and his 300 redcoat regulars. Paralleling them in the river were the warships *Blonde* (a 32-gun sixth rate), the sloops *Otter* (a former French ship of 14 guns), and *Delight* (a 14-gun sloop); plus the galleys *Comet* (a bomb galley), *Adder*, and *Dependence* (one 24-pounder cannon and six 4-pounders).[4]

In 1781, Wilmington was a town of 1,200 people living in 200 homes. Town leaders sent a delegation including James Walker and John Dawson under a flag of truce to negotiate a surrender with Maj. Craig. The British commander received their proposal on January 27. The Wilmingtonians' terms included two things: "**Article I:** The Inhabitants and others remaining there to be Prisoners of War until regularly exchanged;

British Marines landed below Wilmington at Ellis Plantation (south of modern Greenfield Lake) and marched overland to take the town in January 1781.

Article 2: The Inhabitants to remain in town and to have their Property of every denomination secured to them and their Persons protected." Craig declined. The people of Wilmington, he said, must "submit to be prisoners of war at discretion or take the Consequences of resistance, in the former case every exertion will be used to prevent Plunder or Personal ill usage to any Person." It was an ultimatum the people of Wilmington had no choice but to accept.

Wilmington was in chaos. The British fleet was detected off Cape Fear days earlier on January 25, but contrary weather conditions kept the flotilla offshore until the 28th. Col. Henry Young of the New Hanover County Militia had 50 men with him to defend the town. It was not enough. Though efforts to fortify Wilmington had been ongoing since 1776, time had dulled the people's vigilance regarding the threat of a British attack. There were two gun batteries established on the approaches to the town, but short of weapons and ammunition, Young wrote that "we are in great confusion here and very much in Want of Arms." All he could really do was spike the cannon and leave town to prevent it from being shelled by the approaching British warships and galleys.

Wilmington was a supply depot for the American army, and Young evacuated as much of the war material as possible before the British arrived. Cornelius Harnett, himself a wanted man because of his agitation against Crown rule in 1776, fled Wilmington with the town's money to safeguard it from capture by the British. William Hooper left town, too. A high priority target because he was one of North Carolina's three signers of the Declaration of Independence, he was also afraid his salt works and

Finian, William Hooper's house on Masonboro Sound. The house no longer exists.

This contemporary sketch shows the British redoubts Craig's men constructed in Wilmington, as well as Capt. Andrew Barkley's galleys anchored in the river.

other property would be targeted by the British. Fearing for his family, he evacuated them from Finian, their home on Masonboro Sound. Writing to James Iredell, he said "In the Agony of my Soul, I inform you that I am severed from my family - perhaps forever!...I removed my family to Wilmington. Had I attempted to have carried them further I apprehended that they must still have been subject to parties of the enemy who would have been engaged in plundering without the restraint of any officers to check their depredations." Hooper hoped that in Wilmington, his family would be under the protection of Maj. Craig's officers. Hooper and Alexander Maclaine fled to Halifax, where the General Assembly was meeting.

Newlyweds Lucy Bradley and Thomas Brown had only a few short days to celebrate their nuptials when redcoats spoiled their honeymoon. The wedding took place at her father's Wilmington home, but the arrival of Craig's Highlanders of the 82nd Regiment of Foot forced them to flee to the family's plantation in Bladen County. Thomas Bloodworth, brother to gunsmith Timothy Bloodworth and the Wilmington tax collector, grabbed as many of the town's public records as he could lay his hands on and sent them upriver aboard a boat, but the naval contingent of Craig's force managed to capture the vessel and burn it, along with all of the records.[5]

The new redcoat masters of Wilmington instituted great change in the town. Loyalist merchant and former town commissioner Samuel Campbell was made commander of the Tory militia. One of Craig's first orders of business was to require all residents to take an oath of allegiance to the king, something everyone except Thomas Maclaine and John Huske complied with. Dr. Thomas Cobham willingly sided with the British, becoming a surgeon at the naval hospital in Charlestown. Elizabeth Parker opened a boarding house catering to loyalists and British officers, and also provided horses for the redcoats. Those who welcomed the soldiers experienced little disruption to their lives. Indeed, most prospered.[6]

Supporters of the American cause experienced something entirely different. Maj. James Henry Craig, a twice wounded veteran of Bunker Hill, Hubbardton, Vermont, and the 1779 Penobscot Expedition, was described by one of his staff as "…a man who had made his way by varied and meritorious services to a high position in our army. He had improved a naturally quick and clear understanding by study, and he had a practical and intimate acquaintance with every branch of his profession. In person he was very short, broad, and muscular, a pocket Hercules, but with sharp, neat features, as if chiselled in ivory. Not popular, he was hot, peremptory, and pompous, yet extremely beloved by those whom he allowed to live in intimacy with him; clever, generous to a fault, and a warm and unflinching friend to those whom he liked." Craig did not treat the Americans in Wilmington with any such generosity.[7]

Printer Adam Boyd's wife, Mary, was "in a constant state of alarm" and depended on her slaves to keep things on an even keel. Her husband had enlisted in the army and was away from home when Craig arrived. Mary escaped to their plantation, The Oaks, near the mouth of Turkey Creek on the Northeast Cape Fear River and concealed herself in a cellar there with others hiding from the invaders. At dark British gunboats came upriver and seemed about to land. One of the men taking refuge in the cellar, John Brown, made a white flag of truce and went to meet the redcoats to hold a parley. The British fired on him when they saw him, missing Brown but sending him back into hiding. The redcoats shelled The Oaks

Anne Hooper, whose husband William was badly wanted by the British, was forced by Maj. Craig to leave Wilmington with barely the clothes on her back.

from their boats for a time before returning back to Wilmington.

Anne Hooper, William Hooper's wife, along with other rebel spouses, was ejected from Wilmington under the new British management. Hooper lamented his wife's and the other ladies' treatment, saying they were "suffered to carry with them nothing but their wearing apparel...." Craig denied the women carriages, but did allow them the use of a boat. Just before they loaded and departed, the major seemed to change his mind. The women were forced to return to the foot of Market Street and stand in the sun "for several hours" until Craig relented and let them go on their way. Anne made her way to Hillsborough with the help of Capt. Thomas Rutherford, a loyalist captured at the Battle of Moores Creek who was later paroled. Rutherford helped arrange transportation for Anne's baggage and valuables. William Hooper learned of his wife's ordeal when he was finally reunited with her in Hillsborough.

"Mrs. Hooper had been ill for several months before she left Wilmington," he recalled, "and when she came out, was so much reduced by disease that there was very little reason to believe that she would have reached Hillsboro alive. My son Tom was under the influence of a high fever. Craig, immediately upon issuing his edict of expulsion, had ordered a sergeant and a superior officer to take a list of my property, and Mrs. Hooper was enjoined to quit the town in a certain number of hours, under pain of the Provost. She was not allowed to carry out of it a riding carriage, though she had two, nor a horse, though Captain Leggatt and two others offered their horses to forward her to the American camp. In this melancholy situation, Mr. James Walker offered a boat and Mr. William Campbell's hands to row it as high up as Mr. Swann's on the Northeast. The ladies were seated in the boat, and passed through the painful scene of bidding adieu to their few friends, who were not permitted to accompany them, when Craig, who had not yet filled up the measure of cruelty allotted for these distressed women, forbade the boat to proceed. Again they came on shore - no house to shelter them, of their own - few that were hardy enough to receive them into theirs. They stood in the sun for several hours, when my daughter, overcome with the heat, called out 'Mama, let us go home.' Mrs. Hooper, whose firmness never forsook her in the severest moment of trial, answered -'My dear, we have no home.' Betsy could not support it. She burst into tears. Several British officers publicly abused Craig's conduct, and said that such cruelty would disgrace a savage. Craig again shifted like the weathercock, and ordered the boat to go on, but would not suffer any gentleman to attend them, although James Walker requested it. A boy of about ten years old was sent up as their escort."

Despite the circumstances, it seems the journey to Hillsborough was recuperative for Mrs. Hooper. "The back country and exercise...repaired her shattered constitution, and the fatigue of a few months is amply compensated by the accidental consequences of it," William Hooper related.

Those in Wilmington who supported American liberty fled when they could. South Carolina governor John Rutledge commented derisively that when the British arrived, "6 of the Town's people left it, the rest receive the Enemy with 3 huzzahs." In their absence, those loyal to King George III emerged from their post-Moores Creek isolation to take a more active role supporting the king's government. Many local loyalists enlisted to act as scouts or spies for Craig. Others joined new commissary officer Isaac DuBois in rounding up cattle and other seized rebel supplies. From surrounding plantations, a number of slaves ran to embrace their British liberators.

The occupation of Wilmington had an impact on the North Carolina economy too. While the redcoats under Craig held sway in the port town, the people had no access to trade with the surrounding countryside. Yes, the British held Wilmington, but the town was also isolated from the rest of the state by the major rivers that hemmed it in on the coast (the Cape Fear, Northeast Cape Fear, and Northwest Cape Fear). Likewise, the British would increasingly find that those same waterways were obstacles to successfully raiding into the Cape Fear beyond Wilmington.[8]

Under the British thumb they might have been, but the people of Wilmington nevertheless still managed to exercise some agency, even if it sometimes took silly forms. The loyalists who suddenly found themselves at the top of the societal pyramid in Wilmington made sure to reward their redcoat benefactors with plenty of amusements. Balls and receptions offered as much of a social scene as the town could muster. At one such gala, according to E.W. Carruthers, who said the story was told to him by Griffith John McCree, a statuesque young woman named Miss Ann Fergus became the target of a young British swain who sought her attentions. Ann was not a diminutive flower. She stood five feet ten inches in her bare feet, but when in heels could reach six feet. With a brother serving in the American army, Ann's enthusiasm for a British beau was muted at best. When a British officer who was rather on the short side asked her for a kiss, Ann told him, "Yes, he might have one, if he could take it without getting upon a stool." The soldier was game, and leaned in to capture his prize, but every time he did, Ann Fergus raised herself up on her tiptoes. The reward the short officer was seeking might as well have been on Mount Everest. His effort became laughable, and when the gathered men and women did, the soldier fled in embarrassment, never to pester an American woman again.

Craig immediately set about improving the defenses of the town. An anonymous writer provided Gov. Abner Nash with intelligence on the situation in Wilmington in a memorandum dated February 13, 1781. "At the Constitution Hill, there is a strong fortification which Commands the Town [of Wilmington] and its Vicinity. Two Hills between the So. end of the town and the old Battery is also thrown into R. Dobbs. The N. West is also fortified with Baterrys. Garrison not over Vigilant and 450 by count. Inhabitants not to be depended on to the Common Cause of A. 4 Armed Vessels in the River. Small pox in Burguins [Burgwins], Yellow Corner house near J. Walkers. No Rum for -- have arrived. Major Craig Commands and Capt. Ingalls of the *Delight*, 20 Gun Ship."

American defenders were hard pressed to answer the threat posed by 450 redcoats in control of the most important port town in North Car-

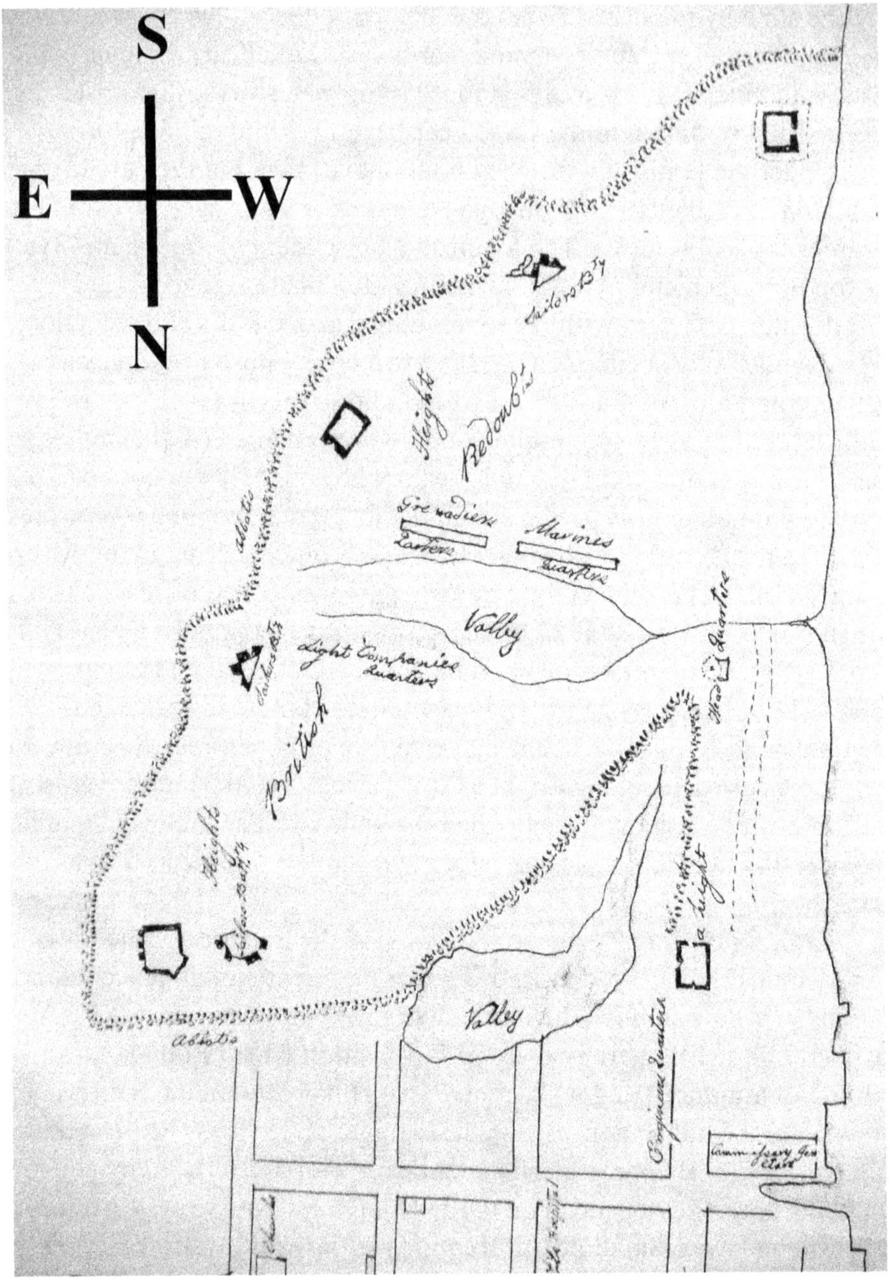

200

A close up detail of the sketch map showing the British fortifications in Wilmington. The northeast corner (top right corner) was anchored by St. James Anglican Church at the intersection of Fourth and Market Streets.

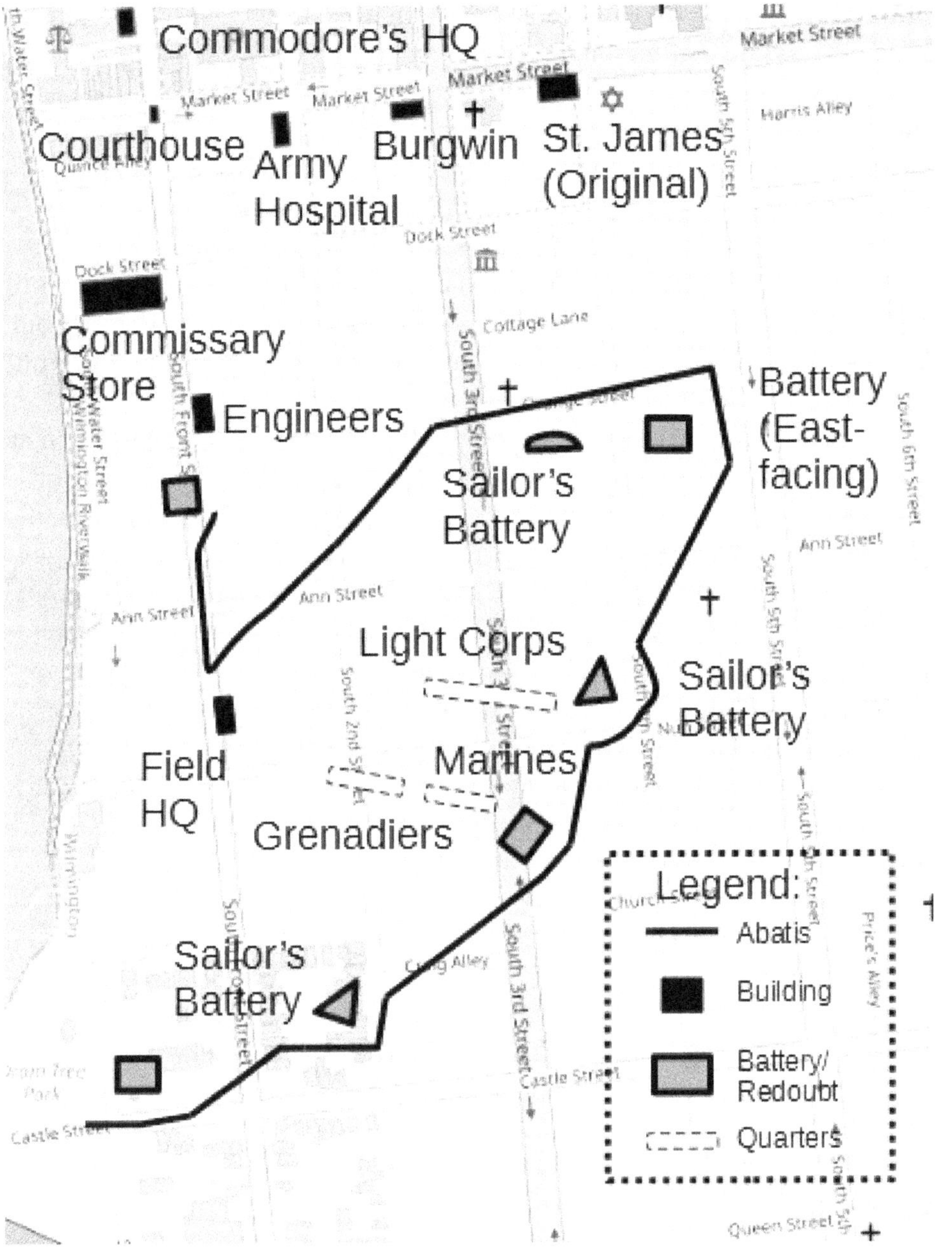

The outline of the British fortifications at Wilmington overlaid on a modern street map. From "The American Revolution Tour of North Carolina™" (AmRevNC.com). Copyright 2020 by AmRevNC, LLC. Reprinted by permission.

olina. On February 19, Col. Thomas Brown of Bladen County reported to BGen. Alexander Lillington his assessment of the situation. "I inclose you Col. [James] Emmet's [also Emmett] letter to inform you how Infamously the Newbern District hath behaved," he wrote, "and I am told cheafly owing to Capt. Thomas; I will gard the river on acct. of the Baggage & as far as lies in my power, but the greatest part of the good people in this County is Engaged back against the Toryes, and seems Very Loth to go Against the British And Leive [sic] their Families Exposed to a set of Villians, who Dayley threattains [sic] their Destruction. I intend seting out for Wilmington on Thursday with what few I can raise; at which time you shall hear from me."[9]

Col. Henry Young, after spiking the town cannons to make them at least temporarily inoperable, withdrew his 50 men to Heron's Bridge, on the Great Duplin Road running from Wilmington to Duplin Courthouse at modern Warsaw, N.C. Heron's Bridge was one of just two drawbridges in America at the time, stretching across the Northeast Cape Fear River at Castle Hayne. The bridge had hinges that allowed the center of the span to swing up to allow vessels to pass. Young established a defensive position on the Duplin County (modern Pender County) side of the bridge. Once Craig settled his men into the abandoned barracks in Wilmington, he turned his attention to securing his position and completing his primary mission of ferrying supplies to Cross Creek for LtGen. Cornwallis. That meant eliminating the threat posed by Brown's men at Heron's Bridge.[10]

The First Battle of Heron's Bridge
Forces Engaged:
British: Maj. James Henry Craig, commanding, British Regulars (250 total): 82nd Regt of Foot (the Hamilton Regt.) - Capt. Colebrook Nesbitt, Capt. Thomas Pitcairn; Capt. Andrew Barkley (Marines); Artillery: 3lb.-cannon (2). Outcome: 7 WIA.
American: Col. Henry Young, commanding, New Hanover District Militia: Wilmington Militia (50 men), Bladen Co. Militia (200 men), Artillery: 3lb-cannon (1). Outcome: 3 KIA, 8 POW

Two days after landing at Ellis Plantation, Maj. Craig mustered 250 soldiers and Marines with two small 3-pound cannons, and set out to deal with Col. Henry Young and his men of the New Hanover County District Militia. The redcoats did not know how many men Young had, or how

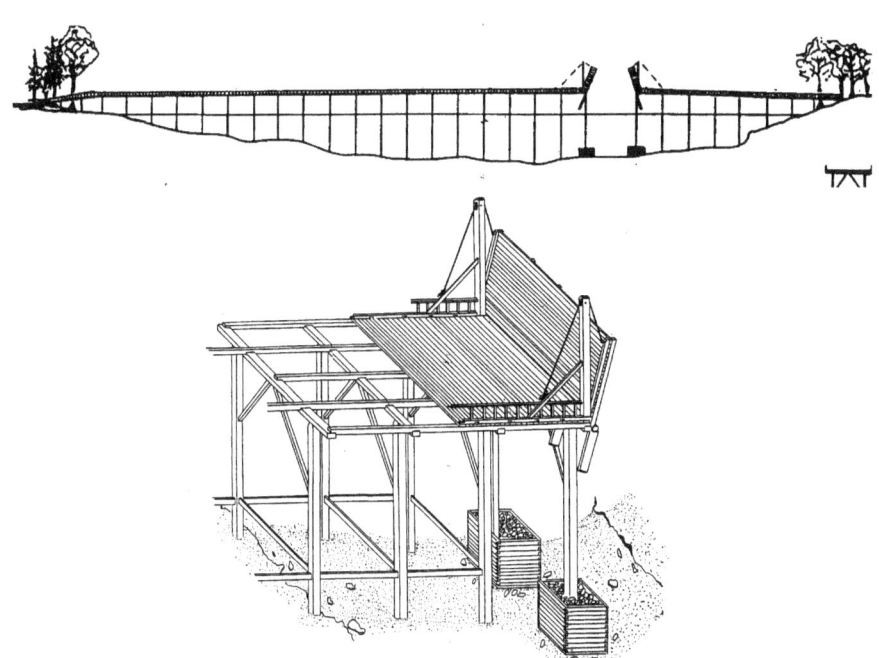

Heron's Bridge (top) was one of only two drawbridges in America in 1781. The span was hinged (bottom) to allow boat traffic to pass on the Northeast Cape Fear River. It was part of the Great Duplin Road that led to the Duplin Courthouse near modern Warsaw. (Credit: Wes Hall, 1992)

they were armed. They simply put their faith in the superiority of British arms and discipline when facing notoriously undependable American militiamen. Leaving Major Daniel Manson, the loyalist Royal North Carolina Regiment, and the remainder of his regulars to hold Wilmington, Craig set out from Wilmington at four in the afternoon on January 30 to cover the ten miles to the bridge.

Benjamin Heron built the single span drawbridge that stretched for 400 yards across the Northeast Cape Fear, emptying onto a causeway over swampy lowland before reaching dry ground on what, in 1781, was the Duplin County side. According to Craig's account, a number of vessels, including one loaded with gunpowder and ammunition, had gathered near the bridge to avoid capture by the British invading the town. That made taking Heron's Bridge all the more important, for Craig would need all the boats he could find to ferry supplies upriver.

The British stopped for the night some distance away, intent on attacking the bridge at dawn. One of Craig's light infantryman managed to capture an American cavalryman before he could raise the alarm. The prisoner provided information that made the British confident they could surprise Young's force and take the bridge with a minimum of casualties. In the morning the redcoats began their stealthy approach to the bridge only to be surprised themselves. A British sergeant and a private were discovered by six American cavalrymen and, unable to seek cover, the redcoats opened fire. The need for silence disappearing with that first volley, the main British force made for the bridge.

At the bridge, Craig's light infantry and grenadiers formed ranks and delivered a withering volley at the guards who challenged them. The Americans were thrown into disarray at the appearance of the redcoats and the violence of their attack. After the first rounds, the British charged, trying to take the span before the Americans could react. Captains Colebrooke Nesbit and Thomas Pitcairne led their companies, supported by Royal Marines, across the bridge while the two British field pieces were set up on the New Hanover County side to cover them. The 400 feet across the Northeast Cape Fear River seemed to stretch forever to some of the British making the crossing, but to their relief they made it to the north side without any real resistance from Young's men. The Americans were retreating, leaving their camp, their belongings, and the bridge in British hands.

In the camp Craig's men found "a number of arms, canteens. some provision, etc." They braced for a counterattack that never came, and eventually returned to the south side of Heron's Bridge. The redcoats set up camp there and rested from their exertions. The butcher's bill was light

The view from the site of Heron's Bridge, looking toward the modern bridge on I-40 crossing the Northeast Cape Fear between New Hanover and Pender Counties.

for the British, who suffered only six wounded. Captain Nesbit was one of them, shot twice in the leg in the Americans' first return fire. Wounded or not, Nesbit continued the attack, and Craig did not realize his officer was wounded until after it was done. The Americans, according to Craig's tally, lost three men dead and eight taken prisoner. Craig ordered the bridge burned, but the torching was only partially successful. Before returning to Wilmington, the redcoats removed the trunions of a captured American field piece and tossed the cannon into the river.

On the same day, BGen. Alexander Lillington was on the PeeDee River at Colston's Mill, building a redoubt to protect the powder magazine being built there. The mill became an important supply depot for Greene's army. Lillington and around 500 men arrived there on January 14, but upon learning of the British landing at Wilmington, they marched to meet the new threat. Lillington did not get there in time to participate in the first fight at Heron's Bridge, but he and his 500 men did arrive in time to stop Craig from doing any more damage. The redcoats spent January 31 marching five miles down the Northeast Cape Fear, burning plantations belonging to Whigs and destroying any stores that might be of use to the American cause.

Signature of Alexander Lillington

With Lillington's superior force in the vicinity, the British withdrew to Wilmington. Taking over from Col. Young, Lillington turned the American defenses at the bridge into something more formidable than what the New Hanover County Regiment's commander had been able to accomplish.[11]

On the way back to town, the British captured five of seven supply vessels on the Northeast Cape Fear. The two they did not capture were run aground and burned. The brig *Rose* was the biggest prize, with a cargo that included two 3-pound cannons and a hold full of rice, tobacco, and bale goods. The *Betsy*, a schooner, had six 9-pounder guns, plus rice, flour, turpentine, and rum. Aboard another schooner, the *Ceres*, was rice, flour, and ammunition. Craig could not help but brag a bit about how his men had performed. "In justice to the troops and marines under my command," he wrote, "I cannot help mention that the town of Wilmington was taken

A British landing party foraging for horse feed was turned back from Bacon's Inlet by Whig militia.

possession of and an extent of country upwards of 45 miles marched over with only one single instance of any article being touched or inhabitant injured in his property." For the British, it was an auspicious way to begin the occupation of Wilmington.[12]

The disruption to everyday life in southeastern North Carolina caused by the presence of Craig's regiment in Wilmington was significant. Courts, for instance, were unable to meet while redcoats held sway there. To remedy the problem, the General Assembly introduced a bill to allow the courts to meet anywhere within the county. By February Craig was sending foraging parties out into the countryside. A priority was forage for the horses of his command, plus meat for his soldiers' mess. For that, he sent two row galleys back to take the cattle he had noticed free ranging in Brunswick County on the way to Wilmington. Major John Cain and Major Samuel Leonard of the Brunswick County Militia intercepted the galleys at Bacon's Inlet. James Holden recalled the short-lived British landing. In his pension application he testified, "...that while at Bacon's Inlet on the coast of Brunswick County, North Carolina, some of the British landed from what were then called row galleys, who fired upon some men of Colonel [Major] Cain, but immediately retreated to their boats." In 1836, Brunswick County militiaman Charles Tharp remembered that "...news

The original St. James Anglican Church, which was incorporated into the British defenses at Wilmington.

was brought by one Robert Bell that the enemy were killing cattle on the marsh near Bacon's Inlet, that a part of the Lockwood Folly Company, this declarant being one, was marched down there under Maj. Samuel Leonard to drive them off - that a small skirmish ensued when the enemy retreated to their row galleys and went out of the inlet."[13]

    The British fortification of Wilmington took into account the force Craig had to defend it with, and the geography of the town. Wilmington was built atop seven hills with a number of streams that run down to the Cape Fear River. The redcoats constructed earthworks around the town and equipped them with sharpened stakes called abatis to repel attackers. They also built a compound stretching from Second to Fourth Streets on

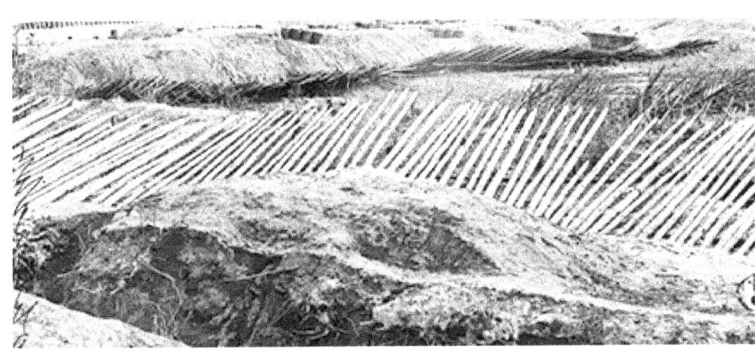

Sharpened stakes like these, called abatis, surrounded the British compound in Wilmington.

the heights south of the town that included St. James Anglican Church. Soldiers knocked holes in the brick church walls to make firing ports. Across from the foot of Market Street, on Eagles Island, Craig fortified a brick house at the ferry landing, adding more abatis to deepen its defenses. Army surgeons set up a hospital at the corner of Market and Second Streets, and fields of fire were cleared around the town and on Eagles Island to provide the British an unobstructed view of any enemy that might approach.[14]

In Bladen County on February 2, loyalists emboldened by the British at Wilmington skirmished with American militia at the plantation home of Col. Thomas Owen. The only known account of this action is in the pension application of Sherwood Fort, submitted in 1832. "There was another troop of Horse," he remembered, "formed in the lower part of the county under Capt. Jarrott Irvin [Jared Irwin] part of Colonel [Thomas] Brown's, and Colonel [Thomas] Robeson's command, with whom we served at times, but more frequently separate...It was during the time of this service, in 3 several engagements with the Tories, one on Raft Swamp in Robeson County, another, at Elizabeth [Town], and the 3rd which took place at Colonel [Thomas] Owen's Plantation on the 2nd of February 1781, 10 days before I received my discharge."[15]

Five days after the fight at Owen's plantation illustrated the heightened activity of Tories in the state due to the presence of Craig's regulars, the General Assembly passed a resolution to raise more militia to "repel the enemy at and near Wilmington." The resolution called for the North Carolina counties to provide a new draft of 2,900 men to counter the redcoats' activity, and to tamp down loyalist militancy. The Assembly assigned each county specific numbers to provide for the common defense: Beaufort - 75; Bladen - 200; Brunswick - 500; Carteret - 75; Chatham - 100; Craven - 150; Cumberland - 100; Dobbs - 125; Duplin - 300; Edgecombe - 100; Hyde - 50; Johnston - 150; Jones - 100; Nash - 50; New Hanover - 150; Onslow - 200; Pitt - 150; Wake - 200. Four days after passing the resolution, on February 11, they also tasked MGen. Richard Caswell, of Moores Creek fame, with raising a regiment of Light Horse from men of the New Bern and Wilmington Districts.[16]

Craig's men surprised a group of Americans while on a foraging party on February 9. The mounted Americans' horses were a prized target for British forces seeking what they could get from the surrounding countryside to help sustain themselves. The shortage of good cavalry horses was a serious concern for Craig, so the capture of the Americans' mounts would be a boon. Capt. Pitcairne reported that the Whigs only stood their ground long enough to fire one volley before galloping off. The incident was one of many that illustrates the challenges facing Maj. Craig at Wilmington.

A day after Pitcairne's men surprised the Americans, Craig wrote his first letter to Lord Cornwallis, providing a snapshot of the situation on the Cape Fear River. The small size of his force meant that local loyalists were reluctant to step forward and assist the occupiers from fear that the redcoats were too few to insure their safety. Despite small numbers, the major reported that he was fortifying the town, and was finding the help of seamen from *H.M.S. Delight* and *H.M.S. Otter* useful to man the town's defenses while Craig's regulars ventured outside Wilmington to forage. While the Northeast Cape Fear River proved effective at preventing American militia from making forays against Craig, he was still compelled to build earthworks around the town to defend the other approaches. Craig briefly entertained the notion of sallying forth from the town and attacking Gen. Nathaniel Greene's forces, the goal being to sandwich the Americans between Cornwallis and himself, but quickly discarded the idea because of the small size of his detachment.

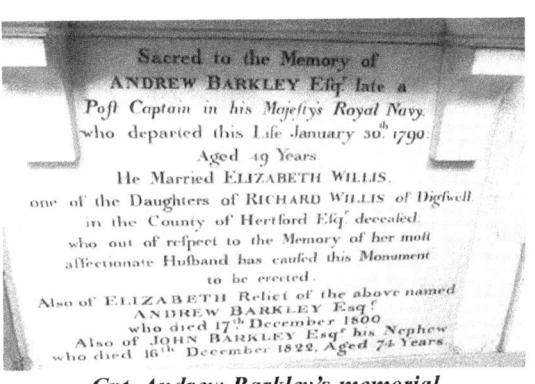

Cpt. Andrew Barkley's memorial.

Craig's manpower woes increased when, on February 18, Captain Andrew Barkley hoisted anchor and left the Cape Fear River, taking most of his Marines and warships with him. He left a number of smaller vessels and galleys to support Craig, but took the significant portion of his flotilla along when his flagship, *H.M.S. Blonde*, crossed the bar for the open Atlantic. Craig and Barkley had clashing personalities, and obviously did not get along with each other. Joint operation command structures of the time usually involved a ground commander and a commander for naval forces, who unless specifically ordered to do otherwise by higher authority, worked independently of each other. With Craig and Barkley at odds - either out of personal dislike or differing opinions on how to accomplish the mission - the major was not sorry to see his naval counterpart go. When writing of it to a superior officer Craig said, "May I beg if you can ever turn the scale relative to his returning here, that it may be in the negative - he & I differ so much in our sentiments that I much fear we can never carry on service together with that cordiality requisite to do it effectively... Pardon me if for your private information I warn you to receive it with caution every thing he tells you - [his] interest will be his chief inducement. I had once thoughts of returning him his marines that he might have no reason for coming back but I could not part with six and twenty fine fellows."

As the ink dried on Craig's letter, North Carolina Governor Abner Nash arrived to survey the situation at Heron's Bridge. Nash reviewed Alexander Lillington's men and promised reinforcements, emphasizing that as long as the militia held the bridge they could keep the British bottled up on the south side of the New Hanover County peninsula, bounded by river and sea. The situation was something of a stalemate. The Americans had superior numbers, but Lillington's men were also short of ammunition and everything else they needed to successfully oust Craig from Wilmington. The British, on the other hand, had superior soldiers and supplies, but in numbers too few to seriously challenge the Americans and break out of the river cordon.

To venture outside of fortified Wilmington was risky for the British. When the 14-gun sloop *H.M.S. Delight* sent ashore a seven-man burial

The site of the Bullpen where Cornelius Harnett, Jr. was held by the British in 1781. Today (2024) it is home to a bank at Second and Market Streets in Wilmington.

party on the west bank of the Cape Fear River to inter a crewman who had died, they were fired upon by American militia hidden in the tall marsh grass. The ambushers killed one sailor and captured three others. The remaining crewmen beat a hasty retreat, as the *Delight* covered their withdrawal with her own guns. The Americans themselves fled as grapeshot from the *Delight* ripped over their heads, allowing the British to free their captive shipmates.[17]

In the southernmost part of Onslow County, Cornelius Harnett was bedridden, a flare-up of gout causing excruciating pain in his lower body. Laid up at Col. John Spicer's plantation home in April, 30 miles north of Wilmington, he could only wait until the inflammation went down enough to allow him free movement again. He hoped it would be soon, for Harnett was one of the most wanted men in North Carolina. A central figure in the resistance to the Crown since 1765, Harnett and Robert Howe were the two Cape Fear men specifically excepted from a blanket pardon offered by the British when their fleet anchored in the Cape Fear River in the spring of 1776. Major James Henry Craig, occupying Wilmington, said of him that "he was employed to the most traitorous purpose; it determined me to turn any risk to seize him." Learning that Harnett had taken refuge at Spicer's, Craig dispatched men to attempt a capture. Harnett's heart must have sunk when redcoats burst into his room and held him at bayonet point while trussing him up for his ride back to Wilmington. One witness who saw Harnett when the British returned him to the town testified that the man Josiah Quincy, Jr. dubbed the "Samuel Adams of the South" came home "thrown across a horse like a sack of meal."

Harnett's headstone

In Wilmington, Harnett was confined in the Bullpen, an open-air enclosure without a roof that the British used to jail prisoners. Exposed to the elements, Harnett took ill and died on April 28, 1781. He was buried at St. James Anglican (Episcopal) Church, where his grave is still visible in the graveyard at Fourth and Market Streets. Harnett was in the company of BGen. John Ashe during his Bullpen stay. Ashe also fled the town when the British arrived, making it to Eagles Island, where he hid out in the rice fields. The militia general was betrayed to the occupying redcoats by a slave, and was shot in the leg while trying to escape. Smallpox laid Ashe low, contracted while he was incarcerated in the Bullpen. Maj. Craig eventually paroled him within the Wilmington town limits, but too late to save his life. The deaths of Harnett and Ashe did nothing to help the redcoats' reputation among the people of Wilmington, and indeed was seen as evidence of their cruelty. As the British settled in, the resentment their cruelty sparked would only get worse.[18]

March arrived with a number of problems for the British in North Carolina. At Wilmington, though Craig and his redcoats controlled the town, the militia at Heron's Bridge and in the vicinity beyond town limits proved a pesky obstacle to British operations. The American rebels tried Craig's patience and drew British blood by racing to the town limits and shooting at any redcoat sentry they saw. When British cavalry pursued, the Americans would wheel about and fire their rifled carbines at the redcoat horsemen while still out of range of the British weapons.

In the pursuit of Nathaniel Greene and his American army, LtGen. Cornwallis took drastic steps to be quicker in the chase. Cornwallis ordered that his baggage trains be destroyed or abandoned to match Greene's speed and agility as the two forces both moved towards Virginia, in what came to be known as the Race to the Dan. To that point, Cornwallis assumed that Craig, in control at Wilmington, was busily carrying out his orders to provide logistical support for the marching British army by ferrying supplies to Cross Creek. He was soon disabused of that notion.

Cornwallis penned a letter to Major Craig on March 1, 1781, with a request for resupply. The British army west of Wilmington needed a variety of things, including shoes, saddles, and boots. Craig was finding it a difficult task to complete. With Lillington's men fortified on the north side of the Northeast Cape Fear at Heron's Bridge, getting supplies to Cross Creek was exceedingly difficult. Added to that, there was a scarcity of shallow draft boats at Wilmington to ferry the supplies. Craig had ordered boats built, but with little success. The green wood the redcoats used was not the best material to make boats from. Then, even if he could get past the militia at the bridge, the Northeast Cape Fear upriver from Wilmington narrows and flows through plenty of places with high banks that provided perfect ambush sites for the rebels. Craig's inability to complete his resupply mission would have major implications for Cornwallis' Southern Campaign.[19]

The Massacre at Rouse's Tavern
(a.k.a. Eight Mile House)

Eight miles along the old New Bern Road (modern Market Street), somewhere near Middle Sound Loop Road in Ogden, N.C., once stood Rouse's Tavern. It was a place where weary travelers could stop for a drink on the road to or from Wilmington. The tavern was also sometimes called Eight Mile House because that was the distance it stood from the town limits. In early March 1781, it was the scene of one the worst slaughters of the war in the Lower Cape Fear.

BGen. Alexander Lillington tasked Major James Love and Captain William Jones of New Hanover County's militia to patrol the New Bern Road for enemy activity. Maj. James Henry Craig, it was said, had a habit of exercising his horse along the road each morning, and Love and Jones thought they might get a lucky shot at the commander of the British forces in Wilmington if they were in the right place at the right time.

Love gathered a couple dozen men and set up an ambush site near Walker's Bridge where it crossed Burnt Mill Creek on the outskirts of town (near the modern National Cemetery in Wilmington), and the next day Craig did, in fact, ride out with an armed escort of 12 or 15 dragoons. To cross the bridge required the redcoats to ride single file, and the thud of hooves across the wooden planks unnerved most of the Americans hidden nearby. They fled, but Love and Jones stayed. Looking down the barrel of his musket, James Love drew a bead on the short, thick officer who was obviously in charge, and took up the slack on his trigger. Just as the hammer was about to fall, the flint striking a spark that would send a .69 caliber ball racing towards the British commander, caution got the better of him. Love realized that with just Jones and himself left in the hide, the dragoons would sweep down upon them before they could get off another shot. It would be suicide. The two men decided to wait for another day, and James Craig rode on unmolested.

Love and Jones caught up with the rest of their men at Rouse's Tavern. They bellied up to the bar, drinking to take the sting out of their missed opportunity. The men who fled did the same, likely to dull the em-

Craig's redcoats massacered Maj. James Love and his men at a tavern along the road to New Bern in what is modern Ogden, N.C.

barrassment of running away from the fight and leaving their commanders behind. One drink led to two, and that led to another, and before long the Americans were well into their cups. Their senses impaired by drink, the danger posed by being so close to the road, where British patrols frequently passed, receded to some place less urgent in their minds. By 12:30 in the morning, the men had sunken to the floor of the tavern to sleep, using their saddles as pillows.

In Wilmington, Maj. Craig learned that Love and his men were at the tavern. Thinking he could catch them unawares, he dispatched 70 men of the 82nd Regiment of Foot with orders to grant no quarter. They arrived around nine in the morning to surround the tavern and try the door, only to find it barred. The captain in command of the British troops ordered it pried open. The noise of the redcoats trying to gain entry to the building woke James Love, who recognized what was happening and decided to sell his life dearly.

Love shouted an alarm and grabbed up his saddle. Using it as a shield he burst out the door, slashing with his saber at the redcoats closest to the entrance. The British soldiers quickly closed in, the 18-inch bayonets on the ends of their Brown Bess muskets prodding at Love, backing him step by step away from the tavern and towards a nearby mulberry tree. Love made it about 30 yards before he was pierced multiple times by enemy bayonets and left to bleed out underneath the tree.

Inside Rouse's, the Americans who were trying to wake up after a night of drinking opened their eyes to the horror of red coated death pouring in through the now open doorway. Some never woke up from their alcoholic slumber, bayoneted by British steel as they slept. Others managed a momentary bit of resistance before bayonets, butt strokes, and musket balls left them dead or dying. One man, named Garrett, survived the onslaught. The redcoats told him he could live if he told them where other American militia were. Garrett, fearing for his life, said that some men were staying at a house a few miles away. The British soldiers killed him anyway.

Eleven men were killed by Craig's soldiers at Rouse's Tavern. One, probably Lieutenant David Jones of the Fourth North Carolina Regiment of the Continental Line who was on recruiting duty, escaped. Not far off, LtCol. Thomas Bloodworth, of the New Hanover County Militia, heard the gunfire and rode with some men to the tavern. The British were gone, but the evidence of their attack was all around. Maj. James Love lay dead in the yard underneath the mulberry tree. Inside, the floorboards were crimson, "covered with dead bodies & almost swimming in blood, & battered brains smoking on the walls." An old woman and a child, both in shock, crouched by the fireplace. Taking it all in, Bloodworth, a friend of the dead James Love, swore he would have revenge for the massacre.

As Bloodworth took in the carnage, George Reed and five other militiamen were resting for the night at the Widow Collier's home, just a few miles from Rouse's Tavern. Reed and the men were driving cattle to the American militia headquarters to feed the troops Lillington had gathered at Heron's Bridge. Based on the tip from the unfortunate Garrett, they soon found themselves prisoners of the redcoats. Reed's 1832 pension application gave this account of the events on the night of the Rouse's Tavern massacre.

"About twenty days before this term of his service was ended, he with five others viz. John Wilkins, John Ferrell, Sandy Rouse, John Loper & William Bowen were staying all night on the Edenton Road about 12 or 13 miles from Wilmington at the widow Colliers house with some cattle which they were driving to headquarters for the use of the American troops," Reed's testimony said. "On the same night a detachment of American troops was staying at Rouse's house [and tavern] on the same road & about four miles toward Wilmington from where he was staying with his five companions.

"On this night, a party of British commanded by Major James H. Craig & [Daniel] Manson attacked this detachment of Americans & defeated them. Major James Love, Capt. John McClamma [Peter McLammy] with several men were killed. Among them was John Ferrell the father of one of the men that was with this declarant. Also among the killed was the quartermaster & a lieutenant whose names he has forgotten.

"A part of this same detachment of British, on the same night, attacked him & his companions at the widow Collier's house &, after a short resistance, they were all taken prisoner by the British. He received from this skirmish two wounds from a bayonet; one on the side & one in the leg below the knee. William Bowen was mortally wounded by a bayonet thrust in the neck & died the next day.

"This same party of British, on the same night, took one Col. Arnett a prisoner at the house of John Spears' where he was there lying sick. This Col. Arnett had, before the war, been a treasurer or collector for the king & he always understood that there was a reward offered for Col. Arnett. He [George Reed] saw him the next day as they took him in a carriage to Wilmington where he, Col. Arnett, died in about a week.

"On the next day, just before night, this declarant was with his other companions, set free on parole & under a promise to the British Major to go into Wilmington & take protection.' This promise they all violated except Sandy Rouse who, he heard, did take protection to save his property.

"This declarant was hauled in an oxcart to his father's which was about forty miles from Wilmington. The wound in his side was dressed by [Lt] Col. Thomas Bloodworth who was a doctor & when he probed it he said it had penetrated to the hollow, this wound, however, soon got well but his wound in the leg below the knee was sore for a long time, the bone was injured by the bayonet & ever since that time that his leg has occasionally broken out causing him a great deal of pain & loss of time & this declarant was unable to serve the balance of his term for which he had volunteered which was about twenty days."[20]

The Second Battle of Heron's Bridge

Forces Engaged:
British: Maj. James Henry Craig leading 200 men of the 82nd Regiment of Foot, augmented by 30 British sailors, and two 3-pound cannons.
American: BGen. Alexander Lillington commanding 400 militiamen, with six cannon.

The crux of the problem was Heron's Bridge. If Maj. Craig had any hope of fulfilling his orders to supply Cornwallis at Cross Creek, Lillington and his men must be ousted from their position at the bridge. Otherwise nothing the British sent upriver would ever make it to its destination in Cumberland County. The bridge had to be taken for other reasons, too. With rebels in control of the crossing, there was no way for Craig's forage parties to get into the countryside to gather the forage and foodstuffs they needed to supplement the rations coming in by ship. Forage for the British cavalry was gone in the Wilmington area. To get more required the redcoats to cast a wider net into New Hanover, Duplin and Brunswick Counties. Craig decided Heron's Bridge had to go.

On March 9, 1781 Craig again led a column of redcoats out of Wilmington along the Great Duplin Road to Heron's Bridge. When they arrived, the British set up their two field guns to cover the bridge and repulse any attack the Americans might make.

Scouts warned BGen. Alexander Lillington of the British arrival. The militia commander devised a plan to sandwich Craig between two fires. It required sending one company of troops downriver to cross the Northeast Cape Fear and circle in behind the redcoats. A second body of troops would cross Heron's Bridge to engage the British from the north. Craig would find his command caught in the pincers of a deadly American vise. The general assigned Col. Henry Young with 60 cavalrymen and Col. Thomas Brown with 70 infantrymen to make the crossing and hit the British from the south.

The militiamen made the crossing to the New Hanover County side of the river undetected and set up a quick camp to await the signal to attack. A Major Dennis was ordered to take a dozen men and set up a picket south of where Young and Brown were, to warn of any approaching redcoats. But Dennis disobeyed the order and stayed in camp, and the British found them there. Maj. Craig related what happened next. "Our

The second battle at Heron's Bridge by artist James C. Horton.

Craig's redcoats unleashed a hail of cannon and musket fire on Lillington's defenders at Heron's Bridge.

Advanced Guard surprised a piquet [guards] of Light Horse most of which was bayoneted or rushed into the River and drowned," he said, "and by the Prisoners taken I learnt that a party under a Colonel Brown consisting of 150 Horse and Foot, were then on the sound." Dennis' detachment suffered one man killed and another drowned when he slipped off the dismantled and burned Heron's Bridge into the Northeast Cape Fear. Craig regrouped his men on a nearby hill, and positioned his artillery to confront the coming attack.

At four o'clock in the afternoon, Lillington gave the nod for his artillery to open fire. Colonels Young and Brown led their men onto the bridge and towards the British positions on the far side. The Americans quickened their pace as the first rounds of British fire began to buzz over their heads. Behind them, Alexander Lillington stood on a high bluff to direct the action. He immediately saw that the Americans were not properly placed to make a strong sortie against Craig's defenses. The British 3-pounders barked out, sending shot and shell into the mass of rebels crossing the river, while redcoat infantry sent volleys of musket balls into the Americans. Militiamen James Malpass and Joseph Humphrey were among those who made the attempt, but like their comrades, they were forced to retreat.

In the aftermath, Col. Thomas Brown was among the wounded, his arm broken so badly that he lost the use of it afterwards. Others, like Private John Edge, who were wounded at the bridge, never fully recovered. Lillington's force lost about 20 men killed, and about 11 taken as prisoners. On the British side, Craig lost two wounded and one cavalryman taken prisoner. The British remained at Heron's Bridge for four days gathering much needed forage before marching back to Wilmington. A month later, Lillington withdrew his men to a position at Rutherford's Mill, near modern Burgaw, N.C. roughly 15 miles away.

Onslow County's Joseph Humphrey, who was among Lillington's 500, offered an account of the action in his 1833 pension application: "...having enlisted in the county of Onslow, under Col. Henry Rhodes, Col. [Maj.] Joseph Scott Cray & Capt. Ephraim Battle, & marched thence to New Hanover County to Rocky Point on the Cape Fear River at Big Bridge - here we lay encamped until we were joined by [Brig] General [John Alexander] Lillington; the British having made their appearance on the opposite side of the river, General Lillington ordered a company to march down the river and cross the same whilst another division should cross the bridge & they attacked the British in front & us in the rear. The British had two large cannons planted facing the bridge, the Lieutenant whom General Lillington ordered to advance across the bridge refused to do so, and the British sentinels having notified them of the advance of the Americans across the river, and great confusion having been produced in consequence of a want of cooperation by the other party refusing to cross the bridge, the British brought on a general engagement, and soon routed the Americans. We retired into the woods and the British made their way back to Wilmington."

Confusion was the deciding factor at the second clash at Heron's Bridge. Craig and Lillington offered hugely different tallies of the killed and wounded. Fighting in swamps meant individual soldiers were focused only on what was going on around them. Craig's account of the battle painted a different picture from the one submitted by Lillington.

"The rebel militia, now between five and six hundred under Brigadier Lillinton' [Lillington] with six pieces of cannon, continue at Heron's Bridge and prevent all communications with that part of the country," Craig wrote to Cornwallis on March 22, "We have dispersed a party of about a hundred that were on the Brunswick side of the river and defeated another of a hundred and fifty a few days ago, killing twenty and taking a few prisoners, but it has no effect on their main body. Both their numbers and position put it out of my power to attack them, nor can I hope to disperse them with my present force. Though our different actions have been attended with very little loss, yet we are much diminished by sickness and desertion…The town of Wilmington itself would require at least six hundred men to garrison it properly. As it was impossible for us to attempt it, we chose a post below the town but commanding it."

Three days later, he continued his report to Cornwallis: "In the middle of March, finding the forage near us consum'd, and it being dangerous to procure it at any distance from the great numbers the rebels might oppose to the small parties I was able to send, I determin'd to march with two hundred men and two three pounders and take post opposite them at the end of the bridge. Their numbers were then at a low ebb, their main body not consisting of more than three hundred and fifty or four hundred with six can[n]on. I intended by this to cover the country while with the assistance of Captain [John] Inglis (who sent me a lieutenant and thirty seaman) I collected forage, and I was in hopes it would have encourag'd the country people to bring in fresh provisions of which the inhabitants were beginning to be in want. Our advanc'd guard surpriz'd a picquet of light horse, most of which were bayoneted or push'd into the river and drown'd, and by the prisoners taken I learnt that a party under a Colonel [Thomas] Brown [of Bladen] consisting of 150 horse and foot were then on the sound. These I meant to have gone in quest of the next night, as I was well acquainted with their usual haunts and did not doubt I should find them. However, they by good fortune prevented me and reduc'd our meeting to a certainty, for deceiv'd by intelligence that we were only a party of fifty men, they came and attack'd us at four o'clock in the afternoon. Our picquet under Lieutenant [Moore] Hovenden of the Legion, doing duty with the 82nd, and a small foraging party under Lieutenant [John] Reeves of the 82nd, who were coming in, receiv'd their attack and repuls'd them, and the light company with the mounted men being order'd to their support, the rebels were pursued between four and five miles. The thickness of the swamps, the near approach of night and the attention I was obliged to pay to the enemy in my front, who can[n]onaded us the whole time, by not allowing me to detach more men after them, prevented our doing greater execution. They left twenty dead and we took an officer and ten prisoners. Their number of wounded by accounts obtain'd since was very considerable, and among them Colonel Brown. Our loss was a serjeant and two men wounded, the former since dead, and one mounted man by engaging too far in the pursuit was taken. We had also two horses kill'd. We remain'd at the bridge four days, when, having collected a sufficiency of forage and finding the other purposes I expected from taking the post were not answer'd, we march'd at nine o'clock in the morning and return'd to this place, but without the enemy's accepting the fair invitation we gave them of following us." [21]

Horace Walpole

Lillington was not blind to the opportunity that was lost in the action. He reported the details of the fight to Gov. Richard Caswell, saying "there was a Most Glorious Opportunity offered when they were at the Bridge, if we that day had the Troops that Major Dennis Carried off we Positively Should have killed & taken Craig & All his little Army - I cannot put it out of my mind." To General Greene he said, "we are not in a situation to drive [Craig's] Troops out of Wilmington & I am afraid we shall not be able to hold this part of the State long, unless we have a timely reinforcement..."[22]

Early in March Nathaniel Greene and his army won the Race to the Dan. Rather than staying in Virginia, they circled back down into North Carolina to set up the climactic set piece battle Cornwallis had been craving, and which Greene had been refusing until he could do it on ground of his choosing. Greene found that ground at Guilford Courthouse, and Cornwallis got his battle on March 15, 1781. The fight was vicious, but in the end the Americans conducted an orderly withdrawal when their ammunition ran low, ceding the bloody field to Cornwallis. Greene's army suffered light casualties all things considered. More importantly, they were still ready and able to fight again.

For the redcoats, the cost was much higher. Horace Walpole observed in Parliament that, "Lord Cornwallis has conquered his troops out of shoes, and himself out of troops." Technically Guilford Courthouse was a British victory, but in claiming that win Cornwallis suffered twenty-five percent casualties. At the end of the battle, the British left the field with only 1,400 men fit enough to fight. Lord Cornwallis had, in effect, ruined his army. The result prompted Member of Parliament Charles Fox to exclaim that another such victory would destroy the British army.

The ragged remains of Cornwallis' command began their staggering march to Cumberland County, the place where Maj. Craig was supposed to have delivered desperately needed supplies, on March 18. Leaving 64 badly wounded men in the care of the Quakers at New Garden Meeting House, the British turned south. Cornwallis wrote to his superiors in London describing the condition of his army. "With a third of my Army Sick & Wounded which I was obliged to carry in Waggons or on horseback," he said, "the remainder without shoes & worn down with fatigue, I thought it was time to look for some place of rest & refreshment."

Charles O'Hara

American forces nipped at the edges of the tired British the whole way to the coast. On March 25, Capt. John Taylor's Granville County militia ambushed Cornwallis' column as they tried to cross Stewart's Creek in Cumberland County (now part of the Fort Liberty U.S. Army base). It was cold, with light snow dusting the ground as dragoons from BGen. Charles O'Hara's lead element approached the crossing. Taylor waited until eight of the mounted redcoats had gathered before opening fire, killing one and capturing three more. O'Hara, crippled due to a wound suffered at Guilford Courthouse, ordered a burly soldier to carry him on his back as he led a counter attack across the creek. Riding the redcoat soldier piggyback, O'Hara fired both barrels of the "double barreled fusee" at Taylor's Americans and killed three. The rest of the Americans melted away.[23]

In January 1781 Cornwallis' army was 3,224 men strong. In the aftermath of Guilford Courthouse, only 2,213 men filled his ranks. Losses at Cowpens, King's Mountain, and Guilford Courthouse, plus the usual enemies of armies in the field such as disease and desertion, had whittled away at the seemingly invincible British campaigners. While the Americans enjoyed the home field advantage of knowing the terrain and being able to replenish their losses relatively easily, Cornwallis found himself a stranger in a strange land. Loyalists in the Carolina interior never materialized in the numbers he had been led to believe they would. In Guilford and Orange Counties, the earl tried to recruit Tories to his army, but he "could not get 100 men in all the Regulator's as Militia." Cornwallis asserted that their zeal was "not so great as had been represented, and that their friendship was only passive."

Gen. Greene shadowed Cornwallis as he marched south. As an example of how much ground the Americans covered and how fast, Joseph Plumb Martin, a member of the Massachusetts Continental Line, recorded in his journal an occasion in which they covered fifty miles in twelve hours, and ninety miles in twenty-four. After Guilford Courthouse, the worn, wounded, and sick British army took six days to cover ninety miles. Greene reached a point where he had to decide whether to continue after the remnants of the army he had fought at Guilford, or turn into the South

The modern incarnation of Barbeque Church.

Carolina backcountry to eliminate the British forts strung like crimson daggers across the frontier. He made his decision, and marched for South Carolina. His former opponent would go in a different direction, soon leaving Cross Creek for Wilmington.[24]

Cornwallis' army threaded their way through Harnett, Cumberland, Bladen, Brunswick and New Hanover Counties to reach Craig at Wilmington. Along the way they took a number of prisoners. The captured Whigs represented more mouths to feed from an increasingly barren larder, so the British more often than not paroled the low value rank and file soldiers, sending them off to their homes. Other times, the redcoats turned a blind eye to Americans "escaping" their captors because it was easier than being responsible for feeding them on the march.

Banastre Tarleton

Under orders from Gen. Greene to make sure there was nothing to provide material support to the British on their march, Alexander Lillington's Wilmington District militia were also instructed to do what they could to obstruct the redcoats as they made their way to the port town. One example of the Americans' doing just that came at Barbeque Church, near the home of William Buie in what is now Harnett County. After camping at Buie's home on March 26, the redcoats resumed their trek and approached the church the next day. In the vanguard, Lieutenant Colonel Banastre Tarleton's British Legion scouted ahead of the column. Lying in wait, Capt. Daniel Buie and his men of the Cumberland County militia saw them coming.

When the two sides clashed, Tarleton's dragoons captured Captain Daniel Buie on the Upper Little River part of the Cape Fear. The green jacketed cavalrymen also took Duncan Buie, Jacob Gaster, John Small, and Laurence Strodder.

A British prison ship was anchored off modern Carolina Beach State Park.

The home of Cross Creek merchant and Continental officer Peter Mallet was looted by the British and loyalists when Cornwallis arrived. The house is now a part of the Methodist University campus in Fayetteville, N.C.

In capturing Duncan Buie, the dragoons "crowned" him, delivering a severe cut to the top of his head and another to his face with a cavalry saber. Buie collapsed to the ground and was left for dead. He wasn't. Duncan recovered and lived to fight another day, while his officer brother Daniel was fated to perish as an inmate aboard a British prison ship in the Cape Fear River, off modern Carolina Beach State Park. Another officer, Capt. Peoples, was held in the Bullpen at Wilmington but managed to escape, while Gaster, Small, and Strodder were eventually exchanged after being held in Wilmington. In his 1832 pension application, Small testified about the prisoners' fates. Small said, "...in 1781 - 27th of March - he was taken by Lord Cornwallis (with one Daniel Buie who raised a small company, and who died between Charlestown and James River) and carried to Wilmington, from thence to Charlestown, and put on board a Prison Ship and carried to Jamestown on James River in Virginia where he was set at liberty, the Term of his confinement was about three months - and returned home either July or August - That he was never wounded."[25]

The British army limped into Cross Creek on March 30. Cornwallis recorded that "500 rebels had taken their position, but who withdrew on our approach, having partly burnt their stores and partly carried them off. The remaining stores of provisions were collected together and distributed amongst the troops." The scant amount of supplies was a far cry from what the general believed would be waiting for him. Cornwallis was dismayed to find that other than the few things the Americans had not been able to remove or destroy on his approach, there was nothing for miles around.

It was a terrible blow. The British who had chased Greene across two states, and finally fought him tooth and nail at Guildford Courthouse, needed just about everything - shoes, saddles, medicines, ammunition, food, uniforms, tents, and all the sundry other items it took to keep an army in the field. Cornwallis wrote, "From all my information I intended to have halted at Cross creek, as a proper place to refresh and refit the troops; and I was much disappointed, on my arrival there to find it totally impossible. Provisions were scarce, not four days forage within twenty miles, and to us the navigation of Cape Fear river to Wilmington impracticable; for the distance by water is upwards of one hundred miles, the breadth seldom above one hundred yards, the banks high, and the inhabitants on each side generally hostile." Cornwallis ordered that runaway slaves who had been flocking to the British camp be organized into foraging parties, but they were hard to control. The general received complaints of "Negroes Straggling from the Line of March, Plunder'g and Using Violence to the Inhabitants." Cornwallis ordered any caught in such behavior be whipped or shot. At any rate, the foraging parties had little success.

Cornwallis had nearly 600 sick and wounded men with him when he arrived in Cross Creek. A third of his army was shoeless. The need to reach Wilmington where medical attention and resupply could be obtained became paramount, but getting there would be difficult. The general was dismayed to find that American militia had removed or destroyed every boat in the area, so floating down the Cape Fear to Wilmington was out of the question - even if the high bluffs along the river where enemy forces could ambush his army as it floated past were not a reality. He determined to stay in Cross Creek no longer than necessary.

The redcoats resumed their march for the coast on April 1, traveling down the same road Donald MacDonald had intended to use five years earlier. While local loyalists provided the British what supplies they could, it was nowhere near what the army needed to right itself after the fight and long march from Guilford. Sick and wounded mixed in with those men still able to walk on their own, carried in litters or on stretchers suspended between two horses. Along the way, the graves of dead redcoats littered the route of march, some victims of the fighting at Guilford Courthouse, others victims of Americans like Cato Riddle and his men, who sniped at

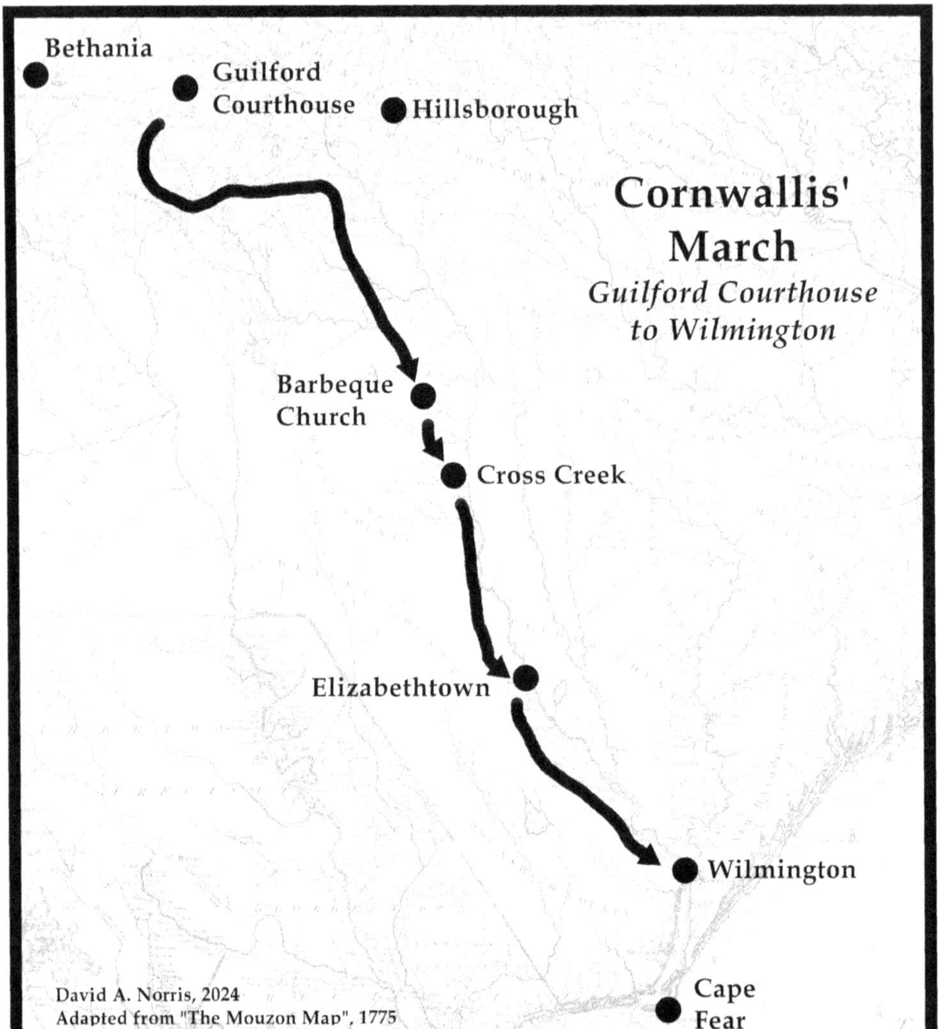
Bethania
Guilford Courthouse
Hillsborough
Cornwallis' March
Guilford Courthouse to Wilmington
Barbeque Church
Cross Creek
Elizabethtown
Wilmington
Cape Fear
David A. Norris, 2024
Adapted from "The Mouzon Map", 1775

them incessantly along the way.

One of those graves belonged to LtCol. James Webster, the popular and capable officer of the 33rd Regiment of Foot. Webster was wounded in the leg at Guilford Courthouse. The wound festered with infection until, two weeks later, it killed him. Webster was a soldier who was liked and respected on both sides, and his loss hit Cornwallis hard. British Sergeant Roger Lamb recorded that "it was reported in the army that when Cornwallis received the news of Webster's death, his lordship was struck with a pungent sorrow, that turning himself, he looked on his sword, and emphatically exclaimed, 'I have lost my scabbard.'" The general penned a letter to Webster's father, Dr. Alexander Webster of Edinburgh, assuring him that, "...You have for your satisfaction that your son fell nobly in the cause of his country, honoured and lamented by fellow soldiers; that he led a life of honour and virtue, which must secure to him everlasting happiness." Webster was buried on a Bladen County plantation just south of Elizabethtown, on the British route of march, in an unmarked grave to protect it from desecration by partisans. [26]

The looming threat of Cornwallis cast a pall over Whig recruiting efforts in the Lower Cape Fear, and the militia that were already embodied were often undependable. The inability of the state to pay its troops the recruiting bonuses they promised when they promised them led men to consider their contracts with the state null and void. In such cases they often just left, returning to their homes and farms. As early as 1778, units were making regular reports about men "hiding themselves in the woods" to avoid serving. The sympathy civilians had for these deserters often compounded the difficulties officers had in keeping their units manned because it was common for the missing men to find willing confederates who kept them hidden. [27]

As Cornwallis continued his march to Wilmington, the earl also had to contend with the biggest killer of soldiers in the Revolutionary War, disease. Fevers and "fluxes," dysentery, typhus, and smallpox all contributed to a death toll few clashes of arms could match. Illnesses of various sorts impacted the ability of both armies to conduct operations. People of the time believed the sicknesses originated in what one historian has called "mysterious effluvia or miasma rising from the swamps." Anyone familiar with southeastern North Carolina can attest that there are plenty of swamps to blame an eighteenth-century army's health woes on. Of

Artist James C. Horton's imagining of the arrival of Cornwallis and his weary troops as they passed by the Burgwin-Wright House in Wilmington in April 1781.

course, modern virologists and health professionals understand that other culprits - like poor sanitation habits and mosquitoes - are the sources of much disease, but the limited knowledge of the time made the swamps of the Lower Cape Fear region an enemy to both armies.[28]

The British column arrived at Maclean's Bluff overlooking the Cape Fear River (modern Navassa) on April 7, after averaging a meager 14 to 16 miles per day on the march. Looking across Eagles Island at the port town, Gen. Cornwallis decided he had been in the Carolinas long enough. Word arrived that Gen. William Phillips had landed a redcoat army in the Chesapeake and was about to undertake operations in Virginia. Cornwallis wrote to him, saying "I assure you that I am quite tired of marching about the country in quest of adventures." While the Carolinas campaign did not turn out as he had hoped, he saw in the arrival of Phillips' army another chance to conquer the South.[29]

The day before Cornwallis arrived, Maj. Craig wrote that he was afraid Capt. Andrew Barkley would take his Marines with him when he departed the Cape Fear. If he did, it would only serve to make Craig's undermanned command weaker. Craig sent his concerns along to the general, with fresh intelligence that the Dutch had joined France and Spain in an alliance with the Americans. This turned the American war into a conflict with implications beyond North America.

The British began ferrying their wounded across the Cape Fear River to Wilmington on April 9, first the badly injured, then those with less serious conditions the next day. Saint James Church had its pews removed so the redcoats could use it as a hospital. The remainder of the army made the crossing between April 11 and April 13. A German officer with the army noted "row-galleys and provision ships were moored in the Cape Fear River not far from the town. The great transports, etc., however, account of the shallowness the water, lay 16 miles further down the river, and most requirements and necessities had to be brought up to the town in sloops." Also returning to the town, the deposed royal governor Josiah Martin and the Black Pioneer Regiment made up of escaped slaves, some of which came from the Cape Fear region.[30]

Although Wilmington offered access to medical aid that simply was not available on the march from Guilford Courthouse, for some it was too late. More men died, such as one Lieutenant von Trott, and were interred in the town. The other thing Wilmington offered (finally) was rest and resupply. Word of the desperate need for virtually everything reached Charlestown, and Nisbet Balfour jumped to do what he could. The lieutenant colonel left in charge of the city where the Southern Campaign began wrote Gen. Clinton of Cornwallis' plight and the steps he took to remedy it.

"I am honoured with your letters of the 2d of January, and 19th of last month," Balfour wrote, "as also with one of the 14th ult. by your Excellency's directions, from Captain Smith. As Lord Cornwallis is in the greatest want of every supply, I have sent him to Cape Fear what can be procured here, and as he will have many calls on the Hospital, in consequence of the late marches and action, I have taken care to furnish a supply of officers and stores to that department at Wilmington; and shall by that way forward to his Lordship your Excellency's dispatches, whenever an occasion offers."[31]

Maj. Daniel Manson met Cornwallis when he arrived in Wilmington on April 9. Craig's second in command noted that the men who followed him were something less than the image of a conquering army. They still had smart ranks and a disciplined march, but their dirty, torn uniforms and too many pairs of shoeless feet told a different story. Manson met Gen. Cornwallis because Maj. Craig was out of town on the raid that captured Cornelius Harnett. The next day Cornwallis sat down to write a dispatch informing of his status and the condition of his command.

"I am now employed in disposing of the sick and wounded," Cornwallis wrote to Gen. Clinton, "and in procuring supplies of all kinds, to put the troops into a proper state to take the field. I am, likewise, impatiently looking out for the expected reinforcements from Europe, part of which will be indispensably necessary, to enable me either to act offensively, or even to maintain myself in the upper parts of the Country, where alone I can hope to preserve the Troops, from the fatal Sickness, which so nearly ruined the Army last Autumn...but North Carolina is, of all the Provinces in America, the most difficult to attack, (unless material Assistance could be got from the Inhabitants, the contrary of which I have sufficiently experienced) on account of the great extent of the numberless Rivers and

Creeks, & the total want of interior navigation..."[32]

Wilmington loyalists, either out of true conviction or self-interest, came out of hiding with the arrival of Gen. Cornwallis and his regulars. They petitioned newly returned Gov. Josiah Martin to be recognized as British citizens, to have their property restored, and to have the protection of the British army. While some were undoubtedly sincere in their declarations of fealty to the king, others were likely following the prevailing winds and declaring their loyalty out of a sense of self preservation.[33]

Not every thought was taken up with military matters. One story says that among Cornwallis' officers was a young lieutenant who set out on the campaign from Charlestown, leaving behind a South Carolina girl he had fallen in love with. Missing her terribly, and unsure when he would see her again, the soldier allegedly used the diamond in his ring to scratch her name on a window pane of John Burgwin's house at the corner of Third and Market Streets. After the war was over, the story says the young man returned to his love and married her. He took his bride home with him to England.[34]

At Rutherford's Mill outside modern Burgaw, Alexander Lillington considered the arrival of Cornwallis' men and what it might mean for

The remains of Lilligton's earthworks north of Heron's Bridge in modern Pender County.

the next stage of the war. Lillington's militia had retreated from Heron's Bridge on April 9, the same day Cornwallis arrived in Wilmington. The situation between the redcoats in town and Lillington's force trying to keep them hemmed in there was something of a stalemate. Lillington's cavalry had managed to bring in about 150 steers to feed his force, but he had also lost ten valuable men at Rouse's Tavern. Meanwhile, the 400-500 men he still had needed to eat if he wanted to keep them. It seemed that so far, 1781 had not been a banner year for the American cause in the Lower Cape Fear. First, the British took the largest and most strategically important town in the state. Then, Lillington's force had been driven back from Heron's Bridge. Most recently, Capt. James Love and his men had been massacred by redcoats who caught them by surprise. The army he had was, as one American observed, a "confused rabble," and Lillington himself confided that "the Militia was not to be depended upon." Alexander Lillington, a hero of the victory at Moores Creek five years earlier, could only hope it was the darkness before dawn brought a new, brighter day.[35]

Lillington kept American troops posted on the north bank of the Northeast Cape Fear River in the vicinity of Heron's Bridge to keep an eye on the British and to interdict any efforts by the redcoats to send supplies upriver. While the British had technically won both clashes at the bridge so far, they had not been able to run Lillington's men off completely. Each time the rebels had scattered into the surrounding woods and swamps, only to creep back in once the British were gone. Craig tried to bluff Lillington into abandoning the position with a letter when he learned Cornwallis was marching for Wilmington.

"Sir," Craig wrote, "as the people under your Command are all militia, whom we always rather...pity than wish to destroy - I will now acquaint you that I have taken Post here, to cut you off from all possibility of escape. In a few hours Lieut. Colonel [Banastre] Tarleton will be upon you with a detachment superior to yours even in Numbers - to spare your People therefore and to Preserve their farms (every one of which whose owners is absent will be Destroyed) I am to propose to you to deliver up your Arms to me, on which Condition your people shall have full Liberty to return home unmolested, & I will take effectual measures to secure their Property from the resentment of Lieut. Colo. Tarleton's Party."

Lillington was not cowed, declaring that it would take more than a threat to dislodge the Americans. He answered, "Were it reasonable to suppose that you were well acquainted with the strength of my Army, & be sure of Lieut. Colo. Tarleton's success in an engagement with us, I should feel the full force of the humane Terms offered my men. But while we have Arms in our hands, and are appraised of your intentions, my prospects of success are very fair. I shall not yield up this post until compelled to it by superior force when my Army shall have an opportunity of signalizing their valour."

Craig tried one more time. He said, "my coming here is the effect of a preconcerted scheme & I beg you to be assured I should not have given you notice of your situation, had my so doing, been in the smallest Degree likely to have Afford you the means of extricating yourself." The American commander again declined.[36]

While the center of the action in the Lower Cape Fear was around Wilmington, it was not the only place where Whigs and Tories clashed. At Drowning Creek (today's Lumber River near modern Fair Bluff), Micajah Vasser described a short, sharp fight that left him with a missing leg and a discharge from service. In his pension application, he wrote that he "...volunteered first of November 1780 under command of Captain Robinson's [Peter Robeson's] cavalry or light horse company...We marched to Wilmington, North Carolina, thence to Georgetown, South Carolina, thence to Fair Bluff on Drowning Creek [now the Lumber River], North Carolina, there had a small skirmish with the Tories; thence to Legat's fields on Rockfish [Creek], there had a severe fight with the Tories, got wounded in the right leg which caused an amputation of the same, below the knee, was discharged in the early part of April 1781..."[37]

With Craig and, for the time being, Cornwallis in command of Wilmington, conducting intelligence was of paramount importance for the Americans. The British knew it too, and actively sought out those who might be spying for the rebels. Brunswick Town blacksmith William Cain was arrested and accused of espionage. Cain had a history of supporting the American cause, having served on the Brunswick Committee of Safety before the war. He had already been captured and paroled once before, but violated the terms of the agreement when he continued to offer material support to the rebel militia. When the redcoats found him "holding a correspondence and giving intelligence" to the enemy, Cain was sentenced to hang. Cain's conviction came on April 11, amid allegations that he had been instrumental in the February 1781 ambush of a landing party from

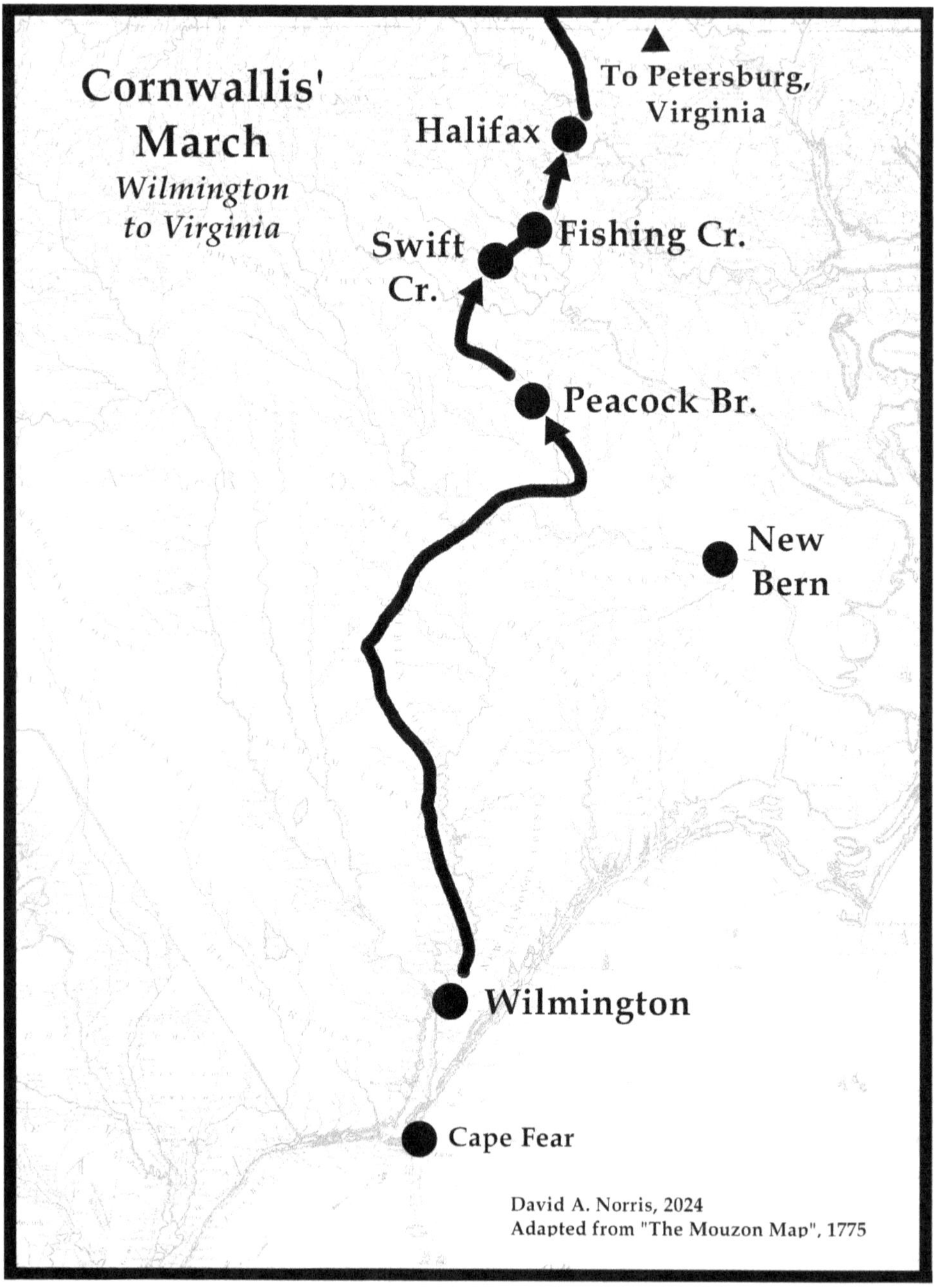
Cornwallis' March
Wilmington to Virginia
To Petersburg, Virginia
Halifax
Fishing Cr.
Swift Cr.
Peacock Br.
New Bern
Wilmington
Cape Fear
David A. Norris, 2024
Adapted from "The Mouzon Map", 1775

H.M.S. Delight. The British thought it poetic justice to hang Cain from the yardarm of the same ship he was accused of helping attack. Once dead, Cain's body was dropped into the Cape Fear.[38]

Among the things on Cornwallis' plate was the possibility of a prisoner exchange. Corresponding with Nathaniel Greene, both sides were anxious to unburden themselves with the extra mouths to feed represented by their prisoners of war. The talks had been ongoing since 1780, but not until the spring of 1781 were the details hammered out. Finally, an exchange was arranged at the South Carolina home of Claudius Pegee on the Pee Dee River.[39]

Resupplying Cornwallis' weary army was also a paramount concern. After two weeks, the British troops were still not completely replenished, but shoes, uniforms, and new arms were distributed to both German and British soldiers. Their discarded muskets were handed over to loyalist militias. In an army where many were barefoot when they arrived in Wilmington, the two pair of shoes they received from quartermaster's stores in Wilmington must have seemed like Christmas come early. One soldier of the Von Bose Regiment took delight in the double ration of rum each man received daily, no doubt used to wash down the plentiful rations of fresh meat and hardtack from ship's stores.[40]

His decision to join Phillips made, LtGen. Cornwallis and those of his men fit for duty, including some of Craig's 82nd Regiment of Foot, marched from Wilmington between April 25-26, 1781. Gossip, based on someone seeing redcoats at Brunswick Town, led some to believe the British intended to march south, but that was soon proved false. When the redcoat column was ferried across the Northeast Cape Fear River at Heron's Bridge and up the Great Duplin Road, an alarm went out to all the militia units in the region alerting them to the movement and calling them to arms. BGen. John Butler, at Ramsey's Mill on April 21, received orders from Gen. Nathaniel Greene to lead his militiamen to Cape Fear and effect a link up with Lillington's men. The Americans responded in good numbers, but few had more than three rounds of ammunition in their cartridge boxes, certainly not enough to take on Cornwallis' recently rested and resupplied professionals. Cornwallis camped at Swan's Plantation on the northern side of the Northeast Cape Fear River that night, before embarking on their march the next morning. The army made stops at Thunder Swamp Bridge in modern Wayne County, as well as at William Reeve's

British soldiers and loyalist troops looted Whig homes all along their march to Virginia in the spring of 1781.

Brooks Swamp plantation near Mount Olive, crossed over Gray's Ford on the Neuse River, then by May 5 were at Nahunta Creek and Cobb's Mill, southeast of modern Fremont. Before reaching Virginia, the British army would march across Duplin, Wayne, Johnston, Nash, Halifax, Edgecombe, and Northampton Counties.[41]

When Cornwallis set out for Virginia, he left behind his wounded and a detachment of German Jaegers and the Royal North Carolina Regiment to reinforce Craig's regulars. Crossing the Northeast Cape Fear at Heron's Bridge, the redcoats continued unmolested up the Great Duplin Road. The earl took with him men of the 23rd and 33rd Regiments of Foot, the second battalion of the 71st Regiment, the Bose Regiment, his Black Pioneers, Tarleton's British Legion, elements of the 82nd Regiment of Foot, and Hamilton's light companies from the Royal North Carolina Regiment. American forces were too small to interdict the British march. The militia at the bridge, under Robert Sloan, prudently pulled their artillery back to Limestone Bridge before repositioning at Kingston.

Along their march, Whig homes in Duplin and Wayne County fell victim to British looting, while Captain Joseph Wade, John Bradshaw, and two others were taken prisoner. Near modern Warsaw, May Ann Buck was forced to feed the British troops occupying her family farm. While soldiers did some of the looting, it was the loyalists who traveled with them who caused most of the damage. Those Tory civilians had little choice but to leave with the British, lest they face the revenge of their Whig neighbors who until then had been muted by the presence of such a large force of British regulars. With their own property confiscated by the state, the loyalists were happy to put the shoe on the other foot and take what they wanted from Whig families who could do little to stop them. The female camp followers were especially bad, according to one militiaman, who called them "a swarm of beings (not better than harpies). These were women who followed the army in the character of officer's and soldiers' wives. They were mounted on the best horses and side saddles, dressed in the finest and best clothes that could be taken from the inhabitants."

William Dickson remembered the fear of the inhabitants as the redcoats advanced. "The whole country was struck with terror," he wrote, "almost every man quit his habitation and fled, leaving his family and property to the mercy of merciless enemies. Horses, cattle, and sheep and every kind of stock were driven off from every plantation, corn and forage taken for the supply of the army and no compensation given, houses plundered and robbed, chests, trunks, etc. broke, women's and children's clothes, as well as men's wearing apparel and every kind of household furniture taken away," Dickson spoke from experience, as his home and those of his brothers were all victims of British attentions. In an effort to safeguard Duplin County's records, Clerk of Court Dickson hid them in a pot and buried it in Goshen Swamp. It was all for nothing, as when the danger passed, he returned to get them but could not find them.[42]

Mary Slocumb, who anecdotal accounts say rode all night to find her husband at Moores Creek in 1776, was again entangled with the British in 1781. Her militiaman spouse, Ezekiel, was away when Tarleton's dragoons, acting as the screening force of Cornwallis' main column, arrived at her Duplin (modern Wayne) County home. Tarleton and his officers quartered themselves in the house, while the enlisted men and their mounts camped in an orchard a short distance away. Eli W. Carruthers recorded what happened next in his *Revolutionary Incidents and Sketches of Character: Chiefly in the" Old North State, Vol. II*:

"Soon after arriving at the place, Tarleton sent out a Tory captain with his company of Tories to scour the country for two or three miles round, and, while thus engaged, Col. Slocum with his little Whig band came upon them. A terrible onslaught followed, and half the Tories were killed or wounded. The Captain was wounded and fled with four or five of his men towards headquarters; and the Colonel, with about the same number of Whigs, went in hot pursuit. So great was their eagerness to kill the captain or take him prisoner that they were in the midst of a thousand British, most of them mounted, before they thought of any danger, or were even aware that the enemy was on the plantation, but by great presence of mind and an act of most daring courage, they dashed through and made their escape. Col. Slocum with a few intrepid and patriotic men like himself, hung on the rear of the British army, cutting off stragglers and sometimes attacking their foraging parties all the way into Virginia, when they made their way to Yorktown and were present at the surrender.[43]

On May 3, Cornwallis sent a dispatch to Nisbet Balfour in Charlestown describing the biggest problem he was having on his march. "The difficulties I allude to are principally the troops becoming sickly and many of the [grinding] mills being useless by the dryness of the season, which prevents my keeping up my stock of provisions so as to enable me to return if necessary from any point of the march to Wilmington," he wrote. The movement of the British towards Virginia was not uncontested, either. The redcoats fought skirmishes at Swift Creek, Fishing Creek, and Halifax. Bladen County militia made the transit more difficult by dismantling several bridges on Cornwallis' route of march. At Peacock Bridge, 15 miles from Wilmington, Tarleton with 180 dragoons and mounted troops of the 82nd Regiment and the Royal North Carolina Regiment ran into 400 Pitt County militia under Col. James Gorham. Gorham's men tried to make a stand at Contentnea Creek, but Tarleton's riders spurred their horses into a charge that scattered the Americans into the woods. A day later, the militia tried again to stop Cornwallis at Swift Creek and Fishing Creek in Nash County, but a charge of British cavalry dispersed them with no damage done. The dragoons galloped across the bridge untouched.[44]

Back in Wilmington Maj. Craig commanded a force of 394 regulars, including the Hesse Cassel jaegers (riflemen) Cornwallis left behind. With Cornwallis in Virginia, Craig realized he had the only professional military force on either side of the war between Charlestown and the Chesapeake. The major decided to take advantage of that. While he did not have enough men to subdue Whig activity much beyond Wilmington, he could provide a base of operations for loyalist militias operating in the interior. The war in North Carolina turned into a true civil war at that point, as neighbors and families on opposite sides of the question of American liberty took up arms in support of their positions, or just to settle old scores.

The man who would become Craig's best weapon in that fight was David Fanning. Originally from South Carolina, Fanning was an orphan who suffered from a scalp condition. The unfortunate boy was left bald and with a scarred head as a result. Eventually he was cured thanks to the kindness and medical knowledge of a woman who took him into her care, but to his enemies David Fanning was often derisively called "Scaldhead Dave." Perhaps self-conscious over his appearance, Fanning eventually went into the South Carolina backcountry and began trading with the Cherokee.

When the war broke out, Fanning proved an enthusiastic supporter of the king. He was a loyalist combatant at the siege of Ninety-Six, and engaged in Tory militia skirmishes and battles on the South Carolina frontier before moving to North Carolina by 1781. Recognizing Fanning's skills, Maj. Craig invited him to Wilmington and commissioned him a colonel of the loyalist militia in Chatham County. Fanning traveled into the territory around Deep River and established a base of operations at Cox's Mill Creek (near modern Ramsour, N.C.). He recruited an initial band of about 50 men, then set out to terrorize the enemies of King George throughout the North Carolina interior. When things got too hot, Fanning and his men retreated to the safety of the British guns at Wilmington, where Major Craig made sure he had everything he needed to carry out his irregular warfare activities.

On May 9, Fanning was back in Deep River with eight of his men. Not long before, Greene's American army was marching back into South Carolina where foragers earned a reputation for treating loyalists they came across harshly. Their actions prompted a reprisal from Fanning's band, in which they captured 18 of the Whig soldiers. When Whig militia in Bladen and Cumberland Counties rode to attempt capturing Fanning, they left the door open for local loyalists to step up their own activity.

Captain John Hinds and his men discovered that Fanning was camped at the Deep River home of a friend. Leading 11 men on a mission to capture him, Hinds surprised the Tory band. Pinned down by Whig musket fire, Fanning made a desperate move. He and his men charged past Hinds' troops, killing one militiaman before escaping into the woods. The Americans captured two of Fanning's men before they could reach the woods, and summarily executed them both. That pattern would repeat itself many times over the coming months, as Whigs and Tories clashed and committed atrocities against each other that drew vicious reprisals.[45]

Cohera Swamp
Forces Engaged:
Loyalists: Capt. Middleton Mobley with 120 loyalist militiamen
Americans: Col. James Kenan, Col. James C. "Shay" Williams with roughly 80 men of the Duplin County Regiment of Militia (20 infantry, 60 light horse)

Two days after Fanning narrowly escaped John Hinds' ambush at Deep River, a small group of Duplin County loyalists grew emboldened by Cornwallis' march through their territory and came together at a small camp in Cohera Swamp on May 11, 1781. The group took pains to make sure their location was a secret, but word reached Col. James Kenan of the Duplin County Regiment of Militia anyway. Kenan gathered 15 men under Captain Robert Merritt, including his brother Owen Kenan, and went to disperse the loyalists before they could get organized and create any mischief.

As Kenan's men crept towards the loyalist encampment, a Tory sentry surprised one of the militiamen. Shots were exchanged, and one round struck home killing Owen Kenan. Private David Tucker was wounded in the thigh. In the confusion, neither side was confident of their numbers so they broke off the engagement and retreated.

When word spread that the loyalists had defeated the Whigs (a debatable claim), as many as 120 more loyalists - some from as far away as Onslow County - joined the Tories in their new camp on the west side of Cohera Swamp at a bridge on the road to Cross Creek. The loyalists chose Middleton Mobley as their leader, and his brother, Biggars, as their second in command. Col. James Kenan and his men, augmented by 60 mounted reinforcements under Capt. James C. "Shay" Williams, trailed the Tories to their new camp. Kenan, angry at the death of his brother, was determined to exact his revenge against the Duplin loyalists.

Kenan moved his men to a camp at Capt. Richard Clinton's plantation, roughly three miles from Mobley's campsite. Learning that Kenan was chasing him with a larger body of men, Middleton Mobley retreated towards Black River under cover of night. The American militiaman caught up to Mobley's band at loyalist Isaac Portivent's mill. William's men, a motley collection of farmers, lumberjacks, and even runaway sailors, attacked with the cavalry in the lead. The horsemen rushed the loyalist encampment, firing pistols from their saddles and slashing with their sabers, some of them made from saw blades. One mounted Tory was hit and fell from his saddle, but Mobley's men managed to put up enough of a resistance to force the Whigs to fall back. Williams reformed his men and launched a counterattack that broke the loyalist's line and forced Mobley's men to retreat into the thick underbrush and bogs of the Cohera.

James Kenan

Williams' mounted pursuers were at a disadvantage in the mire of the swamp, but the respite that bought for Mobley's men was mitigated by the arrival of more militia, this time on foot, from a different direction. The newcomers fired into the loyalists, who returned fire. The Tories continued to flee, making it as far as modern Clinton. The American infantrymen caught up to them again, and the fight became hand to hand, with both sides resorting to knives, fists, and swords in the close quarters clash.

Three miles from Mobley's original Cohera campsite, Col. Kenan caught up with the loyalists again. The Tories ducked behind trees and hugged the ground as the Whigs discharged their weapons, then returned fire as Kenan's men reloaded. On May 13 the loyalists managed to establish a makeshift defensive position near Mayhand's (sometimes spelled Myhand's) Bridge, and Kenan sent some horsemen forward to lure them out. Mayhand's Bridge was actually two spans approached by a long causeway over swampy ground. Mobley's loyalists had pulled up the planks from the first bridge to fortify their positions. When the Tories chased the Whigs across the causeway, Kenan's men opened fire from both sides. Mobley forced a breakout on the left side, allowing his men to escape. Leaving several dead and wounded where they fell, Mobley's men fled again, down the Little Coharie River, before finally making it to Boykins Plantation. Some militia follow them, using dugout canoes to cross the creek. Discovering they were badly outnumbered by the Tories, the Whigs withdrew without engaging. At the plantation Mobley's men looted the Boykin home.

    Back at the loyalist camp, Williams and Kenan were trying to pick up Mobley's trail. Their men, plundering the Tory camp, found bottles of liquor and soon became drunk. One man was bitten several times by a snake in a tree. Hungry, tired, and more than a little relieved to have so far made it through the skirmishes unscathed, the Whigs were grateful for the rest. Kenan and Williams' men doubled up on the horses they had and scoured both banks of the Little Coharie River hunting for Mobley's trail. At a fallen tree in the water they found two bodies entangled with the dugout canoes the loyalists had used to make their escape.

    It was a nerve-wracking chase. A minister who witnessed it described the two sides, saying "The Loyals were neat and groomed. but the pursuers were unkempt and fiercely chin-whiskered." Men on both sides quickly lost their enthusiasm for more fighting. Loyalists from Mobley's band began leaving, trying to reach their homes and safety. Others fled to the protection of the British redoubts at Wilmington. Some of Kenan's militia were ready to call it quits too. Other Tories surrendered to Whig militia they stumbled across. A few snapped off quick shots at Kenan's men when they were discovered, making for tension when the militia happened across a stranger. The Whigs ran the real risk of shooting their own men, as exemplified when two militia groups happened onto each other. One group engaged a band of about a dozen loyalists, attracting a response from more Whig troops who ran to the sound of the gunfire. The weary Americans engaged with the loyalists saw the newcomers and mistook them for more Tories and opened fire. Fortunately, no one was hit. Before the chase wound down, three Americans were dead. Middleton Mobley's loyalists lost a dozen men killed, another 4 wounded, and 12 taken prisoner.[47]

Major Craig saw opportunity in the civil war raging among the North Carolinians. On May 28, he wrote to Balfour in Charlestown.

"This country is in a glorious situation for cutting one another's throats," he confided. "I am sincere in my endeavors to prevent it, which, however, have not in every instance been effectual. The Tories are the most numerous, and was I to give the word, a fine scene would begin. However, I think it cruelty without a certainty of being ready to support them. If I had that, I should soon begin. I am confident, if suffer'd to remain here, I could do much, and want only a few cavalry appointments. The men who were left behind recover fast and tho' not fit for active service yet, are more than equal to our defence, was the whole country assembled together to come against us.

"There is a rascally little place call'd Beauford near Cape Look Out where they fit out a number of little piccarroon [sic] privateers and do much mischief on our coast. There are no less than five row boats fitting out now. I wish to destroy it but dare not undertake it in my present situation. If I remain here, it will be one of the first things I do.

"Lord Cornwallis's idea when here seem'd to be to raise independant [sic] companies and not corps. It is a much better scheme. Governor Martin's corps has got but 50 men. Indeed they have had not much time, but I don't think they will ever compleat. Country people don't like to have their neighbors and former companions for their officers. However, they should have a fair trial, which they have not had yet."[48]

With Greene close by, recruiting for Whig militias was not too difficult. When the Continentals marched back into South Carolina, it became much harder. Not only did the demands of agriculture, bringing in crops and preparing fields for planting hamper recruiting efforts, but loyalists also became emboldened. The redcoats at Wilmington gave backbone to the Tories, and the absence of American professionals cowed the Whigs. Without the support of Greene's army, men joining the American militias risked their lives, their property, and their freedom. The danger was particularly great in and around Wilmington and the lower Cape Fear Valley. When Cornwallis was campaigning in the Carolinas, one technique used to keep the Whigs out of the fight was to conduct small operations that required American militias to stay close to home.

During the summer of 1781 in what are now Duplin and Sampson Counties those operations were mostly small clashes. On the South River, a tributary of the Black River, Private Joseph Williams of the Duplin militia fought one such skirmish against loyalists under an officer named Scarborough. The Tories proved "too much for them," so the Americans retreated to the farm of a Widow DeVane who lived on the Black River. When they fled to the farm, their intention was to surrender when Scarborough caught up to them, but they had a change of heart and laid a trap for the Tories. When the loyalists arrived, the Whigs jumped them without firing a shot, capturing all 11 men in Scarborough's band. Taking the men to the Duplin jail, all of them decided to switch sides except for their commander.

North Carolina leaders began getting word of large numbers of loyalists gathering in Bladen County, especially at Raft Swamp (near modern Red Springs). Governor Thomas Burke received word from BGen. Steven Drayton that Maj. Craig in Wilmington had encouraged Bladen men to take up their arms in the king's cause. Burke was not able to muster many men to counter the threat. In fact, he estimated that of the 15 militia companies in the county, a dozen of them sided with the British. The rampaging of Bladen County loyalists went on all summer long, even to include taking Cross Creek for a time in August 1781. One witness said they were "ravaging the Inhabitants of Cape Fear on both sides, for Considerable Distance up it."

The Americans had effectively lost control over large swaths of eastern North Carolina that summer, with one American officer calling Bladen a "Frontier County." Maj. Craig ventured out of the confines of Wilmington to establish a small fort at Rutherford's Mill on Ashe's Creek near modern Burgaw. With Cornwallis in Virginia, Greene in South Carolina, and Craig providing a safe have at Wilmington, loyalist militia leaders grew more confident they could conduct operations in relative safety.[50]

Craig recognized that the tides of war were turning in his favor. With the Tories turning out in large numbers, the major implored his superiors in Charlestown to give him the support he needed to take advantage of the situation. He wrote to LtCol. Balfour on June 13, 1781.

"I cannot help repeating that expedition is on this occasion of utmost consequence," Craig wrote. "Every day brings fresh accounts of the Tories being in arms in almost every part of the province, but they want both arms and ammunition and leaders. They cannot get to me to be supplied and must fall very soon if left to themselves. The only thing I should be in want of is bayonets to give them a confident superiority over the rebels. Of them I have not one."[51]

What successes the Americans made that summer were small in nature. On June 17, Tory Maj. Micajah Gentry signed a truce with Col. Peter Horry on behalf of BGen. Francis Marion that took Drowning Creek and Pee Dee loyalists out of the fight, at least temporarily. The ceasefire would not last. One Whig said Gentry signed it in the first place only because he was no longer receiving material support from British forces at Georgetown, S.C. For his part, Gentry pointed a finger at some Whigs who failed to live up to the truce terms themselves. Regardless, Gentry and his men were soon back in the fray, with some of them going to Wilmington and enlisting with Craig and Fanning.[52]

There were more summary executions by the militias than were palatable to either Maj. Craig or the leadership of North Carolina. Craig, as a professional soldier, took a dim view of the killing of captured Americans by loyalists, and N.C. governor Abner Nash found them a distasteful aspect of the conflict as well. Yet both men well knew that in the vicious sort of war being fought in North Carolina, neighbor against neighbor and brother against brother, passions ran hot and atrocities were more common than either of them might wish. Craig wrote to Abner Nash on June 20 (Craig did not know that Nash had recently been replaced by Thomas Burke) to decry the treatment of Tories who fell into American hands, and to deliver a threat if the governor could not curb it.

"Sir," he wrote, "I cannot let pass this opportunity of addressing myself to you on a subject which I expect will meet with more attention than I suppose would be paid to it by the perpetrator of the actions I am forced to complain of - the inhuman treatment imposed on the King's friends on every occasion and by every party in arms, obliges me to adopt some serious resolution to put, if possible, an end to it - the deliberate and wanton murders daily committed on them call, I should imagine, as much for your attention as they do for vengeance on my part. It is now my business to assure you, sir, that the former alone can prevent the latter.

"Had I listened only to the first emotions excited by the account of Mr. Caswell's conduct in murdering five men at Kingston who were carried to him from River; Mr. SamL Ashe and his comrades who were put in irons for the purpose would have become the immediate victims to his unwarrantable cruelty. Fortunately for them I am a Soldier and have been taught to look on the deliberate & unnecessary shedding of blood to be repugnant to my principles as such, as the sparing the enemies of my King in the field. I therefore determined to adopt every method I could think of to prevent the necessity which could alone justify to my own mind that extremity, to the world I am sure I should have been fully justified by the cause alone - several instances which have happened since both in that quarter and in Duplin County, have very nearly forced me to have recourse to the expedient I wish to avoid, even without previous representation, which I was at a loss how to make, as I knew not where to address you, and was determined never to have any communication with people capable of ordering such actions, & whose inhumanity gave me every reason to suppose, their answer would be the immediate occasion of the extremity I wished to avoid.

"I now Sir, call on you to use your efforts to put a stop to a proceeding which promises such additional misery, to the people over whom you now preside. I fully discharge my duty in this address and shall think myself perfectly unanswerable for the consequences of its being disregarded. After allowing a reasonable time for the interposition of your authority I shall think myself called on by justice, duty, & I may add ultimately by every consideration of humanity, to give the people who from the most laudable principles of loyalty take arms in the King's favor, ample revenge & satisfaction for every instance of murder committed by any party of Militia on one of them, and for this purpose I shall not hesitate to deliver to them those prisoners who from character or situation are most likely to gratify them in those sentiments, and produce the effect I ardently wish for, of preventing a repetition of those barbarities, however I persuade myself there will be no necessity for having recourse to these means as it will be with the utmost regret I shall aggravate the miseries to which all countries are liable when the seat of war. My wish ever is to soften them as much as is consistent with my duty & in this I know my own wishes to coincide with the intentions of my superiors.

"I am, Sir, Your most Obed. Servant; J. H. Craig, Major, 82nd Regiment, Commanding at Wilmington"

Governor Burke was quick to reply, in a letter dated June 27, 1781:

"Sir, your letter of the 20th instant to my predecessor in office, came to my hands and I am now to return you an answer.

"Being entirely uninformed of the executions you allude to I am unable to say whether they ought to be denominated murders or not, but I will venture to affirm that if they were and wanton and unnecessary, or contrary to the laws and rights of war, they were not tolerated by the government of this state, nor shall such ever be approved by me.

"In several parts of the country, the war has, unhappily kindled the most fierce and vindictive animosity between the those who adhere to the government of Great Britain and those who resolved at all hazards to oppose what they deemed an unconstitutional exercise of power, very lamentable effects have always been apprehended from this disposition, and as the best means for preventing them, a resolution was very early taken to remove out of the state those people together with their property who could not reconcile themselves to the established government and this resolution was in part executed but the legislature was afterwards prevailed on by the entreaties of those very people to dispense in a great measure with the further execution. The animosity still continues and on some occasions when the people have been obliged to take arms has produced reciprocal violences and bloodshed which are entirely unauthorized by the magistrates of the state, and as much reprobated by them as they can be by his Britannic Majesty's officers.

"To this cause may probably be attributed the acts of which you complain and whether it has produced more violence on the one side than the other might prove a very unpleasant and unsatisfactory enquiry, but it is certain that many people have been killed by those whom you are pleased to call the King's friends where nothing could be assigned as provocation or excuse.

"Duty and inclination conspire in determining me to use my utmost efforts for checking and, if possible, entirely preventing those practices which, tho' occasioned by the war, are no way necessary for, nor in my opinion conducive to, its happy termination. To this restitution your letter could not contribute, for the evil was already perceived and threats have no influence on my conduct.

·"With respect to the particular behavior of [Brig.] General [William] Caswell I shall only say that the laws reach every officer of this state and so far as it may depend on me they shall be enforced on all for the prevention of offenses against the law of nations as well as the municipal law.

"I cannot see the justice of your present treatment of Mr. Samuel Ashe and his comrades nor of the future measures which you threaten them with. I believe they do not live in the parts of the country which are infected with the animosity above mentioned nor can I learn that they themselves or any of their connections have even countenanced such practices as you complain of and which are unauthorized and unapproved by this government so far as they come within the description above mentioned, &c. Should you therefore continue your treatment of those citizens or listen to any emotions which may dictate any measures against them on the ground of retaliation which you refer to, I shall find myself under the unhappy necessity of taking similar measures against British prisoners, tho' all such measures are utterly repugnant to my disposition.

"The delivering over of such prisoners as from character or situation are most likely to gratify the vengeance of those enraged people to whom you allude which you are pleased to say you will not hesitate to do so is conformable known of among civilized nations, and should you in any instance put this threat in execution, the effect will be very different from what you expect for altho' we should abhor the following of the example of our Indian savage neighbors in delivering over prisoners to be tortured at the pleasure of a fierce and vengeful kindred, yet the example of a nation so polite and celebrated as Great Britain would meet with more respect, and we should probably imitate it with peculiar advantages should our humanity be obliged to give way to public utility.

"I wish to be favored with your ultimate resolution on this subject because there are at present some prisoners in my power to whom I am much disposed to grant some indulgences which are requested, but which must be delayed until I know the result of your determination.

I concur, Sir, in your wish to mitigate as much as possible the miseries incident to war, and am of the opinion that clemency and humanity should in every instance prevail most liberally except where incompatible with indispensable public utility. I perceive the letters to my predecessor are not directed to him in his official character tho' on an official subject, as I can hold no correspondence with the subject of his Britannic Majesty or other enemies of the United States except in my official character, none will be opened but such as those addressed to me as Governor.

"This, Sir, it will be necessary to observe should I be favored with any future address.

"I have the honor to be, Your Obd. Ser, Thos. Burke."[53]

At the end of June, the redcoats at Rutherford's Mill sortied out into the countryside led by Craig's second in command, Maj. Daniel Manson. BGen. Lillington in Richlands wrote to Maj. Abraham Moulton of Duplin County, alerting him that the British were on the march. "Sir, the enemy are advancing this morning from Rutherford's Mill with about 800 Tories & Regulars," Lillington wrote. "You will please to march forward immediately with all the horse and foot you can muster, not a moment is to be lost. We shall rendezvous at Hines's, where I hope you have a large force this evening. Everything will depend on your quick dispatch."

BGen. William Caswell, the son of former governor Richard Caswell, delivered intelligence on Manson's progress in a letter written to Gov. Thomas Burke from Kingston. "I returned last Night from New River, where it was said the British Troops had taken post," he told Burke. "This account was confirmed by several and by a Capt. Powers, who had command of Hawkin's Horse; but on my arrival at the No. Wt. of New River I found Col. Mitchell posted there and the Enemy at Rutherford's Mill, reaping wheat and collecting Cattle. Their Number when they left Wilmington was about Two Hundred British and Twenty Five Tories, under the Command of Major Manson. Some Few Tories have joined them. Major Craike [Craig] was in Wilmington with about 150 (suppose not above 100). When I found their situation and that the Party commanded by Manson had no cannon, had Determined to attack them or Wilmington instantly, and with that intent left New River to forward on the Troops, but on my return to this Place found your Excellency's orders (thro' Gen'l [John] Butler) to move up towards Wake, which orders I am now Executing and the Troops on their Way. Have no expectation of the British moving nearer this Way, unless the movement of the Troops from this Place should occasion it. Hope to have the pleasure of seeing your Excellency in a few Days, as I intend to set out To-morrow for the Assembly."[54]

Lillington also penned an update to the governor, warning him that unless something changed, it would be difficult for his militia to counter the threat posed by the loyalist bands and Craig's regulars. "Dear Sir," he wrote, "your Excellency will excuse me for taking the liberty of addressing myself to you on this distressing occasion. I am to acquaint you. Sir, that it is not my own opinion, but the principal part of the people of the district of Wilmington, and every other part of the state, intended to fall a sacrifice to the enemy, which is now almost the case, by being lately destitute of every assistance from the other districts. This is too visible not to be seen by the conduct of some of the neighboring counties, where early notice was given to Col. [Francis] Ashe, [of the Jones County Regiment] that the enemy was up at Holly Shelter, and said to be on the march for New Bern. After some days, he at last collected a body of men together and then discharged them. Altho' I had informed him that the Onslow men were embodied and were waiting for the Jones men to join them, and that the Duplin militia were coming on. The troops from Craven [Brig.] Gen'l [William] Caswell wrote me he had ordered on, and the next day he sent orders to have them discharged, on a bare supposition of Col. Avery that the British were gone back to town, which to this moment it is well known that they are not returned, but is now at Wishart Mill, sending out parties collecting all the cattle that is between Holly Shelter and New River [in Onslow County], and it is not known how far they intend [to go] into the country. I am sorry to say that I see nothing to hinder them from going where they please.

"Having lost a great part of property, and I see I am in a fair way to lose all; but if that should be the case l should not regard it, or at least as little as most men, provided we had that justice shown us from other parts of the state, which protection we have an undoubted claim to. But since that justice has not been given us, and no likelihood of ever having any assistance, and it being entirely out of my power and many others who are in the same situation, having no money and in great want and my country not paying me for them. Impressed now over twelve months, and no wages paid, but five thousand dollars, puts it out of my power to remove what little is left any further out of the way of the enemy. Had it not been for the want of money, I should have done myself the pleasure to have waited on your Excellency, as I see that there is no prospect of driving the enemy back into town or that we might get to our homes. I cannot see with what justice our country can blame us to make the best terms we can."[55]

The general was not wrong. There was little his worn and unpaid militiamen could do without help in the face of the emboldened British and their local allies. At Cross Creek, the Deputy Quartermaster General of the South Carolina Continental Line, BGen. Stephen Drayton, wrote to Burke with his own warning that Craig had issued an order to loyalists around Bladen County to stand ready. The South Carolinian assumed "that Maj. Craig intends to fix posts at Elizabeth Town and Cross Creek and to procure grain from the locals in this area." With most militia companies in that area siding with the British, Drayton warned of the coming civil war, "attended with something horrid."[56]

Thomas Bloodworth and the Sniping Tree

Back in Wilmington, a new danger bedeviled Craig's redcoats. In early June, Thomas Bloodworth, former tax collector and gunsmith, decided it was time to exact a measure of revenge against the occupiers in his town. Bloodworth, who operated a ferry between the Wilmington waterfront and Point Peter (also known as Negro Head Point), was on the point hunting when his dog chased a fox into a tunnel beneath a very large cypress, 70 feet up to the first branches. Bloodworth followed his dog and discovered a large chamber inside the base of the tree that reached high up the trunk. It gave him an idea.

Thomas Bloodworth still carried a grudge over the butchering of Maj. James Love at Rouse's Tavern some weeks before. The two had been friends. What the British did to him and his men was a debt Bloodworth was anxious to repay. Looking up into the dim heights of the chamber in the cypress tree, a plan came together in his mind. Returning home, Bloodworth put his gunsmith skills to work, building a rifle capable of delivering a two-ounce .83-caliber ball across the river to the place at Market Dock where British troops mustered for morning formation each day. He spent weeks practicing, with a silhouette drawn on his barn door, firing from a distance equal to that from the tree to the dock, until he could accurately place his shots where he intended them to go. He was ready.

In the first week of July Thomas Bloodworth, along with Timothy Bloodworth and his servant, Jim Paget, crossed the Cape Fear to Point Peter on a hunting trip. Thomas carried his new rifle with him, while Timothy and Jim toted their rations of food and water. Arriving at the tree, Thomas finally let his companions in on his plan. Crawling into the cypress tree chamber, the three men built scaffolding that allowed Bloodworth to get higher. With an auger, he bore a hole in the trunk that would

Point Peter today, where the Brunswick River empties into the Cape Fear across from Wilmington's riverfront.

accommodate his rifle barrel. Thomas counted on distance and the river's prevailing winds, normally blowing downriver, to hide the smoke signature from the rifle shot.

It was the fourth of July when Thomas Bloodworth first took aim at the scarlet-clad men on the far riverbank from his position, and squeezed off his first round. The sound of the shot inside the tree must have been deafening, but Bloodworth watched with satisfaction when a British soldier collapsed at Market Dock. Four others quickly gather up their fallen comrade and carried him inside a store on the riverfront. Bloodworth, reloaded by then, took aim and delivered another round to one of the soldiers standing in the window of Nelson's liquor store. Drums beat a tattoo calling the redcoats to arms, as others scanned the far side of the river trying to locate where the sniper was firing from. Columns began to form up to cross the Cape Fear and hunt down the long-range marksman who had taken two of their own so early in the morning.

Jim Paget asked Thomas if he could try his hand. Scrambling up the scaffold, Jim took the rifle from Thomas and picked a target in one of the columns of redcoats forming up across the river. While it is unclear if Paget's shot hit home, it did have the effect of convincing the men in the British formation that perhaps finding cover might be the smarter tactic.

The redcoats scattered. Search parties scoured the far side of the river on Eagles Island, but it never occurred to them that a rifle was capable of firing with accuracy from the distances Bloodworth shot from. They never approached the big cypress on Point Peter that concealed the Bloodworths and Paget.

Resting overnight inside the tree, the snipers resumed their hunt the next day. When no shots came that morning, redcoats going for their morning rum ration grew slack and clustered around the door of the grog shop as they downed their tots. As the sun reached its apogee, Bloodworth sighted down the rifle barrel and squeezed the trigger. The hammer dropped, and striking flint sparked a flame that ignited the fine grain powder in the rifle's pan, which in turn ignited the powder that sent a ball racing downrange. Across the river, a redcoat tumbled to the ground. The rest of the British scampered inside the closest shops seeking cover. Minutes later, a dragoon rode his mount to the riverfront and peered across trying to locate where the shots were coming from. Bloodworth's shot sent him tumbling from his saddle.

The three Whigs kept their reign of terror up for a week. A loyalist neighbor of Bloodworth's informed Maj. Craig that the former tax collector had been missing from his home for the past week, suspicious that it was him who was causing the mayhem. Craig sent a 20-man detachment over to Point Peter to search for the snipers, but they never found them. Swinging axes, the soldiers clear away smaller trees and underbrush that might offer a sniper concealment. The redcoats considered cutting down the huge old cypress, but realized the day was growing short to undertake such a massive task. Leaving a token squad behind, the rest of the soldiers crossed back over to their Wilmington barracks. When darkness fell and the sentry was sleeping soundly, Bloodworth and his companions crept back to their hidden canoe and rowed across the Cape Fear. They were never caught by the British, though they were suspected of being the snipers.[57]

The surge in loyalist activity west of Wilmington over the summer of 1781 led to real gains for the Tories. Bladen County militia commander Col. Thomas Robeson wrote that his men were in a "Distressed Situation,"

with loyalists in control of most of modern Richmond, Scotland, Robeson, and Bladen Counties, a territory 100 miles by 50 miles wide. Swampy terrain hampered American operations against the Tories too, being suitable only for small bands fighting the guerilla style of combat characterized by hit and run attacks too fast to be countered by more conventional forces. In the face of such Tory aggression, Whigs in the area had to choose between leaving their homes or facing "immediate Destruction."[58]

Maj. Craig commissioned David Fanning as a colonel of loyalist militia on July 5. Fanning's band arrived at the British encampment at Belvedere Plantation in Brunswick County, near modern Leland, with a petition from loyalists in the interior that he delivered to the commander of the British garrison in Wilmington. Fanning's loyalist militia and British regulars shared the use of the estates' spring. An argument set redcoats against militiamen, and three of Fanning's men found themselves under arrest by the British soldiers. David Fanning answered in kind, arresting three redcoats. He sent word to the British commander that when his men were released, he would turn over the British regulars. The angry British officer stormed over to Fanning's tent and confronted the Tory leader with his sword drawn. The redcoat officer took a swipe at Fanning, who ducked the lunge and drew his own sword. In a flash Fanning had his sword tip at the redcoat's throat, pinning him down. Fanning again demanded the release of his men, this time securing their release. With his men back in his camp, Fanning and his band removed themselves to the backcountry around Deep River again. When he left, Fanning's reputation as a man not to be trifled with was firmly established.

The sort of fighting going on in the western counties of the Lower Cape Fear suited Fanning to a tee. When he reached Cox's Mill in the Deep River country, Fanning learned that several leaders of loyalist militia were sentenced to be hanged. Although more than 100 men rallied to Fanning when he arrived in the backcountry, only about a third of them had arms. He kept 53 men and sent the rest back home. Fanning received word that the Tories were to be executed at Chatham Courthouse the next day. Riding through the night, the loyalist militia arrived at the courthouse at seven in the morning. The Whigs returned to carry out the hangings an hour later, only to walk into a trap laid by Fanning. The Tories took 53 prisoners, among them three members of the General Assembly, plus soldiers, lawyers, judges, and other prominent citizens. Prisoner Ambrose

Ramsey wrote a letter to Gov. Burke on July 20, describing his ordeal.[59]

"Sir, on Tuesday last we were captured at Chatham Court House by a party under the command of Col. David Fanning" he reported, "which party we found consisted of persons who complained of the greatest cruelties, either to their persons or property. Some had been unlawfully drafted; others had been whipped and ill-treated, without trial; others had their homes burned and all their property plundered; and barbarous and cruel murders had been committed in their neighborhoods. The officers complained of are Maj. Neal, Capt. [Peter] Robeson, of Bladen, Capt. [James] Crump. Col. [Thomas] Wade and [Col.] Philip Alston, the latter a day or two ago a few miles in our rear took a man on the road and put him to instant death, which has much incensed the Highlanders in this part of the county. A Scotch gentlemen the same day was taken at one McAfee's Mill and ill-treated. He is said to be peaceable and an inoffensive man, in name we do not know. He lives in the Raft Swamp. Should be happy if he could be liberated. Notwithstanding the cruel treatment these people have received we have been treated with the greatest civility and with the utmost respect and politeness by our commanding officer, Col. [David] Fanning. to whom we are under the greatest obligations, and we beg leave to inform your Excellency that unless an immediate stop is put to such inhuman practices we plainly discover the whole country will be deluged with blood, and the innocent will suffer for the guilty. We well know your abhorrence of such inhuman conduct. and your steady intention to prevent it. All we mean is information. We expect to be delivered to Major [James H.] Craig at Wilmington in two or three days, entirely destitute of money or clothes. How long we shall remain so, God only knows. All we ask is that the perpetrators of such horrid deeds may be brought to trial, that prisoners may be well treated in future, and we are your Excellency's most obedient servts, Gen'l Herndon [?], [Col. Ambrose Ramsey, Joseph Hinds, Matthew Ramsey, W. Kinchen, John Birdsong, James Williams, Matthew Jones, Thomas Scurlock, James Herndon, M. Gregory."[60]

Other loyalists were active as well. Hector McNeil, Duncan Ray, and Maturin Colville gathered between 300 and 400 men in Bladen County, driving any potential Whig resistance underground. By July 15, Craig's men had rebuilt Heron's Bridge. Col. James Kenan told Burke, "Sir, the enemy has moved out of Wilmington up to the long bridge [Heron's Bridge] and are rebuilding it. This is said by several gentlemen who have left the town. Their intention is to give no more paroles but will sell every man's property who will not join them and become British subjects. They have about 100 light horse well equipped, and about 470 foot, and are determined to be at Duplin Court House on Monday next. We have no ammunition nor do I know where to get some. We have no account of any assistance coming as yet. Your Excellency will be so kind as to inform me if any is ordered on."[61]

The Skirmish at Stuart's Creek
Forces Engaged:
American: Col. Peter Robeson and 300 Bladen County militia
Loyalist: Col. Hector McNeil and unknown number of Tory militia

At the place where Robeson, Hoke, and Cumberland Counties meet, two miles from Davis' Bridge, Hector McNeil and his loyalist militia came upon Col. Peter Robeson with 300 men of the Bladen County militia at Stuart's Creek on July 26. Stuart's Creek is a tributary of Rockfish Creek that empties into it a mile downstream from Davis' Bridge. Robeson had with him two Tory prisoners that he intended to execute once their breakfast was finished.

When the firing squad was formed up, one of the prisoners, Ralph Barlow, requested time to pray. As he knelt in the dirt before the assembled muskets of the militiamen, Barlow turned what the Americans thought would be a short chat with his Maker into a sermon. As Barlow bowed his head, desperately buying time to avoid the executioner's musket ball, the Americans began to show their irritation. Barlow's God must have been listening because at that moment Hector McNeil with a band of loyalists on horseback burst onto the scene.

An American sounded the alarm, shouting "Red Caps!" and "Tories!" Another shot at Barlow and his fellow prisoner, but his weapon misfired. By that time McNeil and his riders were well upon them, and the Americans scattered to avoid being trampled, slashed, or shot. Barlow broke free of the ropes binding him and jumped headlong into the nearby mill pond, making his escape by swimming across. McNeil's men chased the fleeing Whigs until they lost themselves in the woods.

Elijah Wilkins was one of the Americans surprised by McNeil's band. In his pension application, Wilkins said, "...we reserved our fire until they charged on us, when a few of us fired, and then tried to make our escape. Some undertook to cross the creek below the mill, but the banks being very steep, they were thrown from their horses. It was rather a running fight from there to a fork on Rock Fish, near the junction of the two steams. On crossing Rock Fish our scattered party was pursued by some of the Tories. Two or three of us concealed ourselves in the bushes near to each other, and immediately a mulatto approached us who held some office. When within a few paces of us, he fired at some one who was at a distance, on which one of our party rose and presented his gun. He cried for quarters, but as he uttered the words, I saw a streak of fire pass beyond his body, as the charge passed through, and he fell dead."

The loyalists lost three men killed in the action. American losses are not recorded. Women who lived nearby buried the dead.[62]

The House in the Horseshoe (Philip Alston's house)
Forces Engaged:
American: Col. Philip Alston and roughly 20 militia
Loyalist: Col. David Fanning and roughly 30 militia

Philip Alston was tired. His pursuit of David Fanning after the raid on the Chatham County Courthouse had been a long one with little to show for it. He had been chasing Fanning since the July 17 raid, and his men of the Cumberland County Regiment of Militia were tired, too. Alston's reputation for ruthlessness towards loyalists was well known, and no man in his band wanted to incur his wrath by falling out.

Fanning had led them a merry chase. In the hunt, Alston passed by the home of Tory Thomas Taylor, who uttered a remark that infuriated the Whig officer. Before the words had hardly crossed Taylor's lips, Col. Alston shot him dead where he stood. Meanwhile, Fanning rested for the night at the home of loyalist Kenneth Black, before riding the next day for Wilmington with his prisoners. Black accompanied Fanning and his men for a short distance on the road to Wilmington, and when they parted ways Black traded Fanning his fresh horse for the loyalist commander's own played out mount. The two Tories rode on, before Black turned for home.

Along the route, Col. Alston came across Kenneth Black riding Fanning's exhausted horse. Black tried to make a run for it, but the horse just did not have it in him to outrun the Whig militia with Alston. Black

Philip Alston's House in the Horseshoe, now a N.C. State Historic Site. There are still holes made by musketballs in the front walls.

was wounded during his escape attempt and fell from his saddle. Laying prostrate on the ground he begged for quarter from the Americans, but none came. The Whig militia beat him mercilessly with the butts of their muskets, then left him for dead. But Black did not die immediately. He lived long enough to tell Fanning who had killed him.

After the incident with Black, Alston called off the pursuit of Fanning's band. He and his men headed towards Alston's home on the Deep River. On the way, the Whigs stopped at the home of the notorious loyalist Hector McNeill, where Alston accused him of stealing a slave from him. McNeill denied it, but when the militia commander threatened to hang McNeill if he did not produce the missing bondsman, Mrs. McNeill sent her own slave to find the fugitive and bring him back. Satisfied, Alston and his men rode on.

When he learned of the mortal wounds Alston inflicted on his friend, Kenneth Black, and of the shooting down of Thomas Taylor, Fanning determined to exact his revenge. With 30 men riding with him, Fanning set out for Alston's home tucked into a bend of the river that gave it the local name of the House in the Horseshoe. The Tories crossed the river at Dickson's Ford to reach Alston's home early on Sunday morning, July 27, 1781. They found two of the four sentries set out by Alston asleep and quietly captured them, but before they could reach the other two, one saw the intruders and gave the alarm.

The 20 men riding with Alston rushed into the house and barricaded it. Temperance Alston, the colonel's wife, grabbed her small children and placed them on a small table set inside the brick fireplace to protect them, while she dropped to the floor next to her bed, loyalist bullets whizzing past her head. In the yard, Tory Lieutenant McKay came up with a plan to rush the house. He shared it with his men, then took the lead and leaped over the split rail fence. McKay's leap was poorly timed, as he went over just as Alston's militia gave a return volley, striking the officer down dead and wounding those loyalists game enough to have jumped the fence with him.

Fanning bribed a "free Negro" to set fire to Alston's house and smoke the Whigs out, but the militia saw what he was doing and delivered him a musket ball for his trouble. Just as Fanning began to think the risk was no longer worth the reward, some of his men discovered a hay-filled

Fanning's men lit a fire in a hay-filled cart and began rolling it towards the Alston house.

ox cart in the barn. Fanning instantly came up with a new plan. He set the hay alight, and had his men begin pushing the cart towards the bullet-riddled house. Inside the barricaded home, Philip Alston realized he was out of options. If he continued fighting, it was likely everyone inside the house would perish in the flames once the cart crashed into the front porch and set it on fire too - including his wife and small children. The colonel determined to surrender to the loyalists.

Temperance Alston had other thoughts. She told her husband she would negotiate the surrender on his behalf, and slipped outside to find Fanning. He met her halfway across the yard, where Mrs. Alston bargained for the lives of her husband and his men. "We will surrender, sir, on condition that no one shall be injured;" she told Fanning, "otherwise we will make the best defense we can; and if need be, sell our lives as dearly as possible."

The Tory leader knew that an assault on the house would be costly, and there were already too many of his men nursing wounds. It was also true that the surest way to lose the support of loyalists in the region would be to burn down a house with women and children in it. He agreed to Temperance Alston's terms. Col. Philip Alston and his men were paroled after their surrender.[63]

Craig's Expedition
Forces Engaged:
American: BGen. Richard Caswell commanding 180 N.C. militiamen, Col. James Kenan commanding 150 men of the Duplin County militia
British: Maj. James Henry Craig commanding 250 men of the 82nd Regiment of Foot (the Hamilton Regiment), Capt. John Gordon commanding 78 mounted provincials of the N.C. Independent Dragoons, and elements of the Royal Regiment of Artillery.

As July drew to a close, there were rumors afoot that the redcoats at Wilmington were planning a foray into the countryside. The gossip was lent credence when a British officer was discovered carrying a dispatch from Maj. Craig to Gen. Cornwallis expressing his intention to march on New Bern - or so it seemed, as deciphering the coded missive was beyond the means of the Americans who found it. General William Caswell passed it along to Gov. Burke on July 31.

"Sir, I am happy to have it in my power to enclose your Excellency

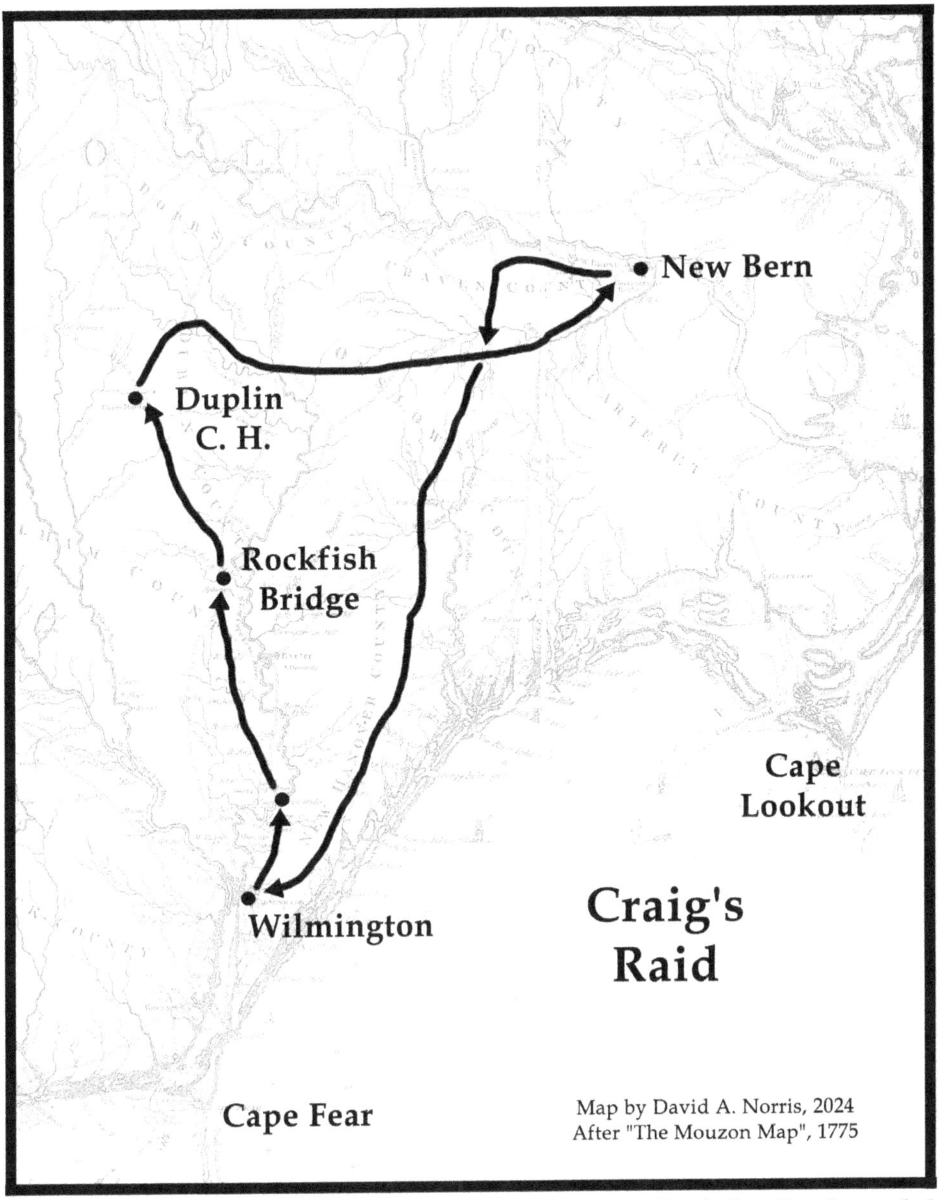

Major Craig left Wilmington to cut a swath through eastern North Carolina that ended up at New Bern. (Map by David A. Norris)

a letter from Major [James H.] Craig to Lord Cornwallis," Caswell wrote, "which I should have been exceedingly glad to have deciphered, but I have it not in my power, it was yesterday taken by some pilots off Core Sound, and the persons mentioned in the forged pass, one J.D. Wilson, says (after his packet was found) that he is a Lieut. in the 82nd Regt and was ordered to rejoin Major Craig at this place, and that the Major would shortly move here...Should those troops from Nash County be discharged, I shall have no men in the field. Should Major Craig move out, I shall raise what men I can arm, but fear it will be very few as arms are very scarce, and grain more so, as there is little or none between Tar River and Cape Fear..."[64]

Craig was, indeed, planning a sortie out from Wilmington to conduct a raid up to New Bern and elsewhere. Had the plan Gen. Nathaniel Greene contemplated in early August come to fruition, it might have prevented a great deal of anguish among Whigs and their families over the coming weeks. Greene even went so far as to dispatch a Capt. Michael Rudolph with some Legion infantry to scout out the territory the American regulars would have to cross to oust Craig from Wilmington. Greene aborted the plan when Gen. Washington informed him of a possible landing of French troops in the Virginia tidewater.[65]

On August 2, 1781, Craig issued a proclamation warning the inhabitants of North Carolina that anyone who refused to take the oath of loyalty to the king would be considered a rebel and would forfeit their property and their life. The proclamation resulted in few takers willing to come to Wilmington and swear the oath. Craig decided that if the people would not come to him, he would go to the people. He gathered his forces and set out to force compliance with his edict.

Rockfish Creek (Duplin County)

The British marched out of Wilmington and up the Great Duplin Road into Duplin County. At Rockfish Creek, dividing New Hanover from Duplin County on August 2, 1781, Col. James Kenan set an ambush with 150 men of the Duplin County militia. Today, the Rockfish Creek site is off Highway 117, near Wallace, N.C. The Americans built earthworks, and were joined by BGen. William Caswell's 180 men of the New Bern District militia and a smaller detachment from Halifax. Though Kenan carried the brevet rank of brigadier general, William Caswell held seniority; but since Kenan knew the territory and came up with the plan for the ambush, Caswell largely deferred to him.

Not long after the New Bern men arrived, Craig's redcoats came up the dusty road. When they entered the kill zone, Kenan and his men opened fire. Craig's men, according to American militia private Arthur Mattis, charged the bridge over Rockfish Creek head on. The British wheeled into ranks and delivered a volley in reply. The clash was sharp and over quickly. Both sides delivered a few rounds before the Whigs withdrew, as their chronic shortage of ammunition and the appearance of British artillery left the Americans unable to engage in a prolonged fight. As the militia pulled back, Craig's dragoons under Capt. John Gordon charged after them with the redcoats' real main thrust, hitting the Americans from the rear. Militiaman John Knowles reported that he was struck by a British dragoon's sword with a blow that nearly took off his arm, and left him handicapped for the rest of his life. Capt. William Hall, of the Nash County Regiment of Militia, was wounded and captured by the horsemen, the only known American officer to be injured in the fight.

Rockfish Creek in Duplin County, where James Kenan's militia tried to stop Craig's redcoats but instead were sent running by British dragoons.

Joining Hall in his captivity were another 20 to 30 Whig militiamen. All told, the Americans suffered 60 men killed or wounded, a particularly high number out of the 300 men who started the ambush in a war where casualties were usually much lower. Col. Kenan wrote to Governor Burke with an account of the fight.

"Sir," he reported, "I embodied all the Militia I could in this county to the amount of about 150 men & was reinforced by [Brig.] Genl. William Caswell with about 180 and took post at a place called Rockfish. The British this day came against me, and the Militia again broke, and it was out of my power and all my officers to rally them. They have dispersed. Before the men broke we lost none. But the light horse pursued and I am afraid have taken about 20 or 30 men. I cannot give you a full acct. But the bearer, Capt [John] James, who was in the action, can inform your Excellency of any particular. He acted with becoming bravery during the whole action. I am now convinced this country, with several others, will be overrun with the British & Tories."

Men who fought behind the American breastworks all described a rout at the hands of the British. One, William Dickson, testified that, "I narrowly escaped being taken or cut down by the dragoons," while the redcoats captured the Americans' ammunition and baggage train. Jacob Wells was captured as he retreated to the safety of Island Creek. Militiaman John Holley remembered the confusion of the withdrawal, saying there was "no regular order in the retreat and the regiment was placed in a scattered condition." Taking refuge in the woods and swamps, Private Joseph Williams lamented that they "subsisted on pork and bread and some days with nothing but cowpeas boiled in bog pond water without salt." Kenan suffered 20 desertions overnight because of the poor prospects of the militia.

Gov. Burke was not happy with Kenan, accusing him of disobeying orders that resulted in the humiliating defeat by a smaller force. The governor had issued instructions to shadow the British, not to engage them in a fight the Americans were unlikely to win. Burke wrote that the defeat "was owing to the want of due precaution and imprudence of attempting a stand under the several disadvantages of inferior numbers, want of cavalry and uncovered flanks, not to mention the want of discipline...In consequence of this indiscreet officer, the country is now uncovered."

Maj. Craig and his redcoats stayed in Duplin County for ten days before marching north. The people who lived along the way suffered depredations at the hands of the redcoat column. Nathan Bryan was one of them, relating that "The British army called on me and took off all my negroes and horses and robbed my house of our clothing. Their mallace was principally against my family as we were the principal sufferers." While Craig was in Duplin, another 300 loyalists joined his ranks, plus some escaped slaves. With such a large force, all the Whigs could do was make small hit and run attacks on the British column's flanks whenever the opportunity arose. Leaving Duplin County behind, the British took aim at New Bern, Jones County, and Craven County. Alexander Lillington, now tasked with keeping them in check, could do little to stop them.[66]

The Piney Bottom Massacre
Forces Engaged:
Americans: Col. Thomas Wade and a Capt. Culp (perhaps Col. Abel Kolb of South Carolina), and Capt. Patrick Boggan, with an unknown number of Whig militia from Richmond and Montgomery Counties
Loyalists: Tory militia including Daniel Patterson, Kenneth Clarke, Alexander McLeod, John Clarke, Daniel McMillan, Duncan Currie, Allen McSweene, Kenneth Black and his family, two daughters of Flora and Allan MacDonald, Alexander Black, and a mulatto named Turner

While Nathaniel Greene was marching his army back into South Carolina, North Carolina militia officers Col. Thomas Wade and a Capt. Culp undertook to leave the Neuse River area and return home to the Pee Dee. The pair crossed the Cape Fear River with a few of their men at Sproul's (later McNeill's) Ferry and spent the night camping by the Lower Little River.

During the night or early the next morning, some of the men with Wade and Culp came across a young girl, Marren McDaniel, hired out to a man named John McDaniel. The Americans stole a piece of cloth from the girl. Loyalist John McNeill, the son of Archibald McNeill, heard of the affront and sent a runner to mobilize area Tories to make a pursuit of the thieves. When the loyalists had gathered, McNeill rode out to find Wade.

Piney Bottom is now a part of the U.S. Army installation at Fort Liberty (formerly Fort Bragg), but in 1781 it was an open area on the west side of Rockfish Creek that divided Cumberland from Hoke Counties, a few hundred yards off the old Raeford Road and about 12 miles from modern Fayetteville. It was there that McNeill's Tories found Wade's sleeping Whigs on August 3.

The loyalists spurred their mounts into a charge that took the Americans by complete surprise. Five or six men were shot dead as they struggled to wake up. The remainder of Wade's band escaped to the surrounding forest. From one of the wagons, a boy Wade had taken under his wing as his protege awoke to the gunfire. The boy dropped to his knees with his hands up, imploring the Tories to spare him. His cries of "Parole me! Parole me!" fell on the deaf ears of an American deserter riding with McNeill. The man told the boy to come out of the wagon and he would parole him. The boy complied, but the turncoat Tory approached him in a way that suggested mercy was not his intent. The boy jumped to his feet and made a break for the trees as the galloping hooves of the Tory's horse thundered behind him. The lad never made the trees. A single swing of the Tory's saber cleaved his head down the middle, one half collapsing onto each shoulder. The surprise was complete. The Tories rifled through the supplies and belongings left behind by the fleeing Americans. For the dead, McNeill's men only provided partial graves.

Revenge came swiftly. American militia went on a rampage, hunting down any loyalist they believed played a role in the butchery at Piney Bottom. Wade and his men camped for the night at the home of old Daniel Patterson, a bagpipe playing loyalist the Whigs suspected of knowing where they could find the rest of McNeill's band. They beat Patterson until he told what he knew. The next day they rode on to Kenneth Clark's house and captured Alexander McLeod. A search of a nearby field exposed Tories John Clarke, Daniel McMillan, Duncan Currie, Allen McSweene, and a British deserter still wearing his scarlet uniform coat. Of the bunch, only Currie and McMillan could be definitively placed at Piney Bottom.

Capt. Patrick Boggan and his Light Horse arrived, drunk off captured alcohol but without any loyalist prisoners of their own. They demanded Wade's prisoners be executed by sword, just as the hapless boy at Piney Bottom had been. Executions of the guilty (and probably some who just were believed guilty) were commonplace. Alexander McLeod fell where he stood, three musket balls in him. Duncan Currie was killed as he tried to escape over a fence. Daniel McMillan was shot in the shoulder, the discharge so close that it set his shirt on fire. He came into the house begging for his life from Boggart's vengeful men. His arm was broken from another musket shot, and he bled from three other wounds. McMillan, like the boy the Tories had butchered, found no mercy that day. He was shot through the chest and died.

Allen McSweene, his hands already bound, tried to hide behind his wife and the baby she carried in her arms, but the Whigs pulled her away. McSweene tried to bolt out the door. He made it a quarter mile before the Americans caught him again, when his head was slit open in the same way the boy's had been. Wade and Boggan ordered the elderly Clarke to bury the dead by the next evening or risk joining them. When they left that night they took the runaway redcoat with them and added him to the death toll sometime in the night. In the morning, the militiamen went in search of David Buchan. Not finding him at home, they torched the place instead.

Kenneth Black's sons were believed to have been participants in the Piney Bottom killings. They went into hiding at the approach of the Americans, but Capt. Culp found them and returned them to the family house. The elder Black was tortured for information, slapped repeatedly with the flat of militia swords, his thumbs screwed into a gunlock, but Kenneth provided no new intelligence. Boggan's riders nudged their mounts into the house and herded the Black family into a corner near the fireplace while others looted their belongings. A chest of china was smashed. Another full of books was shredded.

The Black family lived just four miles north of the home Flora MacDonald had made for her family, not far from where the massacre happened. The Blacks had been dealing with sickness, so two of the MacDonald daughters went to the Black home to see how they were fairing. They were alarmed to discover the house full of armed men. Some of the men grabbed the two young women and robbed them of their jewelry. Using their sword points, they sliced open their dresses and forced the MacDonald daughters to strip.

One man sat impassively on his horse, watching the proceedings. Mrs. Black asked why he was not indulging in the looting, too. He answered that the Blacks had nothing he wanted. The horseman was the father of the boy killed at Piney Bottom. Mrs. Black then turned her anger on the men rifling through her family's things. She told them that they had just recovered from a bought of smallpox, and that all of their belongings likely carried the dreadful sickness too. The alarmed Americans dropped their plunder.

Kenneth Black was forced to guide the Americans to the home of a man named Ray. Many among them wanted to see Black dead too, but Capt. Culp stayed their hand. At Ray's the Whigs split into two bands, one riding to the home of Alexander Graham, the other to Alexander Black's. Graham also had smallpox, so out of fear he was left unmolested. Alexander Black was not so fortunate. He was murdered too.

    The violent rampage sparked by the Tory atrocities committed at Piney Bottom seemed to finally wind down. The last men captured and killed in the Whig vengeance spree were Peter Blue and Archibald McBride. Blue was wounded when the Americans found him, and McBride was killed. One more American died in connection with the Piney Bottom Massacre, when Capt. Culp returned to his home. He had been followed by a mulatto loyalist named Turner, who threatened to burn his house down around him if Culp did not present himself. Capt. Culp appeared on his porch with his two sons. The boys begged for their father's life, but Turner shot him dead anyway, then burned down the Culp home.[67]

    Rested after his raid on the Chatham County Courthouse, Col. David Fanning set out again from his Deep River base camp to stir up more mischief among North Carolina Whigs. When he learned of a raid on Cross Creek, he turned his men in that direction.

    On August 14, Colonels John Slingsby, Duncan Ray, and Hector McNeill rode into the town so quickly that the residents did not have time to either resist or flee. With the addition of Fanning's band, the loyalists fielded several hundred men. Col. James Emmet, Col. Robert Rowan, a Capt. Winslow, and a Mr. Cochrane were among the captured Americans in the Cross Creek raid. From there, Fanning and his men continued down the Cape Fear Valley towards Wilmington where he turned over his prisoners to Maj. Craig. Along the way, the Tories raided and looted at any Whig plantation they came across. Col. Emmet wrote to Gov. Burke a week later with his account of the raid and his capture.

    "I am under the disagreeable necessity of informing your Excellency that, on Thursday last, the 14th inst., between nine and ten o'clock in the morning, this town was, in the most sudden manner imaginable, surprised by a party of the enemy, under the command of Colonels [John] Slingsby, [Duncan] Ray and [Hector] McNeill," he wrote. "They entered the town in so sudden and secret a manner that it was out of the power

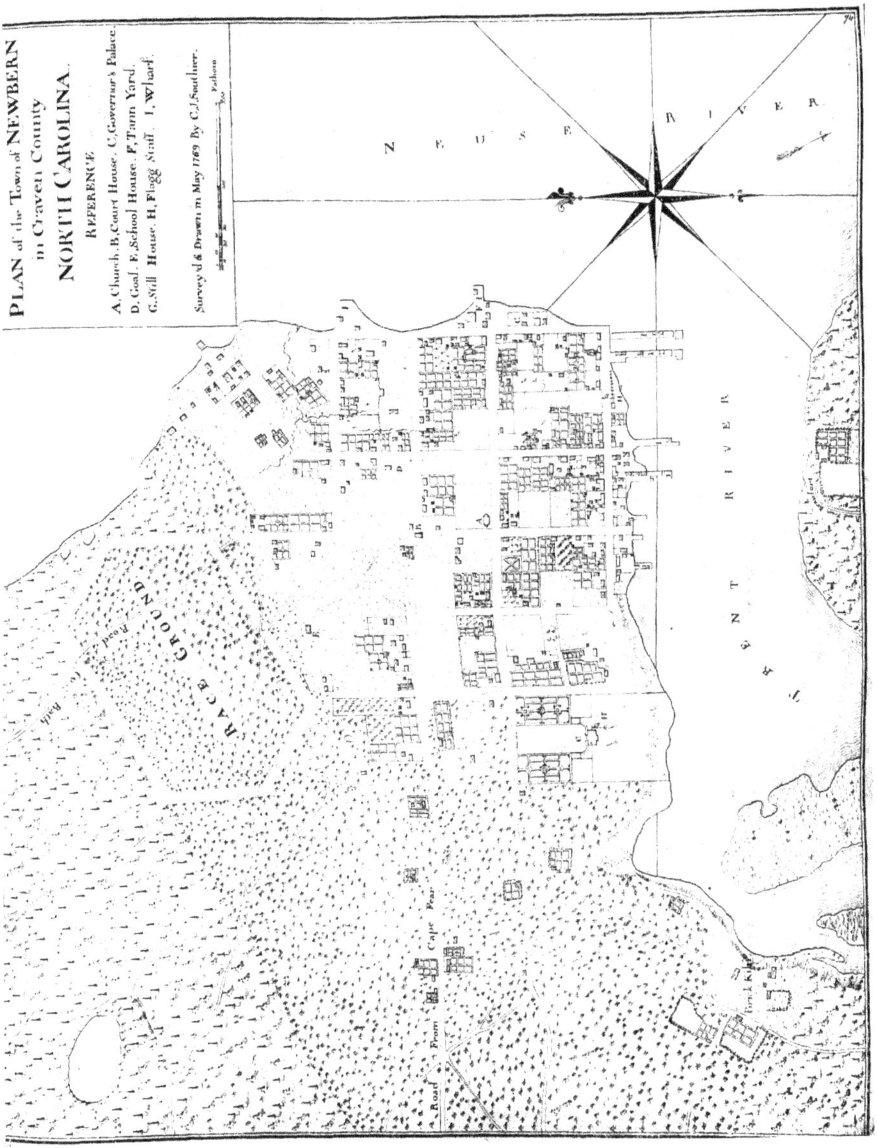

Claude Sauthier's map of colonial New Bern.

of any man who was in it to make his escape. I was at a plantation I have about a mile off, when I was alarmed by a party of about twenty horse. The noise of their horses' feet just gave me time to slip into a swamp, where I lay until the party left the plantation, which they did as soon as they had deprived me of my horses. I then got over the river, when I learned their numbers to be about three hundred. I was likewise informed the same evening, that McNeill, with one hundred men, had gone up the river on the west side, and, not being able to judge where they might intend to cross the river, thought it my best way to keep where I was. Had I done so, I might have kept clear of them, but at such times so many reports are flying, that there is no such thing as distinguishing the true one. At midnight, between the 16th and 17th, word was brought me that a Col. [David] Fanning came down the country with one hundred and eighty men, made a short stay at Cross Creek, had crossed the river at lower Campbleton late in the evening, and at that time was encamped, with an intention in the morning to pursue his march up the river, and so join McNeill on the east side. On this information, I unfortunately crossed the river, early in the morning, and about nine o'clock was taken a prisoner by McNeill, on his return to town."

Thomas Robeson's grave.

James Kenan had disobeyed Gov. Burke's orders when he tried to ambush Craig's redcoats at Rockfish Creek. The undermanned and undersupplied militia were only supposed to shadow the British, nipping at their heels when the opportunity presented itself, not get drawn into a set battle that could only favor the enemy. William Caswell's militia hoped to interdict Craig at Kingston (Kinston) on August 16, but again Gordon's dragoons tipped the advantage to the redcoats and drove off the militiamen. The following day, Alexander Lillington tried to do the same at Webber's Bridge. Repeating a tactic he had successfully used at Moores Creek in 1776, Lillington ordered his men to remove planks from the bridge to impede a crossing. While the work was being done, British scouts came upon the Americans and delivered a surprise fire that killed three men and wounded five more. Mindful of Burke's orders not to get drawn into a costly battle, Lillington and his men withdrew. The way was now open to New Bern.[68]

Capt. Peter Robeson's plantation home fell victim to the Tories on August 17, when Fanning's men burned it down. His brother, Capt. Thomas Robeson, had a home across the river that a detachment sent by Fanning burned down, too. Several men were taken prisoner, added to the growing list of prisoners Fanning intended to deliver to the British at Wilmington.[69]

Two days after the Americans wisely chose not to allow themselves to be drawn into a fight at Webber's Bridge, New Bern was in purposeful chaos. Militia elements tracking Craig's column provided intelligence that made it clear the British had the former colonial capital in their sites. For days residents collected what belongings they might need if necessity dictated they flee the town, hiding valuables from potential redcoat looting. Militia removed things that might be militarily useful to the British, such as the lead gutters of Tryon Palace that could be melted into musket balls. As the former capital, the town had cannon strategically placed to repel a land assault, but what it did not have was ammunition to defeat a sustained attack.

After brushing aside Lillington's men at Webber's Bridge, Craig marched his force into New Bern on August 19. Despite the Whigs' best efforts, there were still considerable stores of food and other useful things in the town. Most of the militia pulled out when the redcoats appeared, but not all. Shooting from concealment in one of the buildings, they took a measure of revenge for the setbacks dealt the American forces at Rockfish Creek and Kingston by shooting down Capt. John Gordon, commander of Craig's provincial dragoons and former Wilmington merchant.

Over the course of two days, the British sacked New Bern. Redcoats set fire to over 3,000 bushels of salt and several ships anchored in the Neuse and Trent Rivers off the town. They destroyed stocks of rum and naval stores, and pillaged the town's shops of whatever they fancied. Several area plantations and homes were put to the torch, too, including Alexander Lillington's. Ships in the New Bern harbor had their rigging cut if they were not burned. Local physician Dr. Alexander Gaston tried to dodge the redcoats by escaping in a small rowboat, but a British soldier shot him down. His wife, Margaret Gaston, who saw it happen, cried out in anguish and tried to shield her husband's bleeding body with her own.

Leaving New Bern, Craig continued cutting a swath through eastern North Carolina. He marched his men 17 miles to Bryant's Mill on the Neuse River, where Col. James Gorham and 150 militiamen tried to block the redcoats. Gorham ordered his cavalry to protect his flank, but like at Rouse's Tavern and other places, alcohol led to fatal neglect by the Americans. The cavalrymen found a stash of liquor and got drunk, allowing

Craig's own horsemen to get around Gorham's defenders. Had it not been for mill owner Bryant showing them a hidden means of escaping through the nearby swamp, the day could have ended very badly for Gorham's force.

Craig was preparing to make an assault on Kingston when word reached him that General "Mad" Anthony Wayne was marching with a force of Continentals to end his rampage, a false rumor as it turned out, so instead he turned his column south for Wilmington. By the last week of August, the redcoats were well on the way back to their safe haven on the Cape Fear. Craig suffered 15 men dead and a like number wounded in the raid, but it accomplished two very important things. One, it struck terror into the Whig population across eastern North Carolina. Two, he nearly doubled the size of his force with the flood of loyalist recruits who flocked to him on his march. Craig re-entered Wilmington on August 24 after a very successful expedition. Not since 1776 had the British and their Tory allies controlled so much of North Carolina.

Among those joining the redcoat column were as many as 500 slaves from eastern plantations and towns. Their loss had real consequences for the American war effort, as slaves did many of the tasks required to keep home and hearth intact while the white men went off to soldier. That loss of laborers had a serious impact on things like farming, construction - military and civilian - and trade. Add to that the fears of whites that the British presence could lead to slave revolts and the exodus of bondsmen to join the redcoats was a serious issue. For the British, the influx of formerly enslaved Africans provided them with the muscle they needed to fortify their own enclaves and support their war effort.[70]

The Battle of Elizabethtown (a.k.a. The Battle of Tory Hole)
Forces Engaged:
American: Col. Thomas Robeson commanding the Bladen County Regiment of Militia, including Col. Thomas Owen, Col. Thomas Brown, Capt. William Ellis, Capt. William G. McDaniel, Capt. Peter Robeson, Capt. James Gillespie of the Duplin County militia, Lt. William Daniel serving under Capt. Peter Robeson, Sgt. James Cain, and Privates Richard Brown, Richard Cheshire, Sherwood Fort, Robert Johnson, Musgrove Jones, Hiram Pendleton, Samuel Pharis, Richard Plummer, James Singletary, Josiah Singletary, Moab Stevens, and Burell Whitehead

Loyalist: Col. John Slingsby with 300 men of the Bladen and Cumberland County Loyalist Militias, including Capt. David Godwin and Capt. Charles Malloy

David Fanning had just left Elizabethtown after passing through on his way to deliver his prisoners to Wilmington. Col. John Slingsby had taken Elizabethtown, on the Cape Fear River in Bladen County, only a short time before. There were still a number of Whig prisoners in town under his control. Fanning warned Slingsby that in his opinion there were too many American prisoners for the force the Tory commander had with him. Slingsby, who even though a Tory was not a harsh man towards his Whig neighbors, listened but did not take Fanning's advice.

Thirty-nine-year-old Sallie Salter was a fixture in Elizabethtown from one of the most prominent families in the county, bringing her eggs and produce to market on a regular basis. When she showed up at Slingsby's camp with a basket of fresh eggs on her arm, no one suspected that her real task that morning was to note the layout of the loyalist defenses for her Whig friends. With her information in hand, Col. Thomas Robeson devised a plan of attack.

During the dark early morning hours of August 27, Robeson and his men crossed the Cape Fear River, probably at Waddell's Ferry. The Americans discovered there were no boats available for the crossing, so they had to waded across with their clothes and weapons held above their heads to reach the south bank below the town. The men were tense, their band of 80 amounting to only about a third of the number of loyalists Slingsby had with him. Not only did they have to cross the exposed river, but they had to keep their weapons and powder dry in the process. The nearly full moon helped the crossing, but the downside was that it seemed like a spotlight as they crossed the dark water. If a random sentry discovered them, they would be easy targets.

Reaching dry ground, the militiamen checked their weapons, climbed up the embankment and crossed the road running parallel to the river. Robeson's men crept into position and engaged the Tory sentries, sweeping them back into town. The Whigs sowed confusion among the loyalists and made them think their attackers were more numerous than they actually were by yelling commands to imaginary units and firing their muskets into the air. The loyalists made a stiff resistance at first, but eventually began to fall back into Elizabethtown proper. The Tories took

Bladen County militiamen crossed the Cape Fear and rushed to surprise Col. John Slingsby's loyalists in Elizabethtown.

up positions inside local buildings, where Slingsby directed their fire. That all came to an end when both John Slingsby and another officer named Godden were shot. Confusion added to the chaos of losing their commanding officers, and the loyalists began to fold. Panicking Tories fled the town, scrambling down the steep vine and cane covered hillside into the deep ravine behind Elizabethtown's main street, trying to escape by way of the river. The pursuing militiamen shot down more than a few from the high ground at the top of the ravine.

The 1832 pension application of Josiah Singletary recalled the Whig attack. "On their countermarch from Lisbon to Sampson County between Colley Swamp and the Cape Fear, about nine miles from Elizabeth [Town] they were met by Mrs. McRee, the mother of Major Griffith J. McRee [a NC Continental officer from Bladen County] of the Continental army, who left home for the purpose of apprising them of the situation of the Tories," Singletary remembered.

"By that time, they had been joined by Colonel [Thomas] Brown, and [Col. Thomas] Owen, and Captain Peter Robeson, and several other Whigs, and in consequence of the information received from Mrs. McRee, an attack on the Tories was determined on - although the whole force of the Whigs did not exceed eighty men.

"They accordingly marched to the Cape Fear, and forded it at night, about half or three quarters of a mile below the village - attacked the Tories at a point called Tory Hole - drove them to the upper end of the village; where the ammunition of the Whigs, having been expended, they were under the necessity of retiring; after having killed or mortally wounded their commanding officer, Colonel [John] Slingsby, Captain David Godwin, and a private named Harrison -Lieutenant Baldwin and several privates were severely wounded.

"'Of the Whigs none were killed, and only two privates, James Singletary and James Cain, slightly wounded."

In the end, Slingsby's Tories lost 17 men killed, including five captains. Robeson's militia only had four men wounded. John Slingsby did not linger long after the shooting stopped. When he passed, despite being well liked by combatants on both sides for his even keeled and lenient nature, his property was still confiscated by the state.[71]

After the raid on Cross Creek, the three main loyalist bands had split up, each heading off to different destinations. Fanning turned towards Wilmington. John Slingsby took his men to Bladen County, running local

The terrain at Tory Hole, just before reaching the Cape Fear River, where Tories fled to escape the American attack.

Whigs out of Elizabethtown (as it turned out only temporarily). Hector McNeill moved to McPhaul's Mill, in modern Hoke County's Antioch Township, near the town of Raeford. When Slingsby was killed at Elizabethtown, it left just Fanning and McNeill's bands as the only organized loyalist forces in North Carolina. It was imperative to British war planners that the Whig guerilla bands of South Carolina, led by leaders like Marion and Pickens, not be allowed to take root in North Carolina. The loyalist militias were a key tool to prevent it. With one of the three main Tory forces eliminated after Elizabethtown, that task became much harder. But the Tories were still effective weapons for keeping American militias from interfering with British operations in any meaningful way. When Fanning and McNeill learned Col. Thomas Wade's Whigs were on the way to deal with Hector McNeill's loyalist force, he rode to support the Tories.[72]

The Battle of McPhaul's Mill (a.k.a. Little Raft Swamp, McFall's Mill, Burnt Swamp, or Beatti's Bridge #2)

Forces Engaged
Loyalist: Col. David Fanning commanding at least 155 men of the North Carolina Loyalist Militia including Captains Benjamin Underwood and John Elrod, and 70 men of the Bladen County Loyalist Militia led by Col. Hector McNeill
American: Col. Thomas Wade commanding roughly 450 men, including those of the Anson County Regiment of Militia with four companies led by Captains Patrick Boggan, John Randle, Stephen Tomkins, and Alexander "Red" McNeill of Cumberland County; Three companies of the Richmond County Regiment of Militia led by Col. Thomas Crawford and Captains William Hunter, John Speed, and William Wall; and a detachment of the Chatham County Regiment of Militia led by Capt. Abner Nash.

David Fanning met with Hector McNeill at the mill owned by John McPhaul on August 29 and determined to mount a pre-emptive attack against Whig militia led by Col. Thomas Wade at Drowning Creek, 18 miles away.

Arriving at Drowning Creek by September 1, loyalist scouts discovered Wade had encamped atop a hill between Beatti's Bridge and a swamp. The Americans' main defensive works faced the swamp. The Whigs outnumbered the loyalists more than two to one, so Fanning or-

The memorial marker at the site of McPhaul's Mill, southwest of modern Fayetteville.

dered his men to space themselves wider than they normally would to make it appear there were more of them than there actually were. Splitting their force, McNeill took his men to ride around the Americans' position and cut off their most likely route of retreat at the bridge. When they were in position, Fanning would launch his attack on Wade's front.

The timing of the plan went out the window when one of Fanning's men slipped from his horse as they moved into position around eleven o'clock, accidentally discharging his musket. The Americans turned to and began firing at the now exposed Tories. The Whig fire took several of Fanning's mounted men down in the first volley, but did not blunt their charge. Fanning leapt from his horse and urged his men to do the same. They began clawing their way up the hill, where Wade's men suddenly found that having the high ground put them at a disadvantage because it caused too many of them to shoot high. The daylight attack also meant that when the Americans rose to fire down at the Tories they became silhouetted against the sky, making them easy targets for Fanning's men.

The loyalists made it to within 20 yards of Wade's position when the Americans began their retreat. The premature launch of the attack after the accidental discharge that started the fight meant that McNeill's horsemen had not been able to get into position at Beatti's Bridge in time to close the door on Wade's escape. The Whigs took to the swamp, where Fanning pursued them for seven miles before giving up the chase. The Tories captured 250 horses and 54 prisoners, including Col. Joseph Hayes, but four of the prisoners died overnight. In Wade's camp, the loyalists counted 19 dead Whigs. Fanning's attackers counted four of their own killed and another 20 wounded.

The fight lasted until one o'clock that afternoon, and proved to be a significant win for David Fanning. Had McNeill, either by intent or circumstance, not allowed Wade's men to escape, it would have been a significant blow to the American cause in North Carolina. The two loyalist leaders split up again after the battle, with Fanning returning to his base at Cox's Mill on Deep River. On the way, Maj. Thomas Dougan of the Randolph County Regiment of Militia was captured by the Tories as he tracked them, trying to gather intelligence on where the loyalists were going. Fanning sentenced him to be hanged, but fortunately for Dougan there were several neighbors of his in the Tory band who spoke up for him. Fanning ignored them and put the bound Dougan on horseback with a noose around his neck. Before he could spur the horse, one of the Tories stepped forward and threatened to shoot the Tory leader if Dougan swung. Fanning backed down and allowed a show of hands vote to determine Dougan's fate. The tally came out in the American's favor, and he was sent along to Wilmington as a prisoner.[73]

North Carolina was a mess as the summer of 1781 drew to a close. Governor Thomas Burke confided to Gen. Nathaniel Greene that the only way out of the situation would be to dislodge Craig and his redcoats from Wilmington. Greene agreed, but admitted he would be unable to do anything about it for the time being. "I perfectly agree with you in opinion that the best way of silencing the Tories is by routing the Enemy from Wilmington," Greene wrote, "for while they have a footing there the Tories will receive such encouragement as to keep their hopes and expectations alive: and their incursions will be continued. Nor will it be in your power to crush them with all the force you can raise as they act in small Parties, and appear in so many different shapes, and have so many hiding places and secret springs of intelligence that you may wear out an Army, and still be unable to subdue them. Strike at the root of the evil by removing the British...I have long had it in contemplation to attempt something against Wilmington; but my force and situation has put it out of my power. I shall be happy to aid you in advice or in any other way which may serve to give success to your plan."

Greene must have had second thoughts about his ability to help North Carolina's governor remove the thorn in his side represented by Craig at Wilmington. Even George Washington recognized the necessity of eliminating the British from the state's chief port. Retaking Wilmington "would be of great Importance in the scale of future Negotiations; as it would in Effect, be the Liberation of another State," he said.

That summer Greene tasked BGen. Griffith Rutherford with mounting an expedition to liberate Wilmington, using militia from the western part of the state to do the job. The eastern militia were tired after being so long in the field fighting both Craig's redcoat regulars and loyalist bands led by men like Fanning and McNeill. It would have to be militia that did it, because no North Carolina Continentals were available. But Rutherford's assignment was cancelled when Greene received word that the French would soon arrive with troops that could be used for coastal operations. That being the case, Greene opted to continue into South Carolina with his force. The trouble was that the French landed in the Chesapeake that fall to aid Washington in the siege at Yorktown. Wilmington would have to wait.[74]

The Hillsborough Raid

In modern Columbus County, a small skirmish occurred at Lake Waccamaw. According to militiaman Joseph Humphrey, it was early September 1781 when his company of the Onslow County Regiment of Militia were dispatched to the settlement in what was then Brunswick County.

Griffith Rutherford

The Tories in that area were creating problems for the Whigs who lived there, and Humphrey and his fellow Onslow County men were ordered to put a stop to it. The militiamen, led by Col. Henry Rhodes, LtCol. Joseph Scott Cray, and Capt. Ephraim Battle, marched to the house of a noted Tory named Simpson. Camping for the night at the Simpson home, the Americans were attacked by a band of loyalists. Capt. Battle took seven pieces of buckshot in the fray, and the militia retreated and returned to the Wilmington vicinity. Battle survived his wound under a doctor's care.[75]

David Fanning was also active in early September. In the first weeks of the month N.C. Governor Thomas Burke and his wife left Halifax for Hillsborough. Elected to the state's top office in June, Burke had a meeting with other leaders to address the growing problem of Tory militia mischief in the state. BGen. John Butler raised a large force of militia to eliminate loyalist activity between the Pee Dee and Cape Fear rivers, consisting of militia from Caswell, Chatham, Randolph, Wake, and Orange

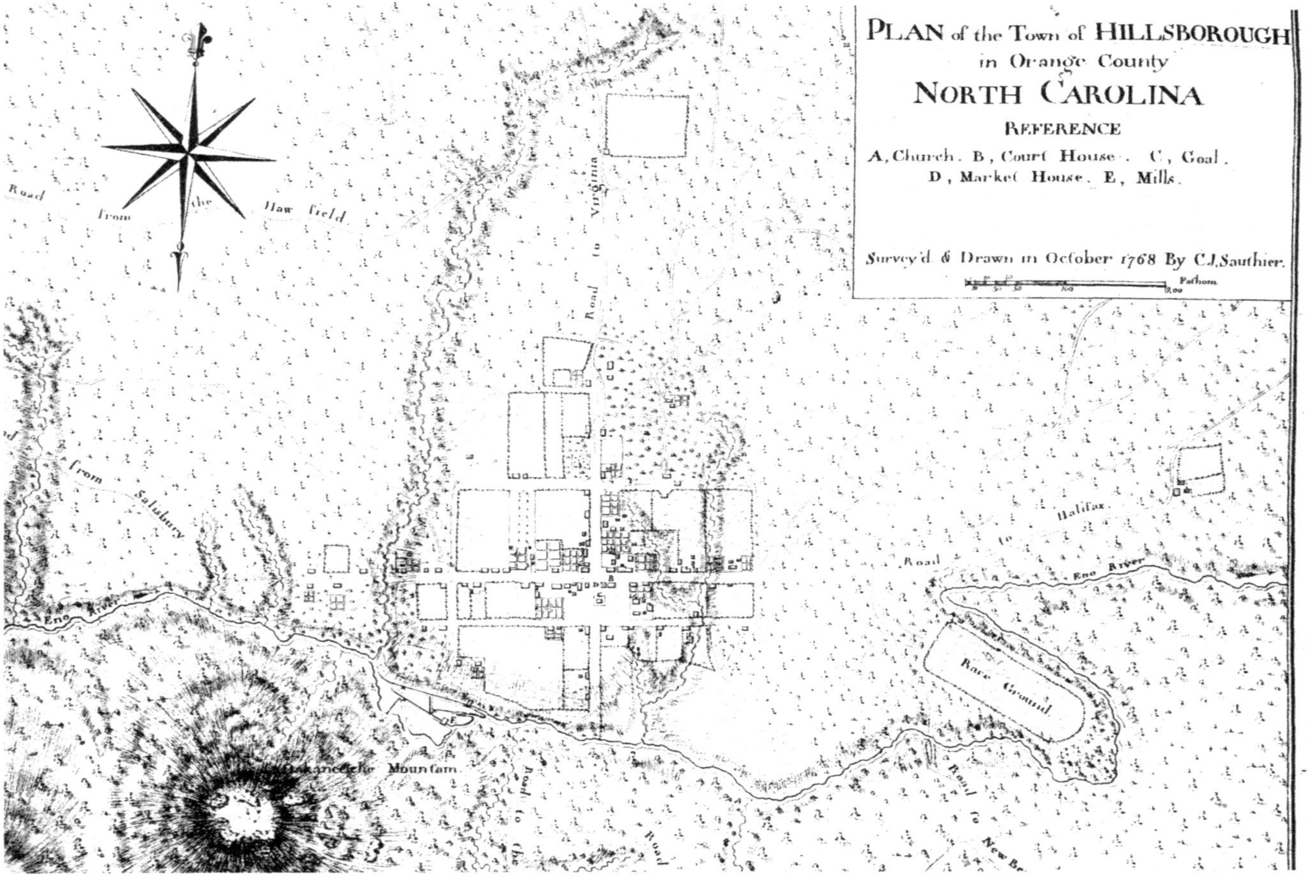

Claude Sauthier's map of colonial Hillsborough.

Counties. Loyalists had placed a price on Burke's head, so the governor ordered BGen. John Butler and a guard made up of Hillsborough District militia to return to the town to provide security for the meeting. Unknown to Butler, David Fanning learned of the meeting and followed him back to Hillsborough.

The loyalists under Fanning were augmented by volunteers who were eager to join up with the Tories after the battle at Little Raft Swamp. While he had almost 1,000 men at his disposal, only a little less than half were equipped to fight. On September 9, Hector McNeill's 70 Tories joined Fanning at Cox's Mill. Cumberland County's Col. Archibald Mc-Dugald brought in 200 men. David Fanning was now in command of the largest force he had ever led, even if they were only partially armed for the coming operation. The loyalists started their march to the state capital and the rebel leaders gathered there on September 11, 1781.

September 12 dawned thick with fog, concealing Fanning and the 500 men with him as they crept into the still sleeping town of Hillsborough. As the Tories burst through doors, people tumbled from their beds and breakfast tables to find themselves at gunpoint, herded into the streets. A small detachment of Continentals in town were quickly overcome after they barricaded themselves inside the town church, and the only resistance the Tories encountered came from the occasional sniper firing from windows and alleys. A handful of Whigs tried to escape by running. Fanning spotted one officer, Col. Archibald Lytle, wearing a military helmet and running for the woods. Fanning spurred his horse to stop him, splitting Lytle's helmet with a blow so hard it broke his sword.

Fanning's men made their way to the Burke home, where the governor and personal guard Capt. John DeCoin put up a fight. Outnumbered, it was a short one. When a British officer with the Tories (some accounts say it was Fanning) gave his word they would be unharmed, Burke surrendered. North Carolina's governor, along with 200 other prisoners, were led away to begin their march to Wilmington. There, Burke would be transported to Charlestown, where he was imprisoned on James Island. Thirty loyalists sentenced to hang that morning were freed by Fanning, as well.

The fighting was over two hours after it began, and Fanning's men began plundering the town. Someone found a supply of liquor and many of the Tories got quite drunk. One teetotaler who did not imbibe was Capt. John Mclean, who was placed in charge of the prisoners while order was restored. From that point on, McLean was known by the nickname "Sober John." By two in the afternoon, Fanning began herding his men and prisoners out of Hillsborough toward his base at Cox's Mill, before continuing on to Wilmington.

    Militiaman William Allen remembered the raid in his 1832 pension application. "While at Hillsborough preparing to go on this expedition, the Tories under the command of David Fanning, and the British under Col. McDougan...came upon us and took three hundred of us prisoner, among whom was Governor [Thomas] Burke. He saw [Lt.] Col. [Archibald] Lytle wounded by a sword in the head by the Tory, Fanning. This transaction took place at Hillsborough as above stated on the 4th [the 12th] Of September 1781. That night we remained near Hillsborough, and were carried the next morning by the British and Tories on to a place called Lindley's Mill, where a pretty severe and well-fought battle took place between a force of the Republicans and the British and Tories, during which engagement the prisoners were kept in a close place with a strong guard around them. He recollects well of seeing there killed the celebrated Tory, Col. [Hector] McNeill. That night after the battle at Lindley's Mill we were forced off by our captors and taken by Wilson's Iron Works to Wilmington, where we were put on board of British ships, which steered towards the West India Islands and then taken and disembarked us at Charlestown, where the greater part remained until peace; but the applicant states he was exchanged on the 11th of August 1782, and came on back home in Orange."

    The Fanning raid on Hillsborough was astoundingly successful, but presenting his trophies to Maj. Craig was not a foregone conclusion.[76]

The Battle of Lindley's Mill (a.k.a. Cane Creek)

Forces Engaged:
American: BGen John Butler, commanding the **Hillsborough District Brigade of Militia**. The brigade included the Chatham County Regiment of Militia led by Col. John Luttrell, Majors John Nall, William Ghoulson, and Roger Griffith. The **Chatham County Militia** had twelve companies led by Captains Alexander Clark, Capt. Hawkins Dye, Charles Gholson, William Griffin, John Hudgins, John Jones, Taverner Marsh, John May-

ben, Richard B. Meacham, James Mebane, Abner Nash and Joseph Rosser. The **Orange County Regiment of Militia** with fourteen companies led by LtCol. Robert Mebane, Maj. William Cage, and Captains Abraham Allen, Lewis Bledsoe of Wake Co., Nathaniel Christmas, Matthew Collier from Wake Co., Charles Crawford from Cumberland Co., Joshua Hadley from Cumberland Co., John Honeycutt from Cumberland Co., Capt. William Jamieson, William Jones, James Kell, Matthew McCullers from Johnston Co., John McFarland from Wake Co., William Ray, and William Smith. The **Randolph County Militia** with four companies led by Captains Edward Beeson, John Johnston, John Knight, and Robert McLane. The **Craven County Regiment of Militia** with three companies led by Captains Nathaniel Dickerson, William Douglas, and Mason Foley. The **Salisbury District Brigade of Militia** detachment under Col. Thomas Wade, with units from the **Anson County Militia** led by Captains Patrick Boggan, Joseph Howell, and Stephen Tomkins; the **Guildford County Regiment of Militia** led by LtCol. John Humphreys and Captains Edward Gwinn and William Gwinn; the **Rowan County Militia** with a detachment led by Capt. Peter Hedrick; one company of the **Surry County Militia** led by Capt. James Gains; and one company of the **New Hanover County Regiment of Militia** led by Capt. Thomas Handley

British: Col. David Fanning and his **Regiment of Loyalists** (435 men) led by Captains John Rains of the **Randolph County Militia**, Benjamin Underwood and William Deaton of the **Chatham County Militia**, Edward Edwards and Stephen Holloway of the **Orange County Militia**; the **Royal North Carolina Regiment of Bladen County** led by Col. Hector McNeill with 70 men; and the **Royal Militia of Cumberland County** (200 men) led by Col. Archibald McDugald and Captains Sober John" McLean and Archibald McKay; and **Gov. Martin's Corps** led by Capt. Alexander McGraw

Leaving Hillsborough, Fanning stopped for the night 18 miles away, near Lindley's Mill in what is now southern Alamance County, east of Snow Camp. BGen. John Butler was made aware of the Hillsborough raid by the Commissary General for North Carolina's militia, BGen. Alexander Mebane, who slipped out of the noose set by Fanning the day before and carried the news to the American camp. Now Butler and 450 men lay in ambush, waiting for Fanning's loyalists to fall into his trap.

Fanning's column crossed the Haw River at Woody's Ford, then continued on towards Cox's Mill, Hector McNeill's loyalist militia scouting ahead of the main body. McNeill's Tories rode into Butler's kill zone near a ford running by the mill, on September 13, 1781. The Whigs were positioned on high ground overlooking the Tory line of march. Their first volley ripped into the loyalists without warning, killing several men. The rest of McNeill's men dismounted and found what shelter they could along the banks of Crane Creek. Col. McNeill ordered his men to fall back beyond the range of the American muskets. Archibald McDugald was furious at the order, and openly challenged McNeill's courage. McNeill switched course, and ordered his men into a charge, with him in the lead. According to the 1846 pension statement of militiaman Isaac Brewer, who witnessed McNeill's death, it came quickly.

"During the action at Lindley's Mills, Colonel McNeill and Major John Nall met in single combat both fired at the same instant," he said. "McNeill's ball struck Nall near the left pap, and Nall's ball penetrated McNeill in the forehead; both died on the spot. A good many men were killed & wounded on both sides."

McNeill's death had come to him in a dream two nights before, and it was one that came true. All told, McNeill took eight musket balls to his body. His mount took five more. Seeing McNeill fall, men cried out that their commander was dead, but Col. Archibald McDugald denounced it as a lie. McDugald knew that such news could turn whatever resolve the Tories had left into jelly. The Tory colonel ordered a disciplined retreat back to the place McNeill had wanted to move to before the charge. His death was a waste that would be felt long after the shooting stopped.

Butler's plan was not simply to ambush the loyalists, but also to free the prisoners Fanning had taken at Hillsborough, including North Carolina governor Thomas Burke and several Continental officers. As the militia focused the Tories' attention on the fire coming from the hilltop, another element of Butler's force was maneuvering in behind Fanning's men to close the trap and liberate the captives. The prisoners jumped to their feet in anticipation of being freed, but Capt. "Sober John" Mclean threatened to kill them all if they did not sit down and be quiet. McLean moved the prisoners to the nearby Spring Friends' Meeting House where they could be more easily contained.

Col. Fanning pulled his men back to the meeting house as Butler's troops tried to get behind them. Archibald McDugald swore that he would

The ridge near Lindley's Mill where Butler's men lay in ambush waiting for Fanning's Tories. *From "The American Revolution Tour of North Carolina ™" (AmRevNC.com). Copyright 2020 by AmRevNC, LLC. Reprinted by permission.*

kill the prisoners before he let them be set free. McDugald was sent to attack the Whigs at Stafford Branch, while Fanning executed an encirclement of his own, getting behind Butler's force. The fighting kept up for four hours. BGen Butler finally ordered a withdrawal, leaving their dead and wounded where they lay. As Butler's militia began pulling back, Continental Army officer LtCol. Robert Mebane took some men and fought a delaying action to allow the rest of the Americans to escape. Powder ran so low among the Americans that Mebane himself went from man to man with coarse gunpowder in his hat to resupply the soldiers.

Just when it looked like Mebane's men would be overwhelmed, David Fanning was wounded when a musket ball shattered the bone in his left arm and tore open an artery. Like when McNeill was mortally wounded, the loss of the Tory leader had an immediate impact on the loyalist fighters. Capt. John Rains assumed command of the Tories and tried to rally them, but soon ordered a withdrawal.

Butler's Americans fell back to Alamance Creek, while the wounded Fanning and his men resumed their slow march to Wilmington. Overall command of the loyalists fell to Col. Archibald McDugald, who was augmented by Col. Duncan Ray's Anson County loyalist militia at McPhaul's Mill. On the battlefield, 200 men of both sides lay dead or wounded. Dr.

John Pyle, then best known for leading his own loyalist band in the disastrous battle known as Pyle's Defeat, redeemed himself among his fellow North Carolinians by caring for the wounded of both armies in the aftermath.

The Tories were fired on again by a small band of Whigs as they forded Rocky River on September 14, but the attack was little more than an irritation to the tired loyalists. After linking up with Ray's men, McDugald turned the American prisoners over to him to continue on to Wilmington. McDugald and Capt. Stephen Holloway accompanied the prisoners traveling with Ray to the British enclave on the coast.

David Fanning survived his wounds and penned this account of the battle at Lindley's Mill:

"About 12 o'clock, I left Hillsborough; and proceeded Eighteen miles further, to Lindsey's [Lindley's] Mill on Cane Creek; where Gen'l Butler and a party of rebels had concealed themselves. Col'n McNeal [Hector MacNeil], who had the advanced guard, had neglected to take the necessary precautions for our safety, and by information of Capt. McLain Cumberland county, Little River; and as soon as I had discovered the situation, we were in, and having so great a number of prisoners, I left my situation, and pushed for the advanced guard; on my coming up with Col'n Mcneal [sic], I inquired the reason of his neglect; and before he could answer, we were fired upon by the rebels. They killed Eight men, among them was Col'n McNeal, who received three balls through him, and five through his horse. I then ordered a retreat back to where I left the prisoners, and after securing them, I made the necessary preparations to attack the enemy; and after engaging them four hours they retreated. I lost twenty seven men killed, and sixty, so badly wounded, that they could not be moved; besides thirty slightly, but so, that they could keep up with our main body. At the conclusion of this action, I received a shot in my left arm, which broke the bone in several pieces; my loss of blood was so great, that I was taken off my horse, and led to a secret place in the woods. I then sent Lieut. Woleston, to my little army, for Col'n Arch McDugald [Archibald McDougald], and Major John Rains [or Reins] and Lu Col'n [Lieut. Col.] Arch[ibald] McKay, to take command; to send to Wilmington for assistance, as I was not able to take any command. I also desired that Major Rains should return as soon as he could leave Col. McDugald; as I thought he might be the means of saving me from the hand of my enemies.

These gentlemen conducted themselves in such a manner, I think they deserve the applause of every loyal subject, both for their valour and good conduct, as Col'n Maybin [Mebane] and Gen'l Butler persued [sic] them all the way until they met Major Craigg [James Craig] coming to their assistance. They made their march god for 160 miles and never lost one prisoner, but introduced Thos. Burk[e], their Governor, and his regiment of rebels, to Major Craigg; who very well accepted them; and Major Craigg introduced his Excellency, and Regiment, to the Provost Master..."

"At the departure of my little army, I was left with three men; and in four days 17 more came to my assistance. I made enquiry respecting the loss of the Rebels, in the late action; and found that the inhabitants had buried 24, and that the wounded they had left were 90, besides those that went off and that my party had taken 10 prisoners. Of the number of the Killed was Col'o Guttrell [John Luttrell], and Major Knowles, who were inveterate enemies to the Loyalists.

"The party we had engaged I found to have consisted of four hundred Continentals under the command of Col'o Maybin and Gen'l Butler. In twenty four days, I found myself able to set up, and then dispateched [sic], four of my Captains Hooker, Rains, Knight, and Lindly, to Wilmington for a supply of ammunition; and before their return I had set out and embodied 140 men, during which time I heard of a quantity of leather, which was prepared for the use of the rebel army, and was ordered for Gen'l Green's quarters at Camden. I went to the place, and finding the leather agreeable to my information, I took enough thereof to equip the company completely, and ordered the rest to be destroyed. On my return to Brush Creek, near where I had been secreted during my illness, occasioned by my wounds, I sent out spies for discovery. Two of them returned, in less than an hour, with information of six hundred rebels, who were advancing for to attack me. But they proved no more than 170. Their accounts disheartened a number of my men. From my being is so weak a state, they apprehended I would not be able to command them. However they lifted me, on my horse, and I formed my men there in two ranks and showed two fronts, as they appeared both in my front and rear; the fire continued for near an hour. I lost three men killed, and three badly wounded. The rebels had one killed, and several wounded. Then they retreated; and rallied and attacked again, after retreating, about a mile, which was so unexpected, that I concluded they had been reinforced. I then retreated;

but without loss, except my baggage. I, then, separated my men into small parties, until the arrival of the four officers, I had dispatched for ammunition, to Wilmington, who brought...5000 cartridges."77

Skirmish at Livingston's Creek (Bladen County)
Forces Engaged
American: BGen John Butler with three companies of the Caswell County Regiment of Militia, led by Capts. Josiah Cole, Shadrack Hargis, and John McMullen
British: Col. Archibald McDugald commanding an unknown number of loyalist militia; Maj. James Henry Craig commanding an unknown number of British regulars of the 82nd Regiment of Foot

While Fanning's loyalists were limping towards Wilmington, BGen Griffith Rutherford was assembling a force at Robinson's Plantation in Montgomery County to finally deal with the British and loyalist presence in North Carolina. The 950 infantry and 200 cavalry, mostly from Guilford, Rowan, and Mecklenburg Counties, were short on experience. The veterans in the force had seen action at Cowan's Ford, Trading Ford, Kings Mountain, and Guilford Courthouse, and Rutherford used them to impart the lessons experience taught and provide some backbone for his untested recruits. Until they could be trained and put into the field, though, the civil war between those who stood for American independence and those who supported King George III in southeastern North Carolina continued.78

In Wilmington Maj. Craig received word of Fanning's raid on Hillsborough and the clash at Lindley's Mill. The capture of Gov. Thomas Burke was a plum the British commander was eager to claim, and he led a column of redcoats from the 82nd Regiment of Foot to meet Col. Archibald McDugald and the rest of Fanning's Tories. The two forces joined at Livingston's Creek in Bladen County's Brown Marsh, southeast of Elizabethtown, on September 23.

It had been a difficult march for the loyalists. After McDugald and Ray rendezvoused at McPhaul's Mill, Whig cavalry pursued them for the next two days. The Tories set up an ambush at Hammond's Creek Bridge to buy time for McDugald to deliver his captives to Craig. Once the

British troops joined the loyalists, the major determined to deal with the Whig horsemen that he believed were led by Col. Thomas Brown, of the Bladen County Regiment of Militia, and end their chase. Four hours after the British linked with the Tories, a body of American horsemen appeared. Craig sent his cavalry and 60 infantry to disperse what he believed to be Brown's mounted militia.

The redcoats surprised the Whigs, who did not expect to see British regulars. Craig's men drove the Whigs back for three miles before they got a surprise of their own. The Americans, some 200 strong, had built a defensive position across the road. The redcoats paused and collected their wits. After evaluating what they were up against, they charged the enemy defenses and successfully sent the American militia into retreat. The British, unsure what they would encounter if they pursued, returned to Craig to make their report. The major quickly sent Fanning and McDugald's prisoners on their way to confinement, first at Wilmington, then later at Charlestown.

It was a wise move. As it turned out, the Americans Craig skirmished with at Livingston's Creek did not belong to Col. Thomas Brown. Instead, they were advanced elements of BGen. John Butler's much larger force that was trying to head off McDugald and free Gov. Burke before he could be delivered to Wilmington. They were unsuccessful, and as a result Speaker of the Senate Alexander Martin assumed the role of North Carolina's chief executive in the captive Burke's place.[79]

The Skirmish at Hood's Creek
Forces Engaged
American: Col. Edward Wingate and LtCol. Jacob Leonard, with three companies of the Brunswick County Regiment of Militia led by Capts. Charles Gause, Thomas Russ, and James Simmons; 30 men including Thomas Smith and Jeremiah Wescoat; Two companies of the Bladen County Regiment of Militia led by Capts. Robert Hayes and Daniel Shipman
British: Maj. Daniel Manson leading 120 men of the 82nd Regiment of Foot, plus an unknown number of loyalists

Maj. James Henry Craig had an itch that needed scratching. American militia had established a camp northeast of modern Sandy Creek in

Brunswick County that was proving bothersome. The Americans there were interdicting supplies intended for the redcoat garrison across the river, and were also preventing area slaves from escaping to British lines. In late September, Craig decided enough was enough.

Intelligence told Craig that the post consisted of Lt.Col. Jacob Leonard and men of the Brunswick County militia camped at the bridge over Hood's Creek. The plan called for a main attack by a detachment led by Maj. Daniel Manson, while a second element circled around behind the Americans to close off any retreat. Manson and his men were instructed to give no quarter. They were to kill any armed American they found.

The orders to kill any armed man the British found disturbed the loyalist guide who was to lead Manson to the bridge, then take the Tory element in behind the Whigs to flank them. Rebels they might be, but the men with Leonard at Hood's Creek were also people he knew. The Tory guide stalled for time, leading the loyalists on a long, winding trek through the woods and swamps northwest of modern Navassa until he believed Leonard's men were alert to Manson's presence. At the bridge, the concealed redcoats grew impatient waiting for the loyalists to get into position behind the rebel militia. They sounded a horn to let the Tories know they were ready.

The horn alerted the Americans too. Leonard sent the two Smith brothers to the bridge as an advance guard to see what was happening. It did not take long for them to find out. When they got to the bridge they saw Manson's redcoats and wheeled their horses about, spurring their flanks to speed their retreat. Their horses may have been fast, but they could not outrun musket balls. One of the brothers, Thomas Smith, tumbled from his saddle with a shot from a British Brown Bess lodged in him. Thomas Smith was wounded, but not dead. British bayonets finished the job, as several of Manson's soldiers ran across the bridge and stabbed him to death. The other Smith brother made it back to camp missing only his hat, shot off his head in the mad minute that took his sibling's life.

When Smith made his report, Leonard and the rest of his men retreated into the surrounding swamps. The lieutenant colonel picked ten men, including Jeremiah Wescoat, to follow and harass the British on their way back to Wilmington. The Brunswick County militiamen would dash from the woods and fire at Manson's column, retreating back into the relative safety of the forest before the redcoats could respond. The Americans hounded the British all the way back, until they reached the Brick House on Eagles Island across from the foot of Market Street in Wilmington.

According to Wescoat, Leonard's retreating men had followers of their own. Loyalists caught up with the rebels and launched an attack at a "Mr. Duncan's" plantation. In the clash there, the Americans lost two men killed and another five wounded.[80]

The Battle of Brown Marsh (Bladen County)
Forces Engaged
American: BGen. John Butler, overall commander and unit commander of the **Hillsborough District Brigade of Militia.** The Hillsborough District Brigade of Militia consisted of four companies of the **Orange County Regiment of Militia** led by Capts. Lewis Bledsoe of Wake County, George Hodge, Matthew McCullers of Johnston County, and Adam Sanders. Also under Butler's command was one company of the **Chatham County Regiment** led by Capt. Alexander Clark; four companies of the **Bladen County Regiment of Militia** led by Cols. Thomas Robeson and Thomas Owen, along with Capts. Jared Irwin, William Leggett, William G. McDaniel, and Capt. James Shipman; six companies of the **Caswell County Regiment of Militia** led by Capts. Josiah Cole, Spillsby Coleman, Mason Foley, Shadrack Hargis, John McMullen, and John Oldham; two companies of the **Duplin County Regiment of Militia** led by Capt. David Dodd and Capt. William Turner; two companies of the **Guilford County Regiment of Militia** led by Capts. Edwin and William Gwinn; two companies of the **Randolph County Regiment of Militia** led by Capts. Edward Beeson and James Woods; one company of the **Montgomery County Regiment of Militia** led by Capt. James Crump; at least one company of the **Brunswick County Regiment of Militia** led by Col. Edward Wingate and Capt. Thomas DeVane; and one company of the **Mecklenburg County Regiment of Militia** led by Capt. Charles Polk

British: Maj. Daniel Manson of the 82nd Regiment of Foot in overall command of 180 men of the Royal North Carolina Regiment of loyalist militia; Col. Duncan Ray leading the Royal North Carolina Militia of Anson County; one detached company of Col. David Fanning's militia regiment led by Capt. Stephen Holloway

In late September, sometime between Sept. 28 and Oct. 1, 1781, loyalist militia leaders Colonels Duncan Ray, Archibald McDugald, and British army Maj. Daniel Manson moved back into the field after a few days of rest and refit at Wilmington. The combined force of Tories came across BGen. John Butler's formidable force encamped at Brown Marsh, south of modern Clarkton, almost on the border between Bladen and Columbus Counties.

Butler had worked his way down the Cape Fear by crossing at Waddell's Ferry near Elizabethtown and marching until setting up camp at Brown Marsh. The entire campaign was a response to Fanning's successful raid on Hillsborough that saw North Carolina's governor, Thomas Burke, captured along with a number of other valuable military and civilian leaders. Butler had hoped to catch the loyalists in time to reclaim the hapless chief executive, but did not manage to pull it off. Now, Butler hoped to at least get some revenge for the humiliation the Americans had suffered at the hands of the loyalists.

The Tories split into three groups and moved into position to attack Butler's camp along modern Red Hill Road. One group, under Duncan Ray, got lost in the swamps, but Manson and Holloway's men made it into position in time. In the darkness before dawn, the loyalists struck, each of the two forces hitting the American flanks. Butler's men had been facing the Brown Marsh swamp, their attention drawn there by the commotion of Ray's lost Tories stumbling around in the mire. When Manson and Holloway hit their unguarded flanks, their surprise was complete. Chaos ensued among the Whigs, with some backcountry men fleeing the rush of redcoats and loyalist militia pouring into the camp. Others held their ground and gave as good as they got while they had ammunition to fight with. Thinking the Tories had artillery with them, Butler ordered a hurried retreat out of cannon range.

Col. John Mebane and Col. Thomas Owen of Bladen County stood their ground. Mebane's refusal to fall back bought time for the rest of Butler's command to reach safety. One American who was at the battle observed that "if it had not been for old Col. Mebane of the Orange [County] Regiment, we would have all been taken prisoner...and a brave officer he was." Another wrote of Mebane and Col. Thomas Owen, "The two Colonels made quite a manly resistance for a while, but were overpowered."

The Americans suffered 20 men killed and an unknown number of men wounded. Another 25 members of the Whig militia were taken prisoner. The Tories only lost three killed and five wounded.

"The Rebels were completely dispers'd leaving twenty dead & five & twenty prisoners," Manson wrote in his after-action report to Maj. Craig in Wilmington. "They had also a number of wounded who in the darkness of the night got off. We took between 30 & 40 horses but the militia the next day got upwards of a hundred more who were running loose in the woods."

The British and their loyalist allies celebrated another victory against the American rebels. September had by and large been a good month for the king's supporters in North Carolina, especially in the southeastern part of the state. Trouble was coming though, in the form of Rutherford's American force, intent on ousting the British from Wilmington and crushing Tory resistance in the Lower Cape Fear for good.[81]

On the first day of October, while BGen. Butler and his men were licking their wounds after Brown Marsh, and while Craig celebrated another victory, BGen. Griffith Rutherford marched his army of newly trained Americans out of the Uwharrie Mountains and headed east for the coast.

It was Acting Gov. Alexander Martin who authorized the expedition to take back Wilmington, following a plan put in place by his predecessor, Thomas Burke, before he was captured. At Cross Creek, Rutherford linked up with Butler's militia, and the two formed a plan of battle. Rutherford placed Butler's Hillsborough District militia under the command of the Wake County militia's Col. John Hinton, Jr. While Butler's men attacked the port town from the east, crossing into Brunswick County and across Eagles Island, Rutherford's men would descend on Wilmington from the north, retaking Heron's Bridge and crossing the Northeast Cape Fear River there. The two forces would put Craig's redcoats in a vise that they would not be able to escape, unless they evacuated by way of their ships in the river.

The Americans marched out of Cross Creek with something approaching 3,000 men, and by October 15 were near the modern town of Red Springs in Robeson County. Rutherford's force had been supplemented by BGen. Alexander Lillington's 18 companies of the Wilmington District Brigade of Militia, most of which were led by Duplin County's

Col. James Kenan. Scouts brought the news that between 300 and 600 Tories were encamped at McPhaul's Mill on Raft Swamp. BGen. Rutherford dispatched a force of cavalry to deal with them.

Battle of Raft Swamp (Robeson County)
Forces Engaged
American: Maj. Joseph Graham, commanding. Graham leads the **N.C. State Legion**, consisting of ten companies led by Capts. Lilly, John Lopp, Charles Polk, John Rogers, Richard Simmons, Frederick Smith, Minor Smith, Robert and Daniel Wright, and Capt. Wynn; one company of the **Anson County Regiment of Militia** led by Capt. Patrick Boggan; one company of the **Bladen County Regiment of Militia** led by Col. Thomas Owen and Capt. Peter Robeson; one company of the **Chatham County Regiment of Militia** led by Capt. Alexander Clark; one company of the **Granville County Regiment of Militia** led by Capt. James Blackwell; four companies of the **Guilford County Regiment of Militia** led by Capts. William Bethel, David Humphreys of Surry County, John McAdow, and Smith Moore; three companies of the **Orange County Regiment of Militia** led by Capts. George Hodge, Baxter King, and William Smith; at least two companies of the **Randolph County Regiment of Militia** led by LtCol. James Dougan and Capt. John Gillespie; and one company of the **Wake County Regiment of Militia** led by Capt. Lewis Bledsoe.

British: Col. Duncan Ray commanding 150 men of the **Royal North Carolina Militia of Anson County**; Col. "One-Eyed" Hector McNeill leading 150 men of the **Royal North Carolina Militia of Bladen County**; two companies of the **Royal North Carolina Militia of Cumberland County** under Col. Archibald McDugald - 300 men led by Captains "Sober John" McLean and Archibald McKay; and an unknown number of men from **Col. David Fanning's regiment** led by Major John Elrod.

At Rutherford's camp at Monroe's Bridge on Drowning Creek, Maj. Joseph Graham gathered the men who would ride with him and set out for Raft Swamp to attack the loyalists gathered there. Loyalist commanders Ray, McDugald, and McNeill had about 600 men. The Hector McNeill with the loyalists was not the same one who had been at the battle at Lindley's Mill. That Hector McNeill had been replaced by Col. "One-Eyed" Hector McNeill in an effort to keep the news of the much-loved

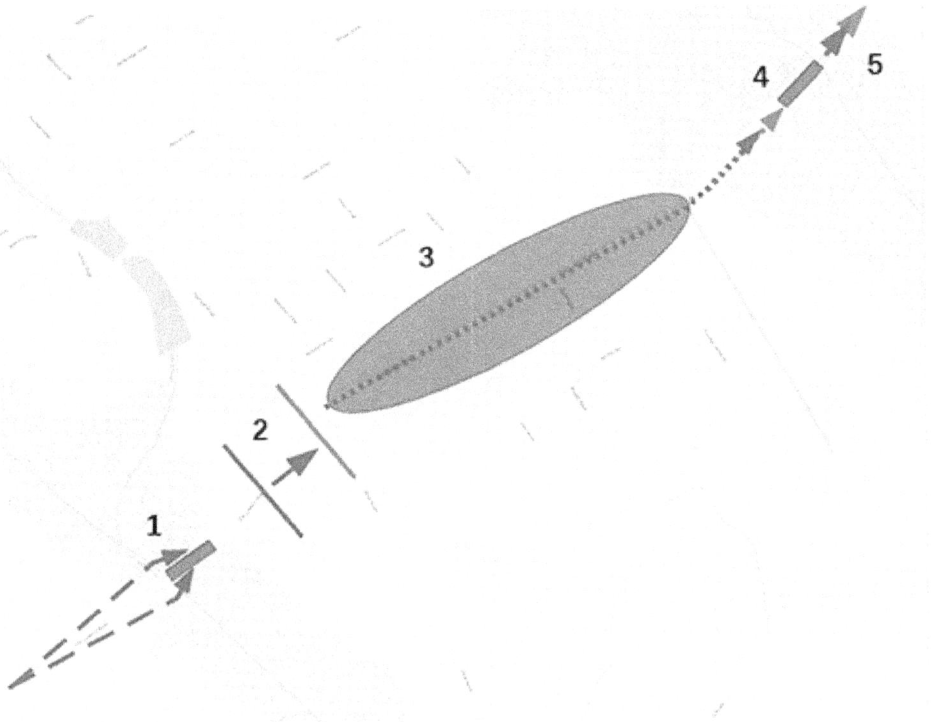

The Battle of Raft Swamp. Troop locations on the hill are approximate. 1) Patriot cavalry ride into swamp and drive back Tories. 2) Some Tories form a line; Patriots form and charge, breaking it. 3) A running battle spreads across the hill. 4) Tories and their horses create a traffic jam, cleared by Patriots. 5) Tories flee and Patriots give chase.
From "The American Revolution Tour of North Carolina ™" (AmRevNC.com). Copyright 2020 by AmRevNC, LLC. Reprinted by permission.

other Hector's demise a secret from the men.

    The Tories crossed Little Raft Swamp and established a camp just across today's Lowry Road on a hill three miles from modern Red Springs. Ray sent scouts to patrol the area south of their position, and it was they who first discovered the approaching Americans. They delivered the news to Ray that the Whigs were closing in. Col. Duncan Ray surveyed his position and decided it was good enough to make a stand on. The Tories occupied a hill that gave them the high ground, with swamp protecting their flanks and a long causeway that emerged from it. The loyalists attempted to slow down the cavalry they knew would be coming by taking up the planks of the bridge crossing the causeway. It proved to be a futile gesture. When Maj. Graham's horsemen emerged from the swamp, they ignored the causeway completely and just rode through the murky waters

Raft Swamp, near modern Red Springs, N.C. From *"The American Revolution Tour of North Carolina ™" (AmRevNC.com). Copyright 2020 by AmRevNC, LLC. Reprinted by permission.*

to reach the loyalists, who were still constructing their defenses when the fight began.

From the north, Graham's detachment swooped down on the Tory scouts, who managed to get off one volley before fleeing the thundering hooves and sabers of the American dragoons. The causeway became packed with loyalists trying desperately to reach the main body of Tories on the hill at the other end. Many did not make it, and the Whigs were in no mood for mercy. Major Graham wrote of it later.

"The enemy broke and fled as best as they could," he recalled. "After their first fire, the enemy thought of no further resistance, but endeavoured to make their escape, and aimed for a branch of Raft Swamp in their front, over which there was a causeway two hundred yards wide. Our troops entered the causeway with them, using saber against all they could reach. As soon as it was felt, the Tories would throw themselves off to each side into the ditch, quitting their horses and making off in the swamp, the dragoons near the front fired their pistols at them in their retreat. By the time the Whigs got halfway through, the causeway was crowded with dismounted ponies for twenty steps before them, so that it was impossible to pass. Two or three stout men dismounted, and commenced pushing them over into the ditch, out of the way. When it was a little cleared, the dragoons rushed over, the front troop, now scattered, pursued the Tories in all directions."

Some brave loyalists tried to make a stand, but they were quickly overwhelmed. In the swamps surrounding the causeway it became something of a shooting gallery, with men who had jumped into the swamp to escape becoming mired in the mud and shot at the Americans' leisure. Thirty-five Tories halted their flight and tried to form a line but were shot down even as some tried to surrender. Scotsman David Bethune tried to rally the loyalists with his bagpipes, skrilling out "The Campbells Are Coming," providing a musical backdrop to the musket shots and screams that punctuated the morning quiet. Many who escaped owed their lives to a small group of Tories who formed a rear guard at Lowry Road that allowed their fellows to escape.

Unit cohesion disappeared as the Tories broke ranks and ran, each man now fighting individually and usually not well. William Watson was cut down as he ran from a Whig dragoon. Not far away, his brother John met the same fate. A third kinsman, Thomas Watson, was wounded in the fray, dying a week later. Bodies were scattered over the battlefield and in the swamp and woods, the landscape littered with the dead and dying, many to be left unburied in the battle's aftermath. From the place it started to where it ended, the Battle of Raft Swamp was a running engagement that covered roughly four miles. It would be that last major fight before the British were ousted from Wilmington.

Major Graham's report continued with details about the effort to round up the fugitive Tories. "As the enemy were much scattered and completely beaten," he wrote, "it was thought inexpedient to pursue the victory further. The men were collected by the sound of the trumpet at the west side of the swamp, and marched back to where [Brig.] General [Griffith] Rutherford had encamped, near McPhaul's Mill, where they arrived about 10 o'clock at night."

With the Whigs in firm control of the countryside after the battle, BGen. Rutherford, who had once himself been a prisoner of the British, determined to exact retribution from those who sided with the Tories. The harshness of his policies and the failure to grant quarter at Little Raft Swamp earned him a cautionary rebuke from Gen. Nathaniel Greene, who wrote, "You are treating the Inhabitants ... with great severity, driving them indiscriminately from their dwellings without regard to age or Sex and laying waste their possessions destroying their produce and burning their houses." The commander of the Southern Army warned Rutherford to show some leniency towards the loyalist civilians.

Capt. John McAdow of the Guilford County militia was the only American killed in the battle. The butcher's bill for the Tories was not as light. Graham's men searched the swamp the next day for survivors but found none. Knowing that the appearance of Rutherford's army in southeastern North Carolina changed the force equation, many of the loyalist militia retired from the field to what they hoped was the safety of their homes.

The day after the bloody work at Raft Swamp, Rutherford's men moved down the east side of the swamp into an ambush. Realizing that the swamps provided a perfect cover for loyalists to make guerilla-style hit and run attacks, Rutherford fanned out his men to root the Tories from the murky bogs. It was exhausting work, the men plagued as much by bamboo thickets and briars as by enemy muskets. In places the Americans waded through water and mud up to their waists, but the loyalists had fled by then. Rutherford marched to Brown Swamp near Elizabethtown, both to show local loyalists that even though the Americans had been dealt a defeat there earlier, the loss could not keep them out of the country; and to rest and train before ousting Craig from Wilmington.[82]

In Wilmington, Gov. Thomas Burke was soon to be put aboard a British ship and transferred to Charlestown. He used the time he had before departure to write a letter to an unknown recipient that detailed his capture and captivity under Craig's command.

"I will not trouble you with a relation of the different extremes of hunger, thirst and fatigue, and the frequent dangers our lives were exposed to while we were in the savage hands of those who were our first captors," Burke wrote, "who, to avoid the pursuit of our friends, traversed by long and rapid marches, vast pathless tracks of intermingled sand and swamp very thinly inhabited and which ought not to be inhabited at all, but will begin with our delivery into the hands of Major [James H.] Craig on the 23rd of September at Livingston's Creek on the North West of Cape Fear [River], by which time we were completely pillaged of everything except the few dirty, worthless clothes we had on, which with regard to myself, were chiefly borrowed. The British officers behaved with frank politeness to us and Maj. Craig treated me with particular respect, in short, we had great reason to rejoice in our exchange of situation, and for the first time after our capture, felt ourselves out of danger of personal violence, with which we had been often threatened, through the savage, ungovernable fury of those people in whose possession we were. Such was the respect paid to me and so easy was my treatment that I began to expect that my confinement would be that of a prisoner of war on the most liberal footing. This continued until the next day after my arrival in Wilmington, in the afternoon of which an officer presented me with a letter from Major Craig expressing his regret at finding himself obliged to secure my person until his superior officers should instruct him whether to consider me as a prisoner of war or of state, and promising to do everything in his power to render my situation as little disagreeable as possible. After I had read the letter he conducted me to a house within the lines, one room whereof was assigned to be my place of confinement and for that purpose was shut up from all communication except by one door leading into the street, there he left me with a sergeant to watch me constantly, and a guard to prevent my escape and all access to me. This room is always dry in fair weather, and warm when the sun shines, and the wind is southerly, it has all the advantage of the northeast winds which may enter freely and must go out the same way; in short it seems calculated to answer the end of a grotto in winter and a hothouse in summer. My traverses, however devious, were in no danger of interruption by furniture and I was likely to have time and subject enough for meditation; my prospect was that of reducing to practice much of what I had read of the Lacedemonian virtue, and I already began to cast my memory back, through the history of that patient austere people in search of some person whom I might propose for my model. I might indeed have chosen any plank I pleased for my lodging, for the sergeant seemed to be too civil a fellow to dispute it with me, and for any other accommodation, I did not know but that, like many other great affairs of this world, it was under the peculiar care of providence. Major Craig visited me in the evening and pathetically lamented the situation in which he had put me, and expressed much concern that he had nothing of his own with which he could accommodate me. He was so obliging as to permit Col. [James] Read to have access to me at all times, and to reside with me. This gentleman's care and attention to me have been with unremitting diligence and his representation of the circumstances I was in, to some friends of his and mine soon procured me the necessaries which my confinement required. Mr. William Campbell furnished me with a bed, some furniture and a negro wench and lent me some money, all which enabled me to keep batchelor's quarters but so different from all I had ever kept before that I now never have any company, and tho' not shut up in a Seraglio, I am almost as difficult of access as his majesty of Constantinople; very few, indeed, are suffered to approach me at all, and every one must converse with me in presence of the sergeant. Col. Read is so scrupulous an observer of his parole that he even does not tell me the news of the day, which indeed I very seldom venture to ask him lest it should reduce him to a dilemma; my good humor which, thank heaven, never forsakes me entirely, suffered an attack which had well nigh disconcerted it, by the refusing of Mr. Strudwick to see me; in truth, Sir, I promised myself great satisfaction from his visit which he informs me by letter, he made principally with a view of serving me, and he has been kind enough to desire I would command anything in his power; as I believe him perfectly sincere, I would freely avail myself of his friendship, if 1 could see in what manner he could serve me, but I cannot see it and he is not at liberty to see me, and therefore cannot well explain himself consistently with the restrictions he may be under. I have not requested permission for him, for altho' Major Craig desired me to apply to him in every case wherein be could indulge me. Yet having made a few such applications which were with great respect & politeness refused, I am unwilling any more to involve him in difficulties between his civility and his duty. My pride, if I have any, has this consolation, that my most trifling movements are considered as dangerous to a prince who is lord of so many brave battalions and so invincible a navy and such inexhaustible resources, as is his majesty of Great Britain, and this perhaps it is that has restored my good humor. I knew before, indeed that I was upon the axeltree of the chariot but never thought I made much of the surrounding dust. You will no doubt perceive, I sometimes smile while I am writing, but I beg you not to conclude from thence that I am upon a bed of roses and that I may well stay there sometime longer..."

  Burke went on to describe the condition of his fellow inmates under British care in Wilmington. "...Our prisoners, my dear Sir, by the want of the necessaries of life in a rigorous confinement call for the assistance and attention of their country at least if I may judge from such as I see daily passing by my window to the spring for water, who might well be taken for skeletons, did they not retain life enough to make them appear too ghastly and some languid unanimated motion that shows they have some small remains of strength. I do not write this as a charge against the commanding officer. I really do not know how they are treated, for I have no means of information except what I have just mentioned. There is no Commissary of Prisoners at this post; no other person has a right to inspect their treatment, but as I am persuaded, they want provisions. I take the liberty to solicit that some be sent for them. I know no other way whereby they can be supplied."[83]

The world turned upside down for LtGen. Cornwallis and the British army on October 17, when George Washington's encirclement and siege of their redoubts at Yorktown, Virginia forced the redcoat army to surrender. Cornwallis could not bring himself to make the submission himself, so he sent his second in command, BGen. Charles O'Hara, to offer the Americans his sword. In Halifax, General Sumner wrote the Commander in Chief of the Continental Army to congratulate Gen. Washington on his victory, and inform him of what had been taking place in North Carolina.

"I rejoice to hear of your approaches against the fortified holds of the Enemy about York, and flatter our expectations that they will soon fall under yr. [your] Power," Sumner wrote. "The Situation of the Southern Camp, about the 27th of September on the High Hills of Santee, were under some apprehensions of the Enemy's Crossing the river Santee upon receiving some reinforcements, which had not jointed them before the affair, at the Eutaw Springs. Genl. Rutherford & Butler with about eighteen Hundred Militia were last Tuesday, within twenty five miles West of Campbleton [modern Fayetteville] on Cross Creek on Cape Fear, that the disaffected were imbodyed [sic] on the head waters of the Wocomaw [Waccamaw] River South of Campbleton....Major Craig who commands in Wilmington about Four Hundred British troops has fortified redoubts and [lacuna] this post has recovered much of the neighboring country..."

It would be another few weeks before word of Cornwallis' surrender reached Wilmington. By then, the wheels were already in motion to take the port town back from the redcoats.[84]

The Evacuation and Liberation of Wilmington

Forces Engaged
American: BGen. Griffith Rutherford, overall commanding officer. With him are 1,500 men including his **Salisbury District Brigade of Militia**, and four companies of the **N.C. State Legion** led by Col. Robert Smith and Maj. Joseph Graham, with Capts. William Bethel, Thomas Kennedy, Richard Simmons, and Robert White; 35 horsemen of the **Bladen County Regiment of Militia** led by Col. Thomas Owen; the **Duplin County Regiment of Militia** with two companies led by Capts. David Dodd and William Kenan; a detachment of the **Mecklenburg Cavalry** led by a Capt. Polk; one company of the **Randolph County Regiment of Militia** led by Capt. John Gillespie, and an unknown number of men form the **Chatham County Regiment of Militia.**

British: Maj. James Henry Craig leading the **Hamilton Regiment of the 82nd Regt. of Foot**; one company of the **2nd Battalion of the 84th Regiment of Foot** (the Royal Highland Emigrants) under Capt. Ronald Mackinnon; the **Royal North Carolina Regiment**; the **North Carolina Highland Regiment**; and the **Loyal American Rangers**.

On October 23, Griffith Rutherford began his march on Wilmington in two elements, one led by himself, the other by Col. Robert Smith. Smith's column, with the N.C. State Legion, was much smaller than Rutherford's, consisting of 100 cavalrymen and 200 mounted infantrymen. Smith's group, designed for speed and shock, was sent to the west bank of the Cape Fear River while Rutherford advanced at a slower, more determined pace. The main column advanced down Negro Head Point Road (a.k.a. the Market Road) until they reached a point where they crossed to the east side of the river and marched on Heron's Bridge, north of the town.

By November 14, the Americans had closed the vise on Craig's Wilmington occupiers. On the march, the Whigs captured two loyalists who said Craig intended to cross the Cape Fear River and attack Rutherford from behind. The attack never materialized. With the approach of the Whig army, Craig pulled his outpost at Heron's Bridge back to the town, where they would be under the protection of his small cannons and the redcoats' walled compound. Across the river from the foot of Market

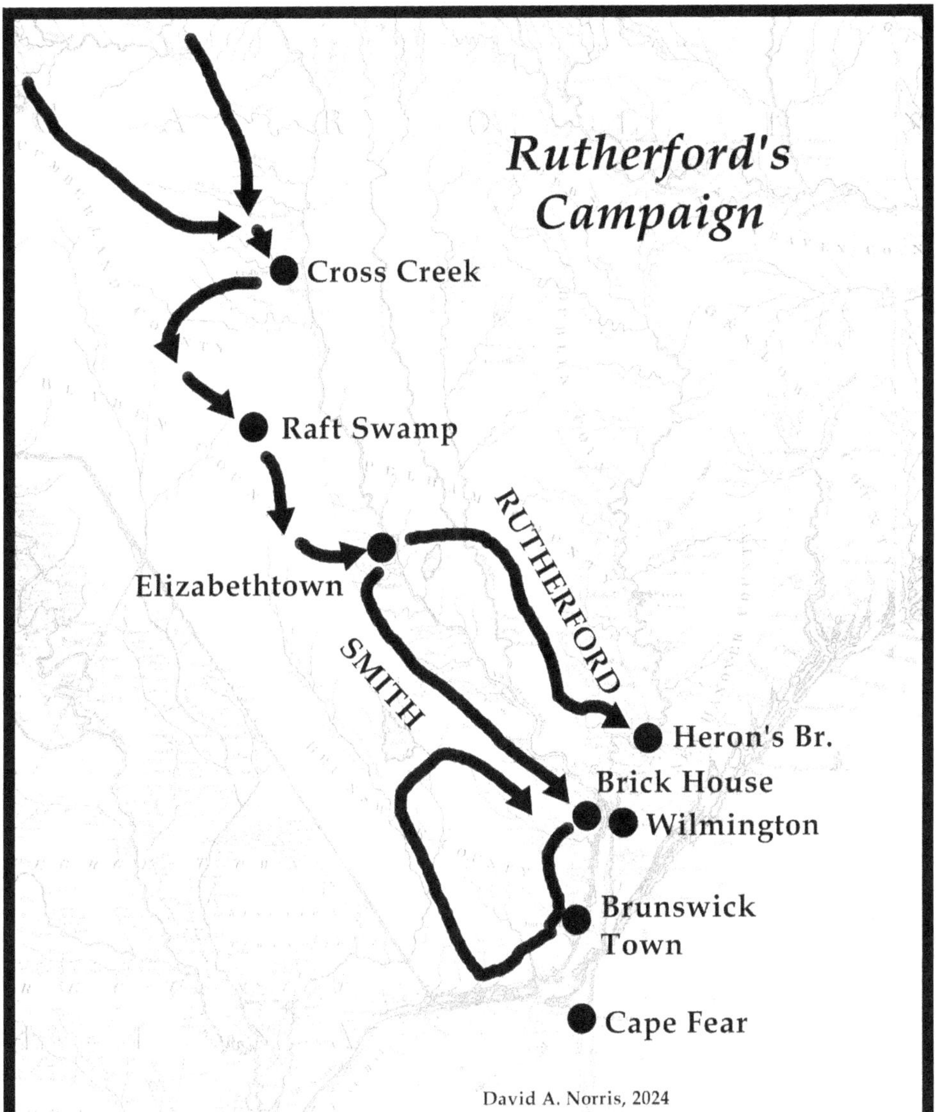

Rutherford's Campaign

Cross Creek

Raft Swamp

Elizabethtown

SMITH

RUTHERFORD

Heron's Br.
Brick House
Wilmington
Brunswick Town
Cape Fear

David A. Norris, 2024
Adapted from "The Mouzon Map", 1775

Street stood the Brick House, its doors and windows boarded up except for firing slits, fortified by the British with abatis and 50 men.

That same day, Col. Smith got word of a party of loyalists gathered at Alfred Moore's Buchoi Plantation and sent Maj. Joseph Graham at the head of a column of dragoons to deal with them. On the way there, a group of Tories rode up to Graham's militiamen, mistaking them for some of their own troops. By the time they realized their mistake, Graham had surrounded and disarmed them. Detaching some men to escort the prisoners back to Col. Smith, Graham continued on to Moore's plantation, a mile south of the ferry at Wilmington on the Brunswick County side of the river. On arrival, Graham's men dismounted and crept into position around the plantation house. The Americans captured two Tories who ventured into the woods for kindling, and learned from them and through observing the enemy encampment that there were about 100 loyalists there.

Graham divided his forces. Capt. Thomas Kennedy led one group, while Capt. William Bethel took another and positioned themselves 30 paces to the right of Kennedy. Capt. Charles Polk's cavalry made up the reserve, positioned 80 yards behind the other two elements. As they got into position, a sharp-eyed loyalist officer spotted them and shouted a warning. Surprise gone, Graham's men attacked immediately. The attack came so swiftly that the Tories never had a chance to get into line and fire. Some of Graham's men took advantage of a causeway 140 yards from the house to deliver accurate aimed fire over the top of a fence. Return fire came in fits and starts from the disorganized loyalists, but to no avail. When Polk's cavalry galloped into the fight, the Tories broke. They raced for the imagined safety of the woods and marshes, chased by mounted Whigs whose sabers slashed down many of the Tories before they could reach cover.

The loyalists lost a dozen men killed, and another 30 wounded. The Americans lost none. Graham's mission was a rousing success. After plundering the Tory camp for supplies, weapons, ammunition, and intelligence, the Whigs returned to Smith's main body.[85]

After their success at Buchoi Plantation, Col. Robert Smith's men were chaffing at the bit to attack the Brick House on the riverfront across from Wilmington's Market Street. The colonel sent men to reconnoiter the British position. The information they brought back was not promising. The scouts described a strongly fortified building whose brick walls would be impervious to the Americans' musket balls. Abatis surrounded it, making any charge on horseback unlikely to be successful. The Brick House had a strong garrison of redcoats to defend it, and the scouts reported more were being ferried across the river from Wilmington. Considering it all, Smith decided the chances of a successful move on the Brick House to be too slim to be worthwhile. Instead, he led his troops back to above Livingston's Creek.

Smith's decision did not sit well with his militiamen. The failure to attack the British post became the main topic of conversation among the men, whose grumbling and prodding led Smith to reverse his decision. On November 15 they returned, sending a flag of truce to Capt. Kennedy, the commander of the British in the Brick House, offering him a chance to surrender and the promise of attack if he did not. Smith gave the redcoats ten minutes to decide but Kennedy did not need that long. He sent his answer back with the truce flag, saying "I disregard your orders: I don't surrender."

The Americans sent one force along the tree line to the left of the Brick House, with Smith leading the rest of the Whigs in a frontal attack. Inside the British defenses, loyalist militia, British redcoats, and Hessian jaegers were delivering effective fire against the Americans, while being almost untouchable behind the brick walls of the house. With the redcoats shooting from firing ports in the windows and doors, the American attackers got the worst of the exchange. After trying for an hour, Smith broke off the attack and returned his men to Livingston's Creek. The Americans lost one man killed and several others wounded.[86]

Upon reuniting with Col. Smith's main body after the raid on Alfred Moore's plantation, Graham received new orders to conduct a reconnaissance deep into Brunswick County to look for other enemy troops and gather information that might be useful to the Americans. Graham and his N.C. State Legion headed south past Brunswick Town, then west towards the South Carolina state line. Along the Waccamaw River at a place known as Seven Creeks, near modern Nakina in Columbus County, Graham's men took planks from nearby homes to make shelters against the cold, rainy night. One hour before midnight on November 16, South Carolina loyalist Maj. Micajah Gainey discovered the Americans and decided to ambush Graham's 90 dragoons. The Tories, 80 strong, surrounded Graham's camp. When Gainey's men delivered their first fire, it took the Whigs by surprise. One man, using a pumpkin for a pillow, narrowly missed death when a musket ball shattered it beneath his head. Graham rallied his men and formed a firing line 30 paces behind their camp. The Whigs made an orderly withdrawal after killing one of Gainey's ambushers and wounding two more. But Gainey's attack exacted its own toll, killing Lt. Clark of the dragoons and several of their horses.

Graham later related that Gainey was supposed to be under a flag of truce agreed to with BGen. Francis Marion in South Carolina, but the loyalist apparently did not think it binding in North Carolina. Dragoon John Smith wrote of the affair in his 1832 pension application, saying, "Major Grimes [sic, Major Joseph Graham] was dispatched with 80 picked men to Waggamaw River [sic, Waccamaw River] 70 or 80 miles, I suppose from Wilmington to disperse some Tories who with the British officers, were reported to be engaged in recruiting men for the British army. We had several skirmishes while we were gone and killed a British Lieutenant and some Tories. Capt Charles Poke [sic, Polk] was in company and killed one or 2 Tories who were found having some of our forces in possession the morning after we had been attacked in the night. We lost one man killed and 2 or 3 wounded. My messmate was killed."[87]

The day after the fight at Seven Creeks, LtCol. Henry "Light Horse Harry" Lee delivered the news of Cornwallis' surrender at Yorktown to Griffith Rutherford's camp. The Americans besieging Craig's redcoats in Wilmington celebrated by firing their weapons into the air and cheering. In town, the British deduced what it meant, too. Craig's options were diminishing fast. There was no way to hold Wilmington against the overwhelming numbers Rutherford had at his disposal. Despite being at a port town, British supplies had dwindled to just two weeks' worth of rations, and clothing and medicine were all but gone too. Forage for their horses was so scarce that Craig ordered all but 20 of them ferried across to Eagles Island where they could graze for themselves. Then the news came that the Americans had crossed the river and advanced to Schaw's Plantation, only four miles from town. Craig had no choice. He instructed his men to prepare for evacuation.

The British had already expelled all Whig women and children from town to ease their supply problems. For weeks, everyone in Wilmington had been suffering the deprivations of being isolated south and east of the rivers that surrounded the town. With the countryside in American hands, there was little chance of venturing out. Prices in town skyrocketed as commodities became scarce. One resident remembered that "every article to be sold in Wilmington is at least three times as high...as usual," and Gov. Thomas Burke, before he was transferred to Charlestown, observed that the barren larders in town were evidenced by the appearance of the people who, "...if I may Judge from such as I see daily passing by my window to the spring for water, who might well be taken for skeletons..." Even Maj. Craig was forced to admit to his superiors that he was "oblig' d to give a more unfavourable report of the healthiness of our men than I have hitherto done - we have more sickness here and lost more men within this month past than during the whole time of our being here before."

Craig's position was obviously untenable. MGen. Alexander Leslie dispatched orders for the evacuation of British forces from Wilmington. Leslie directed that the redcoats who had occupied the port town for ten months embark aboard the transport ships in the Cape Fear River and return to Charlestown. On November 18, Maj. James Henry Craig began carrying out those orders. As the sun broke over the hills to the east where Saint James Anglican Church sat, columns of British soldiers, loyalist militia, and as many of their families and supporters as could be crammed aboard the ships, snaked through town to the harbor. Highland kilts were interspersed with trouser-clad redcoats as the soldiers moved towards the waiting vessels along the Wilmington wharves. It would be a race to see if they could make it out before Rutherford's forces caught up to them.

In Rutherford's camp the knowledge that the Americans were finally about to eject the hated British from the state's largest town was tempered with a hunger for revenge for the many acts of terror and destruction their presence had caused among the Whigs and their families. They wanted not just to chase away the British, but to exact a measure of retribution, too. Scouts rode into camp and delivered the news that the British were evacuating. Rutherford ordered his cavalry to advance into the town.

The British were still making their way to the ships when a cloud of dust arose over the rise of Market Street beyond John Burgwin's house. The thunder of hooves announced the arrival of the Whig light horse, tearing down Market Street towards where the British were still going aboard transports tied up at the riverfront. A Wilmington loyalist stepped out into the road and raised his hand as if to wave a welcome to the mounted newcomers. Cavalryman Thomas Tyler saw the Tory, and recognized him as the man who had hanged his father earlier in the war. He wheeled his horse out of the American column and rode down on the waving Tory. Tyler swung his saber, and "with one blow by a vertical cut laid his head open, the divided parts falling on each other."

The rest of the cavalry continued on to crash into the column of evacuees, their sabers drawing the blood of the startled redcoats. One witness described it, saying the Americans "dashed thro' this like lightning, hacking and hewing to the right and left receiving in turn a scattering of fire from the broken column, which did but little mischief; slightly wounding two or three of the horsemen." The British ships fired into the town as they made their way downriver, but by that point the Whig cavalry had already departed. Meanwhile, Col. Robert Smith and his men boarded boats and floated downriver to join Rutherford's soldiers, who had already been in town for an hour.

Rutherford's main force could see the topmasts of the British transports making their way downriver above the Wilmington rooftops as they entered town. The general established his headquarters at the home of a Mr. Hill, and began issuing orders to bring the town fully under American control. The unlucky loyalists who were unable to get aboard one of the evacuating ships, or who decided to take their chances on the mercy of the victorious Americans, soon found themselves besieged by vengeful Whigs. One of Rutherford's officers interceded, placing a militiaman outside the doors of each loyalist family to insure their safety. Nevertheless, the much put-upon citizens of Wilmington were not in the mood to let bygones be bygones with their Tory neighbors, and tensions remained high.

The Whig dragoons and infantry began rounding up loyalists and stragglers who did not make it aboard one of the evacuation ships, marching them to a fence rail pen near Saint James Anglican Church at Fourth and Market Streets. In the enclosure, boys amused themselves taunting the Tories whose fortunes had taken such a turn for the worse. Those sentenced to hang for treason were later exchanged for American prisoners held by the British. The people of Wilmington were finally able to view their foes in captivity. The ships disappearing down the river, headed for the Atlantic Ocean and Charlestown, carried the last British regulars in North Carolina with them.[88]

Aboard the British ships making for Charlestown, a mix of British soldiers, loyalist refugees, runaway slaves, and camp followers gazed for the last time at the landscapes along the Cape Fear River. For some, it was the only home they had ever known, and there was great sorrow at the upheaval in their lives that the Whig victory created. For others, their time in the Lower Cape Fear had been nothing but trouble.

There was drama on the wharves of Wilmington as desperate people scrambled for a place aboard the transport ships. Lavinia, the slave of North Carolina Declaration of Independence signer William Hooper, escaped from Hooper's home and made for the British encampment in a bid for freedom. Lavinia was among the throng waiting to go aboard a British ship when she was recognized by a friend of Hooper's and returned to him. James Rogers secured his place and took his last looks at the Cape Fear as his ship made for the bar at Old Inlet. Rogers played host to Capt. Alexander McLeod on the evening before he was killed in a hail of Whig gunfire at Moores Creek in 1776. He had been sentenced to hang in Wilmington before being rescued by David Fanning earlier in 1781. Merchant Joseph Titley, the surviving business partner of killed loyalist cavalry leader John Gordon, boarded one of Craig's transports carrying "all the books, notes, bonds & other Securities belonging to the Copartnership" in his bid to start over someplace else. Janet Murchison became a camp follower of Cornwallis' army after the Battle of Camden. Her husband was one of the unlucky loyalists captured at Moores Creek, sent to Philadelphia as a prisoner, and who came back to Carolina when the British took Charlestown in 1780. John Murchison died of wounds he got at the Battle of Camden, leaving his wife to fend as best she could, trailing after Cornwallis' redcoats. When Cornwallis marched out of Wilmington for Virginia, illness caused Janet to be left behind. Like other loyalists, Janet Murchison lost all of her property in Anson and Cumberland Counties as a result of being on the losing side of the war. Others, like Tory Rigdon Brice, complained that "by the hurry and confusion of this evacuation, I lost most of my Baggage & Effects." Loyalist grocer John Mackay echoed Brice, saying "Goods and Effects of considerable value, part of which he was obliged to leave on the wharfs, and what he put on board the Transports was Plundered & destroyed by the Soldiers, Sailors, and Negroes, on the passage." Many, like Arthur Benning's family, left Wilmington "without anything, but their wearing Apparel."

William Hooper urged lenience for the loyalists left behind. Hooper foretold that "there will be a time, and I hope it is not of a great distance, when the distinction of Whig and Tory will be lost" and grudges will "die away." If shared misery knitted people together, then the days after Craig left town should have been a time of common cause. Both

Whig and Tory citizens found themselves in the same boat in the aftermath of the British evacuation, when Rutherford's militia looted civilian homes and businesses regardless of who their owners had supported.

Hooper recounted his own experience at the hands of Wilmington's liberators. "Two nights before I arrived in Wilmington, Rutherford's militia had broken open my house, cut open the feather beds that remained, plundered the tickings, and given the feathers to the wind. My library, except as to law books, is shamefully injured, and above 100 valuable volumes taken away. What vexes me most of all is that they have broken several sets of books, where the volumes were so necessarily dependent on each other, as to make what remains useless lumber. You know my partiality to my books -of course my chagrin at the loss of them."

A dispatch sent to Acting Governor Alexander Martin in December, 1781 complained of "depredations committed by Western militia upon friends and foe," which were "scarce to be paralleled." The writer informed the governor that American militia were impressing the locals' fodder, their slaves, and otherwise being disruptive to the people of Wilmington.

BGen. Rutherford ordered guards be placed around town to safeguard the persons and property of locals in Wilmington. Wagons were brought from Heron's Bridge and abandoned British stores were confiscated for the army and state. Soldiers were paid off in salt, which they preferred over a receipt for their service to be redeemed later. Salt could be bartered immediately, a promissory note could not. Yes, the British were gone, but there were still problems to solve. It would be a while yet before the Lower Cape Fear found peace.[89]

Endnotes

[1] Brinkley, 5; Sherman, 25. By 1781, the name "Whig" was being replaced by the name "American" or "republican." To the British, it was still just "rebels."

[2] Sherman, 344, 350. Nathaniel Greene replaced Horatio Gates as commander of the American army in the South after Gates' terrible showing at Camden...Gen. Leslie did not depart Camden until January 9...Drowning Creek is in modern Marion County, S.C. Its name was later changed to the Lumber River...Another reason to take Wilmington was that it was a major source of supplies for Greene's American army.

[3] Dunkerly, 141.

[4] J.D. Lewis, *NC Patriots 1775-1783: Their Own Words, Volume 2, The Provincial and State Troops (Part 1), Second Edition* (Stocksdale, N.C.: Carla G. Harper, 2021): 321.

Hereafter cited as Lewis V2. Wilmington was armed with 9 and 12-pounder cannons... Thanks to Jim McKee for the names and armament of the ships that accompanied Craig's force.

[5] Dunkerly, 141-145. One soldier wrote just a day or so before the British arrived that he had been ""to an old fort and repaired it for use." That fort, according to historian Robert Dunkerly, likely was at the river end of Wilmington's modern Northern Boulevard on the Cape Fear River.

[6] Watson 1861, 91-92. Samuel Campbell later moved to Charlestown, where he was made commandant commander of all loyalist militia in the Southern District. After the war he evacuated to Nova Scotia, and his property in North Carolina was confiscated by the state...Cobham went with the British to New Providence, Bahamas after the war. His property, too, was seized... Maclaine and Huske were eventually harassed until they were forced to leave town.

[7] Sherman, 81-82.

[8] Watson 1861, 91-92; Dunkerly, 150-151; Henry Jay MacMillan, "Living Archives," Lower Cape Fear Historical Society, Inc. Bulletin, Vol. III, No. 1, (October 1959). Hereafter cited as LCFHS. Anne Hooper was the sister of Thomas Clark, Jr., from an affluent colonial family. Thomas Clark, Jr. would become a brigadier general in the Continental Army.

[9] Carruthers V1, 161.

[10] Sherman, 373-374; Dunkerly, 169-170. The British redoubt in Wilmington occupied the territory roughly encompassed by Water, Dock, Third, and Nun Streets.

[11] Lewis V2, 321. The Great Duplin Road was described by Janet Schaw as being as wide as the Tay of Perth, one of Europe's most famous roadways. It roughly parallels modern Interstate 40, and was said to be wide enough to march 50 men abreast...The site of Heron's Bridge was roughly 300 yards to the right of the modern bridge crossing from New Hanover to Pender County on I-40 as one travels towards Raleigh.

[12] Dunkerly, 146-148; Lewis V2, 321-322; Sherman, 375. Craig's letter to Cornwallis about the skirmish at Heron's Bridge (also called Big Bridge by people at the time), dated April 12, 1781: "On our taking possession of Wilmington on the 29th of January, which in conjunction with the gallies we did without opposition, I found that a body of militia had retir'd to a very strong post about ten miles off and that several vessels loaded with provisions and other stores had gone up the river with them. The report of their number varied so much that I was at a loss to form any judgment of it. However, as Captain Barkley, senior officer of the navy, had at my request landed the marines of His Majesty's ships with us, I did not hesitate to march immediately to endeavor at best to make ourselves masters of the boats. The facility with which we drove the party of the enemy on this side the bridge encourag'd me, notwithstanding the peculiar strength of the ground, to attack their main body posted in the most advantageous manner on the opposite side. Captains Nesbitt and Pitcairne with their companies led the attack, supported by the marines, while the companies of the 82nd remain'd to cover the bridge. After a short resistance the enemy fled and left us masters of their camp, but, being favour'd by the darkness of the night, a few only were kill'd and seven or eight taken. Many were wounded and went to their homes, as did most of the remainder. On our side Captain Nesbitt and seven privates were wounded...The next day all the vessels [sic] fell into our

hands. The two largest, loaded with ammunition, were burnt, and the remainder, together with a brig taken by a galley...brought here. We then march'd between 40 and 50 miles thro' the country, destroying such stores as might be of use to the rebels, and arriv'd here without seeing any other enemy."

[13] Dunkerly, 148.
[14] Maass, 95; Lewis V2, 324.
[15] Dunkerly, 153.
[16] Lewis V2, 328.
[17] Lewis V2, 330-331.
[18] Dunkerly, 149-152; Sherman, 399. The reinforcements Nash promised came in part when MGen. Richard Caswell ordered his hometown militia from Kingston (modern Kinston) to join Lillington at Heron's Bridge. Caswell was once again commanding the state's militia, and busy trying to raise more troops in the Wilmington and New Bern districts.
[19] Dunkerly, 153; Joseph Parsons Brown, *The Commonwealth of Onslow: A History* (OG Dunn, 1960): 35-36. Hereafter cited as Dunn. John Spicer was a well-known public servant in Onslow County. He represented his neighbors in the Colonial Assembly, the Provincial Congress, and in the Second Regiment of the North Carolina Continental Line, seeing service at Charlestown. He was part of the committee that drafted the Bill of Rights that was such a key part of the North Carolina constitution...The Bullpen was located on the northeast corner of Second and Market Streets in Wilmington, where a bank building sits in 2023.
[20] Dunkerly, 153-154.
[21] Lewis V2, 342-344; Dunkerly, 191-193; Patrick O'Kelley. *Nothing But Blood and Slaughter: The Revolutionary War in the Carolinas-Volume Three 1781* (Booklocker.com Incorporated, 2005): 166-170 . Hereafter cited as O'Kelley V3. While some details in the various accounts of Rouse's Tavern vary, the main points of the story align...Historian Robert M. Dunkerly gives the name of the man with James Love at Walker's Bridge as Young...According to the account related by Dunkerly, James Love's brother, Thomas, witnessed the Rouse's Tavern massacre from the mulberry tree under which his brother died. Thomas had climbed the tree to sleep off the drinks he had consumed with the other men, and was still high in its branches when he woke to the sound of thundering British horses and clashing sabers...Alexander Lillington later wrote that the men killed at the tavern were not supposed to be there, but rather were under orders to be on patrol and helping to guard the Americans' beef supply...Dunkerly's account says of the 11 Americans at Rouse's Tavern, two survived with bad wounds.
[22] Dunkerly, 154-158; Sherman, 425-426. Maj. Dennis was court martialed at Mulberry Plantation near Beaufort's Bridge sometime at the end of March. He protested his innocence, but was found guilty of dereliction of duty anyway. BGen. Lillington wrote that Dennis had "shamefully neglected his duty," and was "incapable of holding any Office of our trust." With the conviction, Dennis was dismissed from the service of his country... Lillington's account says only one man was killed and two wounded, but he may have been downplaying the Americans' losses.
[23] Dunkerly, 157-158.
[24] O'Kelley V3, 164-165.

²⁵ Brinkley, n. 55; Ross, 142; Dunkerly, 163-166, Sherman, 21; Maass, 224. Marching to Wilmington gave Cornwallis options. He was reluctant to march back into South Carolina, covering the same ground he had already trekked across after leaving Charlestown. By going to Wilmington, where Craig was in control, he could rest and mend his exhausted men. Then he could plan his next move. If evacuation was required, Wilmington offered the safe port he would need to load his men and equipment and sail away to someplace where they would be more effective. If operations in Virginia looked promising, he could deliver his army there either by sea or by a march up the coast. Wilmington was centrally located to make all of that possible.

²⁶ Eli Washington Caruthers, *Revolutionary Incidents: and Sketches of Character: Chiefly in the" Old North State, Vol. II"* (Wilmington, N.C.: Dram Tree Books, 2010): 108. Hereafter cited as Caruthers; Lewis V2, 374; Dunkerly, 160. With a shortage of manpower, keeping prisoners was a problem for the British. In addition to the Bullpen at Second and Market Streets, they also had a prison ship, *H.M.S. Forbay* (sometimes spelled *Forby* or *Torbay*). Captured rebels like Capt. Daniel Buie, who died there, was one of its inmates. The ship also held 160 prisoners taken at the Battle of Camden.

²⁷ Dunkerly, 168.

²⁸ Dunkerly, 166-167; Carruthers V2, 110; Sherman, 452; Lewis V2, 375; O'Kelley V3, 215; Babits-Howard, 174. Hereafter cited as Babits-Howard. Other losses along the road to Wilmington included Capt. William Schurz of the Guards Regiment, and Capt. Alexander Wilmonsky of the Regiment Von Bose. Wilmosky died at Alston's Plantation on the Cape Fear.

²⁹ Maass, 304.

³⁰ Sherman, 21. Diseases like smallpox claimed victims of all ranks. Commanders James Hogun, James McCall, William Campbell, and William Phillips all died of the disease while in service during the war.

³¹ Dunkerly, 168; Babits-Howard, 180, 186; Sherman, 475. Cornwallis intended to link with Phillips and BGen. Benedict Arnold, whose treason had earned him a command in the British army. If their combined force could take Virginia, Cornwallis could split the North and South and deprive the American army of the larder that kept it fed. "I was firmly persuaded that until Virginia was reduced we could not hold the more Southern provinces; " Cornwallis said, "and that after its reduction they would fall without much resistance and be retained without much difficulty."...Gen. Charles O'Hara, Cornwallis' second in command, wrote to the Duke of Grafton from his "camp near Wilmington," that "A report prevails this morning that Green[e] with his Army has march'd into South Carolina, if that should prove true a general Revolt will take place and we shall certainly loose the Carolina's forever -- it will be impossible for Lord Cornwallis to return by Land to South Carolina and equally impracticable for us to remain here. I believe we shall endeavor to join Major General [William] Phillips who is said to be at Petersbourg [sic] at the head of the James River in Virginia."

³² Dunkerly, 169. Just south of Eagles Island the Cape Fear gets very shallow at a place that is marked on most maps as The Flats. Before modern dredging opened a channel to the Wilmington waterfront, most large vessels had to stay below that point. Ships that drew less water could, alternatively, sail up the west side of the island on the Brunswick River and then down past Point Peter to Wilmington.

[33] Sherman, 460. After Cornwallis left Wilmington, Saint James Church was used as a stable for Craig's cavalry horses.

[34] Lewis V2, 377-378.; Babits-Howard, 6. Clinton understood how important cooperation and support from loyalists were to the success of the British army in the South, and how after Moores Creek and their experience with the British since had not worked in their favor. "The good will of the inhabitants is absolutely requisite to retain a country after we have conquered it," Clinton declared. "I fear it will be some time before we can recover the confidence of those in Carolina, as their past sufferings will of course make them cautious of forwarding the Kings interests before there is the strongest certainty of his army being in a condition to support them." The original plan had been for Cornwallis to march through an area and liberate it for the king's loyal subjects. He would turn administration of that area over to the loyalists, and march off to do the same somewhere else. Instead, when the redcoats liberated an area and the loyalists came out to cheer them, the Tory men too often found themselves drafted into the army, leaving their families exposed to retribution from the recently deposed Whigs. As a result, the loyalists were shy about coming into the open to support Cornwallis.

[35] Dunkerly, 171.

[36] Lewis Philip Hall, *Land of the Golden River: Historical Events and Stories of Southeastern North Carolina and the Lower Cape Fear, Volume II and Volume III* (Wilmington N.C.: Wilmington Printing Company, 1980): 27-29. Hereafter cited as Hall.

[37] Dunkerly, 182.

[38] Dunkerly, 157.

[39] Lewis V2, 378.

[40] Dunkerly, 158-159.

[41] Dunkerly, 171.

[42] Dunkerly, 172.

[43] Lewis V2, 38; Sherman, 475; Seielstad, 68-69. Cornwallis on the reasoning that led to his decision to go to Virginia: I came to this resolution principally for the following reason: "I could not remain at Wilmington, lest General Greene should succeed against Lord Rawdon [who was left in command in South Carolina]...From the shortness of Lord Rawdon's stock of provisions and the great distance from Wilmington to Camden, it appeared impossible that any direct move of mine could afford him the least prospect of relief...I was likewise influenced by having just received an account from Charlestown of the arrival of a frigate with dispatches from the commander-in-chief, the substance of which then transmitted to me, was that General Phillips had been dispatched to the Chesapeake and put under my orders, which induced me to hope that solid operations might be adopted in that quarter; and I was finally persuaded that, until VA was reduced we could not hold the more southern provinces, and that after its reduction, they would fall without much difficulty."...When Cornwallis' troops crossed the Northeast Cape Fear, Craig sent his gunboats to cover their crossing. Banastre Tarleton's dragoons had crisscrossed the countryside to gather what boats he could to facilitate the crossing.

[44] Dunkerly, 173-177. Units with Cornwallis came from a letter Banastre Tarleton wrote.

[45] Sherman, 491. The Slocumb home was near modern Dudley, N.C.

[46] Sherman, 494-497; O'Kelley V3, 136-159.

[47] Dunkerly, 182; O'Kelley V3, 232 ; John Hairr, *Colonel David Fanning: The Adven-*

tures of a Carolina Loyalist. (Averasboro, N.C.: Averasboro Press, 2000): 16. Hereafter cited as Hairr.

[48] Lewis V2, 392, 398-400; Dunkerly, 183-186. Mayhand's Bridge no longer exists, but in 1781 it was located near the Sampson County Airport, west of Clinton...The Americans began firing on anyone who approached them, resulting in one man wounding his own brother.

[49] Sherman, 522.

[50] Dunkerly, 187-189; William A. Graham, *General Joseph Graham and his Papers on North Carolina Revolutionary History* (Raleigh: Edwards and Broughton, 1904): 354. According to Graham, one reason locals may have favored the British was a lack of salt. To get it, they had to submit to Craig's authority at Wilmington.

[51] Sherman, 534. Craig originally requested 400 men to augment his garrison at Wilmington, and to make arrangements to return Cornwallis' convalescents to Charlestown.

[52] Sherman, 535. Georgetown was evacuated by the British in May, 1781.

[53] Lewis V2, 406-409.

[54] Lewis V2, 416; Sherman, 552. Manson's expedition left Rutherford's Mill on June 28, 1781.

[55] Lewis V2, 423-424.

[56] Lewis V2, 424.

[57] Lewis V2, 420-422; Dunkerly, 194-195; O'Kelley V3, 278-279. Thomas Bloodworth (sometimes spelled Bludworth) sold his firearms at Richard Clinton's trading post and tavern.

[58] Dunkerly, 195.

[59] Maass, 325; Lewis V2, 431-432. Fanning paroled all of the prisoners except fourteen men, including Col. Ambrose Ramsey, Maj. William Cage, Capt. Edward Douglas, Joseph Hinds, W. Kinchen, John Birdsong, James Williams, Matthew Jones, Thomas Scurlock, M. Gregory, and Private George Herndon. All of those not pardoned were marched to Wilmington and turned over to Maj. Craig.

[60] Lewis V2, 432.

[61] Lewis V2, 430.

[62] Dunkerly, 195-196.

[63] Lewis V2, 440-441; Dunkerly, 196-198.

[64] Lewis V2, 445.

[65] Sherman, 586. Rudolph's mission was a false one. It was intended to make the British think the Americans were going to make a move against Maj. Craig, when they really were intended to hide the fact that Greene was moving Continentals to join Lafayette against Cornwallis in Virginia.

[66] Crow, 77; Lewis V2, 448; O'Kelley V3, 306-307; Dunkerly, 199-203. Capt. John Gordon was a Wilmington merchant who allied himself with the British and became Craig's cavalry commander.

[67] Oates, 793-794; J.D. Lewis, "The American Revolution in North Carolina." https://www.carolana.com/NC/Revolution/ (accessed 12/23/23). Hereafter cited as Lewis Carolana. McBride, already on parole, had not been at Piney Bottom.

[68] Dunkerly, 203. New Bern had been the provincial capital under Tryon and Martin. The American state capital was at Hillsborough.

[69] Sherman, 594; Oates, 149.

[70] Dunkerly, 203-204; O'Kelley V3, 147; Sherman, 598. Gov. Thomas Burke was sorry to see New Bern opened up to the British, but took comfort that its loss would little effect the war effort...Gordon had been the business partner of Joseph Titley in Wilmington.

[71] Dunkerly, 206-207; Carolana, https://www.carolana.com/NC/Revolution/revolution_tory_hole.html.; Lewis V2, 471-473. John Slingsby was originally from England, but came to North Carolina and became a wealthy Cross Creek merchant. He served in several public offices, including the Provincial Congress, the Wilmington Committee of Safety and in the colonial militia before switching sides to the loyalists in 1775...According to Dunkerly, there is confusion among historians as to who exactly commanded the Americans at the Battle of Elizabethtown. Some say it was one or the other of the Robeson brothers, whose homes had been torched by Fanning. Historian J.D. Lewis contends it was Col. Thomas Robeson, Jr....The river road in 1781 follows roughly the same track as modern N.C. Highway 87...The American attack was aided by several men among Slingsby's Whig prisoners who managed to conceal weapons upon their capture. When Robeson's attack began, they joined it.

[72] O'Kelley V3, 320.

[73] Lewis Carolana, https://www.carolana.com/NC/Revolution/revolution_little_raft_swamp.html (accessed 1/7/2024); Dunkerly, 213. Drowning Creek is located west of Fayetteville, near Camp Mackall (part of Fort Liberty U.S. Army Base)...There is some conjecture that Hector McNeill intentionally let the Americans slip the noose at Beatti's Bridge because his cousin, Alexander, was an officer in Wade's force...Joseph Hayes was identified by Capt. Elrod of the loyalists. Elrod claimed Hayes was responsible for plundering his home and mistreating his family. Hayes was immediately hanged, but cut down after fifteen minutes. Fanning's surgeon detected a pulse and worked to revive the Whig officer, at which point Elrod decided he could live. Hayes and the other prisoners were delivered to the British at Wilmington.

[74] Dunkerly, 213; Lewis V2, 479-481.

[75] Lewis V2, 479.

[76] Lewis V2; O'Kelley V3, 358-362. The Continentals at Hillsborough were mostly recruits for Greene's army in S.C...Lytle may have been desperate to escape because he was on parole after being captured when Charlestown fell in 1780...Some of Fanning's men were so drunk they fell out along the march, only to be captured themselves by pursuing Whigs.

[77] Lewis Carolana, https://www.carolana.com/NC/Revolution/revolution_battle_of_lindleys_mill.html; Lewis V2, 494-495;Sherman, 621. Thomas Lindley, owner of the mill where the battle was fought, was a septuagenarian loyalist who, according to historian J.D. Lewis, died of a heart attack or stroke on the same day after seeing members of his family fighting on opposite sides against each other...William Allen of Orange County was one of the Hillsborough prisoners, who offered this recollection of Lindley's Mill and the fate of the captives afterward: "...While at Hillsborough preparing to go on this expedition, the Tories under the command of David Fanning, and the British under Col. McDougan [the Loyalists were under Col. Archibald McDugald of Cumberland County] came upon us and took three hundred of us prisoner, among whom was Governor [Thomas] Burke. He saw [Lt.] Col. [Archibald] Lytle wounded by a sword in the head by the

Tory, Fanning. This transaction took place at Hillsborough as above stated on the 4th [no, the 12th] of September 1781. That night we remained near Hillsborough, and were carried the next morning by the British and Tories on to a place called Lindley's Mill, where a pretty severe and well-fought battle took place between a force of the Republicans and the British and Tories, during which engagement the prisoners were kept in a close place with a strong guard around them. He recollects well of seeing there killed the celebrated Tory, Col. [Hector] McNeill. That night after the battle Lindley's Mill we were forced off by our captors and taken by Wilson's Iron Works to Wilmington, where we were put on board of British ships, which steered towards the West India Islands and then taken and disembarked us at Charlestown, where the greater part remained until peace; but the applicant states he was exchanged on the 11th of August 1782, and came on back home in Orange."

[78] Dunkerly, 224.
[79] Lewis Carolana, https://www.carolana.com/NC/Revolution/revolution_livingstons_creek.html; Sherman, 623; Lewis V2, 501-502. Livingston's Creek is located in the lower southwestern corner of Singletary Lake State Park...Militiaman Isaac Rainey said in his 1832 pension application statement that "... in 2 days afterwards the Tories took possession of Hillsboro; and that he was called upon by Captain McMullen again and was marched to Hillsboro and on in pursuit of said Tories and that the American troops overtook the Tories at Livingston's Swamp that he was in an engagement at that place with said Tories and British Light horse; and that the latter gave way; and that he was then placed in a company of volunteer infantry under the command of Captain Spillsby Coleman; Captain McMullen having disgraced himself and was dismissed and sent home; He says he was marched to a place called Brown Marsh where he says he was in another engagement with the British in the night time for more than an hour; and that 7 or 10 Americans were killed and about 60 head of horses; and 35 of the British were said to have been killed at said battle."
[80] Dunkerly, 213-214; Lewis V2, 478-479. In the account told by militiaman Jeremiah Wescoat in his pension application years later, the two men who crossed the bridge were Capt. James Simmons and Thomas Smith.
[81] Lewis Carolana, https://www.carolana.com/NC/Revolution/revolution_brown_marsh.html; Dunkerly, 218-219; Lewis V2, 501-503; O'Kelley V3, 368-370. Capt. James Shipman of the Whig militia wrote of the battle, "The backcountry men fled immediately. The Bladen Militia under Col. Owen & the Sampson Militia under Capt. Dodd, stood their ground until their ammunition was expended. A man by the name of Sigourres, a brave soldier belonging to the Bladen Militia was killed; a lad by the name of Stephens belonging to his company, was also killed, by my side. The backcountry Militia lost a great many of their horses."
[82] Lewis Carolana, https://www.carolana.com/NC/Revolution/revolution_raft_swamp.html; Dunkerly, 224-228; Lewis V2, 509-510. One witness wrote of Bethune's piping that "This encouraged the Tories so much that they extricated themselves from the surging crowd of Whigs and succeeded in assembling across the swamp in an old field where the little piper had begun his tune."...A quarter century later, workmen doing repairs on Lowry Road found spent musket balls and bones marking the place where the battle took place.
[83] Sherman, 638; Lewis V2, 511-513.

[84] Sherman, 642.
[85] Dunkerly, 228; Lewis V2, 514-515. Abatis are sharpened poles placed around a position to ward off infantry or cavalry, who cannot attack it without running the risk of being impaled.
[86] Dunkerly, 230.
[87] Lewis V2, 516.
[88] Dunkerly, 231, 234; Lewis V2, 517-517. The North Carolina Highland Regiment was likely the only unit serving in the state that still wore kilts as part of their uniform. Most British regiments had traded the traditional Scottish garb for trousers earlier in the Southern Campaign...One witness to the liberation of Wilmington described that day: "I was standing where the old Court house used to stand, just as the sun was rising; and looking up Market Street in the direction of the old church; when I saw a cloud arising on the hill; in a moment the trampling of horses was heard all around me. It was the Whig light horse, who came thundering down the street, and at full speed. There was a noted Tory who had lagged behind the embarking columns, not dreaming of danger. He seemed petrified with fear as the cavalry approached, and in a state of apparent mental hallucination walked forth with his hand strechd out, as if to salute the troop. A young man left the ranks, drew his hanger [sword], rushed upon him, and with one blow by a vertical cut laid his head open, the divided parts falling on each shoulder."
[89] Dunkerly, 232-233.; Maass, 322; LCFHS, 1-4. John Gordon's widow, Margaret, petitioned North Carolina governor Thomas Burke for permission to go to Charlestown to settle her dead husband's estate. Burke granted her permission, but on the condition that she did not return to Wilmington...William Hooper's home was ransacked by both Craig's redcoats and Rutherford's Whig militiamen.

1782

Redcoat troops row out to waiting transports and galleys during the evacuation of Wilmington in 1781.

1782

For James Henry Craig, the loss of Wilmington represented a strategic blunder on the part of his superiors. After Yorktown, Craig commanded the only professional military force on either side between Charlestown and the Chesapeake. With capable and enthusiastic provincial militias led by men like David Fanning, Craig understood the chance they had to cause real damage to the American cause in North Carolina. He requested reinforcements on at least two occasions that would have allowed him to assume something more than the defensive posture his small force dictated. Craig ruminated on what might have been when he wrote, "had I the 4 or 500 more men I had so long wished for I would hope to give this Province a blow they would not easily recover."

Just because Maj. Craig's redcoats were gone did not mean that violence came to an end in North Carolina. Loyalist bands like the one led by David Fanning still roamed the countryside, and it was not just the Tories that people needed to worry about. There were plenty of Whigs who went on campaigns of retribution, too.

During the last week of November 1781, Whig Capt. Thomas Kennedy looted loyalist homes in Chatham County, taking some horses and household furnishings. Fanning's Tories chased the American band for five miles before capturing him and nine of his men and all of the things they had taken.

Ten days into December 1781 Col. Elijah Isaacs of the Wilkes County Regiment of Militia was on the way home with 300 Whig militia when they arrived at Cox's Mill on Deep River. Cox's Mill was the home base of Col. David Fanning's Tory band, but Fanning wisely avoided Isaacs' larger force and moved his band towards the southeast. Isaacs had been imprisoned at St. Augustine the previous year after his capture at the Battle of Fishing Creek in South Carolina. His grudge against loyalists was considerable. The Americans torched several Tory homes and meted out revenge, including hanging a man named David Jackson. One of Isaacs' officers, Capt. James Stinson, executed Jackson in retribution for things done by the loyalist back in 1776. Captured at Moores Creek that February, Jackson was made prisoner along with Col. John Pyle and sent to jail at Halifax, but managed to escape from there.

Isaacs announced that Acting Governor Martin had declared a pardon for all loyalists who would assemble and accept it, with the exclusion of those guilty of murder, robbery, and housebreaking. Many took advantage of the promise of official forgiveness, only to be detained by Isaacs and marched to jail in Salisbury. One Tory was shot while on the way.

While the Americans tore through Fanning's Tory neighbors, Fanning answered in kind. Captain John Cox lived near modern Carthage, not far from his father, Robert Cox, whose house sat at the forks of Big Jumper and McClendon's Creek in Cumberland County. When Fanning arrived at John Cox's home, the captain was not there. Fanning ordered the home put to the flame. Moving on, the loyalists arrived at Robert Cox's place around midnight and rushed the house. John Cox was, indeed, at his father's. He and fellow Whigs Robert Lowe and William Jackson heard Fanning's approach and fled into the woods. Fanning burned down Robert Cox's house just as he had John's. Cox and his companions crept back to see what Fanning was doing, and were discovered by a Tory guard. Fanning ordered them seized and sent men to capture the Americans.

The Whigs saw the loyalists coming for them and ran, stealing horses from the dismounted Tories to make their escape. Cox made it to the safety of the woods. Jackson, pursued by Fanning and another loyalist, turned and fired from the saddle and killed the man with Fanning. Fanning returned fire and killed Jackson. Lowe was wounded and dragged back to the loyalist commander. Robert Lowe found himself in serious trouble. Earlier in the war he had ridden with Fanning's Tories, but switched allegiances later. Now Fanning recognized him as a turncoat. The loyalist leader ordered Lowe executed, and a firing squad was assembled to carry out the sentence. When the Tory marksmen failed to kill him with their volley, Fanning drew his pistol and finished Lowe off himself.

Fanning continued terrorizing Whig homes and farms for several days until pausing for rest. It was during this period when word reached him of Craig's evacuation of Wilmington. The news cast a pall over the loyalist band. Fanning and his men realized that without British support in the form of arms and other supplies, and without Wilmington as a refuge when things got too hot for the Tories, their chances of surviving were effectively zero. Without Craig, the only support he had now was that offered by loyalists in the countryside. Sooner or later, they would all be hunted down by the Americans.[1]

When the British were ascendant in 1780 and 1781, there were many people in the Carolinas who accepted paroles from them in order to protect home and hearth from the consequences of not appearing to support King George III's rule. It was apparent to the Whig leaders who were confirmed in power once the British left that most of those people were not really loyalists. Those people state leaders were happy to exclude from a new law that ordered the confiscation of loyalist property.

John Burgwin, the wealthy Wilmington merchant who owned the grand house at the corner of Third and Market Streets, was one of them. Burgwin petitioned the General Assembly to return to North Carolina in 1779, after leaving on doctor's orders four years earlier. Burgwin sailed for England in 1775, but for health reasons was not able to return to America in time to take the required oath of allegiance. To some, Burgwin's absence was proof of loyalist sympathies, which under the new confiscation law put his entire estate at risk. The Assembly eventually granted his petition, but lingering suspicions about his allegiances contributed to difficulties Burgwin had for some time afterward.

Robert Hogg was another North Carolinian impacted by the confiscation laws and the Whig desire for retribution. Hogg had lived in the Cape Fear for two decades, building a successful mercantile business and serving in various civic capacities including the Wilmington Committee of Safety in 1775. He resigned from the committee that year and left for the backcountry. He went to England in 1776, and managed to refuse or avoid making any loyalty oaths to the new Whig government in the state. Hogg took advantage of a part of the new law that allowed him to sell off at least part of his property, but when the rest of his estate was at risk he returned to North Carolina in 1778. The House voted unanimously to allow Hogg to return as a citizen, noting that the merchant had instructed his agent in the state to sell part of his property to support the Whigs. In the upper house it was a different story. Some there objected, and it was by the slimmest of margins that Hogg's petition was passed.

Unlike Hogg, his partner Samuel Campbell suffered for his choices. Campbell had served with MacDonald's loyalist army in 1776. In the aftermath of the defeat at Moores Creek, Campbell took the loyalty oath to the Whigs and an independent North Carolina, and tried hard to keep a low profile. Once Craig's redcoats occupied Wilmington, Campbell's Tory sympathies came to the fore once again and he actively supported the enemy. When Craig evacuated the town in November 1781, Campbell left with him. He eventually landed in Canada, where he claimed £2,000 in lost property confiscated by the Whigs. Campbell never returned to North Carolina.[2]

New Year's Day 1782 opened with the sale of loyalist property in towns across North Carolina, including Edenton, Halifax, Salisbury, Hillsborough, and at Wilmington in the Lower Cape Fear. With the British gone, and the American forces either discharged or moved off to other areas, it was open season on Tory belongings left behind when the loyalists fled the state.

Many women whose Tory husbands were either killed, evacuated with the British, or banished from the state were left to fend for themselves as North Carolina leaders confiscated their property. James Devane was a Whig militiaman tasked with escorting a number of such women to Wilmington from their homes in the countryside. It was a duty Devane found distasteful at best, his pity for the forlorn women almost outweighing his fear of disciplinary action if he refused to do it.

The treatment of the Tory women was shameful to many people. During Craig's occupation, Whig wives were expelled, often with just the clothes on their backs, from their homes by British and loyalist forces. They knew something of what it was to be tossed into the world with nothing to sustain them. Twenty-one women of the Lower Cape Fear penned a petition to end the expulsions, but officials ignored it. The women's argument, based on their own first-hand experience, was that none of the loyalist women had any say in the actions and policies of their men - it was not their fault - so they should not be punished for it. Many notable women signed the petition asking for mercy on the loyalist women's behalf.

Loyalist bands orphaned when Craig evacuated did not lay down their arms immediately, and the civil war in North Carolina continued. Middleton Mobley, the Tory leader from Duplin County (modern Sampson County), was finally arrested in Martin County in 1782. He was charged with skirmishing with Whig militia near Clinton and the Black River. Mobley was taken to Wilmington where he was tried and executed.

In March 1782, loyalist Maj. John Eliot and his band came across two armed Whigs in violation of the parole they had accepted when Craig's men still held Wilmington. Eliot had saved his friend, Whig officer Col. Thomas Dugan, from hanging when Craig had confined him aboard a prison ship at Wilmington. Eliot intervened on Dugan's behalf and saved his life. Now, an enraged Eliot and his men attacked the two Whigs, killing one named Henry Johnson. The other American managed to escape while Eliot and his men beat and shot Johnson. When Dugan found out about what Eliot had done, he and his company of militia set out to capture his old friend, despite owing his own life to him. When Dugan found Eliot and his band, they tied them to trees, shot them, and left their bodies as a warning to others who might want to follow their example.

That same month, David Fanning raided American militia on Deep River and was so successful that the Whigs agreed to a temporary truce. Truce or not, Fanning and his men were getting desperate. They continued raiding Whig homes for sustenance and revenge, including one belonging to Asheboro's Andrew Balfour. Balfour was away when Fanning arrived, but his sister, Margaret, was not. Six months later she recalled the attack, when "...about twenty-five Ruffians came to the house with the intention to kill my brother. Tibby and I endeavoured to prevent them, but it was all in vain. The wretches cut and bruised us both a great deal, and dragged us from the dear man then before our eyes. The worthless, base, horrible Fanning shot a bullet into his head, which soon put a period to the life of the best of men, and the most affectionate and dutiful husband, father, son and brother. The sight was so shocking, that it is impossible for tongue to express any thing like our feelings, but the barbarians, not in the least touched with our anguish, drove us out of the house, and took everything that they could carry off except the negroes..."

Fanning had been making peace overtures since January. His fellow Tory leaders, Col. Archibald McDugald and "One-Eyed" Hector

McNeill, had both moved to the truce lands in South Carolina. In Fanning's negotiations, he demanded that loyalists be allowed to return to their homes unmolested, that they be under no compulsions to either serve against the king's forces or pay taxes to support the war against King George's troops. On January 7, lawyer James Williams delivered Fanning's offer to the Americans. More than a few of the Whigs were amenable to the deal. The terms were delivered first to BGen. John Butler at Hillsborough, then to Acting Governor Alexander Martin for their consideration.[3]

In April Fanning was to be married. Sarah Carr agreed to wed the notorious Tory in the same ceremony that married friend Capt. William Hooker and her brother, Capt. William Carr. The day before the wedding, Hooker was killed by American militia, so the nuptials went ahead with just the two couples. Fanning allowed himself two days of married bliss, then he and Carr hid their wives away from the Whigs. Fanning admitted in his autobiography that at that point he was getting tired. "I concluded within myself that it was Better for me to try and settle myself being weary of the disagreeable mode of Living I had Bourne with for some Considerable time."

Fanning and his wife moved to a territory on the Pee Dee known as the truce land, negotiated by Francis Marion for the Whigs and Micajah Gainey for the Tories. Within its boundaries, neither side was allowed to pursue armed conflict. It attracted people from both sides of the war who just wanted to live in peace. Fanning tried to negotiate something similar in Cumberland County, North Carolina but was unsuccessful.[4]

Raids began to peter out as the year came to an end. In one of the more notable episodes, Capt. Robert Raiford of the Continental Army and 30 followers disrupted the trial of a loyalist at the Bladen County Courthouse in Elizabethtown. Raiford attacked defense attorney Archibald MacLaine with a sword and beat the court clerk for good measure. From there Raiford and his men set out to purge Bladen County of any remaining Tories. Raiford was later arrested, but the jury would not convict him. In another incident, loyalist Capt. William Lindley quit Fanning's band and made for the North Carolina mountains. Two of his former comrades in the loyalist militia followed him. They found Lindley and hacked him to death with their swords. Fanning learned of the killing and had the two men, William White and John Magaherty, hanged.[5]

Fanning was not the only Tory who sought refuge in the truce lands. More than 100 Bladen County loyalists fled there when the protection offered by the redcoats in Wilmington disappeared. The refugees were not content to simply start their lives anew in South Carolina. Instead, they began raiding into North Carolina, to the consternation of state leaders like Gov. Thomas Burke. "It is our misfortune to have among us a large Settlement of people who were never thoroughly United with us, and who have always become very dangerous Instruments in the hands of the Enemy," he wrote in March 1782. "Under Cover of that Settlement Numbers of the Outlaws of every State have Collected in this, and even many deserters from both armies. These under pretence of bearing Arms in British Interest Commit the most inhuman Barbarities and most atrocious Crimes. The injured People are provoked by those Outrages into Acts of desperate revenge and the Country is in many places filled with Assassinations... no Efforts can be Expected from a State in such Circumstances." North Carolina authorities complained to Francis Marion, but he confessed there was little he could do to stem the Tory raids. Marion confided that "there will be few men on the North line who was not under controle of Either party will yet settle them in such a manner that will Leave that part of the District in peace for the future."[6]

Tory banditry was not eliminated in North Carolina until 1783, but when it was the Americans got busy carrying out laws targeting the losing loyalists. In the courts, the sparse records of 1783 show a noticeable increase in trials for treason that lasted for the next two years, but by 1785 the prosecutions dwindled to almost nothing. Most cases were settled with the guilty paying a fine, though the penalties could include banishment or worse.[7]

The war in North Carolina spanned seven years, but in truth it began more than a decade earlier with the resistance to what colonists considered an unjust tax, continued through a rebellion against extortion by government officials in the backcountry, peaked with the British occupation of North Carolina's largest town, and ended when the last loyalist holdouts finally sheathed their swords in the face of diminishing alternatives. The Cape Fear was ground zero for much of the war in North Carolina, from Cross Creek, to Wilmington, to everywhere in between. It was America's first civil war, and the residual grudges of it lasted for generations after the shooting stopped. Wilmington would play an integral part in another civil war almost a century later, one that looms larger in the consciousness of most North Carolinians than that earlier conflict did; yet the Revolutionary War fought in the Cape Fear was arguably more important because it paved the road to securing our independence in the first place.

As noted at the beginning of this work, when it comes to the American Revolution, there is a saying among historians that while the famous battles of that war were fought up North, the decisive ones were fought in the South. If Patrick Ferguson had not died at King's Mountain, would Nathaniel Green's army have beaten Cornwallis in the Race to the Dan? Did Daniel Morgan's militia performance at the Cowpens finally show the militia that they could fight and win against British regulars? Did it have an influence on that later, more consequential battle at Guilford Courthouse? And by preventing Maj. James Henry Craig from accomplishing his primary mission of ferrying supplies to Cross Creek for Cornwallis, did a handful of North Carolinians lining the banks of the Cape Fear and Northeast Cape Fear Rivers force changes to Southern Campaign that led to the British surrender at Yorktown? Historians debate that sort of thing all the time, but the fact that there are such arguments lends credence to the assertion that North Carolinians, especially those in southeastern North Carolina, played a major role in winning American independence.

Endnotes

[1] Dunkerly, 234; Lewis V2, 518-520.

[2] Maass, 366. There were those in the upper house who objected to Hogg's readmittance because "when Mr. Hogg left this Country he was generally deemed unfriendly to the public Measures of this & the United States; that he returned under the protection of the King of Great Britain and hath not taken the Oath of Allegiance to this State; and lastly because Mr. Hogg hath not shown or offered in his own behalf any mitigating Circumstances to induce the General Assembly to admit him as a citizen and restore him to his property."

[3] Lewis V2, 528.

[4] Dunkerly, 236. The truce lands included South Carolina's modern Marlboro, Dillon, Marion, and Horry Counties.

[5] Lewis V2, 528.

[6] Maass, 368.

[7] Maass, 433; Dunkerly, 235. Signers of the petition asking for leniency included Anne

Hooper, wife of Declaration of Independence signer William Hooper; Mary Allen; Sarah Nash, widow of BGen. Francis Nash; Mary Nash, wife of N.C. governor Abner Nash; Ann Towkes; M. Hand; S. Willings; Mary Moore, widow of Col. James Moore; E. Nash; Sarah Moore; M. Lloyd; Catherine Young; J.M. Drayton; E. Wilkings; M. Lord; Isabella Read; Sally Read; Mary Grainger; Jane Ward; Hannah Ward; and Kitty Lord...Gov. Burke sent an expedition to capture or kill Fanning, but it failed. He also took the precaution of stationing more guards at Hillsborough to deter a repeat of Fanning's raid from earlier in the war.

Bibliography

Primary Sources

Documenting the American South: Colonial and State Records of North Carolina, https://docsouth.unc.edu/csr/. (accessed 2/18/22)

Price, William S., Jr. *Not A Conquered People: Two Carolinians View Parliamentary Taxation*. N.C. Department of Cultural Resources Archives & History, 1975.

Schaw, Janet. "Journal of a Lady of Quality: Being the Narrative of a Journey from Scotland to the West Indies, North Carolina, and Portugal, in the Years 1774 to 1776." *(No Title)*(1939).

Southern Campaigns Revolutionary War Pension Statements & Rosters, https://revwarapps.org (accessed 10/22/23)

Saberton, Ian. "The Cornwallis Papers: The Campaigns of 1780 and 1781 in the Southern Theatre of the American Revolutionary War." (2010): 2-320. Vol. III/Vol. IV/Vol. V

Secondary Sources

Angley, Wilson. *A History of Fort Johnston on the Lower Cape Fear*. Southport, N.C.: 1996.

Ashe, Samuel A. *Biographical history of North Carolina from colonial times to the present*. CL Van Noppen, 1906.

Brown, Joseph Parsons. *The Commonwealth of Onslow: A History*. OG Dunn, 1960.

Bell, Karen Cook. *Running from Bondage: Enslaved Women and Their Remarkable Fight for Freedom in Revolutionary America*. Cambridge University Press, 2023

Bennett, Charles E., and Donald R. Lennon. *A Quest for Glory: Major General Robert Howe and the American Revolution*. University of North Carolina Press, 1991.

Buchanan, John. *The Road to Guilford Courthouse: The American Revolution in the Carolinas*. Wiley, 1997.

Buchanan, John. *The Road to Charleston: Nathaniel Greene and the American Revolution.* Charlottesville, VA: University of Virginia Press, 2024.

Babits, Lawrence Edward, and Joshua B. Howard. *Long, obstinate, and bloody: the Battle of Guilford Courthouse*. University of North Carolina Press, 2009.

Butler, Lindley S. *North Carolina and the Coming of the Revolution, 1763-1776.* N.C. Department of Cultural Resources Archives & History, 1976.

Caruthers, Eli Washington. *Revolutionary Incidents and Sketches of Character: Chiefly in the" Old North State, Vol. I"* Wilmington, N.C.: Dram Tree Books, 2010.

Caruthers, Eli Washington, *Revolutionary Incident and Sketches of Character: Chiefly in the" Old North State, Vol. II"* Wilmington, N.C.: Dram Tree Books, 2010.

Connor, Robert Digges Wimberly. *Revolutionary Leaders of North Carolina*. No. 2. The College, 1916.

Connor, R. D. W. "The Colonial and Revolutionary Periods, 1584-1783." *Volume I of History of North Carolina, by RDW Connor, William K. Boyd, JG de Roulhac Hamilton, and Others (Chicago and New York: The Lewis Publishing Company, 6 volumes 1919).*

Crow, Jeffrey J. *The black experience in revolutionary North Carolina.* Vol. 16. North Carolina Division of Archives, 1977.

Dann, John C., ed. *The Revolution Remembered: Eyewitness Accounts of the War for Independence.* University of Chicago Press, 1980.

Dauphinee, Andrew D. *Lord Charles Cornwallis and the Loyalists: A study in British pacification during the American Revolution, 1775-1781.* Temple University, 2011.

Dunkerley, Robert M. *Redcoats on the Cape Fear: The Revolutionary War in Southeastern North Carolina.* Dram Tree Books, 2008.

Fraser, Flora. *Flora Macdonald: "Pretty Young Rebel."* New York: Alfred A. Knopf, 2023.

Fryar, Jack E. Jr. *Charles Towne on the Cape Fear: The Rise and Fall of the First Barbadian Settlement in Carolina.* Wilmington, N.C.: Dram Tree Books, 2019.

Ganyard, Robert L. *The Emergence of North Carolina's Revolutionary State Government.* N.C. Raleigh: N.C. Department of Cultural Resources Archives & History, 1978.

Graham, William. *General Joseph Graham and his Papers on North Carolina Revolutionary History* (Raleigh, N.C.: Edwards and Broughton, 1904).

Hairr, John. *Colonel David Fanning: The Adventures of a Carolina Loyalist.* Averasboro, N.C.: Averasboro Press, 2000.

Hall, Lewis Philip. *Land of the Golden River: Historical events and stories of southeastern North Carolina and the Lower Cape Fear, Volume II and Volume III.* Wilmington N.C.: Wilmington Printing Company, 1980.

Hartsoe, Kenneth David. *Governor Josiah Martin and his 1772 journey to the North Carolina backcountry.* San Jose State University, 2001.

Howell, Andrew Jackson. *The Book of Wilmington*. AJ Howell, 1979.

Jackson, Claude V. III; Fryar, Jack E. Jr., ed. *The Big Book of the Cape Fear River*. Dram Tree Books, 2008.

James, William Dobein. *A Sketch of the Life of Brigadier General Francis Marion*. Dram Tree Books, 2008.

Johnston, Peter R. *Poorest of the Thirteen: North Carolina and the Southern Department in the American Revolution*. Haverford, PA: Infinity Publishing, 2001.

Kars, Marjoleine. *Breaking Loose Together: The Regulator Rebellion in Pre-Revolutionary North Carolina*. University of North Carolina Press, 2002.

Lanning, Michael Lee. *Defenders of Liberty: African Americans in the Revolutionary War*. New York: Citadel Press, 2000.

Lee, Enoch Lawrence. *The Lower Cape Fear in Colonial Days*. Chapel Hill, N.C.: University of North Carolina Press, 1965.

Lennon, Donald R., and Ida Brooks Kellam, eds. *The Wilmington Town Book, 1743-1778*. Raleigh, N.C.: Division of Archives and History, 1973.

Lewis, J.D. *NC Patriots 1775-1783: Their Own Words, Volume 1, The NC Continental Line*, Second Edition (Stocksdale, N.C.: Carla G. Harper), 2021.

Lewis, J.D. *NC Patriots 1775-1783: Their Own Words, Volume 2, The Provincial and State Troops (Part 1)*, Second Edition (Stocksdale, N.C.: Carla G. Harper), 2021.

Little, Ann Courtney Ward. "Columbus County, North Carolina: recollections and records." (1980).

Lossing, Benson John. *Lossing's Pictorial Field-Book of the Revolution in the Carolinas & Georgia* (Wilmington, N.C.: Dram Tree Books) 2005.

McIlvenna, Noeleen. *A Very Mutinous People: The Struggle for North Carolina, 1660-1713*. (Chapel Hill: University of North Carolina Press) 2009.

MacDonald, James M. *Politics of the personal in the old north state: Griffith Rutherford in Revolutionary North Carolina*. Louisiana State University and Agricultural & Mechanical College, 2006.

Moore, Louis Toomer. *Stories Old and New of the Cape Fear Region.* Wilmington, N.C.: Broadfoot Publishing, 1999.

Oates, John Alexander. *The story of Fayetteville and the Upper Cape fear*. Dowd Press, 1950.

O'Kelley, Patrick. *Nothing But Blood and Slaughter: The Revolutionary War in the Carolinas-Volume One 1771-1779*. Booklocker.com Incorporated, 2005.

O'Kelley, Patrick. *Nothing But Blood and Slaughter: The Revolutionary War in the Carolinas-Volume Two 1780*. Booklocker.com Incorporated, 2005.

O'Kelley, Patrick. *Nothing But Blood and Slaughter: The Revolutionary War in the Carolinas-Volume Three 1781*. Booklocker.com Incorporated, 2005.

Oller, John. *The Swamp Fox: How Francis Marion Saved the American Revolution*. Da Capo Press, 2016.

Pedlow, Franda D.; Fryar, Jack E. Jr. *The Story of Brunswick Town & Fort Anderson*. Wilmington, N.C.: Dram Tree Books, 2005.

Powell, William S., James K. Huhta, and Thomas J. Farnham, eds. *The regulators in North Carolina: a documentary history, 1759-1776*. Raleigh, N.C.: State Department of Archives and History, 1971.
Rankin, Hugh F. *The North Carolina Continentals*. Chapel Hill: UNC

Press, 1971.

Ross, Malcolm. *The Cape Fear*. New York: Holt, Rinehart and Winston, 1965.

Russell, David Lee. *Victory on Sullivan's Island: The British Cape Fear/Charles Town Expedition of 1776*. Infinity Pub, 2002.

Schenck, David. "North Carolina, 1780-1781: Being a History of the Invasion of the Carolinas by the British Army Under Lord Cornwallis in 1780-1781." (1889).

Sprunt, James. *Chronicles of the Cape Fear River, 1660-1916*. Dram Tree Books, 2005.

Stick, David. *Bald Head: A History of Smith Island and Cape Fear*. Bald Head Island: 1985.

Troxler, Carole Watterson. *Farming Dissenters: The Regulator Movement in Piedmont North Carolina*. Raleigh: Office of Archives and History, North Carolina Department of Cultural Resources, 2011.

Watson, Alan D. *Wilmington, North Carolina, to 1861*. Jefferson, N.C.: McFarland, 2016.

Watson, Alan D. *Wilmington: Port of North Carolina*. Columbia: University of South Carolina Press, 1992.

Watson, Alan D., ed. *African Americans in Early North Carolina: A Documentary History*. Raleigh, N.C.: Office of Archives and History, NC Department of Cultural Resources, 2005.

Watson, Alan D. *General Benjamin Smith: A Biography of the North Carolina Governor*. Jefferson, N.C.: McFarland, 2011.

Watson, Alan D.; Lawson, Dennis, R.; Lennon, Donald R. *Harnett, Hoop-*

er & Howe: Revolutionary Leaders of the Lower Cape Fear* (Wilmington, N.C.: Louis T. Moore Commission of the Lower Cape Fear Historical Society, 1979).

Wheeler, John Hill. *Reminiscences and memoirs of North Carolina and eminent North Carolinians*. Columbus print. works, 1884.

Williams, Isabell M. and McEachern, Leora H. *Salt, That Necessary Article*. Wilmington N.C. 1973.

Theses/Dissertations

Brinkley, William D. *Back to the Future: The British Southern Campaign, 1780-1781*. ARMY COMMAND AND GENERAL STAFF COLL FORT LEAVENWORTH KS SCHOOL OF ADVANCED MILITARY STUDIES, 1998.

John R. Maass. "A COMPLICATED SCENE OF DIFFICULTIES": NORTH CAROLINA AND THE REVOLUTIONARY SETTLEMENT, 1776-1789. PhD. dissertation, Ohio State University, 2007.

Massey, Gregory De Van. "The British Expedition to Wilmington, North Carolina, January-November, 1781." PhD diss., 1987.

Seielstad, Kristen M. ""Upon secrecy, success depends" intelligence operations during the southern campaign of the American Revolution." PhD diss., College of Charleston, 2010.

Journals/Periodicals

Alexander, Clayton Brown. "The Training of Richard Caswell." *The North Carolina Historical Review* 23, No. 1 (January 1946): 13-31.

Alexander, C.B. "Richard Caswell: Versatile Leader of the Revolution." *The North Carolina Historical Review* 23.2 (1946): 119-141.
Alexander, C.B. "RICHARD CASWELL'S MILITARY AND LATER

PUBLIC SERVICES." *The North Carolina Historical Review* 23.3 (1946): 287-312.

Crittenden, Charles Christopher. "The Seacoast in North Carolina History, 1763-1789." *The North Carolina Historical Review* . Vol. 7, No. 4 (1930): 433-442.

Frech, Laura Page. "The Wilmington Committee of Public Safety and the Loyalist Rising of February, 1776." *The North Carolina Historical Review*, Vol. No.1 (1964): 21-33.

DAYS OF DEFIANCE: RESISTANCE TO THE STAMP ACT IN THE LOWER CAPE FEAR Author(s): Lawrence Lee Source: The North Carolina Historical Review, Vol. 43, No. 2 (April, 1966), pp. 186-202

General Robert Howe and the British Capture of Savannah in 1778 Author(s): Alexander A. Lawrence Source: The Georgia Historical Quarterly,Vol. 36, No. 4 (December, 1952), pp. 303-327

Harrell, Isaac S. "North Carolina Loyalists." *The North Carolina Historical Review* 3.4 (1926): 575-590.

Lawrence, Alexander A. "General Robert Howe and the British Capture of Savannah in 1778." *The Georgia Historical Quarterly* 36.4 (1952): 303-327.

Lee, Lawrence. "Days of Defiance: Resistance to the Stamp Act in the Lower Cape Fear." *The North Carolina Historical Review* 43.2 (1966): 186-202.

MacMillan, Henry Jay. "Living Archives." *Lower Cape Fear Historical Society, Inc. Bulletin*, Vol. III, No. 1, (October 1959):1-4.

NORTH CAROLINA LOYALISTS Author(s): Isaac S. Harrell Source: The North Carolina Historical Review, Vol. 3, No. 4 (October, 1926), pp. 575-590

THE SEACOAST IN NORTH CAROLINA HISTORY, 1763-1789 Author(s): Charles Christopher Crittenden Source: The North Carolina Historical Review, Vol. 7, No. 4 (October, 1930), pp. 433-442

Stumpf, Vernon O. "Josiah Martin and His Search for Success: The Road to North Carolina." *The North Carolina Historical Review*, Vol. 53, No. 1 (1976): 55-79.

Van Loan Naisawald, L. "Major General Robert Howe's Activities in South Carolina and Georgia, 1776-1779." *The Georgia Historical Quarterly* 35.1 (1951): 23-30.

Watson, Alan D. "Women in colonial North Carolina: Overlooked and underestimated." *The North Carolina Historical Review*, Vol. 58, No. 1 (1981): 1-22.

Watson, Alan D. "Impulse Toward Independence: Resistance and Rebellion Among North Carolina Slaves, 1750-1775." *The Journal of Negro History*, Vol. 63, No. 4 (1978): 317-328.

Watson, Alan D. "The origin of the Regulation in North Carolina." *The Mississippi Quarterly,* Vol. 47, No. 4 (1994): 567-598.

Watson, Alan D. "Household Size and Composition in Pre-Revolutionary North Carolina." *The Mississippi Quarterly*, Vol .4 (1978): 551-569.

Watson, Alan D. "Benjamin Smith: Brunswick County" General" and North Carolina Governor, 1810—1811." *The North Carolina Historical Review* Vol. 87, No. 1 (2010): 28-56.

Watson, Alan D. "The Committees of Safety and the Coming of the American Revolution in North Carolina, 1774-1776." *The North Carolina Historical Review* Vol. 73, No. 2 (1996): 131-155.

Online Sources

Lewis, J.D., "The American Revolution in North Carolina." https://www.carolana.com/NC/Revolution/ (accessed 12/23/23)

"The Regulator Movement," https://en.wikipedia.org/wiki/Regulator Movement (accessed 10/19/23)

Sherman, William Thomas. "Calendar and Record of the Revolutionary War in the South: 1780-1781." (2003). https://www.americanrevolution.org/warinthesouth.php (accessed 10/25/23)

"Dictionary of North Carolina Biography, University of North Carolina Press." *NCpedia*, https://www.ncpedia.org/category/entry-source/dictionary-no. (accessed 3/9/23)

NHCo Rev Plantations: http://genealogytrails.com/ncar/newhanover/plantations.html

JH Craig Article: https://allthingsliberty.com/2017/10/james-henry-craig-pocket-hercules/

Cornelius Harnett biography: https://www.ncpedia.org/biography/harnett-cornelius-jr

Index

82nd Regiment of Foot (British) - 3, 181, 192, 196, 202, 214, 217, 221, 237, 238, 240, 248, 262, 264, 290, 291, 304, n. 313
Abercromby, Robert - 149
Aberdeen (NC) - 183
Alamance, Battle of - 2, 50, 60, n. 160, 59-63
Alamance County - 285
Alamance Creek - 60, 287
Alexander Hostler & Co. - 17, n. 25
Allen, Abraham - 285
Allen, Thomas - 131
Allen, William - 284, n. 318
Alston, Philip - 257, 259, 260, 262
Alston, Temperance - 261, 262
Ancrum, John - 75, 160
Anson County - 56, 124, 125, 278, 285, 288, 293, 296
Antioch Township - 278
Armstrong, James - 131
Ashe, Francis - 252
Ashe, John - 37, 40, 59, 62, 65-66, n. 69, 76, 84, 88, n. 105, 119, 121, 126, 131, 141, 145, 155, 158, 171, 212
Ashe, John Baptiste - 175, 177, n. 187
Ashe, Samuel - 76, 97, 113, 158, n. 160, n. 187, 250
Asheboro (NC) - 317
Ashe's Creek - 246
Association Test - 81-83
Averasboro (a.k.a. Devo's Ferry) - 138
Avery, Col. - 252
Bald Head Island (Smith Island) - 2, 7, n. 24, 144, 146, 148, 151, 156, 157, 158, n. 164, 193
Balfour, Andrew - 317
Balfour, Nisbet - 191, 192, 232, 240, 245, 246
Ball, John Coming - 182
Barlow, Ralph - 258
Barre, Isaac - 33
Battery Island - 144, n. 164
Battle, Ephraim - 220, 281
Beaufort County - n. 26, 59, n. 105, 208
Beeson, Edward - 285, 293
Bell, Thomas - 22
Bellfont (Russellborough) - 37, 40, , 42, 43, n. 45, 145, 150
Belvedere Plantation - 256
Benning, Arthur - 311
Bethel, William - 296, 304, 306
Bethune, David - 299
Bethune, Laughlin - 137
Berry, Charles - 299
Birdsong, John - 257, n. 317
Black, Alexander - 267, 270
Black, Kenneth - 259, 260, 267, 269, 270
Black Pioneers Regiment - 21, 238
Black River - 126-128, 182, 243, 246, 317
Blackwell, James - 296
Bladen County - 114, 123, 183, 186, 196, 202, 208, 229, 240, 246, 253, 255, 257, 258, 274, 275, 276, 278, 285, 290, 293, 294, 296, 304, 318, 319
Bledsoe, Lewis - 285, 293, 296
Bloodworth (Bludworth), Timothy - 143, n. 164, 196, 253
Bloodworth (Bludworth), Thomas - 196, 215, 216, 253, 254, n. 317
Blue, Peter - 270
Boggan, Patrick - 267, 268, 278, 285, 296
Boyd, Adam - n. 45, 66, 196
Boykins Plantation - 244
Brandywine, Battle of - 170
Brewer, Isaac - 286
Brice, Rigdon - 311
Brick House - 208, 293, 306, 307
Brier Creek (GA) - 175, 177
Brig *Resistance* - 172
British fleet in the Cape Fear (1776) - 2, 142-152
British raid on Brunswick - 148-153
Brockington, John - 184
Brown Marsh - 290, *battle of* 293-295, n. 319
Brown, Richard - 274
Brown, Thomas - 131, 195, 202, 298, 217, 220, 221, 276, 291
Brunswick Committee of Safety - 235
Brunswick County - 62, 66, 79, 81, 85, 91, 97, 114,

115, 122, 123, 148, 206, 207, 256, 281, 292, 295, 306, 307
Brunswick Town - 2, 3, 7, 10, 13, n. 24, 31, 36, 37, 39, n. 45, 62, 91, n. 104, 1120, 122, 143, 145, 147-150, 235, 237, 307
Bryan, Nathan - 267
Bryant, Needham - 59
Buchan, David - 269
Buchoi Plantation - 306
Buncombe, Edward - 75
Burgaw (NC) - 220, 234, 246
Burgwin, John - 14, n. 25, 68, 114, n. 160, 199, 233, 309, 315
Burgwin-Wright House - 3
Burke County - 16
Burke, Thomas - 152, 169, 246, 247, 249, 251, 253, 257, 262, 266, 270, 272, 280, 281, 283, 284, 286, 290, 291, 294, 295, 300, 302, 309, n. 318, n. 320, 329, n. 331
Burnt Mill Creek - 213
Burnt Mill Run - 123
Burrington, George - 12
Butler, Gen. John - 237, 251, 281, 283-291, 293-295, 303, 328
Butler, William - 53-55, 56, 62, n. 69
Buzzard's Bay - 156, 157
Cain, James - 236-237
Cain, Sgt. James - 274, 277
Cain, Maj. John - 206, 207
Cage, William - n. 317
Camden (SC), Battle of - 181, 184, n. 187, 311, n. 312, n. 315
Camden County Militia - 186

Cameron Hill - 92
Campbell, Alexander - 137
Campbell, Archibald - 175
Campbell, Farquahard - 83, n. 106
Campbell, James - 16
Campbell, John - 127, 131, 134, 137
Campbell, Samuel - 196, n. 313, 326, 16, n. 105, 114
Campbell, William - 21, 151, n. 160, 166, 184, 198, 302, 315
Campbellton - 125, n. 162
Cape Fear immigration - 13, 15, 52, 92, 112
Cape Fear Mercury newspaper - n. 45, 65, 66
Cape Fear river pilots - 116
Cape Lookout - 245
Captain's Mills - 328
Carr, Sarah - 328
Carr, William - 328
Caskill, Murdock - 131
Caswell County - 283
Caswell County Militia - 290-293
Caswell, Richard - 66, 77, 79, 117, 118, 125-134, 136, 140, 141, 145, n. 160, n. 162, 163, 208, 222, 251, 262, n. 314
Caswell, William - 247, 249, 251, 252, 262, 264-266, 272
Charles Towne (NC) - 10, n. 26, n. 186
Charlestown (SC) - 23, 111, 138, 141, 144, 151, 153, n. 159, n. 164, n. 165, 169, 172, 173, 178-181, 184, 191, 196, 226, 232, 240, 241, 245, 246, 283, 289, 291, 300, 309, 310, 311, n. 313, n.314, n. 318, n. 319,

n. 320, 323
Chatham County - 241, 278, 284, 285, 293, 296, 304, 323
Chatham County Courthouse - 259, 270
Cherokee Indians - 153-154, 211
Cheshire, Richard - 274
Child, Thomas - 53
Christmas, Nathaniel - 285
Clark, Alexander - 267
Clarke, John - 267, 268
Clarke, Kenneth - 267
Clarkton (NC) - 294
Clayton, Francis - 75
Clinton (NC) - 122, 123, 185, 243, n. 317, 327
Clinton, Sir Henry - 96, n. 106, 143-151, 153, 177, 178, 180, 191, 232, n. 316
Clinton, Richard - 243, n. 317
Cobham, Dr. Thomas - 18, 59, 196, n. 313
Cochrane, Mr. (Tory) - 270
Cochrane's Mill - 146
Cogdell, Richard - 65
Cohera Swamp - 242
Colbreath, Neil - 136
Cole, Josiah - 290, 293
Coleman, Spillsby - 293, n. 319
Columbus County - 183, n. 187, 281, 294, 307
Collett, Capt. John Abraham - 20
Collier, Matthew - 285
Colvin's Creek - 129, 138
Colville, Maturin - 257
Contentnea Creek - 240
Continental Army - 85, 97, 169, n. 187, 276, 287, 303, n. 313, 328
Continental Frigate *Raleigh*

- 172
Cooper River (SC) - 179
Corbett's Ferry - 126, 127, n. 164
Corbin, Francis - 53
Core Sound - 264
Cornell, Samuel - 61
Cornwallis, Gen. Charles - 2, 3, 96, 111, 113, 142-144, 148-150, 180, 181, 185, 186, n. 187, 191, 192, 202, 209, 212, 213, 217, 221-227, 229, 231-235, 237, 238, 240, 241, 245-248, 251-253, 255, 257, 262-267, 270, 272-274, 280, 281, 284, 289-292, 295, 300-303, 308, 309, 311, 312, n. 313, n. 315, n. 316, n. 317, n. 320, 323, 325, 326
Cotton, James - 124, 125, 131, 132, 136, 138, n. 161
Cowan's Ford - 290
Cox, John - 324
Cox, Longfield - 138
Cox's Mill - 241, 256, 280, 283, 284, 286, 324
Craig, Maj. James Henry - 3, 181, 192-199, 202-217, 219-223, 225, 231-235, 237, 238, 240, 241, 245-248, 251-253, 255, 257, 262-267, 270, 272-274, 280, 281, 284, 289, 290-292, 295, 300-303, 308, 309, 311, 312, n. 313, n. 315, n. 316, n. 317, n. 320, 323, 325, 326
Crane Creek - 286
Craven County - 57, 131, 145, 267, 285
Crawford, Charles - n. 107, 285
Crawford, Thomas - 278

Cray, Joseph Scott - 220, 281
Cray, William - 97, 122, 131
Cross Creek, N.C. - 3, 7, 15, 16, n. 25, 92, n. 106, 113, 115-117, 119, 120, 121-126, 131, 138, 139, 146, n. 161, n. 162, 181, 191, 202, 212, 217, 225-227, 242, 246, 253, 270, 272, 277, 295, 303, n. 318, 330
Crump, James - 257, 293
Cruden, James - 121
Cruden, John - 121
Culloden, Battle of - 92, 94
Culp, Capt. (Whig officer) - 267, 269, 270
Cumberland County - 80, 82, 87, 94, 97, n. 106, 119, 123, 217, 223, 225, 259, 275, 278, 283, 285, 288, 296, n. 318, 324, 328
Cumberland County Committee of Safety - 120
Cunningham, Walter - 146
Currie, Duncan - 267, 268
Cusan, Adam - 184
Dalrymple, Capt. John - 40-43, n. 46
Davidson, George Lee - 131
Davis' Bridge - 258
Davis, John - 97
Davis, Thomas - 97
Davis, William - 131, 148, 149
Deaton, William - 285
Declaration of Independence - 1, 19, 57, 66, 141, 195, 311, n. 331
Declaration of Rights and Grievances - 34, 158
DeCoin, John - 283

Deep River - 241-242, 256, 260, 270, 280, 324, 327
Delaware Continental Line - 178, 181, 182
DeRossett, Elizabeth Catherine - 114
DeRossett, Lewis - 20
DeRossett, Moses John - 36, 37, 40
DeVane, James - 326
DeVane, Thomas - 293
DeVane, Widow - 246
Dickerson, Lt. (Royal Navy) - 156, 157
Dickerson, Nathaniel - 285
Dickson's Ford - 261
Dickson, William - 239, 266
Dixon, Henry "Hal" - 131
Dobbs, Arthur - n. 25, 36
Dodd, David - 293, 304, n. 319
Dollison's Landing - 128
Dougan, Thomas - 280
Douglas, William - 285
Downie, Donald - 121
Dr. Forster, British surgeon - 150
Drayton, Steven (Stephen) - 246, 253
Drowning Creek - 183, 192, 235, 247, 278, 296, n. 312, n. 318
Dry, William - n. 25, 39, 40, 42, 43, n. 46, 145, 150
DuBois, Isaac - 154, 192, 198
DuBois, Jean - 154
Dugan, Thomas - 327
Dunbibin, Jonathan - 79
Dunmore's Proclamation - 20
Duplin County - 37, 62, 130, 137, 138, 154, 185, 202, 203, 239, 242, 248,

251, 264, 267, 296, 327
Duplin County Militia - 242, 262, 264, 274, 293, 304
Duplin Courthouse - 202, 203
Dye, Hawkins - 285
Eagles Island - 91, 122, 145, n. 161, 208, 212, 231, 255, 293, 295, n. 315
Ebert, Samuel - 173, 175
Edwards, Edward - 285
Edwards, Isaac - 56, 65
Elizabethtown (NC) - 126, n. 161, 229, 290, 294, 300, 328
Elizabethtown, Battle of (Tory Hole) - 274-278, n. 318
Ellis Plantation - 193, 202
Ellis, Robert - 97, 113
Ellis, William - 274
Elrod, John - 278, 296, n. 318
Emmett, James - 202
Eutaw Springs (SC), Battle of - 22, 318
Fallon, Dr. James - 83
Fanning, Col. David - 3, 241-242, 247, 256-291, 293, 296, 311, n. 317, n. 318, n. 319, 323-325, 327-329, n. 331
Fanning, Col. Edmund - 54-59, n. 68
Fayetteville Arsenal - 124
Fayetteville (NC) - 7, 22, n. 27, 86, 92, n. 162, 226, 268, 279, 303, n. 318
Fergus, Ann - 199
Fergus, John - 177
Ferguson, Maj. Patrick - 180, 181, 184, n. 187, 330
Fields, William - 113, 116
Fishing Creek (SC), Battle of - 240, 324
Foley, Mason - 285, 293
Forster, John - 113
Forsyth County - 16
Fort George - 148, 151, 156-157
Fort Hancock - 172
Fort Johnston - 15, 20, 40-44, n. 46, 64, 67, 73, 79, 84-91, 93, 95, 99, n. 104, n. 105, n. 106, n. 107, 116, 119, 138, 143-145, 147, 148, 150, 156, n. 161, 193
Fort Sullivan (SC) - 153
Fort Liberty (former Fort Bragg) - 223, 267, n. 318
Foy, James - 137, n. 163
Franklin, Benjamin - 54
French & Indian War - 1, 2, 8, 23, 32, 33, n. 46, n. 68, 98, n. 106
Frigate *Randolph* - 22
Frohock, Thomas - 54
Gage, Gen. Thomas - 21, 59, 89, 94, 111
Gainey, Micajah - 307-308, 328
Gains, James - 285
Gaston, Alexander - 273
Gaston, Margaret - 273
Gates, Gen. Horatio - n. 311
Gause, Charles - 291
Gentry, Micajah - 247
Germantown, Battle of - 170
Gillespie, James - 274
Gillespie, John - 296, 304
Ghoulson, William - 284
Godden (Tory officer) - 276
Godwin, David - 275, 277
Goodrich, John Sr. - 172
Goose Creek (SC) - 10, n. 26, n. 69
Gordon, John - 262, 265, 272, 273, 311, n. 317, n. 318, n. 320
Gorham, James - 240, 273, 274
Grady, John - 137, n. 163
Graham, Alexander - 270
Graham, Joseph - 296-300, 304, 306-308, n. 317
Graham, William - 146
Grainger, Joshua Sr. - 296
Great Bridge (VA), Battle of - 101, 103, n. 107
Great Duplin Road - 202, 217, 237, 238, 264, n. 313
Great Savannah (SC) - 181
Great Swamp (NC) - 186
Great White Marsh - 183, n. 187
Greene, Nathaniel - 191, 205, 209, 212, 222, 224, 225, 227, 237, 241, 245, 246, 264, 267, 280, 281, 300, n. 312, n. 316, n. 317, n. 318
Greenfield Lake - 123, 193
Gregory, M. - 257, n. 317
Griffin, William - 285
Griffith, Roger - 284
Guilford County - 16, 113, 117, 131, 138, n. 160, n. 162, 186, 224, 290, 293, 296, 300
Guilford Courthouse, Battle of - n. 187, 222-224, 229, 232, 290, n. 315, 330
Gwinn, Edward - 285
Gwinn, William - 285, 293
Haddrell's Point (SC) - 153
Hadley, Joshua - 285
Halifax (NC) - 39, 53, 101, 102, 117, 131, 138, 139, 141, 146, 152, 153, 159, n. 162, n. 163, n. 187, 195, 238, 240, 265, 281, 303, 324, 326

Halifax Resolves - 146
Hall, William - 265
Hamilton, Ninian Bell - 54
Hammond's Creek Bridge - 291
Hammond, Isaac - 22, n. 27
Handley, Thomas - 285
Hargis, Shadrack - 290, 293
Harrell, Isaac S. - 113, n. 160, n. 187
Harrell, Richard - 136
Harnett, Cornelius Jr. - 14, 15, 40, 43, 50, 64-66, 76, 78, 81, 88, 98, n. 104, 117, 118, 119, 121, 148, n. 162, n. 164, 169, 184, 210-212, 232
Harnett, Cornelius Sr. - 10
Harnett County - 225
Harris, Tyree - 55
Harvey, John - 65, 66, 75, 77
Haw River - 7, 60, 286
Hayes, Joseph - 279, n. 318
Hayes, Robert - 291
Haymount - 124
Hedrick, Peter - 285
Henderson, Richard - 57, 59, n. 69
Hepburn, James - 94, n. 106, 129, 130
Herndon, James - 257, n. 317
Heron, Benjamin - 13, 203
Heron's Bridge - 3, n. 166, 202-205, 210, 212, 215, 217-226, 234, 237, 238, 257, 295, 304, 312, n. 313, n. 314
Hesse Cassel Jaegers - 238, 240, 307
Hewes, Joseph - 65, 66, 77, 79, 118, 141, 142, n. 163
Higgins, Michael - 12
Hill, William - 78

Hillsborough (NC) - 16, 54-57, 59, 62, n. 68, n. 69, 124, n. 162, n. 164, 197, 198, 285, 286, 288, 293, 295, n. 318, n. 319, 326, 328, n. 331
Hillsborough Raid - 281-284, 290, 294
Hilton Plantation - 64-65
Hilton, William - 7
Hinds, Joseph - 242, 257, n. 317
Hinton, John Jr. - 295
Hinton, Johnson - 59
Hinds, John - 242
HMS *Defiance* - n. 23, 156, 157
HMS *Diligence* - 35, 36, 38, 40, 41, n. 45
HMS *Falcon* - 149, 156, 157
HMS *General Gage* - 145
HMS *Mercury* - 143
HMS *Pallas* - 148
HMS *St. Lawrence* - 147, 151
HMS *Scorpion* - 88-89, 99, n. 107, 116, 123, 152, n. 163, n. 164, n. 165
HMS *Solebay* - 169-170
HMS *Sovereign* - 147
HMS *Viper* - 31, 38, 38, 40, 41, 42, n. 45, 89
Hodge, George - 293, 296
Hogg, Robert - 16, n. 25, n. 69, 75, n. 105, 114, 160, n. 161, 325-326
Hogun, James - 178, 179, n. 315
Hoke County - 258, 268, 278
Holley, John - 266
Holloway, Stephen - 285, 288, 293, 294
Holly Shelter - 252

Honeycutt, John - 285
Hood, Charles - 22
Hood's Creek - 291-292
Hooker, William - 289, 328
Hooper, Anne - 197-198, n. 313, n. 330-331
Hooper, George - 75
Hooper, William - 19, n. 26, 57, 65, 66, n. 69, 76, 77, 79, n. 104, 118, 141, 146, n. 164, 169, 194, 195, 197, 311, 312, 320
Horry County (SC) - n. 330
Horry, Peter - 179, 181, 183, 247
House in the Horseshoe (Philip Alston's House) - 259-262
Houston, Dr. William - 37, 38, 42, 43, n. 45
Howard, Martin - 58, 59, n. 69, n. 187
Howe, Robert - 43-44, n. 46, 62, 65, 66, 67, 75, 76, 81, 88, 89, 97, 98, 102, n. 105, n. 106, n. 107, 121, 144, 148, 149, 150, 152, 153, 156, n. 164, 165, 172-175, n. 186, n. 187, 211
Howell, Joseph - 285
Howell, Rednap - 54, 56, 62, n. 68, n. 69
Huger, Isaac - 175, 179
Humphrey, Joseph - 220, 281
Humphreys, David - 296
Humphries, John - 285
Hunter, James - 54, 56, 57, n. 69
Hunter, William - 278
Hudgins, John - 285
Husband, Herman - 54-56, 58, 61-62, n. 69
Huske, John - 196, n. 313
Indiantown (SC) - 182

Iredell, James - 76, 195
Irwin, Jared - 208, 293
Isaacs, Elijah - 324
Jacobite Rebellion - n. 25, 91, 92
Jackson, David - 131, 324
Jackson, William - 324
James Island (SC) - 153, 283
James, John - 266
James, William Dobein - 182-183
Jameson, John - 179
Jamieson, William - 285
Johnson, Henry - 327
Johnson, Robert - 274
Johnston, Gabriel - 12, 13, 15, n. 25
Johnston, John - 285
Johnston, Samuel - 57, 58, 63, 65, 66, 73, 87, 95, 97, 101, 141
Jones, Allen - 171
Jones County - 252, 267
Jones, Frederick - 97
Jones, John - 285
Jones, Matthew - 257, n. 317
Jones, William - 213, 285
Jumping Run - 123
Kell, James - 285
Kenan, Felix - 130
Kenan, James - 97, 131, n. 160, 192, 242-244, 257, 262, 264-266, 272, 296
Kenan, Owen - 242
Kenan, William - 304
Kendal Plantation - 148, 149
Kennedy, Primrose - 149
Kennedy, Thomas - 304, 306, 307, 323
Kettle Creek (GA) - 175
Kinchen, W. - 257, n. 317
King, Boston - 21

King Charles II - 9
King George III - 1, 8, 21, 23, n. 24, n. 67, n. 69, 77, 82, 83, 86, 92, 94, 95, 96, 111, 112, 113, 140, 148, 154, 156, 198, 241, 290, 325, 328
King, Violet - 21, n. 27
Kings Mountain - 184, n. 187, 290
Kingstree (SC) - 182
Kolb, Abel - 192, 267
Knight, John - 285, 289
Knox, William - 131
Knowles, John - 265, 289
Lachlan, James - 179
Lake Waccamaw - 152, 281, 303
Lanier, Ben - 135, n. 163
Laurens, Henry - 173
Lavinia (slave) - 311
Leland (NC) - 256
Lee, Gen. Charles - 144, 152, 156
Lee, Henry "Light Horse Harry" - 308
Leech, Joseph - 59
Leggett, John - 131
Leggett, William - 293
Lenud's Ferry - 179
Leonard, Jacob - 291-293
Leonard, Samuel - 206, 207
Leslie, Alexander - 192, 309, n. 312
Lexington and Concord - 9, 81, 82, 86
Lillington, Alexander - 3, 40, 62, 97, n. 106, 117, 119, 126-131, 140, n. 162, n. 163, 202, 205, 210, 212, 213, 215, 217, 219, 220, 222, 225, 234, 235, 237, 251, 267, 272, 273, 296, n. 314
Lilly, Capt. (Whig officer)

- 296
Lincoln, Benjamin - 173, 178, 179, 180
Lincoln (Tryon) County - 16
Lindley's Mill - 56, 284
Lindley's Mill, Battle of (a.k.a. Cane Creek) - 284-290, 296-297, n. 319
Lindley, Thomas - 56, n. 318
Lindley, William - 328
Linzee, John - 156
Little Coharie River - 244
Little Raft Swamp, Battle of (9/1/1781) - 278-281, 283, n. 318
Livingston's Creek - *skirmish at* - 290-291, 301, 307, n. 319,
Lobb, Capt. Jacob - 38-42, n. 46
Lockwood's Folly - 143
Lomax, John - 22
Long, Nicholas - 102, n. 163, 171
Lopp, John - 296
Lord Bute - 35, n. 45
Lord Dartmouth - 88, 89, 93, 96, 99, 111, n. 159
Lord George Germain - n. 25, 111
Lord Grenville - 32, n. 44
Lord North - 95
Lords Proprietors of Carolina - 9, n. 23
Lossing, Benson J. - 31, 37, 52, 60, 61, n. 68, 124
Lost Colony - 7
Love, Capt. James - 154, 213-216, 234, 253, n. 314
Lowe, Robert - 324
Lowry Road - 297, 299, n. 319
Loyalist property confisca-

tion - 66, 74, 141, 325
Luttrell, John - 284, 289
Lynch's River - 182
Lyon, John - 15
Lytle, Archibald - 283, 284, n. 318
McAfee's Mill - 257
McAlister, Alexander - 97
McArthur, John - 137
McBride, Archibald - 270, n. 317
McCrary, Duncan - 137, n. 166
McCree, Griffith - 170-171
McCree, Griffith John - 199
McCullers, Matthew - 285, 293
McDaniel, John - 267
McDaniel, Marren - 267
McDaniel, William G. - 274, 293
McDonald, Angus - 132
McDonald, Hugh - 134
McDonald, James - 131
McDonald, Kingsborough - 131
McDugald, Archibald - 285-291, 294, 296, n. 318, 327
McFarland, John - 285
McFarling, Capt. - 172
McGraw, Alexander - 285
McGuire, Thomas - 42
McIntosh, George - 149
McKay, Archibald - 261, 285, 288, 296
McLane, Robert - 285
McLean, Alexander - n. 105, 114, 115, 132, 133, n. 160, n. 161
McLean, "Sober" John - 284-286, 296
McLeod, Alexander - 43, 131, 267, 268, 311
McLeod, Donald - 116, 119, 120, 124, 127, 131-135, 137, n. 162-163
McLeod, John - 132, n. 159
McMillan, Daniel - 267-269
McMullen, John - 290, 293, n. 319
McNeill, Archibald - 267, 268
McNeill, Alexander "Red" - 278
McNeill, John - 267
McNeil, "One Eyed" Hector - 296, 297, 328
McNeill (McNeil), Hector - 260, 270, 272, 278-281, 283-286, n. 318, n. 319
McPhaul, John - 278
McPhaul's Mill - 278, 290, 296, 299
McPhaul's Mill, Battle of (a.k.a. Little Raft Swamp, McFall's Mill, Burnt Swamp, or Beatti's Bridge #2) - 278, 279, 288
McRae, Alexander - 131, 134, 137
McRae, Murdock - 137
McSweene, Allen - 267-269
McTier, William - n. 105, 114, 121
MacDonald, Allan - 91-94, 131, 133, 267
MacDonald, Donald - 94, i5, n. 106, 116, 117, 119-121, 123-131, 138, n. 161, n. 162, 227, 326
MacDonald, Flora - 91, 94, n. 106, 124, 267, 269
MacDonald, Hugh - 124
Mackay, John - 311
Mackinnon, Ronald - 304
Maclaine, Archibald - n. 69, 75, 97, n. 104, 195, 328
Maclaine, Thomas - 196, n. 313
MacLeod, Donald - 116
Magaherty, John - 328
Magill, Capt. - 80
Malcolm, Donald - 60
Malloy, Charles - 275
Manson, Daniel - 203, 216, 232, 251, 291-295, n. 317
Marion, Francis - 181-184, n. 187, 247, 278, 308, 328, 329
Market Dock - 253, 254
Martin's Fiery Declaration - 95
Martin, Alexander - n. 107, 291, 295, 312, 328
Martin, James - 126, 131, 138, n. 162
Martin, Josiah - 20, 63, 65, 67, 75, 84, 86, 89, 92, 95, 99, n. 104, 111, 113, 114, 115, 139, 142, 151, n. 163, n. 164, 178, 233
Maryland Continental Line - 178, 181, 182
Mattis, Arthur - 265
Mayben, John - 285
Meacham, Richard B. - 285
Mebane, Alexander - 285
Mebane, James - 285
Mebane, John - 294
Mebane, Robert - 285, 287, 289
Mecklenburg County - 113, n. 160, 290, 295, 304
Mecklenburg Resolves - 95, n. 105
Mercantilism - 16
Mercer, Joseph - 138
Mermaid's Point - 7
Micklejohn, Rev. George - 56
Military Ocean Terminal Sunny Point - 148

Millar, Ralph - 113, 143
Militia:
Whig
Bladen County - 131, 202, 208, 240, 255, 258, 274, 278, 291, 293, 296, 304, n. 319; Brunswick County - 66, 143, 206, 207, 291, 293; Camden County - 186; Carteret County - 59; Caswell County - 283, 290, 293; Chatham County - 283, 284, 293, 296, 304; Craven County - 131, 285; Cumberland County - 259, 278; Duplin County - 131, 185, 242, 246, 252, 262, 274, 293, 304; Granville County - 223, 296; Guilford County - 131, 138, 186, 285, 293, 296; Halifax - 131; Hillsborough - 283, 284, 293, 295; Montgomery County - 267, 293; Mecklenburg County - 293, 304; N.C. State Legion - 296, 304; Nash County - 265; New Bern - 117, 202, 225, 296; New Hanover County - 36, 373, 59, 116, 131, 194, 202, 203, 213, 215, 285; Onslow County - 131, 281; Orange County - n. 68, 186, 283, 285, 293, 296; Pitt County - 240; Randolph County - 280, 283, 285, 293, 296, 304; Richmond County - 267; Rowan County - 186, 285; Salisbury - 285, 304; Sampson County - n. 319; Surry County - 131, 285; Tryon County - 146; Wake County - 283, 284, 295, 296, 304; Wilkes County - 324; Wilmington - 117, 202, 225, 296

Loyalist
Anson County (Loyalist) - 124, 278, 285, 296; Anson Highlanders - 131, 288; Bladen County (Loyalist) - 123, 131, 186, 274, 296; Chatham County (Loyalist) - 131, 278, 285; Cotton's Corps of Moore County - 131; Cross Creek - 123; Cumberland County (Loyalist) - 123, 131, 225, 274, 296; Fanning's Regiment - 296; Gov. Martin's Corps - 285; Highlander Light Horse - 131; Loyal American Rangers - 304; N.C. Provincials - 131; Orange County (Loyalist) - 285; Randolph County (Loyalist) - 285; Regulators - 131; Richmond County (Loyalist) - 278; Royal Highland Emigrants - 131, 304; Royal N.C. Regiment - 203, 285, 293, 296, 304;

Minute Men - 81, 97, 102, n. 106, 122, 123, 128
Mobley, Biggars - 242
Mobley, Middleton - 185, 186, 242-244, 327
Monroe's Bridge - 296
Montgomery, Capt. - 61
Montgomery County - 16, 92, 267, 290, 293
Moore, Alfred - 131, 143, n. 186, 306, 307
Moore, George - 40
Moore, Col. James - 42, 50, 59, 62, n. 69, 75, 76, 83, 88, 97, 99, n. 105, 117, 119, 121, 123, 124, 128, 136, 138, 144, 145, 154, n. 163, n. 164, 170, n. 331
Moore, Louis Toomer - 31
Moore, Maurice - 10, n. 24
Moore, Judge Maurice - 34, 43, 56, 58, 59, 62, n. 69, 116
Moore, Roger - 15, n. 24, n. 25, n. 69, 149
Moore, Smith - 296
Moores Creek, Battle of - 131-139
Morrison, Alexander - 132
Morrison, Donald - 134
Moseley, Edward - 12
Moseley, Sampson - 97
Moulton, Abraham - 251
Moultrie, William - 177
Mount Pleasant - 179
M'Queen, Mr. - 22
Muhlenberg, Peter - 152, 153
Murchison, Janet - 311
Murchison, John - 311
Murchison, Kenneth - 137
Murray, John (Lord Dunmore) - 98, 99, 101-103, n. 107
Myhand's (a.k.a. Mayhand's) Bridge - 185, 244
Mylne, George - 97
Nakina (NC) - 307
Nall, John - 284, 286
Nash, Abner - 83, 84, 181, 199, 210, 247, 278, 285, n. 314
Nash County - 208, 238, 240, 264, 265
Nash, Gen. Francis - 22, n. 106, 170
Nash, Mary - n. 331
Nash, Sarah - n. 331
Navassa (NC)
N.C. Continental Regiments - (General referenc-

es) 156, 171, 178, 281; First Regt. - 119, 154, 131, 148, 149, n. 164, 179; Second Regt. - 102, 131, n. 164, 179, n. 314; Third Regt. - 143, 156; Fourth Regt. - 143, 156; Fifth Regt. - 143
N.C. Outer Banks - 9, 172
Neal, Maj. (Whig officer) - 257
Neale, Capt. - 59, 172
Negro Head Point Road (a.k.a. Market Road) - n. 162, 253, 304
Nelson's Ferry - 181
Nelson's Liquor Store - 254
New Bern - 10, 13, 14, n. 45, 50, 53, 57, 59, 64, n. 68, n. 69, 76, 79, 84, 94, 114, 117, 128, 153, n. 160, n. 164, 208, 252, 262, 264, 267, 273, n. 314, n. 318
New Bern Committee of Safety - 84, 91, 94, 95, 117
New Bern Raid - 264, 272-274
New Hanover Committee of Safety - 79, 80
New Hanover County - 13, 17, n. 24, 66, 79, 85, n. 104, n. 105, 154, n. 164, 193, 194, 204, 210, 217, 220
New River - 251, 252
Newkirk, Abraham - 135, n. 163
Ninety-Six (SC) - 241
North Carolina Gazette newspaper - 37, 43, n. 45, 58
Nova Scotia - 21, n. 27, 34, 39, 117, 120, 140, n. 160, 192, n. 313
Nutbush Address - 54

Oak Island - 7, n. 24, 118, 144
O'Hara, Charles - 223-224, 303, n. 315
Old Inlet - 12, 118, n. 159, 311
Old Mother Covington and her Daughter - 1126, 128, 130, 131, 134-136
Oldham, John - 293
Onslow County - 50, 97, 122, 131, n. 161, 208, 211, 220, 242, 252, 281, n. 314
Orton Mill - 143; *skirmish at* - 148
Orton Pond - 149
Oscar (Marion's servant) - 184
Overmountain Men - 184
Owen, Thomas - 208, 274, 276, 293, 294, 296, 304, n. 319
Paget, Jim - 253-255
Pardo, Juan - 7
Parker, Sir Peter - 2, 96, 142, 143, 147, 151, 159
Parry, Capt. Francis - 86, 118, 122, 132, 143, 147, 156
Parliamentary taxation/acts: Coercive Acts of 1774 - 74; Declaratory Act (a.k.a. American Colonies Act) - 49, 73; Molasses Act - 23; Navigation Act - 33; Stamp Act - 2, 14, 32, 33, 34, 35, 36, 37, 38, 39, 42, 43, n. 44, n. 45; Sugar Act - 23, 32; Townshend Act - 49-51, n. 67; 1773 Tea Act - 2, 49, 51, 67, 74, 75, 77, 78, 80
Patterson, Daniel - 267, 268
Peacock Bridge - 240
PeeDee River - 205
Pendleton, Hiram - 274

Pennington, William - 42, 43
Pensacola (FL) - 172
Peters, Clairy - 21
Peters, Sally - 21
Peters, Thomas - 21, n. 27
Pettifort, John - 22
Pharis, Samuel - 274
Philadelphia (PA) - 13, n. 45, 62, 75, 77, 138, 139, 154, n. 163, 169, 178, 311
Phipps, Capt. Constantine - 36, 40, 41, 42, n. 46
Piney Bottom Massacre - 267-270, n. 317
Plummer, Richard - 274
Point Peter (a.k.a. Negro Head Point) - 91, n. 161, 253, 254, 255, n. 316
Polk, Charles - 293, 296, 304, 306, 308
Polk, Thomas - 156-157
Pollock, Abraham - 101
Portevent, Samuel - 154
Portivent's Mill - 243
Powers, Capt. (CO of Hawkins Horse) - 251
Prevost, Augustine - 172
Proclamation Line - 23
Pugh, James - 61, n. 69
Purviance, William - 97, 122, n. 161
Pyle, John Jr. - 131, n. 161, 288, 324
Pyle, John Sr. - 131
Quash (slave) - 175
Quince, Parker - 74, 75, n. 104
Quince, Richard - 81, 97, 113, 122
Quincy, Josiah Jr. - 64, 65, 98, 211
Raft Swamp, Battle of (10/15/1781) - 296-300
Raiford, Robert - 328

Rains, John - 285, 287, 288, 289
Ramsour (NC) - 241
Ramsey, Ambrose - 257, n. 317
Ramsey, Matthew - 257
Ramsey's Mill - 237
Randle, John - 278
Randolph County - 280
Rawdon, Francis Lord - 101, 148, n. 316
Ray, Daniel - 138
Ray, Duncan - 257, 270, 288, 293, 294, 296, 297
Ray, William - 285
Read, James - 82, 302
Red Hill Road - 294
Red Springs (NC) - 246, 295, 297
Regulator Advertisement #1 - 54
Regulator Rebellion - 2, n. 46, 50, 52, 53-63, n. 68, n. 69, n. 70, 92, 95
Reid, Thomas - 146
Revels, Louie - 22
Rhodes, Henry - 97, 220, 281
Richlands (NC) - 251
Richmond County - 278
Robeson County - 16, 208, 256, 258, 295, 296
Robeson, Peter - 235, 257, 258, 272, 274, 276, 296
Robeson, Thomas - 97, 131, 208, 256, 272, 274, 275, 277, 293, n. 318
Robinson's Plantation - 290
Rockfish Creek - n. 25, 124, 125, 235, 258, 264-266, 268, 272, 273
Rocky River - 288
Rogers, James - 127, 132, n. 162, 311
Rogers, John - 296

Roman, Robert - 131
Rosser, Joseph - 285
Rouse's Tavern (a.k.a. Eight Mile House) - 213-217
Routledge, Thomas - 97
Rowan County - 56, 113, 186
Rowan, Robert - 131, 270
Rudolph, Michael - 264, n. 317
Russ, Thomas - 291
Rutherford, Griffith - 3, 281, 290, 295, 299, 304, 308
Rutherford's Mill - 220, 234, 246, 251, n. 317
Rutherford, Thomas - 97, 123, 131, 132, 136, n. 161, 197
Rutledge, John - 181, 182, 192, 198
St. Augustine (FL) - 324
St. James Anglican (Episcopal) Church - 13, 14, 200, 207, 208, 211
St. John's River (GA) - 172
St. Mary's River (GA) - 172
St. Philip's Anglican Church - 31, 32
Salisbury (NC) - 52, 56, 59, 60, 61, 97, n. 162, n. 164, 324, 326
Salt - 79, n. 104, 113, 118, 121, 139, 154, 155, 158, n. 160, 172, 184, 195, 266, 273, 312, n. 317
Salter, Sallie - 275
Salutary Neglect - 1, 8, 23, 32
Sampson County - 185, 246, 276, n. 317, 327
Sanders, Adam - 293
Sandy Creek - 54, 292

Sanford (NC) - 7
Savannah (GA) - 22, 172-175, 181, n. 187
Scarborough (Whig officer) - 246
Schaw, Alexander - 111
Schaw, Janet - 18, n. 24, n. 26, 73, 81, 82, 97, 98, n. 104, 170, n. 313
Schaw, Robert - 59
Schaw's Plantation - 308
Schoepf, Johann David - 19
Schooner *Little Dick* - 170
Scot Highlanders 15, n. 25, 90, 92-96, n. 106, 112, 113, 115, 119, 120, 126, 128, 129, 130, 132, 133, 137, 152, n. 160, n. 161, n. 162, 196, 257
Scotland County - 15, 16, 256
Scurlock, Thomas - 257, n. 317
Senf, John - 186
Seven Creeks (Brunswick County) - 307, 308
Siege of Charleston (SC) - 179
Shane, David - 115
Shallow Ford - 186
Shelby, Isaac - 184, n. 187
Shelling of Norfolk (VA) - 103
Sherwood Fort - 208, 274
Ship *America* - 118
Ship *Ruby* - 38, 39, 40, 42, n. 46
Shipman, Daniel - 291
Shipman, James - 293, n. 319
Sierra Leone - 21, 22, n. 27
Simmons, James - 291, n. 319
Simmons, Richard - 296, 304

Simpson, Alexander - 31
Sims, George - 54
Singletary, James - 274, 277
Singletary, Josiah - 275, 276
Slavery in the Cape Fear - 17-23, n. 26, 38, n. 45, 159
Slave revolts (Stono Rebellion, etc.) - 17, 20, n. 26, n. 105, 274,
Slingsby, John - n. 105, 114, 131, n. 161, 270, 275, 276, 277, 278, n. 318
Slocomb, Ezekiel - 138, 239
Slocumb, Mary - 138, 239, n. 316
Sloop *Dobbs* - 38-40, 42, n. 45
Sloop *Patience* - 38-40, 42, n. 45
Sloop *Ranger* - 38-40, 42, n. 45
Sloop *Speedwell* - 169, 170
Smith Creek - 65, 123
Smith, Frederick - 296
Smith Island *(see Bald Head Island)*
Smith, John - 97, 308
Smith, Minor - 296
Smith, Thomas - 146, 291, 292, n. 319
Smith, William - 285, 296
Smithville (NC) (a.k.a. Southport) - 2, 7, n. 45
Snow Camp - 285
Society in colonial N.C. - 15
Sons of Liberty - 50
South Carolina - 10, 17, 21, 22, 50, 60, n. 69, n. 70, 91, 111, 154, n. 164, 172, 178, 180-184, 191, 198, 225, 233, 235, 237, 241, 245,
278, 281, 307, n. 315, n. 316, 324, 328, 329
Spanish Florida - 7, 9, 18, 117, 138, 154, 172, 173, 191
Spanish Raid on Brunswick Town - 84
Speed, John - 278
Spring Friends' Meeting House - 286
Sproul's (McNeill's) Ferry - 267
Stafford Branch - 287
Stamp Act Resistance - 32-46
Stevens, Moab - 275
Stewart (Steuart), Alexander - 37, 43, n. 45, 66, 131
Stewart, William - 137
Stiles, Ezra - 140
Stinson, James - 324
Stone, Benjamin - 97
Strudwick, Mr. - 302
Stuart, John - 116, 117
Stuart's Creek - 258
Sugarloaf - 12
Sullivan's Island (SC) - 152, n. 165
Sumner, Jethro - 170, 182, 303
Surry County - 16, 131, n. 160, 296
Swan's Point - 143, 237
Swann, Samuel - 97, 198
Swift Creek - 240
Tar River - 264
Taverner Marsh - 285
Taylor, Thomas - 259, 260
Tea Parties - 2, 43, 74, 78, n. 104
Thackston, James - 126
The Flats - 91, 122, n. 315
The Sniping Tree - 253-255
Thompson, Dugald - 17
Thompson, William - 59
Thresal, Robert - 17, n. 25
Titley, Joseph - 311, n. 318
Tomkins, Stephen - 278, 285
Trade restrictions/non-importation agreements - 49
Trading Ford - 290
Transport *Glasgow Packet* - 147, 150
Transport *Palliser* - 99, 100
Truce Lands - 328, n. 380
Tryon Palace - 53, 273
Tryon, William - 2, 20, 31, 34, 36, 38, 40-44, n. 45, n. 46, 50, 51, 53, 56-64, 67, n. 68, n. 69, n. 70, 84, 113, n. 318
Turner (mulatto) - 267, 270
Turner, William - 293
Tybee Island (GA) - 173
Tyler, Thomas - 309
Underwood, Benjamin - 278, 285
VA House of Burgesses - 8, n. 67, 75
Vance, John - 130, 131
Vassall, John - 10
Waccamaw River - 183, 303, 307, 308
Waddell, Col. Hugh - 40, 42, n. 46, 59, 60, 61
Waddell's Ferry - 275, 294
Wade, Thomas - 131, 239, 257, 267-268, 278-280, 285, n. 318
Walker's Bridge - 213, n. 314
Walker, John - 69, 131, n. 161, 193, 198, 199
Wall, William - 278
Wallace (NC)m - 264
Washington, George - 2, 8, 9, 85, 101, 154, 169, 179, 180, 280, 303
Washington, William - 179

Watson, Elkanah - 19
Watson, John - 14
Watson, Thomas - 299
Watson, William - 299
Wayne, Gen. "Mad" Anthony - 274
Webber's Bridge - 272, 273
Wells, Jacob - 266
Wescoat, Jeremiah - 291, 292, 293, n. 319
West Indies - 17, 77, 154, 155, 191
Wigfall, John - 182
Whiskey Rebellion - 62
White, Anthony - 178
White, John - 7
White, Robert - 304
White, William - 328
Whitehead, Burrell - 275
Whitehurst, Thomas - 31, 32
Wilkins, Elijah - 258
Wilkinson, William - 15
Wimble, James - 12, 13
Winston, Joseph - 131
Wilcox, James - 151
Williams, James - 257, n. 317, 328
Williams, John C. "Shay" - 185, 186, n. 187, 242-244
Williams, Joseph - 246, 266
Williams, Otho - 182
Williams, Samuel - 131, 161
Williamsburg (VA) - 8, 144
Wilmington, Evacuation of - 304, 309-312, n. 315, 325
Wilmington mercantile businesses - 14-16
Wilmington Committee of Safety - n. 26, 76, 78, 80, 82, 84, 87, 88, 91, 99, 100, 101, n. 105, n. 106, 121, 143, n. 160, n. 161, n. 162,
n. 164, n. 318, 325
Wilmington, N.C. (a.k.a. Watson, New Carthage, New Liverpool, New Town, Newton) - 2, 3, 7, 9, 12, 13, 14, 15, 16, 17, 18, 20, 21, n. 24, 26, 34, 35, 36, 37, 38, 39, 40, 44, 45, 50, 59, 62, 74, 76, 78, 80, 81, 82, 83, 84, 85, 87, 89, 90, 91, 92, 93, 95, 99, 100, 103, n. 104, 105, 106, 113, 116, 121, 122, 128, 132, 137, 140, 141, 152, 154, 155, n. 160, 161, 162, 163, 178, 179, 181, 182, 191, 192, 194, 195, 197, 199-202, 204, 205, 206, 207, 208, 210, 211, 212, 213, 214, 217, 220, 221, 225, 226, 227, 229, 231, 232, 234, 237, 240, 241, 245, 246, 251, 253, 255, 256, 259, 264, 270, 273, 274, 275, 278, 280, 281, 283, 284, 287, 288, 289, 290, 291, 292, 293, 294, 295, 296, 299, 300, 303, 304, 306, 307, 308, 309, 310, 311, 312, n. 312, n. 313, n. 314, n. 316-320
Wingate, Edward - 291, 293
Wilson, J.D. - 264
Winslow, Capt. (Tory officer) - 270
Wishart Mill - 252
Witherspoon's Ferry - 182
Woodford, William - 101, 102, n. 107
Woods, James - 293
Woody's Ford - 286
Wright, Daniel - 296
Wright, Sir James - 175
Wynn, Capt. (Whig officer) - 296
Yeamans, Sir John - 10, n. 24
Yorktown (VA) - 2, 240, 281, 303, 308, 323, 330
Young, Henry - 3, 21, 194, 202, 203, 217

Jack E. Fryar, Jr. is the author or editor of more than 30 books of North Carolina and Cape Fear history. He holds Masters degrees in History and Teaching from the University of North Carolina Wilmington, and has taught high school history, most recently at Cape Fear Community College. He has worked as a broadcaster, bookseller, publisher, book reviewer, and graphic designer.

Photo: Belinda Keller

Endnotes